LOOKING INTO PROVIDENCES:
DESIGNS AND TRIALS IN *PARADISE LOST*

Looking into Providences: Designs and Trials in *Paradise Lost*

RAYMOND B. WADDINGTON

UNIVERSITY OF TORONTO PRESS
Toronto Buffalo London

Toronto Buffalo London
www.utppublishing.com

ISBN 978-1-4426-4342-0 (cloth)

Library and Archives Canada Cataloguing in Publication

Waddington, Raymond B.

Looking into providences : designs and trials in Paradise Lost / Raymond B. Waddington.

Includes bibliographical references and index.
ISBN 978-1-4426-4342-0

1. Milton, John, 1608–1674. Paradise lost. 2. Providence and government of God in literature. I. Title.

PR3562.W33 2012 821'.4 C2012-901840-6

University of Toronto Press acknowledges the financial assistance to its publishing program of the Canada Council for the Arts and the Ontario Arts Council.

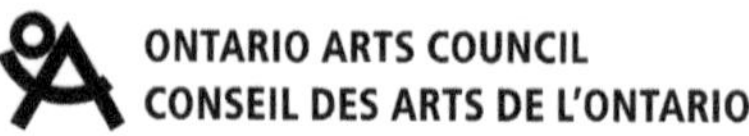

University of Toronto Press acknowledges the financial support of the Government of Canada through the Canada Book Fund for its publishing activities.

Kathie's book, yet once more,
and in memory of Jackson Cope and John Shawcross,
my first and last Milton mentors.

Contents

Illustrations and Tables

Note on Texts and Abbreviations

Milton's poetry is cited from *John Milton: Complete Poetry and Major Prose,* ed. Merritt Y. Hughes (New York, 1957). To supplement the notes in Hughes, I have consulted *Paradise Lost,* ed. Alastair Fowler (2nd ed. Harlow, 1998); and *The Riverside Milton,* ed. Roy Flannagan (Boston, 1998). For the three major poems I have employed the familiar abbreviations (*PL, PR,* and *SA*). For the prose I have used the Yale edition, *Complete Prose Works,* gen. ed. Don M. Wolfe, 8 vols (New Haven, 1953–89), cited as *CPW,* except for the original Latin and instances where I have preferred the Sumner translation of *De Doctrina Christiana* (cited as *DDC).* For this I have quoted the Columbia edition, *The Works of John Milton,* gen. ed. Frank Allen Patterson, 18 vols (New York, 1931–8), cited as *Works.* Marvell's poetry is quoted from *The Poems of Andrew Marvell,* ed. Nigel Smith (rev. ed. Harlow, 2007). The *Oxford English Dictionary* is cited as *OED.* The King James Bible is quoted, except where indicated. For Milton's earliest Bible, I have used *The Geneva Bible: A Facsimile of the 1560 Edition,* intro. Lloyd E. Berry (Madison, WI, 1969).

Journal Abbreviations

CH	*Church History*
ELR	*English Literary Renaissance*
HLQ	*Huntington Library Quarterly*
JEGP	*Journal of English and Germanic Philology*
JHI	*Journal of the History of Ideas*
JMRS	*Journal of Medieval and Renaissance Studies*
JWCI	*Journal of the Warburg and Courtauld Institutes*
MLQ	*Modern Language Quarterly*

MP	*Modern Philology*
MQ	*Milton Quarterly*
MS	*Milton Studies*
P&P	*Past and Present*
PMLA	*Publications of the Modern Language Association*
PQ	*Philological Quarterly*
RenQ	*Renaissance Quarterly*
SCJ	*The Sixteenth Century Journal*
SEL	*Studies in English Literature*
SP	*Studies in Philology*
UTQ	*University of Toronto Quarterly*

Acknowledgments

First, a confession. Even though when I was bringing home bags of theology books my wife would eye me suspiciously and ask if I was having a religious conversion, I am not a spiritual person or a churchgoer. In fact, I admire former Minnesota governor Jesse Ventura who asserted, 'Organized religion is a sham to delude weak minds.' He was not re-elected. The book that follows here is the result of a long engagement with the epic that Milton called 'of highest hope, and hardest attempting.' It attempts to understand *Paradise Lost* on its own terms as a religious poem, providing an 'account of what [his] mind at home in the spacious circuits of her musing hath liberty to propose to her self.'

As with any project long in the works, I have accumulated more debts, both intellectual and practical, than can easily be enumerated. Individual chapters or chapter sections have been read and improved by Don Beecher, William den Boer, Bob Fallon, Rhodri Lewis, Jim Nohrnberg, Kyle Pivetti, Beverley Sherry, Tom Sloane, Paul Stevens, Michael Walton, and Joe Wittreich. John Shawcross read several chapters with his customary engagement and incisiveness; Catherine Gimelli Martin read the whole thing more than once, an unerring critic on clarity of argument and on structure. John and Catherine were struggling, not with angels, but their own recalcitrant manuscripts at the time; the three of us formed an email mutual support group, from which I benefited considerably. I owe a particular debt to the generosity of theology and religious history experts – William den Boer, Loren Stuckenbruck, and David Whitford – who kindly answered questions and shared in-press works. Once again I have relied on Charles Robb for his exemplary skill in photography, and as always Winfried Schleiner has been my resource on matters German.

Portions of this have been read at the International Milton Symposia in York, Pittsburgh, and London; the 'Ars Reminiscendi' symposium in Ottawa; the Sixteenth Century Studies Conference; and the Rocky Mountain Medieval and Renaissance Association. I am grateful to Don Beecher, Al Labriola, and Michael Walton for invitations to speak. Earlier versions of some parts, now much revised and expanded, have appeared in *Modern Philology, Milton Studies,* and *Ars Reminiscendi: Mind and Memory in Renaissance Culture,* ed. Donald Beecher and Grant Williams (Toronto: Centre for Reformation and Renaissance Studies, 2009). I thank the editors for permission to use this material. I also appreciate the help that I received from the efficient staffs of several libraries and museums in obtaining illustrations. At the University of Toronto Press, I wish particularly to thank Suzanne Rancourt and Ron Schoeffel, now with this second book old friends, for their interest and enthusiasm.

Throughout, I have been buoyed by the encouragement of good friends: Luba Freedman, Bruce Golden, Margherita Heyer-Caput, Frances Huemer, Manny Schonhorn, Tom Sloane, Stan Stewart, Joe Tucker, Michael and Phyllis Walton. Catherine Martin, astute critic, faithful email correspondent, and California soulmate, has to be singled out as *prima inter partes.* My son Ray demonstrated a remarkable knack for finding useful books at the right time, most notably the 1827 *De Doctrina.* My daily companions for nearly all the writing were Marmalade, peerless hunter and occasional lap cat; and Spock, grand survivor, who never left his workstation beside the desk.

A slowly gestating study inevitably has its casualties, and I regret the losses of three Miltonists: Hugh MacCallum and Al Labriola, both of whom took a heartening interest in my work; most recently, John Shawcross, sometime colleague at Madison, Wisconsin, lifetime friend, and invaluable resource on this project. Somewhere John will be shaking his head at my having fallen into the trap of believing that Milton was an Arminian. I hope my late colleague Louis Owens would approve the excursus on Amerindian conversion. On postcolonial theorizing, Louis always corrected firmly, 'Just colonial. My country is still colonized.'

Although she complained that Milton was far less fun than Aretino, who was like having a bad uncle around the house, my wife Kathleen uncomplainingly again provided computer support, listened to ideas, made suggestions, and without her this book would not exist.

LOOKING INTO PROVIDENCES: DESIGNS AND TRIALS IN *PARADISE LOST*

Introduction

Seventeenth-century England still was a pervasively religious society, which meant that manifestations of God's will, in events both large and small, were matters of absorbing interest; and in his poetic fascination with the workings of providence, John Milton was, as we shall see in the following chapter, a man of his age.[1] The Nativity Ode encompasses the sweep of history, from Creation (st. 12–13) to Last Judgment (st. 17), even presenting the Peace of Augustus (st. 3) as an act of extraordinary providence preparatory to the greatest such historical event, the Incarnation. Sonnet 7, 'How soon hath Time,' takes a perennial favourite for its subject, the problem of having the 'grace' to discern 'the will of Heav'n.' 'Lycidas' grapples with a puzzling and seemingly unjust providence, the death of Edward King, resolving (not solving) the problem by 'transform[ing] that death into an instrument of providential salvation.'[2] With *Paradise Lost* the workings of providence become the entire poem.

Everyone knows that the 'Argument' of Milton's epic – in rhetorical terms, the subject or thesis that the poet intends to prove – is to 'assert Eternal Providence' (*PL* 1: 26). That acknowledged, however, often attention drifts away,[3] as the second half of the proposition, 'And justify the ways of God to men' (1: 27) seems to exert an inexorable pull on the scholarly mind. Granted this is an engrossing topic in its own right;[4] frequently discussion of it devolves into a bewildering array of epithets for Milton's fictive or personal deity: good God, bad God, tyrannical God, rational God, Hebraic God, and so on. The very diversity of opinion might in itself suggest that the poem presents a God unknown in any direct sense.[5] He is 'invisible,' 'inaccessible,' so 'Dark with excessive bright' that even the seraphim can approach him only with veiled eyes (*PL* 3: 375, 377, 380–2); the Son sits by the Father, 'Amidst as from a flaming Mount, whose top / Brightness had made invisible' (5: 598–9). This God is knowable only through his works, which include the Son, placing the entire determination squarely on providence.

Whereas in Milton's prose writing the word 'providence' appears more than fifty times, it occurs in *Paradise Lost* only five times with the variant 'provident' twice. Most memorably it is the alpha and omega of the epic, the first assertion of the 'great Argument' (1: 24–5) and the closing fadeout of its human actors with 'Providence thir guide' (12: 647). Very quickly Satan announces his counterplot: 'If then his Providence / Out of our evil seek to bring forth good, / Our labor must be to pervert that end' (1: 162–4). For the apostate angels, alienated from God, the term already has become incomprehensible; reasoning 'high / Of Providence' they find themselves 'in wand'ring mazes lost' (2: 558–9, 561). Even earlier in Heaven Satan's blasphemous stump speech had been challenged by Abdiel: 'Yet by experience taught we know how good, / And of our good, and of our dignity / How provident he is' (5: 826–8). The rebels, ironically, are likened to a swarm of monarchial bees (1: 768–76); but the newly created world allows the possibility of a commonwealth, suggested in the 'provident' emmet, 'Pattern of just equality perhaps / Hereafter' (7:485, 487–8; cf. *CPW* 7: 427). Then there is the wisdom that Adam has absorbed from Michael: 'ever to observe / His providence, and on him sole depend, / Merciful over all his works' (12: 563–5). An exquisite economy and, as the entire poem is an assertion of providence, nothing more is needed.

Certainly there have been recognitions that the epic contains manifestations of providence. Joseph Summers long ago called attention to one implication of the shift from ten to twelve books in the 1674 edition: the centre of the poem becomes the war in Heaven and the Creation, 'the divine image of God's ways at their most providential.'[6] A generation after Summers, John Shawcross devoted a chapter to showing how the thesis of the epic is 'Eternal Providence.'[7] Whereas most passing comments on providence within the poem leave the concept at the broadest level, Milton's *De Doctrina Christiana* is unusually precise in its discrimination of three kinds: 'general' or ordinary providence oversees the orderly governance of the creation; 'special' pertains to angels and humans, both rational beings with free will; and 'extraordinary' designates divine acts outside the normal laws of nature and those directed at individuals. When one considers particular events and cases the distinction between 'special' and 'extraordinary' providence can be very fine-spun; in seventeenth-century providential discourse commonly *De Doctrina*'s 'special' is omitted and its 'extraordinary' is termed 'special' or 'particular.' With that caveat in mind, I have thought it nonetheless useful to retain Milton's own terms.

In more recent Milton scholarship two studies deserve recognition here. Despite obscuring the distinction between ordinary and extraordinary providence, Joan Bennett writes illuminatingly about 'providences,' testing situations requiring interpretation, choice, and action. She discusses the responses to some such trials of the loyal angels and the Book 9 separation scene of Eve and Adam, emphasizing the continuing process: 'each event, or outcome, is a providence to be read in preparation for the next effort, which will then result in an "event" or outcome.'[8] Her too brief discussion might be extended to many other providences in the poem, none more wonderful than the first granted to a human. Adam, reasoning out the differences between himself, his Creator, and the lesser creatures, respectfully argues his need for a companion. The Creator responds approvingly, 'Thus far to try thee, Adam, I was pleas'd,' 'for trial only brought, / To see how thou could judge of fit and meet' (8: 437, 447–8). Although God had foreseen and made provision for Adam's need, he uses that need as a first trial of Adam's judgment. Both special and extraordinary providence in one divine event.

In a bold and imaginative study John Rogers has traced the convergence of providential causation and contemporary vitalist science with the consequence that God's will, expressed in general providence, and natural law become, he argues, coterminous. Rogers finds 'competing narratives' in the epic, one naturalistic 'at the heart of the poem's attempt to ground in the authority of science a new logic of individualism.' In the postlapsarian books this is contested by 'an assertion of the strong arm of providential control,' which 'disappointingly orthodox faith' Rogers exorcises by negating extraordinary providence with the departure of Adam and Eve from the garden.[9] Much of this is theologically dubious and simply distorts the poem (problems to which I shall return in chapter 7); nonetheless Rogers provocatively confronts the subject too often shunted to the margins.

Despite such promising overtures, in the past two decades the main stream of Milton scholarship has taken a turn away from religion. The two dominant currents have been driven by topical relevance on the one hand (e.g., women, gender, ecology, war, colonialism, violence, terrorism) and, on the other, seventeenth-century politics, republicanism in particular. How much of the first category is for all time or only of an age remains to be seen. It has had the effect, when providence gets noticed at all, of sometimes looking at it through the wrong end of the telescope. One scholar, recognizing that both the Virginia colonist Captain John Smith and the poet John Milton employ providential discourse, concludes, 'Milton is the garden of Eden's John Smith.'[10] Salmons in both, as Shakespeare's Fluellen would say. Scholarship on Milton's politics and particularly on republicanism has a more clearly enduring value, although this new 'orthodoxy,' particularly as it is defined through his disillusionment with Cromwell, has so far swept the field that there are signs of an emerging backlash.[11] Historians have been praiseworthy in their awareness that religion and politics were inseparable during the Civil War and Interregnum period, whereas literature scholars, in their eagerness to embrace republicanism, have been more prone to slight religion.

Recently, paralleling the reconsideration of Milton's republicanism, there have been indications of a pendulum swing toward religion – sometimes, however, with disconcerting effect. Judging from the absence of a personal conversion experience and 'the apparent absence of a conviction of sin,' Stephen Fallon contends that, 'while Milton is a theological poet, he is not a religious poet.' Although he acknowledges 'One might argue' that Milton's Arminianism accounts for these absences, that possibility is quickly dismissed; his book goes on effectively to restage the Synod of Dort with Milton in the defendant's chair and Fallon acting as a Calvinist judge.[12] Fallon appears to have a somewhat limited comprehension of how Arminianism affected Milton's thought, certainly as it concerns providence. Although my subject is the poem and the poet only tangentially, I would point to Milton's experience of providence as the area of religious sensibility corresponding to the Puritan touchstones that Fallon correctly finds missing.

This study is an exercise in historical interpretation. It draws heavily on recent scholarship in history, religion, and theology, running the risk of seeming obvious or superficial to experts in those fields. But a primary task has been reconstructing a variety of intellectual contexts, a number of which are likely to be less familiar to Milton readers and scholars. Like Rogers, I am interested in exploring the ways that providentialism infiltrates various kinds of discourse, ranging from military to medical, political to philosophic, theological to thaumaturgic – to steal a phrase from John Goodwin, 'the theater of Discourse.' For the reasons just rehearsed, Milton scholarship from earlier decades frequently has proven more relevant than that in the past twenty years;

nonetheless, I do take advantage of, correct, or dispute current work wherever it becomes pertinent.

Undertaking what, to the best of my knowledge, is the first monograph-length study of providence in the epic immediately poses a problem of strategy since, from a seventeenth-century perspective, providence could be said to account for everything in the poem. Rather than attempting an encyclopedic and unavoidably repetitive coverage, I have chosen a prismatic approach, examining significant facets of the subject. After an introductory chapter on providence, the following chapters on *Paradise Lost* attempt to do two things: first, to demonstrate the variety of implicit organizational structures – 'designs' to use a term contemporary with it – that give the vast poem the firm coherence to which readers respond.[13] Milton surely believed as firmly as did Sir Thomas Browne that there are underlying principles of order in everything created; his poetic simulations of them, however, are more varied and subtle than Browne's relentless pursuit of the quincunx. Second, they explore in depth the nuances of individual episodes or narrative sequences, particularly at some points seen as textual cruxes, in which the characters of the narrative, angels and humans alike, are faced with trials and choices. It is suggested throughout that the distinction between design and trial, despite sometimes being as hazy here as it was in the seventeenth century, conforms to the difference between ordinary and extraordinary providence. Large designs will be most evident in chapters 2 and 7, framing the intervening chapters which focus on the 'trials' of characters in the order that they are introduced – Satan, the Son, Eve, Adam – arranged in a loose progression through the poem.

By synthesizing the work of various historians, chapter 1 demonstrates the centrality of providence to seventeenth-century thought and life. It then argues that Milton's own conception of providence was deeply influenced by his Arminianism, which suffuses the poem in important ways. Although there is general agreement that on major points Milton's theology closely paralleled that of Jacob Arminius, I argue for a direct indebtedness. To clearly differentiate Milton's views on providence from those of English Calvinism, the next section compares his beliefs to those of the Englishman most thoroughly and famously identified with providence, Oliver Cromwell. Lastly, it suggests an evolving, implicit dialogue between Milton and Andrew Marvell on the subject, focusing on the figure of Cromwell.

Chapter 2 attempts to imagine or conjecture just how the blind poet responded to the most intimidating of personal trials, using the poetic talent that was his own providence, and which he dared not bury, to compose *Paradise Lost*. It argues that in the composition he drew on his knowledge of the classical art of memory and on the medieval tradition of *sacra memoria*, an amalgam of meditation and classical mnemonics that gave him a method of 'unfolding' scripture. Within the epic the architectural backdrop for memory places and images becomes cosmic; those places – Paradise, Hell, Heaven – shade into a complementary scheme, the Last Things, completing it with Death and Judgment, the two things that are acts or conditions rather than places. The poet's response to his personal providence thus was to recreate the design of God's providence at large.

Milton's Arminian conception of free will and providential trials embraces angels, as well as humans, and chapter 3 looks at what Satan does with the freedom extended to him by God's permissive will. It examines the two tactics by which Satan seeks to achieve the subversion of Adam and Eve. In contemporary discourse force and fraud were inescapably identified with a particular kind of godlessness, Machiavellianism. The first section on force examines Satan's use of and identification with a particular military tactic from the Civil Wars; both literally and figuratively he is a 'Forlorn Hope.' The section on fraud looks at Satan's disguises, which invariably reveal more than they conceal, discussing the related problems of hypocrisy and of the curse on the serpent. Because the danger of Satan should be penetrable by beings made 'sufficient' to stand, providence converts his disguised assaults to good ends in two ways: first, as trials and then, if the responses are right, to defences.

Chapter 4 introduces the embodiment of the providence to which Satan already has sworn his opposition. Even though the entire design of the epic is predicated on his future incarnation as Jesus Christ, the Son of God is the most intangible of characters within the action of the poem, audible as a voice and visible as a blaze of light. Milton symbolizes his mediatorial and providential function through an extended sequence of sight and light imagery, culminating particularly in the homonymic identification of sun with Son. Satan, continuing his voyage to the new world, is afforded a sequence of providences, opportunities to respond to the Son, all of which he rejects. Instead, in his Book 4 soliloquy to the sun, he reaffirms his hopelessness, his hatred, and intimates his future course as a negative parallel to the Son – his incarnation through Antichrist.

Chapter 5 turns to the humans over whom the Son and Satan, providence and antiprovidence war, and particularly to Eve, the hero of Book 10. It defines her relation to Adam in the pattern, informed by Milton's Arminianism and traducianism, of creation, separation, trial, and reunion through dialogue. Then it explores the Book of Tobit frame-story, which implicitly casts Eve and Adam as Sarah and Tobias, whose chaste marriage was modelled on their progenitors'. Milton uses the lore and discourse of demonic possession and exorcism as a palimpsest underlying Eve's temptation by Satan-Asmodeus. She responds wrongly to the Book 9 trial and temptation, but in Book 10 she rallies Adam from despair and sets them on the path to redemption, a righteous providence.

In the epic reordering of the Last Things, Hell, Heaven, and Judgment all appear before the human encounter with Death. Chapter 6 focuses on Adam's confrontation, in the vision of Abel's murder, with the fact of death and the legacy he passes to his descendants. The compact description evokes the tradition of Abel and Cain as types of Jesus and Judas; contemporary discourse on the circulation of the blood and on the soul in the blood; and Milton's own belief in mortalism. Adam, terrified by the sight that he only partially understands, does not yet realize that death itself is a beneficent work of providence.

Chapter 7 examines the entire span of Christian history, its larger providential design, and the actions of extraordinary providence, the sequence of trials that Adam experiences. It considers the nature of Christian time, which the design of the final books represents as both linear and recurrent by typologically paralleling the six visions in Book 11 to the six ages or 'days' of the week in Book 12. The shift from vision to narration accommodates the belief that Adam should not see beyond the first day in which his physical life ends. When drowned in tears at the sight of the Flood, he undergoes a symbolic death and baptism. Lastly, Books 11 and 12 follow the pattern of a conversion narrative. The climax occurs with Adam's acceptance of Christ as his redeemer, a truly extraordinary providence that Eve, it is implied, shares.

Alert readers will notice that certain speeches and events recur in several chapters to be examined from different perspectives. Rather than repetitiousness or my indecisiveness, this might be seen as further evidence that *Paradise Lost*, like all great poems, is inexhaustible in its linguistic richness. There is no last word on any of its words. I have kept in mind Milton's own example and tried not to harp incessantly on the argument of providence; the poem itself is that argument, as well as the extraordinary providence, both exceptional talent and trial, that the poet was granted in its creation.

And now, to borrow a line from Oliver Cromwell, 'My dear friend, let us look into providences; surely they mean somewhat.'[14]

Chapter One

Providence and Providences

> So ubiquitous was providentialism indeed, and at times so repetitive and predictable in its expression, that our familiarity with it may breed, if not contempt, then at least neglect. Conventional providentialism belongs to conventional piety, and conventional piety, the bread and butter of so much seventeenth-century thinking, can easily be mistaken for mere literary decoration.[1]
>
> Blair Worden

In chiding his fellow historians for neglecting the engine primarily driving 'seventeenth-century political argument and decision-making,' Blair Worden felt he had to refute the modern assumption that cynicism underlay the ubiquitous explanations of and appeals to providence. Literary scholars have been equally as neglectful, if for a different reason; for many of them, it appears that evocations of providence do seem 'mere literary decoration,' something too banal to require further attention. To the contrary, Alexandra Walsham maintains that, far from being a marginal feature of the culture, providentialism had 'nearly universal' acceptance: 'It was a set of ideological spectacles through which individuals of all social levels and from all positions on the confessional spectrum were apt to view their universe, an invisible prism which helped them to focus the refractory meanings of both petty and perplexing events.'[2] That being the case, providential discourse, whether in sermons, political tracts, scientific treatises, or poems should be understood as penetrating to the marrow, not remaining simply a decorative surface.

A Primer on Providence

At the simplest level, divine providence is 'The foreknowing and benevolent care and government of God (or of nature, etc.), divine direction, control, or guidance' (*OED*, s.v. 3), but it immediately becomes more complicated. Seventeenth-century writers customarily distinguished general from special providence, the government of the natural world by laws set in motion at the time of creation from God's particular concern for humans.[3] The eighth chapter of *De Doctrina Christiana* on God's providence seems, in this respect, entirely conventional, stating: 'the GOVERNMENT OF THE UNIVERSE . . . is either GENERAL or SPECIAL.'[4] 'General' pertains to the observation, preservation, and governance of all created things; 'special' is not a separate category but denotes a particular concern with angels (chap. 9) and humans (chap. 10) as the most superior of creatures, a superiority established by their free will. Chapter 8, however, introduces a further distinction; general providence is either 'ordinary,' maintaining the system of causality, or 'extraordinary' ('ordinaria vel extraordinaria'). The latter produces an effect 'outside the normal order of nature' or 'gives to some chosen person the power' to do so (*CPW* 6: 340–1). Understandably, in common usage distinctions are less strict and such terms tend to be used interchangeably; outside theological discourse 'special' most frequently compresses *De Doctrina*'s 'special' and 'extraordinary' into one.

God's eternal vigilance works in tandem with his omnipotence, but exactly how could be a mystery, causing the boundaries between general and special, special and extraordinary to blur, making the entire concept rather fluid and subjective. George Herbert's poem concisely expresses his sense of the relation as a seamless partnership: 'O Sacred Providence, who from end to end / Strongly and sweetly movest, shall I write, / and not of thee, through whom my fingers bend / To hold my quill?'[5] Whereas ordinary providence moves 'from end to end,' is it special or extraordinary providence that motivates the smallest physical action, without which he could not hold the pen to become 'Secretarie of thy praise' – that is, recorder of God's secret ways (*OED*, 'secretary,' 1.c)? Matthew 10: 29–31 was a universally favourite proof text; and Hamlet can say confidently, 'There is special providence in the fall of a sparrow' (V. ii. 219–20);[6] however, others might see the 'divinity that shapes our ends' (V.ii.10) as the process of ordinary providence.

The manifestation of general providence commences with or from creation and the provision of natural law, 'that constant and ordered system of causes which was established by [God] in the beginning' (*CPW* 6: 340), extending to the end of the temporal order. The Christian perception of history is by definition providential because the advent of Jesus Christ 'marks the direct entrance of God into the historical process,' giving radically new significance 'to the entire range of human events, past as well as future.'[7] Oliver Cromwell advised his son Richard, 'Recreate yourself with Sir Walter Raughleye's History: it's a body of history, and will add much more to your understanding than fragments of story.'[8] Cromwell's unstated assumptions might be glossed with Bacon's more explicit statement that 'while the mind of man looketh upon second causes scattered, it may sometimes rest in them; confederate and linked together, it must needs fly to providence and deity.'[9] Thus far, there might be universal assent. But how does one account for aberrations in the natural order? Were meteors and comets, floods, earthquakes,and plague freaks of nature programmed into the system or demonstrations of extraordinary providence?

With the rise of the mechanical philosophy later in the century, some spoke 'as if God's providence consisted solely in the original act of creation and that thereafter the world had been left to be governed mechanically by the wheels which the Creator had set in motion.'[10] The Cambridge Platonist Henry More, convinced that God could not create anything less than the best possible world, posited a 'Spirit of Nature' to attend its operation, leaving the distant Creator, perhaps – to quote James Joyce – 'above his handiwork, invisible, refined out of existence, indifferent, paring his fingernails.' This restriction on God's free will was too much for Robert Boyle. Not only was he capable of making an even greater world if he so desired, 'God, by his right of dominion, might without any violation of the laws of justice, have destroyed and even annihilated *Adam* and *Eve* before they had eaten of the forbidden fruit, or had been commanded to abstain from it.'[11]

Most contemporaries would have sided with Boyle by envisioning an active, interventionist, or voluntarist God, who freely dispensed with his own rules as he saw fit. Richard Sibbes chided, 'God doth not put things into a frame, as we do clocks.'[12] Although *De Doctrina* does not specify when extraordinary providence came into effect, logically it might be understood as a consequence of the Fall. Yet the prohibition on the tree of knowledge provided warrant for believing that God decreed either special or extraordinary trials of humans from the outset, an option of which *Paradise Lost* takes full advantage. Herbert may have grasped the balance of ordinary and extraordinary providence in

Figure 1. Title-page engraving by William Marshall to Sir Thomas Browne, *Religio Medici*, printed for Andrew Crooke, 1642, pirated edition. In 1643 Crooke printed the authorized edition. EC65. B8185R.1642. Houghton Library, Harvard University.

his own life, but advised the Country Parson to instruct his parishioners: 'considering the great aptnesse Countrey people have to think that all things come by a kind of naturall course,' he must labour 'to reduce them to see Gods hand in all things, and to believe, that things are not set in such an inevitable order, but that God often changeth it according as he sees fit, either for reward or punishment.'[13] 'Gods hand' or, alternatively, 'the hand of Heaven' was perhaps the most common metaphor used to express extraordinary providence, the activity of this extremely 'hands-on' deity. William Marshall's title-page engraving for Sir Thomas Browne's *Religio Medici* provides a graphic example:[14] a young man falls from a rocky pinnacle toward surging waves that crash against its base; a hand emerging from clouds reaches out to save him (fig. 1). It may suggest falling away from the church and evokes New Testament accounts of providential salvation from stormy seas (e.g., Matt. 14: 24–33; Acts 27: 13–44). The inscription *à caelo salus* (salvation from heaven) plays on the literal sense of *salus* (health), appositely for the religion of a physician.

Such interventions were 'providences,' events either immediately positive ('mercies' and 'deliverances') or negative ('judgments' and 'afflictions') – in Herbert's phrase, 'reward or punishment' – which must be understood as signs and portents. The meanings of the latter seldom were as unmistakable as Marshall's engraving; again, the difficulty was in interpreting them.[15] Affliction, for example, might be a deserved punishment or, conversely, a sign that God thought someone was worthy of particular attention. In the throes of a near-fatal illness, John Donne famously discovered that 'affliction is a treasure, and scarce any man hath enough of it.'[16] Herbert agreed, 'Affliction then is ours; / We are the trees, whom shaking fastens more, / While blustering windes destroy the wanton bowres' ('Affliction (V),' 19–21). To John Bunyan afflictions were 'dark providences' and always impelled by 'the hand of God.'[17] The teen-aged Dubliner James Ussher, later to become archbishop of Armagh, brooded over the possibility that the absence of affliction in his life was a sign of God's disfavour.[18]

However much sermons warned that, while God occasionally made the meanings of his providences clear, for the most part his ways were inscrutable, the temptation to search for signs of grace and election was irresistible for many. And so irresistibly dramatic are the accounts of their efforts that modern scholarship often leaves the impression providentialism was a particularly Puritan phenomenon. In fact, 'All post-Reformation theologians taught that nothing could happen in this world without God's permission.'[19] The practical effect was that most Protestants exhibited an intense preoccupation, if not obsession, with providence as a consequence of the now direct relation between God and the individual. Whereas Puritans were motivated by their acceptance of the total depravity and impotence of humans, high church 'Arminians' felt much the same anxiety about salvation. Worden distinguishes royalist or Anglican providentialism from the Puritan type as being less preoccupied with grace and election, and 'neither as frequently nor as intensely expressed.'[20] Yet Charles I went through the Civil Wars haunted by the possibility that his weakness in consenting to Strafford's execution had provoked God's judgment in punishment, a conclusion the justice of which he acknowledged in his scaffold speech: 'Many times [God] does pay justice by an unjust sentence; that is ordinary. I will only say that an unjust sentence that I suffered for to take effect is punished now by an unjust sentence on me.'[21] Moreover, Clarendon's wartime advice to the king, as well as his subsequent interpretation of events in *The History of the Rebellion*, was strongly shaped by his own providential thinking.[22] Walsham reduces the difference between camps to a matter of 'temperature': 'puritans were simply the "hotter sort" of providentialists.' In her view, English providentialism 'played a pivotal role in forging a collective Protestant consciousness, a sense of confessional identity which fused anti-Catholicism and patriotic feeling and which united the elite with their social inferiors.'[23]

During the Civil Wars and their aftermath, both sides strenuously attempted to control the discourse of providentialism, dismissing often with rancorous contempt each other's claims to divine guidance. Reporting the storming of Basing House (14 October 1645), Hugh Peters with uncharacteristic thoughtfulness remarked, 'Doubtless this providence of God hath a double voice, the one unto the enemy, and the other unto us.'[24] Nonetheless, the opposing camps were in large agreement as to the nature and requirements of providence. An activist and interventionist deity who constantly tested and schooled humans with providences expected them to respond actively to those signs and portents. In the spirit of Paul's exhortation, they were to 'Trye all things, *and* kepe that which is good' (1 Thess. 10: 21) in the effort to understand God's will and act upon it.[25] God values 'Triers' and 'Doers.' As Thomas Taylor asserted, 'We teach that only Doers shall be saved, and by their doing though not for their doing.'[26] To be sure, there were obvious hazards in this wrestling to understand God's intention, not the least of which was the danger of overconfidence. This form of hubris was the target of the Familist Hendrik Niclaes, whose personified figure of 'Searching Providence' attempts to surpass God.[27] Yet the alternative of inactivity was more terrible, as Charles's compliance in the face of Strafford's sentence witnesses. Interior activity, of course, need not be mistaken for passivity. 'Waiting on providences' or 'waiting on God' for a sign of the right moment to act was a matter of exacting, prayerful deliberation, characteristic of Cromwell's decision-making and exemplified in the celebrated discipline of the New Model Army. 'We should neither outrun nor be wanting to providence,' Sibbes advised, for 'when things are clear, and God's will is manifest, further deliberation is dangerous.'[28] Properly understood, the resolution of Milton's Sonnet 19 is not a resigned acceptance that blindness has forestalled his poetic plans, but an acknowledgment that God will tell him when to resume them: 'They also serve who only stand and wait.'[29] The readiness is all.

Arminius and Milton on Providence

Over the course of the seventeenth century, English theology underwent a sea change, from Calvinism to Arminianism. The Dutch theologian Jacobus Arminius (Jacob Harmensz, 1559–1609) evolved from Philipp Melancthon and his Danish follower Niels Hemmingsen a belief, challenging Calvin's theory of predestination, that election is conditional on faith. In the view of Arminius, God 'decreed to receive into favour those who repent and believe, and, in Christ, for his sake and through him, to effect the salvation of such penitents and believers as persevered to the end, but [to] leave in sin and under wrath all impenitent persons and unbelievers, and to damn them as alien from Christ.'[30] Grace is available to all; those who choose to accept it are the elect, and those who refuse are the damned. Election is thus contingent on divine foreknowledge of faith; Christ's atonement is universal; grace is resistible; and the elect can fall from grace. Arminius's major work, *The Declaration of Sentiments* (*Verclaringhe*) was published only the year before his death, but in 1610 his adherents published *Remonstrance*, addressing five issues: predestination, redemption, total depravity, grace, and perseverance. Calvinist orthodoxy struck back at the Synod of Dort (1618–19), which condemned these teachings and the Remonstrants were expelled from the Dutch Reformed Church.[31] Among the English delegates was an observer, the 'ever memorable' John Hales, who confided to a friend, '*There, I bid John Calvin good-night.*'[32] A portent of things to come.

Reacting against the regnant Whig and Marxist accounts of the Civil War period as a class revolution, Nicholas Tyacke turns Christopher Hill's world upside down, neatly reversing the paradigm.[33] In his account, the Royalists were the revolutionaries and the Puritans the reactionaries. Whereas the latter were rock-ribbed Calvinists, from his ascension onward Charles had promoted an 'Arminian' religion, first in the writings of Richard Montagu and Thomas Jackson, and later, with the appointment of William Laud to archbishop of Canterbury

(1633), by the implementation of its policies. Although the Church of England's theology was Calvinist at the time of Laud's ascension, its prayer book was a Catholic adaptation, an opening that he exploited to give English Arminianism a high church inflection alien to its namesake: a renewed emphasis on the sacraments, baptism and the eucharist, auricular confession, the conversion of communion tables to altars at the east end, conformity to the prayer book. More than the theology, it was the revival of Catholic practices that so alarmed Puritans and made the word 'Arminian' an expression of bitter contempt during the late 1630s and 1640s. Because English Arminianism was so inextricably associated with episcopacy and with the absolutist monarchy that Charles espoused, perhaps only when those threats were contained could the theology be assessed more dispassionately. In 1647 Richard Baxter began writing *The Saints Everlasting Rest*, when he had a sudden illumination, a 'clear apprehension,' that led to *The Aphorismes of Justification* (1649). Although John Goodwin may have preceded Baxter and others would follow, William Lamont describes his as being the most significant defence of Arminianism as 'a tenable Protestant doctrine.'[34] Baxter later acknowledged that his earlier hostility to the doctrine resulted from the bogeyman of the false 'Laudian Arminianism' during the prelude to civil war:

> I did ignorantly think that Arminianisme (which Dr. Heylyn maketh the chief matter of the strife) had bin a more intolerable pernicious evill to the Church than since I found it; and I proved in my Catholicke Theologie (to this day unanswered) that it is of lesse consequence than I then imagined. And this conceit made me think the Bishops more injurious and former Parliaments accusations of Arminianisme more necessary than they were.[35]

By the 1650s, Lamont argues, 'A Puritan Arminianism was, thus, possible . . . and liberty could be given an altered dimension accordingly.'[36]

Although this 'altered dimension' has some obvious implications for providentialism, discussions of Arminianism in England tend to focus exclusively on the subversion of Calvinist predestination. Arminius himself thought deeply about the issue of providence, devoting four disputations to the subject and commenting on it in various other writings.[37] Providence he defines as 'the solicitous, everywhere powerful, and continued [*intuitus*] inspection and oversight of God, according to which he exercises a general care over the whole world, and over each of the creatures and their actions and passions.'[38] Two keynotes emerge strongly from these works: his desire to vindicate divine justice and his belief in human free will. To this end, rather than God's absolute omnipotence, he emphasizes its potential, which is regulated by justice; God engages in a covenant with humans to enable their 'spontaneous, free and liberal obedience, according to . . . stipulations and promises' (2: 67). He denies that grace was a corrective response to the Fall; rather, it was present from the beginning in the Creation. Providence Arminius conceives to be subsequent to creation, God's activity within the temporal order, which is either ordinary or extraordinary (2: 69). Neither can providence 'impinge against creation,' nor 'inhibit or hinder the use of free will in man' (2: 488). Reacting against the line of Reformed theology that subordinates providence to predestination, Arminius takes pains to refute the implication that God was the author of sin. He does so through explanations of divine permission, which follows logically from the 'liberty of choice, which God, the Creator, has implanted in his rational creature' (1: 513). Providence can guide through hindrances – such impediments to sinful choices as commandments and moral laws – but a just god cannot abrogate free will by preventing sin; there must be divine concurrence to every human act: 'For it is right and proper that the obedience of the creature should be tried, and that he should abstain from an unlawful act and from the desire of obeying his own inclinations, not through a deficiency of the requisite divine concurrence' (1: 517–18). In conclusion to the disputations on the relation of sin to providence, Richard Muller summarizes, 'Arminius returns to his originally stated theme – the vindication of divine justice and the assertion of the existence of providence despite the existence of sin.'[39] Finally, Arminius's God is a God of love. Explaining the attributes of God that are analogous to human affections and passions, he writes: 'Love is an affection of union in God, whose objects are not only God himself and the good of justice, but also the creature [*referens Deum*] imitating or related to God either according to [*imaginem*] likeness, or only according to [*vestigium*] impress, and the felicity of the creature' (2: 45). 'This relationship of the divine love to the divine goodness,' Muller concludes, 'has profound ramifications for the whole of theology.'[40]

More precisely, William den Boer has shown that at the foundation of Arminius's mature theology is the concept of *duplex amor Dei*: God's love for justice, which assumes priority, and his love for humans. Arminius rejected the Calvinist doctrine of predestined election regardless of merit because it reverses the proper order, placing humans before justice. As he explains the 'mutual relation' between the two: 'The latter species of love, which expends itself to the creatures, cannot come into exercise, except so far as it is permitted by the former' (1: 234). The love for justice is satisfied by the Son's Atonement, negating the disobedience of sin and allowing the love for humans to be freely expressed as the grace available to all those who accept it.[41] Keith Stanglin concurs with den Boer, 'For Arminius, God's *duplex amor* toward righteousness and the sinful creature is the foundation of the Christian religion, and thus, of salvation and assurance as well.'[42] One recalls that Hales's conversion occurred from the 'well pressing' by the Remonstrant Simon Episcopius of John 3: 16, 'For God so loved the world, that he gave his only begotten son, that whosoever believeth in him should not perish, but have everlasting life.' God manifests his twofold love through providence, most centrally in the gift of his son, who inseparably links the two.

Unlike Hales, Milton does not tell us just when he bid Calvin goodnight and embraced the views that so distinctly make *Paradise Lost* an Arminian poem.[43] His putative first reference to Arminians (1641) exemplifies the knee-jerk reaction to Laudian innovation; the rhetorical bracketing, 'doctrines of Popery, Arminianisme, and Libertinisme' (*CPW* 1: 975) says it all. The comment, 'that sect among us which is nam'd of *Arminius* are wont to charge us of making God the author of sinne' (Feb. 1644, *CPW* 2: 293), reflects accurate knowledge of either Peter Baro or Arminius himself, while firmly placing himself with the Calvinists. But *Areopagitica* in November of that year tantalizingly raises the possibility of thought in transition. 'It is not forgot, since the acute and distinct *Arminius* was perverted merely by the perusing of a nameless discours writt'n at *Delf't*, which at first he took in hand to confute' (*CPW* 2: 519–20). The allusion to the 'nameless discours' proves, Maurice Kelley believed, that Milton had access to Arminius's Latin *opera* by this date. His mixed assessment, 'acute and distinct' versus 'perverted,' may convey a mind balanced between approval of free will and reluctance to let go of absolute predestination. The memorable defence of divine permission and radical free will that follows a few pages later, however, could be read as an eloquent restatement of Arminius's colourless theological discourse: 'Many there be that complain of divin Providence for suffering *Adam* to transgress, foolish tongues! when God gave him reason, he gave him freedom to choose, for reason is but choosing' (*CPW* 2: 527).[44] Milton's final direct comment on Arminius defends him from 'that Imputation' of 'setting up free will against free grace,' and insists that he 'grounds himself largely upon Scripture only' (*CPW* 8: 425–6), Milton's approved method.

About the general Arminianism of *Paradise Lost*, it is difficult to find serious disagreement, but hardly a consensus on what that means. One still encounters confusions with the Laudian variety, attempts to enlist Milton among the sectarian 'free-willers,' and efforts to distinguish sharply his views from those of Arminius on particular issues.[45] Kelley long ago showed that both the epic poem and *De Doctrina Christiana* were Arminian in their theology, setting a possibly unfortunate precedent in argumentation by using the treatise as a 'gloss' on the poem.[46] While such cross-referencing can be useful, it sometimes distracts readers from concentrating on just what the poem does say. The narrator explains that divine concurrence is extended to the fallen angels: 'Through God's high sufferance for the trial of man' (1: 366; cf. *Areop.* above). In his first speech the Father declares unequivocally human sufficiency, free will, and divine permission, denying that 'Predestination over-rul'd / Thir will, dispos'd by absolute Decree / or high foreknowledge' (*PL* 3: 114–16). In the sense of 'difficult to comprehend' (*OED* s.v. II: 6), 'high' may indicate 'middle knowledge'; *De Doctrina* recognizes the role of contingent circumstances in God's foreknowledge.[47] Near the end of Michael's tutorial, he instructs Adam in the doctrine of resistible grace redeeming 'as many as offr'd life / Neglect not' (*PL* 12: 425–6). Not surprisingly, most attention has been focused on the Father's deliberate evisceration of Calvinist election in Book 3: 173–202. The passage begins with the announcement of universal grace 'freely voutsaf'd' (175), and continues, wheeling the Trojan Horse into position, with the stunning declaration, 'Some I have chosen of peculiar grace / Elect above the rest; so is my will' (183–4).

Already this may not be what it immediately seems. Whereas Stephen Fallon argues that here Milton specifies 'a Calvinist super-elect,' in fact Calvin never uses the phrase 'peculiar grace.'[48] Although Kelley offered Erasmus as a source for *gratia peculiaris*, Milton very probably took the phrase, as well as the rhetorical manoeuvre, directly from Arminius. In the *Examen . . . Perkinsiani* (1599–1602), his lengthy response to William Perkins's *De Praedestinationis Modo et Ordine* (1598), Arminius addresses the question of a peculiar grace: 'Of what importance to this matter is it, whether he may have obtained the offered blessing by the aid of common or of peculiar grace, if the former, as well as the latter, has obtained the free assent of man, and it has been foreknown by God that it certainly would obtain it?' As if entertaining a hypothesis, he concedes that peculiar grace might manifest a greater love from God, but insists that, like common grace, it would be consistent with human free will and therefore conditional and resistible.[49] In short, it does not matter. There are only two categories – those who accept grace are the elect and those who refuse, the reprobate. To be clear about the implications for the Father's speech: whereas Fallon sees a 'trifold' division of souls – those elect by special grace, by common grace, and the reprobate – I would reaffirm with Kelley the older reading of two categories, those who accept the offered grace and those who refuse it. Nor does one need to go as far as Erasmus for substantiation; it is right in Arminius.[50]

Fallon may well be right in calling peculiar grace 'Calvinist,' if one qualifies that as English Calvinism, which was, *mutatis mutandis*, more Catholic than the pope. Of Arminius's opponent William Perkins (1558–1602), Thomas Fuller said, 'He would pronounce the word *Damme* with such an emphasis as left a dolefull Echo in his auditours eare a great while after.'[51] Perkins was a disciple of Theodore Beza, and made predestination the centre of his theology. A supralapsarian, Perkins believed in absolute, double predestination, the ultimate zero sum game. Calvin, explaining Matthew 22: 14, 'For many are called but few are chosen,' distinguished between two callings, a universal grace and a special grace, 'which [God] deigns *for the most part* to give to the believers alone' (*Institutes* 3: 24, 8, italics added), thus allowing possible exceptions. Perkins hardened this into common and special (*specialis* or *singularis*), given exclusively to the predestined elect. Thomas Corns has remarked that '"peculiar" is a word of some currency in Calvinist discourse,' noting that it occurs in Norton's 1561 translation of the *Institutes*.[52] Certainly it was in play a century later. *Redemption Redeemed*, the Arminian John Goodwin's extended argument for universal redemption, asserts 'Election, not of individualls, but of Species,' scoffing at the notion of 'particular persons' elect or reprobate before the Creation.[53] This reduced Richard Resbury to sputtering rage: 'and if that peculiar grace which for the present [Goodwin] so soundly despiseth, and so boldly bid defiance to, shall yet magnifie it selfe in saving him, though by fire, yet let the zeal of the Lord for his own most precious truth burne his worke, for it is stubble.'[54] When Milton used the phrase, it must have been with full consciousness that he was doing so *épater le calviniste*, just as Arminius had done with Perkins.

Alternatively, the adjective 'peculiar' need not mean 'exclusive' or 'individual'; rather, it may reflect the recurrent formula of the Israelites as God's 'peculiar people,' a usage adapted by Paul to Christian believers: Jesus Christ 'gave himself for us that he might redeem us from all iniquity, and purify unto himself a peculiar people' (Titus 2: 14).[55]

Milton twice uses the phrase 'peculiar people' (*CPW* 2: 718, 7: 449); quotes it directly from Deuteronomy 14: 2 (*CPW* 2: 619); coins such variants as 'peculiar favour' and 'God's peculiar' (*CPW* 1: 747, 837); and the epic itself gives us 'one peculiar Nation to select / From all the rest' (PL 12: 111–12). God bestows 'peculiar mercy' on 'his people, so long as they remain his' (*CPW* 3: 325). '*Brittains* God,' Milton was convinced, 'hath yet ever had this Iland under the speciall indulgent eye of his providence' (CPW 1: 704).[56] If 'chosen of peculiar grace' refers to the special providence extended to the English people, this 'election' is again conditional, dependent on their remaining his, faithful to their covenant; it is still nothing like special election for chosen individuals.

Following on the heels of the 'peculiar grace' provocation is the fully Arminian explanation of conditional election through individual response to the grace that is universally accessible, from which only those 'who neglect and scorn' (3: 199) are excluded.[57] The 'Some' distinguished as 'Elect above the rest' makes clear Milton's view that, just as his poem will 'fit audience find, though few' (7: 31), the majority of people will spurn the offered grace. In this he expresses a belief shared by most English Protestants; John Jewel, bishop of Salisbury, predicted, 'We shall not go in routs; for we shall be but few.'[58] The concept of fallible persistency acknowledges that there can be backsliders among those who do choose rightly. Even past their initial acceptances God does provide hindrances to such apostasy: 'I will place within them as a guide / My Umpire *Conscience,* whom, if they will hear, / Light after light well us'd they shall attain, / And to the end *persisting*, safe arrive' (3: 194–7, my emphasis). This guide, reminding them of God's commandments and moral laws, is not fully identified until the very end of the poem when Adam and Eve, newly exiled from Eden, set off 'to choose / Thir place of rest and Providence thir guide' (12: 646–7). Complementing the thesis of providence is the love which John Shawcross identifies as the theme of the epic: 'Once we understand God's love of man, we understand Providence; once we understand Providence, we see God's justice; once we see God's justice, we should love God with all the attendant responsibilities of that love.'[59] His very formulation unconsciously underscores the twinned principles of Arminian theology, justice and love.

Arminius certainly was not the only theologian to focus on this pair of concepts;[60] he does, however, give them an individual inflection that accounts for the prominence of providence in his theology: 'Humanity was created for fellowship with God, an affirmation that Arminius's opponents did not predicate to all humanity.'[61] Although Milton does not quote directly or refer demonstrably to specific points in the writings of Arminius, an identikit of features is strongly suggestive. Consider: Arminius's insistence on the inviolability of human free will, which is endowed at Creation and never rescinded; his articulation of the order and intimate connection between the two loves through the Son's sacrifice, an act at once satisfying justice and expressing love; then his conception of providence as the agency by which these principles are coordinated and enacted. In short, a combination of characteristics very like those embodied in *Paradise Lost*. A distinctive aspect of Arminius's theology is his understanding of providence as a temporal act of God, 'not [*peractus*] completed in a single moment, but continued through the moments of the duration of things' (2: 68).[62] This concept lends itself well to the treatment of extraordinary interventions, 'providences,' as a continuous process of testing and learning, rather than the Calvinist 'judgments' and 'mercies,' individual signs of vindication or punishment. It may go too far to suggest that Milton consciously envisioned his poem as a demonstration of the *duplex amor Dei*, but his reading of Arminius appears to have reached to the core of his thinking about its theological foundations.

Arguing with Cicero in the *Artis Logicae*, Milton pronounced a correction; fortune properly should be called divine providence, 'the first cause of all things,' then paused for a side reflection: 'fate or divine decree does not force anyone to do evil, and on the hypothesis of divine foreknowledge all things are certain, to be sure, but not necessary' (*CPW* 8: 229).[63] He thus shares Arminius's concepts of divine permission and concurrence, enabling a condition of radical free will in a world governed by providence. In consequence the sense of personal liberty, the freedom to think and act whether rightly or wrongly which permeates the epic, emanates from an Arminian concept of volition: 'many there be that complain of divin Providence for suffering *Adam* to transgresse, foolish tongues! when God gave him reason, he gave him freedom to choose, for reason is but choosing; he had bin else a meer artificiall *Adam*, such an *Adam* as he is in the motions' (*CPW* 2: 527). It is complemented by the 'providences,' equally Arminian in their logic, the continuous trials experienced by humans and angels from Satan to the Son, affording them opportunities to choose in exercising that free will. The distinctive character of Milton's position can be illustrated by comparison with the contemporary Englishman who was most closely identified with providence.

Cromwell and Milton on Providence

Lamenting the untimely death of the Lord Protector, Henry Dawbeny affirmed, 'Now the greatest favourit of fortune, or properly speaking, the dearest Darling of Divine Providence, that ever the Christian World produced, was this most excellent person, his late most Serene Highnesse.'[64] For quite a number of years many fellow Englishmen shared Dawbeny's conviction that Oliver Cromwell was, in the idiom of a more flippant age, 'Destiny's Tot'; from the mid-forties through the fifties his status as an interpreter and beneficiary of providence was legendary – or, to some, notorious. Milton seems always to have been more cautious than Cromwell (and, to be fair, most contemporaries) about interpreting current events providentially: 'The hidden wayes of his providence we adore & search not; but the law is his reveled wil' (*CPW* 2: 292). He would have thoroughly approved Benjamin Whichcote's warning that there was 'a great danger of making false interpretations of providence.'[65] Battle victories during the Civil Wars and the contentious question of executing the king particularly excited providential rhetoric from both sides. In *The Tenure of Kings and Magistrates* Milton mocks the conveniently manipulatable providentialism of Presbyterian divines, 'Providence the word of command, that calls them from above, but always to som larger Benefice, or acts them into such or such figures, and promotions' (*CPW* 3: 255). *Eikonoklastes* scolds Charles for presuming to interpret events as God's judgments: 'He, who without warrant but his own fantastic surmise, takes upon him perpetually to unfold the secret and unsearchable Mysteries of high Providence, is likely for the most part to mistake and slander them' (*CPW* 3: 564; and see 528–9). This appears at odds with the perhaps obligatory assumption that Parliament's victory had God's approval, a position Milton is at pains to qualify circuitously: 'He would fain bring us out of conceit with the good *success* which God has voutsaf'd to us. Wee measure not our Cause by our success, but our success by our cause. Yet certainly in a good Cause success is a good confirmation' (3: 599). Since both sides believed their causes to be good, this may be a distinction without a difference, but Milton presumably could not disavow the Commonwealth position in the first of his official defences.[66] By the time of the *Second Defense*, he was far less politic.

Nine years older than Milton, Cromwell was born into a well-to-do family and attended the Huntingdon Free School wherein he was instructed by Dr Thomas Beard, author of *The Theatre of God's Judgements*

(1597). A collection of histories from various sources illustrating God's active and continuous intervention to punish sinners, *The Theatre* was one of the most popular English 'judgment books,' expanded in three editions (1612, 1631, 1648) and abridged in one (1618). It seems likely that Beard first instilled Cromwell with the belief that the acts of special providence, contemporary events equally with past history, are a means of divine revelation, a turn away from Calvin's insistence that providence in post-biblical history is unknowable.[67]

This particularly English view wrenched providential discourse throughout the Civil Wars; both sides gave lip service to the inscrutability of God's purposes, but inevitably celebrated victory in battle as a sign of the Lord's favour.[68] *The Souldiers Pocket Bible* (1643) marshalled scripture to 'shew the qualifications of his inner man, that is a fit Souldier to fight the Lords Battels.'[69] In *Anglia Rediviva* (1647), his narrative of the victorious New Model Army, Joshua Sprigge is forthright about his thesis: 'I hope *GOD* is drawn through all, and *Providence* is in the *fairest colour*, and the *greatest letter* in the Book.' Negotiating the surrender of Charles's Western Army, Sir Thomas Fairfax credits 'the good hand of God continuing with us' and his opponent Sir Ralph Hopton concedes, 'God hath indeed of late humbled us with many ill successes, which I acknowledge as a very certaine evidence of his just judgment against us for our personall crimes.'[70] Despite his own burden of personal guilt, Charles had no doubt about being in the right, once declaring to Prince Rupert, 'As a Christian, I must tell you that God will not suffer rebels to prosper or this cause to be overthrown.'[71] After the victory at Marston Moor, Cromwell wrote, chillingly if biblically, 'God made them as stubble to our swords.'[72] This was typical of Cromwell's interpretation of his victories; but, if less stridently, providential discourse was equally a feature of Fairfax's battle reportage. At Marston Moor when isolated from his troops, he attributed his unrecognized and unharmed passage through royalist horsemen to 'GOD's goodness.' More in Cromwell's spirit perhaps, earlier at Adwalton Moor Fairfax reported 'a remarkable passage of Divine Justice,' in which four soldiers who stripped the body of an enemy officer were promptly struck by a cannon ball.[73] In the heightened atmosphere of wartime, every act, every event was fraught with divine significance.

In what has been described as 'the mid-seventeenth-century heyday of providentialism,' that vision of life as a continuous, if not always translatable, semiotic communication of God's will was embodied, publicly and vocally, by Cromwell, informing his religious belief, his politics, his military strategy. In his 'brief character' of the Lieutenant General, Sprigge reported: 'It was observed GOD was with him, and he began to be renowned: insomuch that men found, that the narrow room whereunto his first imployments had confin'd their thoughts, must be enlarged to an expectation of greater things, and higher imployments, whereunto divine providence had designed him for the good of this Kingdom.'[74] The 'greater things, and higher imployments' led to Lord General, Lord Protector, and the offer of a crown that he refused, saying, 'I would not seek to set up that that providence hath destroyed and laid in the dust, and I would not build Jericho again.'[75]

Providentialism sometimes effectively settled political disputes, as was the case with the Engagement Controversy (1649–52), Parliament's attempt to secure loyalty by an oath of allegiance to a government that many believed illegitimate. John Dury urged, 'God's appointment of a power over us, is a just caus to oblige us to submission thereunto, whether hee doth it Providentially or Preceptively; or both waies.'[76] For Cromwell, however, persuading recalcitrant parliamentarians to accept his vision could be far more frustrating than pursuing the royal army; the temptation was always there to resolve the problem, following the example of Pride's Purge, by calling in the army – as he did in expelling the Rump Parliament. Men of good will were able to interpret this as an act of providence. Although bewildered by the sudden dispersal, 'like down blown off a thistle,' John Hall of Durham still believed, 'that the ways of Providence are unscrutable, and as such, though they seem to us unexpected and temerarious, yet are carried on with such a strange and supreme kind of design.'[77] It may have become harder to credit providence as Barebone's Parliament proved no more satisfactory to Cromwell, leading to the Protectorate and eventually the dissolution of the first Protectorate Parliament.

Yet it was not the multiplying political critics who finally shook the Protector's faith in his divine sustentation, but the one area in which he must have been most confident. In July 1655 came the news that the expedition to capture the island of Hispaniola in the West Indies had suffered a humiliating defeat, the only such disaster of his military career. As Cromwell felt keenly, in warfare 'a benevolent providence on one side is necessarily a judgment upon the other.'[78] Worden argues that this loss had 'a profound and lasting effect on him,' one from which 'he never fully recovered.' The following year a fast day was declared in recognition that 'the Lord hath been pleased in a wonderful manner to humble and rebuke us, in that expedition to the West Indies.' The rebuke provided a need to ponder whether 'we may have either failed in the spirit and manner wherewith the business hath been undertaken, or that the Lord sees some abomination, or accursed thing, by which He is provoked thus to appear against us.' The 'accursed thing,' Worden shows convincingly, alludes to Joshua 7: 1 and the entire chapter in which, after the fall of Jericho, the children of Israel suffer God's wrath until the hidden sinner Achan is exposed and punished, the implication being that Cromwell himself might be the 'abomination or accursed thing' for which England suffers. The Lord Protector became preoccupied with the penitential Psalm 85, reciting it to Parliament in September 1656, and later twice a day reciting to himself Psalm 71, 'O God, thou has taught me from my youth: / and hitherto have I declared thy wondrous works. / Now also when I am old and grayheaded, / O God, forsake me not' (Ps 71: 17–18). What had once been 'clear and unclouded' had become 'the dark paths through the providence and dispensations of God.'[79] Not long after,

> That Providence which had so long the care
> Of Cromwell's head, and numbered ev'ry hair,
> Now in its self (the glass where all appears)
> Had seen the period of his golden years:
> And thenceforth only did attend to trace,
> What death might least so fair a life deface.[80]

Andrew Marvell's tribute begins with a characteristic ambiguity that the Lord Protector might have appreciated. Starting with the allusion to Matthew 10: 30, the stanza can be read as an assertion of providence's lifetime care for Cromwell; equally, it can imply a hiatus after his golden period, departing with the Protectorate and attending again only at his death.

Milton's personal contacts with Cromwell were minimal, likely limited to a couple of short spans between campaigns when the general was able to attend meetings of the Council of State. Before Cromwell had come to take a prominent role in the government, Milton's increasing blindness already had restricted his secretarial responsibilities.[81] His writings address Cromwell only twice. The sonnet, 'Cromwell, our chief of men,' has the deleted manuscript title 'To the Lord Generall Cromwell May 1652 On the proposals of certaine ministers at ye Commtee for Propagation of the Gospell.'[82] Although the power of the New Model Army had repelled the Presbyterian-dominated Westminster

Assembly's proposal of an Established Church, the idea was revived in the Rump. The committee was formed at the instigation of John Owen, Cromwell's military chaplain in 1649–50 and his appointee in 1652 as vice-chancellor of Oxford University, sometimes derisively called 'Cromwell's Archbishop.' Owen proposed to regulate the ministry by expelling preachers with heretical beliefs, a need further demonstrated by a petition against the recently printed *Racovian Catechism*; Parliament duly responded with an order to burn the book in public. Milton was required to explain his judgment in licensing the *Catechism*; his interest, or lack thereof, in its contents has been considerably debated. Because Owen's personal bête noire was the evil of Socianism, its anti-Trinitarianism particularly has been the focus of attention; perhaps equally interesting is its opposition to predestination and commitment to free will – i.e., Arminianism.[83] In April Parliament approved compulsory maintenance of ministers, paid by tithes. The situation thus posed threats to a complex of Milton's beliefs: separation of church and state, freedom of religious belief, the liberty of the press, the evil of a hireling ministry. His sonnet reviews Cromwell's career, significantly naming only his victories over the treacherous Scots Presbyterians, before turning to his appeal: 'new foes arise / Threat'ning to bind our souls with secular chains / Help us to save free Conscience from the paw / Of hireling wolves whose Gospel is their maw' (11–14). Naming Cromwell's successes at Preston, Dunbar, and Worcester is not simple flattery. The poet reminds the Lord General of his providential guidance in 'rear[ing] God's Trophies' and pursuing 'his work' in order to prick awareness that religion is threatened in peacetime, perhaps the more endangered because less obviously so than on the battlefield.

It is difficult to imagine that Milton was not aware that, despite the Lord General's public commitment to toleration, Owen was unlikely to have advanced a proposal that did not have Cromwell's tacit support.[84] The appeal to 'Help us' must have been conceived as a gamble, an attempt to make him interpret rightly a different kind of trial. Perhaps he thought Cromwell would understand that a state-supported ministry evinced a distrust of providence, whereas, Milton later would maintain in his treatise *The Likeliest Means to Remove Hirelings*, 'they may securely be committed to the providence of God and the guidance of his holy spirit' (CPW 7: 304). Whether or not Cromwell ever saw the poem, Milton turned to a more secure source of support. Sir Henry Vane the younger, frustrated by his quest for religious freedom in Massachusetts, returned to England where he was elected to the Long Parliament and commenced a remarkable political career. Appointed Treasurer of the Navy and member of the Council of State, he was a leader and close ally of Cromwell in the Rump Parliament. Vane's eclectic theology may have been 'a unique hybrid, part-Trinitarian as well as part-Socinian, part-Calvinist but also part-Arminian and part-Antinomian'; however, his firm principles on religious policy could only have caused Milton to cheer: 'a rooted distrust of clerical power, whether of bishops or presbyters, and a belief that the State should abstain from interference in church matters altogether.'[85] Milton's sonnet, presented to Vane on 8 July (*CPW* 4, pt. 1: 174) is constructed on rhetorical antitheses that are resolved in the man's character: 'Both spiritual power and civil, what each means, / What severs each, thou hast learnt, which few have done. / The bounds of either sword to thee wee owe' (9–12). Confident in Vane's judgment and integrity, 'on thy firm hand religion leans' (13), Milton need not make an overt appeal for his help because, unlike Cromwell, Vane surely would be alert to this danger.

Times change, power shifts, alliances falter. Less than a year later, 20 April 1653, an outraged Cromwell launched into a tirade at the House; and, by pre-arrangement,

> Turning to [Major General] Harrison, he said, 'Call them in; call them in.' At Harrison's orders, the doors opened, and some thirty or forty soldiers . . . entered the House. At this point, Vane intervened, rising to speak: 'This is not honest,' he cried, 'yea it is against morality and common honesty.' Whereupon Cromwell cried, 'O Sir Henry Vane! Sir Henry Vane! The Lord deliver me from Sir Henry Vane!' (*CPW* 4, pt. 1: 216)

The Rump was dissolved; some would say that providence departed with the expelled MPs. Vane rusticated himself to write, first *The Retired Man's Meditations* (April 1655), and then *A Healing Question Propounded* (May 1656). The pamphlet attacks the military dictatorship, arguing that sovereignty should be placed in all the supporters of the 'Good Old Cause' and the army subjected to their authority; with power monopolized by a faction or an individual 'this is that anarchy that is the first rise and step to tyranny.' Rather than healing balm, the Lord Protector must have regarded this as salt rubbed in a wound. For his 'seditious book,' Vane was summoned before the Council, arrested, and imprisoned nearly four months. After Oliver's death, seemingly providence returned; Vane was elected to Richard Cromwell's Parliament, an outcome that was, he announced to the House, 'a special testimony of God's Providence.'[86]

Quite possibly Milton began writing *Pro Populo Anglicano Defensio Secunda* (May 1654) before Cromwell commenced the Protectorate; his response to the *Regii Sanguinis Clamor* (August 1552), undoubtedly slowed by his now complete blindness, both defends past actions and reflects present reality. Worden in fact believes that '*Defensio Secunda* was essentially written under the Rump,' revised following its dissolution and further revised during the Protectorate, but acknowledges the need to register its impact as published, 'which is to give the work the character of dramatic irony.'[87] The *Second Defense* pivots on two notable 'characters,' Milton's refutation of the personal attack on himself in the *Clamor* and his character of Cromwell. The two are linked thematically by the concern for 'real and substantial liberty' in all its varieties, 'namely ecclesiastical liberty, domestic or personal liberty, and civil liberty' about which Milton has written (CPW 4, pt. 1: 624) and his implied fear that these are threatened by the Protector's autocratic reign. After deserved praise for his achievements, acknowledgments that Cromwell has been the instrument of providence and that 'On you has fallen the whole burden of our affairs' (671), comes a direct appeal, 'restore to us our liberty, unharmed and even enhanced' by *not* ruling alone, instead admitting the proven republicans to his counsel (674). Some of those recommended would hardly have been welcomed; Robert Overton, 'linked to [Milton] with a more than fraternal harmony' (676) already had expressed his reservations about the Protectorate.[88] Similarly, with the separate praise of John Bradshaw, 'a name which Liberty herself, wherever she is cherished, has entrusted to eternal memory' (637–8); possibly a family connection of Milton's, Bradshaw had presided over Charles's trial and the Council of State, opposing Cromwell in the dissolution of the Rump and establishment of the Protectorate (see 261–2).[89] Some warnings are blunt: 'honor yourself, so that . . . you may not permit [liberty] to be violated by yourself or in any degree diminished by others' (675).

Some of the thrusts are more veiled. Milton interrupts the encomium of Cromwell to praise Fairfax for having 'defeated not only the enemy, but ambition as well, and the thirst for glory which conquers all the most eminent men' (669). Ostensibly addressing 'my fellow countrymen,' he delivers the *sententia*, 'Many men has war made great whom peace made small' (680). Then there are the specific recommendations on liberty. Civil: aside from taking counsel and sharing leadership, propose fewer new laws. Ecclesiastical: separate church and state; do 'not permit two powers, utterly diverse, the civil and the ecclesiastical, to make harlots of each other' (678). Domestic: 'take more thought for education and morality.' 'Next, may you permit those who wish to engage in free inquiry to publish their findings' (679). And again there is the question of whether providence will continue to favour Cromwell.[90] If he were to slip into 'royalist excess and folly,' 'Then in truth, as if God had become utterly disgusted with you – a horrid state – will you seem to have passed through the fire only to perish in the smoke' (681). It would take a careless reader to register the *Second Defense* as simply a glowing tribute to a Lord Protector in whom Milton has full confidence. Alexander More, no friendly reader but not likely a careless one, was taken aback by Milton's attitude toward the Protector, 'whom you address familiarly, without any preface of honor, whom you advise under the guise of praising, for whom you dictate laws, set aside titles, and prescribe duties, and to whom you suggest counsels and even present threats if he should act in any other fashion.'[91] After the *Second Defense,* Milton was silent on the subject of Cromwell for the next five years.[92]

In August 1559 *Considerations Touching the Likeliest Means to Remove Hirelings out of the Church* was published, addressed to the Parliament restored by the Army only months before. Milton salutes the MPs as 'recoverers of our libertie' (*CPW* 7: 275) and lauds them as

> . . . next under God, the authors and best patrons of religious and civil libertie, that ever these Ilands brought forth. The care and tuition of whose peace and safety, after a short but scandalous night of interruption is now again by a new dawning of Gods miraculous providence among us, revolved upon your shoulders. (*CPW* 7: 274)

A lively debate has focused on the referent of the phrase 'a short but scandalous night of interruption,' particularly Austin Woolrych's argument that it alludes to the six-year gap between the expulsion of the Rump and the present restoration (see 7: 85–7). This question has distracted attention from the rest of the sentence, celebrating an extraordinary providence, 'a new dawning of Gods miraculous providence' that nonetheless will be a trial, 'revolved upon your shoulders.' The end of the Protectorate meant to Milton not only the possibility of changes in policies such as a tithe-supported ministry, but, less tangibly, the end of a Cromwellian reign guided by a so-called providence that he had come to regard as deeply suspect. In this he shared the views of such friends as Henry Vane and Moses Wall, who wrote, 'In the time of the wars against the late King, I thought I saw God clearly . . . but upon this unhappy grasping of power into the hands of the late usurper, god withdrew and hid himself, and the body of the Nation proved apostaticall.'[93] Disappointingly, the 'new dawning' proved to be a false one. As the drift into a restored monarchy picked up momentum, Milton could maintain stoutly that those committed to liberty were 'reserved, I trust, by Divine Providence to a better end [than bondage]; since God hath yet his remnant' (CPW 7: 363; cf. Zeph. 3: 13), but only weeks later that sentence vanished from the second edition of *The Readie and Easie Way*.

It may be useful at this point to draw a rough balance sheet. For Calvin predestination and providence were inextricably connected, effectively one and the same: 'It is difficult, if not impossible, to separate Calvin's doctrine of predestination from his view of special providence.' Although he grants the existence of general providence, 'his chief interest is in particular providence or individual election.' His commentary on Isaiah asserts: 'God presides over individual acts, as they call them, so as to move men, like rods, in whatever way he pleases, to guide their plans, to direct their efforts; and, in a word, to regulate their determinations, in order to inform us that everything depends on his providence.'[94] Calvin's position undoubtedly accounts for the widespread phenomenon of self-scrutiny for signs of election and for the parallel anxiety over interpreting providences. The conflation of predestination with providence opens Calvin to the charge of making God the author of sin, and has the effect of limiting severely Christ's mediatorial role. He exists as a means to confirm the salvation of those whom God predetermined to be the elect.

Cromwell's Calvinist God was a judgmental deity in the spirit of Psalm 28: 5 ('Because they regard not the works of the LORD . . . he shall destroy them'). Regarding the sack of Wexford, the General explained that they had intended to spare the town, 'yet God would not have it so; but by an unexpected providence, in His righteous justice, brought a just judgment upon them.'[95] Well and good so long as you were the instrument of providence, smiting those who aroused the Lord's wrath, but anguishing if the judgment turned against you. Attempting to reconcile John 3: 16 to the 'abhorrence' with which God regards sinners, Calvin carefully qualified: 'With respect to us, the commencement of his love has its fountain in the sacrifice of Christ. For when we contemplate God without a Mediator, we cannot conceive Him otherwise than angry with us.'[96] Yet, if Christ is mediator only for the predestined elect, what most humans experience is the judgmental God of wrath. The Laudian Robert Sanderson, reflecting on the doctrine of predestination, concluded that it 'might be consistent with power but not with love.'[97] In contrast to Cromwell's Calvinism, Milton's Arminian God of love mercifully extends grace to all, hardening his heart only against those who refuse it (*CPW* 6: 176–96). For Arminius providence was not an instrument of predestination but an agency of universal grace and guidance toward redemption. Calvin and Arminius read the same Bible, but with quite distinct emphases and inflections.

Both Englishmen firmly believed that providences were trials requiring an active human response – in Milton's words, 'that which purifies us is triall' (*CPW* 2: 515) – but parted company on the nature of the response. For Cromwell this meant either receiving a sign or waiting until one intuited that the moment to act had come: he believed that mercies and judgments were best 'when they have not been forecast, but sudden providences.'[98] For Milton the correct response to providential trial was the use of right reason in the exercise of free will: 'reason is but choosing' (*CPW* 2: 527).[99] Whereas for Cromwell providences were vindications or humiliations, for Milton such trials were processive, challenges to choose rightly, learn from the experience, and apply the lessons to the next trials. However hard-won, Cromwell's confidence that he was the agent of God's will served him best on the battlefield; during the Protectorate it became a club with which to silence political opponents by declaring them among the ungodly. Vane's *A Healing Question* seized on the Achan analogy to assert that Cromwell's dictatorial and self-interested rule had caused God's wrath; only when it ended would God once more 'become active and powerful in the spirits and hearts of honest men, and in the works of his providences.'[100] The more circumspect Milton appears to have arrived at a like conclusion. The dangers of Cromwell's identification with God's will were amply demonstrated for him by its use to disable friends whose politics he admired – Vane, Overton, Bradshaw, indeed Parliament itself. Cromwell's behaviour impressed Vane, Wall, and Milton as a confirmation that, like Niclaes's allegory of 'Searching Providence,' he presumed to usurp God's will.

Marvell and Milton: A Conversation about Providence

Having examined two powerful influences, one positive and one negative, on John Milton's thinking about providence, we will conclude by looking more conjecturally at a mutual influence. During the span of time that Milton guardedly observed the progression of Cromwell's political career, his thinking on providentialism very likely was honed by the friendship that he formed with the most intelligent poet of the younger generation. With the exceptions of three public sonnets, Milton was composing his arguments in prose, most often controversial or diplomatic writings (the latter often in Latin). Andrew Marvell already was tracing his responses to Cromwell's symbiotic relation with providence in English poetry, the medium, we recall, that Milton thought more nuanced, 'simple, sensuous and passionate,' for the expression of feelings. We know that Marvell assiduously read and admired one of Milton's Latin treatises, as he later would the great epic. Surely Milton had access to Marvell's three Cromwell poems; it defies probability that the younger man did not, however diffidently, present copies or, with the older man's vision failing, read aloud his poems. One might speculate that the Horatian Ode was one stimulus to the reflections on providentialism that appear in Sonnet 16 and in the *Second Defense*, whereas that treatise almost certainly influenced Marvell's 'First Anniversary.' David Norbrook comments, 'By now the two men's relationship seems to have been close enough for reciprocal influence.'[101] The further modulation, subtle but discernible, in the elegy on Cromwell's death 'reveal[s] the growing influence of Milton' (Smith, *Poems of Andrew Marvell* 302), now his colleague. In conversation and in writing, it seems possible to postulate, each poet's thought on providence was affected by the other's. This is not the place for a full discussion of Marvell's Cromwell poems; instead, providentialism will be the Ariadne's thread through an implicit intellectual dialogue.[102]

Marvell's 'An Horatian Ode upon Cromwell's Return from Ireland,' set in the days before the expedition against the Scots (July 1650), emerges from the context of the Engagement Controversy with its exacerbated and polarized allegiances.[103] Marvell represents Cromwell as an agent of both extraordinary and general providence. First, ''Tis Madness to resist or blame / The force of angry heaven's flame' (25–6); then, in the common equation of ordinary providence with natural law: 'Nature that hateth emptiness, / Allows of penetration less: / And therefore must make room / Where greater spirits come' (41–4). Paradoxically, in the face of the implied identification with the 'forward youth' obligated to 'forsake his Muses dear' and enlist in the campaign (1–8), Marvell instead did just the opposite, following the example of the man who would be his first patron. Lord General Fairfax, refusing to lead a pre-emptive attack on Scotland, resigned his commission, creating that void in nature filled by Cromwell; he retired to Appleton House where for nearly two years (1651–2) Marvell would be the tutor of daughter Mary Fairfax.[104] 'Upon Appleton House, To My Lord Fairfax' regretfully considers what might have been: 'And yet there walks one on the sod / Who, had it pleased him and God, / Might once have made our gardens spring / Fresh as his own and flourishing' (st. 44, 1–4). The order, *him* first and *God* second, touches the possibility of human preference, rather than God's will; the central section of the meadow (sts 47–60), however, views the wars from the perspective of the mowed, rather than Cromwell's exultant mower. Two decades later Marvell's view of the 'Massacre' did not change: 'upon considering all, I think the Cause was too good to have been fought for. Men ought to have trusted God.'[105] He thus endorses Fairfax's choice to 'ambition weed, but conscience till' (st. 45, 2), as the poet narrator emulates his master by 'retiring from the flood' (st. 61, 1) of civil war.

We do not know how Marvell scraped acquaintance with Milton, only that the 'forward youth,' after wrestling with his conscience in contemplative retirement, elected the active life and, with unerring judgment, placed his future in the hands of the arch-activist. On 21 February 1553 Milton wrote to Bradshaw, President of the Council of State:

> There will be wth: you tomorrow upon some occasion of business a Gentleman whose name is Mr: Marvile; a man whom both by report, & ye; converse I have had wth: him, of singular desert for ye: state to make use of; who alsoe offers himselfe, if yere: be any imployment for him . . . he com's now lately out of ye: house of ye: Lord ffairefax who was Generall, where he was intrusted to give some instructions in ye: Languages to ye: Lady his Daughter. (*CPW* 4, pt. 2: 859–60)

Commending Marvell's competence in modern languages and scholarship in classical authors, Milton concludes that, if the 'Councell shall thinke yt I shall need any assistant in ye: performance of my place . . . it would be hard for them to find a Man soe fit every way for yt purpose as this Gentleman.' Unfortunately from the standpoint of poetic truth, the dissolution of the Rump thwarted the appointment, but the recommendation may have paid off unexpectedly. In that summer Cromwell, acting as informal guardian to William Dutton, placed the young man to lodge in the house of John Oxenbridge, Fellow at Eton; quite possibly remembering the qualifications detailed in Milton's letter, Cromwell hired Marvell as the young man's tutor.[106] Reporting directly to the Lord General, this 'rational amphibian' had landed with one foot still in the retired life, but the other in the active.

Marvell was fortuitously placed at Eton in other ways as well. He met there and commenced a friendship with John Hales, whose epithet 'ever memorable' proved literally true for the younger man. In 1672 he wrote of Hales, deploring 'his Sufferings in the late times': 'I account it no small honour to have grown up into some part of his Acquaintance, and convers'd a while with the living *remains* of one of the clearest heads and best prepared brests in Christendom.'[107] Although Marvell's religion can seem as elusive as his lyric poems, Lamont has used the *Remarks upon a Late disingenuous Discourse* (1677), in which Marvell defends the Nonconformist minister John Howe by 'the reasonableness of Arminian doctrine,' to argue for a continuity of interests extending back to the Protectorate.[108] Marvell's connection with a pioneering convert to Arminianism, therefore, is the more suggestive for his affinity with Milton, who may also have known Hales (see n. 32). Meanwhile the busy tutor continued to cultivate Milton's friendship, calling on him in London and gaining a reputation as one of Milton's 'particular friends,' a 'learned familiar acquaintance.'[109]

Three days after the publication of the *Second Defense*, Marvell wrote to 'my most honoured Freind,' enlarging on a preceding brief message about his delivery of a copy to 'my Lord,' possibly John Bradshaw, inquiring cryptically about 'Colonell Overtons businesse,' and expressing pleasure and envy that Cyriack Skinner was in London near Milton. Skinner's and Marvell's families were on good terms; Overton had served under Fairfax and was known to Marvell through his position as governor of Hull; Bradshaw presumably he would have met through Milton. The letter indicates that Marvell was thoroughly embedded in Milton's circle. It also declares his own admiration for Milton's treatise:

> I shall now studie it even to the getting of it by Heart: esteeming it according to my poor Judgement (which yet I wish it were so right in all Things else) as the most compendious Scale, for so much, to the Height of the Roman eloquence. When I consider how equally it turns and rises with so many figures, it seems to me a Trajans columne in whose winding ascent we see imboss'd the severall Monuments of your learned victoryes.[110]

Marvell only can have been pleased by the praise of Fairfax, which reads almost as a prose distillation of his own in 'Upon Appleton House.'

Both Englishmen very likely had seen Trajan's Column in their respective visits to Rome, and Marvell uses the column as an appropriate figure for Milton's successive polemical triumphs. Although he does not mention the Cromwell section directly, approval may be implied; Filarete's well-known *Treatise on Architecture* (ca. 1461–4) praises the sculptor of the column for his skill in representing historical persons 'as if they were alive.'[111] Milton and his friends already seem to have complicated Marvell's view of his new patron. Hardly surprising, then, that six months later 'The *First* Anniversary Of the Government Under *His Highness* The Lord Protector' would be 'extremely close' to the *Second Defense* 'both in its general assumptions and in its political stance.'[112]

Drawing on a traditional image of providence (rudder or helm), the poem lauds Cromwell as the alert 'lusty mate' who seized the helm when the Rump left the ship of state adrift (273–6). Co-opting a Royalist trope, it presents the Protector as an Amphion who 'tuned the ruling Instrument' of Government (68), a 'protecting' roof whose weight holds the House of the Commonwealth together (98), ironically just weeks before the collapse of Barebone's Parliament. As in the *Second Defense*, Marvell acknowledges Cromwell's past accomplishments; his political dominance, 'Him as their father must the state obey' (282); and his providential direction: 'What since he did, an higher force him pushed / Still from behind, and it before him rushed' (239–40). He can envision optimistically the effect of its continuation: 'Hence oft I think, if in some happy hour / High grace should meet in one with highest power, / And then a seasonable people still / Should bend to his, as he to heaven's will' (131–4). Yet, less bluntly but similarly to Milton, the realistic qualification follows: 'But a thick cloud about that morning lies, / And intercepts the beams of mortal eyes, / That 'tis the most which we determine can, / If these the times, then this must be the man' (141–4). The conditional 'if's intimate the poet's reservation. Christopher Wortham comments, 'The remarkable thing about these lines is that . . . Marvell's hope for Cromwell is so doubtfully expressed.'[113] The ends of providence are unknowable and the man Cromwell still is on probation.

Marvell continued as Dutton's tutor at least through 1656, as the two were known to be in France at the Protestant bastion of Saumur from January through August of that year. 'On the Victory obtained by Blake over the Spaniards in the Bay of Santa Cruz,' written sometime after the 20 April 1657 sea battle, may well be wrongly attributed to Marvell. The triumphal narrative indirectly credits the victory to Cromwell's beneficent providence: 'For your resistless genius there did reign, / By which we laurels reaped ev'n on the main. / So prosperous stars, though absent to the sense, / Bless those they shine for, by their influence' (145–8).[114] Nonetheless, if Worden is correct about the devastating effect of the Hispaniola debacle on Cromwell, even Blake's daring success could have been only cold comfort to the Protector.

On 2 September Marvell finally was appointed Latin Secretary to the Council of State, possibly equal in rank to Milton's original appointment as Secretary of Foreign Tongues.[115] Almost immediately he was pressed into service, writing marriage songs for the November wedding of Mary Cromwell, daughter of the Protector whom he figures in a perhaps double-edged compliment as 'Jove himself.'[116] Then a bare year later it was over. Cromwell died 3 September 1658, and, weeks after, the two secretaries, sober public men swelling the scene of a tragic action, walked together in the state funeral procession.[117] As we have seen above, Marvell's 'Poem upon the Death' perhaps inevitably begins with providence and just perceptibly raises the possibility that it had abandoned the Protector. That possibility comes back more forcefully later in the elegy:

> Not much unlike the sacred oak which shoots
> To heaven its branches, and through earth its roots:
> Whose spacious boughs are hung with trophies round,
> And honoured wreaths have oft the victor crowned
> When angry Jove darts lightning through the air,
> At mortal's sins, nor his own plant will spare. (261–6)

The construction does not allow a judgment as to whether the Protector has been scapegoated for the sins of his people or whether this 'inverted tree' himself has become 'the accursed thing' that must 'be burnt with fire' (Joshua 7: 15). Like some shifting perspective from 'Upon Appleton House,' the demise of the 'sacred oak' alters reality, again equivocally: 'The tree erewhile foreshortened to our view, / When fallen shows taller yet than as it grew' (269–70). Granting that familiarity foreshortened the public's view of the living Protector, does death bring a just or an exaggerated perception of his stature? Keeping his own counsel, Milton wrote no poem on the occasion.

Milton's distrust of interpreting the 'hidden wayes' and 'unsearchable Mysteries' of providence may well have been reinforced and refined in dialogue, both social and poetic, with Marvell while they observed Cromwell's government as fringe participants. Marvell's willingness to accept de facto sovereignty in a 'mixed' government differed from Milton's resolute commitment to a representative government, however constituted. This division in politics has been seen as stemming from their respective views of providence. The younger poet's tendency to regard providence as a force to be accepted stoically, "'Tis madness to resist or blame,' contrasted sharply with Milton's activist vision that, when one is confronted with providences, the appropriate response must be reasoned questioning and choice. Comparing the two, Catherine Gimelli Martin writes, 'Milton's much more conditional providentialism made him reluctant to identify the kingdom of God with any single party or "hero."'[118] His scepticism about the Protector's mantle of providence may have become more pronounced against the foil of Marvell's earlier reluctance 'to resist or blame,' whereas their association plausibly moved Marvell to the refined questioning of his hero that is evident in the 'First Anniversary' and 'Upon the Death,' even to the political activism that the MP from Hull displayed in the Restoration. Both men thus seem to have benefited from this quiet but searching intellectual dialogue on the fallen, one-time darling of providence.

Responding to Royalist tormentors at his execution, Major General Thomas Harrison retorted, 'Wait upon the Lord, for you know not what the Lord is leading to, and what the end of the Lord will be.'[119] The two poets would have believed as firmly as Harrison that God 'will make for his own glory and the good end of his people,' while doubting that either side could penetrate his will during the course to that end. In the major poems then gestating, Milton therefore took a position that Calvin would have recognized: we can understand divine providence in sacred history; what lies beyond the Bible still is a work in progress.

If John Aubrey's chat can be credited, it was in the year of Oliver Cromwell's death that Milton turned to sustained work on the long contemplated and deferred epic poem.[120] Whether he confided the project to Marvell is, as Sir Thomas Browne might say, 'not beyond all conjecture.' Marvell's 1674 commendatory poem, 'On Mr. Milton's *Paradise Lost*,' suggests that he did not. It records Marvell's response to first reading the 1667 edition: 'the argument / Held me a while misdoubting his intent / That he would ruin . . . / The sacred truths . . . / Yet as I read, soon growing less severe, / I liked his project' (5–8, 11–12).[121] Amid the turmoil of personal tragedy and political upheaval, Milton may have been understandably guarded about the poetic project. Milton's sense of his poetic vocation, the necessity of using the 'talent' or '*ingenium*' that he was granted has been much discussed.[122] This endowment itself was a providence, a trial requiring a response in kind. An early entry in Milton's commonplace book records his delight in the first of English poets: 'A wonderful and very pleasing little story is told by Bede about an Englishman who was suddenly made a poet by divine Providence' (*CPW* 1: 381). Milton's response to his own providence was, in Marvell's words, to 'unfold' the 'vast design' of providence itself; however, although like Caedmon he would sing Creation from the beginning, his lot was to have nothing of suddenness in doing so. Chapter 2 begins at the beginnings, not just the subject of Genesis but attempting to describe how, by fusing his classical and biblical learning, the sightless poet would have set about composing his epic through mnemonic techniques. 'Its very completion,' a non-academic writer observes perceptively, 'must have seemed liked divine Providence to Milton.'[123] Just so. Equally, the entire thing – Milton's ability, inspiration, subject, and his responses to all of these in the composition – exemplifies the processes of providence at work.

Chapter Two

Memory and the Art of Composition

> This is the beginning.
> Almost anything can happen.
> This is where you find
> the creation of light, a fish wriggling onto land,
> the first word of *Paradise Lost* on an empty page.
>
> Billy Collins, 'Aristotle'

> . . . This is the cause I grope after in the works of Nature; on this hangs the providence of God.[1]
>
> Sir Thomas Browne

In modern times there have been two great feats, equally remarkable and remarkably different, of memorial composition by blind geniuses: *Paradise Lost* and *Finnegans Wake*. Although James Joyce may well have had memory training in his Jesuit schooldays, his method, surely, was the more arbitrary. Samuel Beckett recounted one experience of taking dictation from Joyce:

> There was a knock at the door which Beckett didn't hear. Joyce said, 'Come in,' and Beckett wrote it down. Afterwards he read back what he had written and Joyce said, 'What's that "Come in"?' 'Yes, you said that,' said Beckett. Joyce thought for a moment, then said, 'Let it stand.'[2]

In this chapter I wish to consider, sometimes speculatively, how Milton would have used his memory training to assist in the composition of his great poem.[3] By 'memory training' I mean not just the patient memorization necessary to dictate each verse paragraph newly composed in his mind to whomever was at hand. I also mean the use of mnemonic systems, the 'art of memory,' to organize his presentation of the vast subject – a principle of structure, if you will, enabling him to see imaginatively the larger design into which the individual parcels of verse would fit. Poetry itself obviously has been a mnemonic device since times immemorial; Bacon pithily advised that poetry sticks and is learned by memory more easily than prose.[4] By scorning 'Rime' with its 'jingling sound of like endings' ('The Verse,' 1668 note), however, Milton also rejected the simplest memory aid. Instead, he drew primarily on the system of recollection in which places containing images associated with ideas are visualized.[5] Moreover, I will suggest that, given a culture for which knowledge of scripture still was engrained from sermons and private devotions, he used mnemonics to evoke the reader's own memory of biblical texts and lessons to reinforce his poetic expansions and amplification of them. In doing so, he assuredly did not bury the talent with which providence had burdened him, but returned it tenfold, enlarging the lyric sketch of the Nativity Ode, which from the memory place of the Incarnation glances back to Creation and forward to the Last Judgment. We shall review the fusion of classical mnemonics with meditation in the medieval tradition of *sacra memoria* before proceeding to the architectural and cosmic system of memory places that works in tandem with the homely and familiar Last Things to order Milton's biblical recollections. He responds to the trial of his own providence by recreating God's grand providential design.

Milton first would have encountered the *ars memorativa* in the classical texts – Cicero's *De oratore*, Quintilian's *Institutio oratoria*, and the *Rhetorica ad Herennium* long attributed to Cicero – all of which he certainly knew.[6] Donald Lemen Clark's patient reconstruction of grammar school curricula provides evidence that Milton most probably became familiar with all three early on; we know that the seven Cambridge prolusions were memorized for delivery, and *Of Education* recommends that political orations should be 'got by memory' (*CPW* 2: 401). Writing well before the important, revisionist work of Paolo Rossi, Frances Yates, and Lina Bolzoni, Clark himself gave minimal attention to memory training, remarking (mistakenly) that the art 'was all but forgotten in the Renaissance.'[7]

Two more directly related factors may have caused scholars to discount the lasting effects of the memory training that Milton exhibited at Cambridge. First, there is the seemingly awkward presence of Milton's

Ramistic *Artis Logicae* (published 1672, but written earlier), awkward because Ramus famously banished memory from its place in rhetoric. As both Walter Ong and Frances Yates have shown, however, Ramus conceived his system of logic in the *Dialectica*, of which Milton's own logic is an adaptation, as an art of memory: 'the real reason why Ramus can dispense with memory is that his whole scheme of arts, based on a topically conceived logic, is a system of local memory.'[8] It may be pertinent that the organization of the *De Doctrina Christiana* manuscript in its earliest form suggests that of a place logic without images: 'It was divided into physically distinct fascicles, each containing a chapter, and it retained that structure through the complex process of revision.'[9] This would have been an appropriate choice for a theological treatise, if not for a poem. Second, and a question even more readily dismissed, since classical mnemonics is a profoundly visual art, would not the consequences of Milton's blindness have impaired its usefulness to him? Such an objection would miss the essential point that, despite Giulio Camillo's quixotic enterprise of building an actual memory theatre, the assignment of vivid images to memory places, locations in a larger spatial construct, is an act of the imagination. As Hamlet might say, 'In my mind's eye, Horatio.'

Sacra Memoria: Memory, Meditation, and the Cosmic Theatre

We lack the immediacy of a Samuel Beckett's eyewitness testimony for Milton's compositional procedures; however, his earliest biographers are informative. His nephew Edward Phillips's recollection of copy-editing, 'in a parcel of ten, twenty, or thirty verses at a time, which being written by whatever hand came next, might possibly want correction as to the orthography and pointing,' indicates a process of dictation not unlike Joyce's. Whether consciously or not, both authors follow the practical advice of Quintilian for *memoria ad verba*: one should memorize a long speech by breaking it into manageable parts. The difference between them is suggested by John Aubrey's observation, '[Milton] had a very good memory; but I believe that his excellent method of thinking and disposing did much help his memory.' In other words, invention and disposition; his natural memory was enhanced by artificial memory.

Perhaps most interesting for its record of Miltonic word-play is the anonymous biographer's account: 'He, waking early (as is the use of temperate men), had commonly a good stock of verses ready against his amanuensis came; which if it happened to be later than ordinary, he would complain, saying *he wanted to be milked*.'[10] As Mary Carruthers has explained, *ruminatio*, the metaphor of digestion and regurgitation, describes the process of reading, '*memoria* as well as *meditatio*, the two being understood as the agent and its activity.' Reflecting on his youthful study of the classics, Petrarch observed, 'I ate in the morning what I would digest in the evening; I swallowed as a boy what I would ruminate upon as an older man.' John Donne counselled himself, 'digest, / My Soule, this wholesome meditation.' Equally, however, the metaphor applies to the act of composition; both Augustine and Caedmon, the first of providentially inspired English poets, use *ruminatio* to describe their compositions. Milton, 'the uncouth Swain' of 'Lycidas,' clearly enjoys converting the Latin bovine metaphor to homely English, a cow chewing her cud, but shifts the application from process of composition, the benefit to the author, which Carruthers summarizes: 'the memory is a stomach, the stored texts are the sweet-smelling cud originally drawn from the meadows of books [and} chewed in the palate.'[11] Rather, Milton emphasizes the product, nourishment for the reader, and probably intends the metaphor of the gospel as 'milk of the word' for 'babes in Christ' (see I Cor. 3: 1–2; 1 Pet. 2: 2). His digestion of the sources becomes part of himself, which he offers, to the reader, applying the lessons drawn from his providence to evoke the reader's memories and understanding.

In formulating the project of composing a Christian epic, Milton denied that the required inspiration can

> . . . be obtain'd by the invocation of Dame Memory and her Siren daughters, but by devout prayer to that eternall Spirit who can enrich with all utterance and knowledge, and sends out his Seraphim with the hallow'd fire of his Altar to touch and purify the lips of whom he pleases: to this must be added industrious and select reading, steddy observation, insight into all seemly and generous arts and affaires. (*CPW* 1: 820–1)

Editors have puzzled over the apparent lapse in making the sirens, rather than the Muses, daughters of Memory, and, because Milton had alluded to them in 'Arcades' and 'At a Solemn Music,' tended to assume that the reference here is to Plato's sirens (*Republic*, 617–18). It makes better sense, perhaps, to think of Homer's seductive sirens; Bacon, considering the allurements of pleasure, judged Ulysses' passive resistance inferior to the active response of Orpheus: 'For they that chaunt and resound the praises of the Gods, confound and dissipate the voyaces and incantations of the *Syrenes*; for divine meditations do not only in power subdue all sensual pleasures; but also far exceed them in sweetness and delight.'[12] Rather as his Jesus later would do (*PR* 4: 286–364) Milton rejects classical learning, turning away from the memory art that he knows and has used to the inspiration of prayer and 'divine meditation.' At the same time, the image of the angel touching Isaiah's lips with the burning coal (Isa. 6: 6–7; Nat. Ode, 26–7) is exactly the kind of bizarre or grotesque image used to stock memory places; and the poet's obligations of industrious and discriminating reading, observation, and insight, are requirements the prophet escaped.

Louis L. Martz's landmark study, *The Poetry of Meditation* (1954), made us conscious of the extent to which formal devotional procedures profoundly influenced seventeenth-century religious poetry. Discerning a significant development in Catholic meditational methods during the Counter Reformation, Martz concentrated in particular on the *Spiritual Exercises* (1548) of St Ignatius Loyola to illuminate the structures of argument and imagery in such poets as Donne and Herbert.[13] From the distance of a half-century, it might be fair to say that Martz slighted the indebtedness of meditation to classical rhetoric and exaggerated the difference between the Counter Reformation type and the earlier traditions of meditation.[14] Only in the 'Preface to the Second Edition' does he state that the 'three powers of the soul' – memory, understanding, and will – which govern the tripartite structure, composition of place, analysis, and petition or prayer, are not a Jesuit innovation but have their 'prime source' in Augustine's *De Trinitate*.[15]

Milton is a missing presence in *The Poetry of Meditation*, mentioned occasionally in contrast because the Calvinist temperament 'was not at all conducive to . . . the art of meditation.'[16] Martz reconsidered this position in *The Paradise Within* (1964), which finds meditative qualities in both narrative poems, more confidently in *Paradise Regained*, where, with the poet's direct authority, 'His holy Meditations thus pursu'd' (1: 195), he can assert that *Regained* 'is a meditation on the entire life of Jesus . . . as he meditates on the meaning of his existence.'[17] Less successful is the long section on *Paradise Lost*, which, despite a few dutiful references to meditation, simply is an appreciative, if somewhat idiosyncratic, ramble through the first ten books, followed by a depreciation of the 'failed' last two. In contrast to the somewhat overly schematic, but usefully tangible, argument of the first book, the thesis of an Augustinian method in this one is so nebulous ('an intuitive groping back into regions of the soul') that it gives Martz no purchase on this poem.[18] In looking beyond Loyola to an earlier tradition, his instinct was right; however, limiting it to Augustine also restricts it to the elements that Loyola found most congenial, not just the three powers of the soul, but the emphasis on the arousal of emotions. In his *De Doctrina Christiana*, for example, Augustine describes how the fear of death can make the skin crawl and turn one toward God, a means of salvation more congenial to Donne than to Milton.[19] Moreover, as Carruthers has remarked, in all of his comments on memory, 'Augustine makes no mention of an art of memory.'[20] Certainly Milton knew and used Augustine, but his authority was only one of many in a broader tradition of *sacra memoria* that might be described as an amalgam or fusion of writings on meditation and prayer, on the faculty of memory, and the classical rhetoricians on the art of memory. In such a system meditation and artificial memory really are inseparable parts of the same process. The nexus between scriptural meditation and classical rhetoric is plain in the domestication of locus or topos to place, both a storehouse for invention ('commonplaces') and 'a particular part, page, or other point in a book or writing' (*OED*, s.v., 7), which to the devout meant habitual ransacking of the Bible for 'places' relevant to one's spiritual state.[21] For Milton the long tradition of sacred memory would be augmented and enhanced by his own knowledge of classical mnemonics. *Paradise Lost* is a poem devoted to memory in both its subject and its creation.[22]

A starting point for the latter might be Carruthers's admonition, '*Memoria* is most usefully thought of as a compositional art.'[23] One side of composition involves *memoria ad verba*, the kind of memorization Milton displayed in reciting verse paragraphs of the epic for his amanuensis. Cicero had prescribed that the orator, after deciding what to say (invention) and arranging his arguments with proportionate weight (disposition), must 'next go on to array them in the adornments of style; after that keep them guarded in his memory.'[24] Style and memory provide insight to the procedure by which Milton had meditated and ruminated in conceiving his poem. His method probably resembled what Hugh of St Victor called *evolvere*, the 'unrolling' or 'opening' of a text; Hugh defined meditation as 'the ability of a keen and curious mind to explore obscurities and unfold perplexities' in the Bible,[25] suggestively like the 'unfold[ing]' of Milton's 'vast design' that Marvell discerned ('On *Paradise Lost*,' 2).

In expanding or illuminating such obscurities the first tactic might be to seek clarification through other scriptural loci. Here the beginning of Milton's *De Doctrina*, is highly suggestive: 'In this treatise then no novelties of doctrine are taught; but for the sake of assisting the memory, what is dispersed throughout the different parts of the Holy Scriptures is conveniently reduced into one compact body, as it were, and digested under certain heads.'[26] The modest compiler disclaims teaching anything new, only helping the reader's memory by gathering ('leguntur') verses scattered through the Bible and arranging them by topic ('locos'). In rhetorical usage, 'digesta' means to arrange systematically; however, the purpose of aiding memory activates the figurative sense of digestion: recollection becomes *ruminatio*.[27] Similarly, *De Doctrina* reflects on the Sabbath as God's commemoration of the Creation and speculates that Moses back-read the fourth commandment into Genesis 2: 3, 'And God blessed the seventh day, and sanctified it,' thus 'reminding' readers of its meaning (*CPW* 6: 354).[28] In this sense both the Bible and *Paradise Lost* can be understood as narratives of recollection, designed to enable and deepen the reader's memory of God's providence through a collaborative exfoliation.

The impulse behind such recollecting is akin to that which caused Nicholas Ferrar, George Herbert's friend and literary executor, to instruct his pupils in the Little Gidding community by having them construct 'Harmonies,' Bible verses cut, reorganized, pasted, and colour-coded into hand-made volumes.[29] Herbert himself, lauding the Bible as 'the storehouse and magazene of life and comfort,' advised the Country Parson to perform 'a diligent Collation of Scripture with Scripture.'[30] His use of the familiar terms 'storehouse' and 'magazine' implies that the Bible is the repository of all memories. The scriptural cross-referencing of the Little Gidding 'Harmonies' and the citations marshalled by topic in the *De Doctrina* manuscript undergo a sea change with the compression of poetic language. Herbert's own poetry is as much a tissue of biblical quotations and echoes as is Milton's, both poetic acts of recollection in their distinct voices. Nor would the task of 'unfolding' obscurities and textual difficulties through recollection restrict a writer to scriptural gatherings; in dialogue with Augustine, Petrarch asserts that one finds good matter in poets as well as philosophers, citing the *Aeneid* for proof; in the *Summa theologia* Aquinas quotes not only Virgil, but Ovid, Juvenal, Terence, and Seneca as authorities. Recollection might best be seen as the medieval and early modern equivalent of 'what we now call "using our imagination," even to the point of visionary experience' and helps account for the origins of the extraordinary allusiveness in Milton's poetic style.[31]

Complementing memory for words and obviously prior in the process of composition was *memoria ad res*, the large-scale organizational process of remembering and arranging the topics of the poem. Several memory systems were popular in the Middle Ages, including the numerical.[32] This is worth a passing thought, since anyone with a casual knowledge of Renaissance number symbolism might think that, at least occasionally, Milton has exploited the conventional symbolic values as a mnemonic for his topics. Book 3, less emphatically than Herbert's 'Trinitie Sunday' (with its three three-line stanzas and three rime sounds) but no less appropriately, houses the Godhead. Book 4, the number of 'man,' introduces the first humans; five is the marriage number, and what could be more married than entertaining the first dinner guest? The assignment of the creation narrative to Book 7 seems an inescapable choice. And there appears to be general, if sometimes grudging, acknowledgment that the Book 6 ascension of the Son, now called 'Messiah,' in 'The Chariot of Paternal Deity' at the centre of the poem cannot be accidental.[33]

Nonetheless, the examples of number symbolism clearly leave this mnemonic procedure in a place subordinate to the architectural system advocated by Cicero and explained at length in the *Ad Herennium*, revived in the thirteenth century and popular throughout the Renaissance. The foundational myth of Simonides remembering the seating order of a banquet provided an expandable and adaptable model for memory places, as Quintilian remarks: 'What I have spoken of being done in a house can also be done in public buildings, or on a long journey, or in going through a city, or with pictures. Or we can imagine such places for ourselves.'[34] Donne memorized his sermons using such images as progression through a palace and progression through a gallery of pictures, and Herbert, University Orator at Cambridge before he became a priest, presents *The Temple* as a tour through the 'places' of a church rather grander than his modest holding at Bemerton.[35] Side by side with the continued utility of the architectural model, some monastic writers took their memory places from the Bible, 'divine structures . . . such as the Ark, the Tabernacle, the Temple, the Heavenly City, the map of the world, the cosmos itself.'[36]

The ambition of Milton's subject clearly dwarfed any building. Not just Heaven Hell, and Paradise, but the cosmos itself, the setting of Camillo's famous memory theatre. 'In ways somewhat suggesting the epic, which incorporates the life-world of an entire culture, memory theaters were cosmological in their sweep.' Ong continues, explaining their operation:

> They related to both the microcosm and the macrocosm, since their symbols were drawn from and referred to both the world of man, the microcosm or 'little world,' and the universe exterior to man, the macrocosm or 'great world.' Standing in imagination (or sometimes in reality) in the middle of a 'theater' of mnemonic icons, the mnemotechnician could readily feel himself a 'little world' with which the 'great world' (the entire universe around him) was aligned, point for point, through the mediation of the symbols along the walls standing between him and it.[37]

Milton, poet and not 'mnemotechnician,' I would suggest, had the imaginative genius to fuse cosmic memory theatre with epic, the little world of his particular providence with the great world of God's providential design.

Long cherished belief held that Moses was the first and finest poet, who in writing Genesis translated into words the perfection of God's own creation. Pico della Mirandola pronounced, 'This is the model, this is the pattern for perfection in a writer. Not only . . . does this kind of writing copy and emulate nature, but also, among the Scriptures, that is greatest and holds the apex of all perfection which in the fewest words both fittingly and deeply encompasses all things.'[38] This is why Milton must seek the inspiration of the 'Heav'nly Muse, that . . . / . . . didst inspire / That Shepherd, who first taught the chosen Seed, / In the Beginning how the Heav'ns and Earth / Rose out of *Chaos*' (1: 6–10). He must emulate the achievement of the perfect poet and, thereby, of the God whom he calls 'the sovran Architect' (5: 256) and Raphael speaks of as 'the great Architect' (8: 72). In his *Poetria nova* (13th c.) Geoffrey of Vinsauf advised poets to emulate their maker by following the procedure of the architect, first laying out mentally the design of the whole composition: 'As a prudent workman, construct the whole fabric within the mind's citadel.'[39]

The concept of *Deus artifex* or *architectus* goes back to Plato and Cicero, receiving powerful corroboration from three biblical loci: Job 26:10, 'He hath compassed the waters with bounds'; Proverbs 8:27, 'When he prepared the heavens, I was there: when he set a compass

Figure 2. Creator with Compass and Scales, Eadwi Gospels, fol. 9v. Possibly painted at Winchester, ca. 1025. Museum August Kestner, Hanover. W.M. XXIa, 36.

upon the face of the depth'; and Wisdom 11: 21, 'thou hast ordered all things in measure and number and weight' (*sed omnia in mensura, et numero, et pondere disposuisti*). These inspired two traditions of biblical illustration; those deriving from the Old Testament verses represent the act of creation with a compass, whereas those depending strictly on Wisdom image both compass and scales. The illustrator of the Eadwi Gospels (Winchester? ca. 1025) shows the hand of God hovering over the newly created world; one leg of the compass projects from his palm to the right. The scales are suspended from the curved middle finger by a neatly tied knot; the spread first and second fingers seem intended to evoke numbers. However awkward the image, God in his providence creates by measure, number, and weight (fig. 2).[40] During the Renaissance, moreover, Wisdom 11: 21 had a significant part in formulating a biblical poetics and enhancing the poet's status as a god-like creator.[41]

The description of the Son's beginning Creation by taking up 'the Golden Compasses' (7: 225) understandably has led to the assumption that Milton follows the Job-Proverbs tradition, and yet the scales already have been announced. When the captured Satan squares off against Gabriel, God forestalls a rewriting of human history by giving him a providence, displaying the scales on which the consequence of fighting is weighed. Gabriel, sounding as confident as Cromwell's 'let God judge between you and me,'[42] interprets the sign, and Satan flees. Here the initial description is pertinent: God 'Hung forth in Heav'n his golden Scales . . . / . . . / Wherein all things created first he weigh'd / The pendulous round Earth with balanc'd Air / In counterpoise' (4: 997, 999–1001). Thus, Raphael's later account of the Creation needs to be rethought. The Son and the life-giving Spirit first 'view'd the vast, immeasurable Abyss' of Chaos; the Son silenced the warring elements, then:

> He took the golden Compasses, prepar'd
> In God's Eternal store, to circumscribe
> This Universe, and all created things;
> One foot he centred, and the other turn'd
> Round through the vast profundity obscure,
> And said, Thus far extend, thus far thy bounds,
> This be thy just Circumference, O World. (7: 225–31)

Next life and order is given, 'And Earth self-balanc'd on her Centre hung' (7: 242). The instrumental detail omitted here had been supplied earlier. Before the earth was balanced in equilibrium, it was weighed 'with balanc'd Air / In counterpoise' (4: 1000–1). Measure, number, and weight. Marvell was quite right in his analysis: 'Thy verse created like thy theme sublime, / In number, weight, and measure needs not rhyme' ('On *Paradise Lost*,' 53–4). The word play on 'number' as metrics is typical Marvellian wit, but the significant point, cued also by 'Where could thou words of such a compass find?' (41), identifies the underlying principle of Wisdom 11: 21, and marvels at its embodiment in words.

As must have been true of the Scales, the Compasses were prepared in 'God's Eternal store,' causing one editor to ask, not entirely facetiously, 'who prepared the compasses and from what . . . warehouse in Heaven they came.' One of the two age-old metaphors for the trained memory – and the one that, through the *Ad Herennium*, had the most enduring influence – was *thesaurus* (treasury or storehouse).[43] The 'store' obviously is God's memory, which in itself creates perplexity since through his foreknowledge the storehouse is stocked with memories of the future. Moreover, by the concept of 'middle knowledge,' that stock contains possible acts and choices that will not occur, as well as those that will. Primed by the Father, Raphael tells Adam what the future might be, whereas Michael both reminds him what could have been and reveals what will be. The sociable angel explains and God confirms (7:176–9, 154–5) that the creation of the world really was instantaneous and the work of the divine week only an accommodation to the limits of human understanding: 'In human minds, time exists, and yet by disciplined thought we can withdraw from it and in some way imitate the eternal present of God.'[44] This is Milton's trial. God's memory of how to, in Adam's word, 'build' the world is the poet's human memory, both accommodation to his audience and expression of gratitude to the Lord 'Who remembered us in our low estate' (Ps. 136: 23), a remembrance of the future in God's mind, thereby motivating his providential alternative to that estate before it occurs in human time.

Seeking to meet the daunting challenge of his own providence, the poet must 'unfold' or 'open' the Genesis story for the reader by recollecting and collating his own storehouse, the lessons of human history brought to bear on the entire Bible, thereby glorifying God's goodness. Carruthers suggests that recollection and imagination might be regarded as synonyms. Milton likely would demur, replacing imagination with divine inspiration, and yet the root sense of a mental image is worth keeping. He populates the heavens with memory images – 'The Chariot of Paternal Deity,' 'golden Compasses,' 'Eternal store,' 'golden Scales,' 'This pendant world' – all emblems of providence by which to locate and stimulate his own and the reader's recollections.

The first act of the builder is measurement, laying out the dimensions of the structure, and so it is in the architectural mnemonic. The possibility of a cosmic memory construct had been recognized by the ancients; Metrodorus of Scepsis was said to have used the zodiac for his system, a claim derided by Quintilian: 'Which makes me wonder all the more how Metrodorus can have found three hundred and sixty places in the twelve signs through which the sun moves.'[45] Nonetheless, Thomas Bradwardine (ca. 1300–49) recommended using the zodiac for placing images, as did later Johannes Romberch, Cosimo Rosselli, Giordano Bruno, and Robert Fludd.[46] Possibly Milton nods to such predecessors when he identifies the golden scales with Libra, 'yet seen / Betwixt Astrea and the Scorpion sign' (4: 997–8), while indicating that the world remains balanced between justice (Astraea) and treachery (Scorpio). The 360 memory places that so aroused Quintilian's scepticism make it clear that Metrodorus envisioned the cosmos as a circle, the same circle of perfection that the Son measures out with the golden compasses.

As the Ciceronian orator would follow his *exordium* with *narratio*, a statement of his purpose, so Milton follows the invocation with his: 'That to the highth of this great Argument / I may assert Eternal Providence / And justify the ways of God to men' (1: 24–6). 'Argument,' as much as 'cause' (1: 28), announces that rhetoric and logic underlie the narrative structure of the poem; his end will be to 'assert Eternal Providence'; doing so will 'justify the ways of God to men.'[47] Six years before the poem's first printing, *A Letter of Resolution Concerning Origen* had assured its readers that '*thou will not be offended with anything . . . which justifies the waies of* [God's] *Providence*';[48] yet the word 'justify' does cause modern readers difficulty. Another recent editor observes, 'In the poet's claim that he will *justify* God's actions lies the remarkable assertion not only that he is able to do this but also that God's ways are in need of justification.' This is a somewhat flat response to one of the most resonant words in the poem. The verb 'justify' appears only once more, but the variant forms are legion – 'justification' once; 'justly' ten times; 'justice' seventeen; and 'just' (adj. and n.) a remarkable fifty-two – an evolving definition that carries us through the poem.

Immediately, 'justify' signals a rhetorical function: along with the obvious demonstrative and deliberative modes (praising God, moving the reader to reform), the poem will have a forensic dimension, evaluating a past action. Any presumption in the undertaking might be cancelled for most seventeenth-century Protestants by the word's evocation of the doctrine that Luther formulated in his wrestling to comprehend Romans 3, justification by faith alone through 'one greater Man.' *Areopagitica* offers an eloquent Arminian rationale for the existence of sin: 'This justifies the high providence of God' (*CPW* 2: 527), because providence creates the conditions under which virtue is defined by trial and free choice. Nonetheless, 'in religion whatever we do under the gospel, we ought to be therof perswaded without scruple; and are justified by the faith we have, not by the work we do' (*CPW* 7: 266). Through his voluntary sacrifice as Jesus Christ, the greatest of providences, the Son simultaneously fulfils his Father's twofold love of justice and humanity – his work, not theirs. If we can entertain the multiplicity of reference, 'justify' might also glance at Milton's awareness that he is composing an epic to be printed; God's ways will be set forth in type exactly for his reader.[49]

To consider again the evolving definition, it may be helpful to invoke the other great compass image. When Donne vowed, 'Thy firmness makes my circle just,' he promised not simply to return from his present journey but to make his life course right and true. Arminius asserted, 'God is just in himself, he exists as the *Iustitia* itself, he does nothing, indeed, can do nothing, except what is most thoroughly in agreement with that nature of his.'[50] The Son's command, 'This be thy just Circumference, O World' (7: 231), declares the creation of a righteous, moral world through God's foresight. As with Arminius, justice comes first in the very act of lovingly creating a place for humans. Providence is both means and cause of Creation as after the Fall the Son, now Jesus, will be the means and cause of redemption, a re-Creation.[51]

Although he opted for a more complex principle of composition, Milton surely understood Walter Ralegh's declaration:

> The examples of diuine providence, every where found . . . haue perswaded me to fetch my beginning from the beginning of all things, to wit, Creation. For though these two glorious actions of the Almightie be so neare, and (as it were) linked together, that the one necessarily implieth the other: Creation inferring Prouidence . . . and Prouidence presupposing Creation.[52]

Arminius, like Milton, believed the Son was generated from the Father, but accepted creation *ex nihilo,* keeping a clear separation of the Godhead and his creatures. Milton, in a rare difference from the theologian, affirmed creation *ex deo,* permitting the Son's enhanced role within the poem, both the first creation and the creator of angels and humans.[53] Consequently, he has a mediatorial and providential role from the beginning, fusing Creation and providence as one. At the very outset the poet appeals, 'say first what cause / Mov'd' our parents to fall (1: 28–9), a question echoed by Adam to Raphael: 'what cause / Mov'd the Creator in his holy Rest / Through all Eternity so late to build / In *Chaos*' (7: 90–3)? Adam's question was almost the first thought to enter his mind: 'But who I was, or where, or from what cause, / Knew not' (8: 270–1). The most direct answer comes not to Adam but the reader in the image of the Son, whose face visibly expresses his Father's will, 'Love without end, and without measure Grace' (3: 143). Raphael's answer to Adam simply is his narration of the Creation story, 'inferring Providence,' as Ralegh put it, 'and Providence presupposing Creation.'

First and Last Things

With his purpose firmly asserted and the most grand of all memory spaces for a canvas, we can look at the memory loci that Milton 'places' in his recollection of the Genesis story.[54] One is named in the title of the epic; the adjective that follows defines the perspective or condition of himself and his audience – existing in time, marked by original sin – which positions them nearer the end than the beginning.[55] This causes him, I suggest, to take the remaining places from a mnemonic familiar to every English man, woman, and child and as cherished as 'Remember, remember the Fifth of November.'[56] Question: 'What are the Four Last Things to be ever remembered?' Answer: 'The Four Last Things to be ever remembered are Death, Judgment, Hell, and Heaven' (*The Penny Catechism*). One might say the scheme is First and Last Things. An early reader who appears to have responded to this dimension was Joseph Trapp, now remembered for his Latin translation of Milton's epic, *Paradisus Amissus* (vol. 1, 1741; vol. 2, 1744). A decade earlier, however, Trapp wrote *Thoughts Upon the Four Last Things: Death; Judgement; Heaven; Hell. A Poem in Four Parts* (1734–5), which overtly was influenced by *Paradise Lost*.[57]

Although death and judgment certainly figure prominently in the action of the poem, obviously they are not places; Paradise, Hell, and Heaven are. These 'places,' the existence of which was not doubted by most Protestants, are a far cry from those of classical rhetoric, but completely congruent with the fusion of mnemonics and meditation in the tradition of *sacra memoria*. The sequence above, incidentally, arranges them in an order that the poem does not follow. A particular advantage of the architectural (here cosmic) system for the memory of things is that, having created the places and stocked them with the vivid images that secure them to one's memory, they can be shuffled like a pack of cards. The orator can take a different course through the building and rearrange his topics at will; Augustine offered the example of a friend who could recite Virgil in reverse order.[58] Approaching the Last Things in his journey within 'The Church' Herbert takes us through 'Death,' 'Dooms-day,' 'Judgement,' but famously elides Hell and goes directly to 'Heaven.'

In *Paradise Lost*, the order is Hell, Heaven, Paradise, Judgment, Death, last first and first last. Celebrating the Creation, the angelic choir lauds divine providence: '[Satan's] evil / Thou usest, and from thence creat'st more good / Witness this new-made World, another Heav'n / From Heaven Gate not far' (7: 615–18). Milton's unorthodox insertion of a third place at the centre focuses the design on the human characters and the poignancy of their loss, 'another Heav'n.' Whereas Heaven and Hell are beyond time, Paradise is the liminal place wherein the wrong responses to temptations change what might be called natural to mortal time, activating the entire compensatory scheme of providence that will be completed only at Judgment Day. The transition, appropriately, is marked by a judgment that foreshadows the final one. To convey a firmer sense of the poem's design, in the remainder of this chapter I wish to review somewhat more closely these places and things, following the order in which we encounter them.

The meagre biblical sources for a description of Hell, the most lurid of memory places, are the 'everlasting fire, prepared for the devil and his angels' (Matt. 25: 41), 'the lake of fire and brimstone' (Rev. 20: 10), and a few ancillary verses such as the fiery mouth of Leviathan (Job 41: 19–21), the 'pit' of Hell (Isa. 14: 15), and the burning of Tophet (Isa. 30: 30, 33). These were elaborated by centuries of hellfire sermons as the church found fear a powerful deterrent to both secularism and sinful behaviour. At the time Milton was writing his great poems, in intellectual circles the doctrine of Hell was beginning to be seriously questioned, but at the popular level the old tradition continued undiminished.[59]

Perhaps conditioned by the precise and detailed descriptions of Dante's *Inferno*, some readers have found the Hell of *Paradise Lost* vague and inconsistent.[60] The vagueness is congruent with the Reformed reaction against 'the absurdity of the Catholic geography of the afterlife.'[61] Protestants, nevertheless, were committed by the Apostles' Creed and the Thirty-Nine Articles to believe that Jesus descended into Hell; the meaning of his descent was noisily contended, but Hell remained a place.[62] Again unlike Dante and the medieval tradition, Milton refused to locate his Hell at the centre of the earth, '*but in a place of utter darkness, fitliest call'd Chaos*' (bk 1, 'Argument'). Beyond those large differences, the descriptions of Hell touch the familiar stops. Satan has been

'Hurl'd headlong flaming from th' Ethereal Sky / With hideous ruin and combustion down / To bottomless perdition' (1: 45–7) within a 'hollow abyss' (2: 518). Although, nicely, he is himself associated with Leviathan (1: 197–209), his awareness that 'a lower deep / Still threatening to devour me opens wide' (4: 76–7) reflects a vestige of the 'Hell mouth' tradition.[63]

Satan comes to consciousness 'rolling in the fiery Gulf' (1: 52) or 'burning lake' (210), 'a fiery Deluge, fed / With ever-burning Sulphur unconsum'd' (68–9) by the 'four infernal Rivers' of classical mythology (2: 575–86). Even the celebrated, oxymoronic descriptor of what strikes his appalled vision, the flames that emit 'No light, but rather darkness visible' (1: 63), has proven to have impeccable antecedents.[64] Land differs only in burning 'With solid, as the Lake with liquid fire' (1: 229), except for the 'frozen Continent' where 'cold performs th' effect of Fire' (2: 587, 595). During the Middle Ages volcanic eruptions and exhalations of vapour were taken as scientific evidence that Hell lurks below at the centre. In his *Rhetorica Novissima* (1235), Boncompagno da Signa drew upon his own experience for a memory aid:

> *On the memory of the infernal regions.* I remember having seen the mountain which in literature is called Etna and in the vulgar Vulcanus, whence, when I was sailing near it, I saw sulphurous balls ejected, burning and glowing; and they say that this goes on all the time. Whence many hold that there is the mouth of Hell. However, wherever Hell may be, I firmly believe that Satan, the prince of Demons, is tortured in that abyss together with his myrmidons.[65]

The most distinctive geographic feature of Milton's Hell is anticipated by a Virgilian simile, comparing the windswept landscape to that of volcanic eruption:

> . . . as when the force
> Of subterranean wind transports a Hill
> Torn from Pelorus, or the shatter'd side
> Of thund'ring AEtna, whose combustible
> And fuell'd entrails thence conceiving Fire,
> Sublim'd with Mineral fury, aid the Winds. (1: 230–5)

When we reach the volcano itself, 'a Hill not far whose grisly top / Belch'd fire and rolling smoke' (1: 670–1), the sublimated minerals have prepared for the gold, 'metallic Ore / The work of sulfur' (673–4), fool's gold even if genuine, that Mammon and his brigade mine, violating an unnatural nature to compound Hell with hellishness. The *Ad Herennium* dictates that the memory place should be a relatively neutral container, a generalized image to set off the vivid image that it houses. In Books 1 and 2 the familiar signifiers attest that this indeterminate and really unimaginable place is Hell, a foil to set off the most arresting image of the poem, Satan himself. As critics have noticed, the incoherence of its geography – 'Rocks, Caves, Lakes, Fens, Bogs, Dens, and Shades of death' (2: 621) – externalizes the mental and moral chaos of its new inhabitants, a state that they come to display physically in Book 10, when they are transformed into obscenely swarming, 'complicated,' serpentine monsters (10: 504–84).[66]

Commenting on the function of memory images in the *Ad Herennium*, Frances Yates wrote: 'Our author has clearly got hold of the idea of helping memory by arousing emotional affects through these striking and unusual images, beautiful or hideous, comic or obscene. And it is clear that he is thinking of human images, of human figures . . . dramatically engaged in some activity – doing something.'[67] Substitute 'fallen angel' for 'human' and this is not a bad description of the range of readers' reactions provoked by Satan and his demonic energy; it might be appropriate, therefore, to ask what idea or complex of ideas readers should remember through Satan. The full complex would require a book in itself; to focus more narrowly one can say with certainty that a key theme of the Hell books simply is loss.

The modern reader may feel teased or set up with the discovery that, even after Satan has found his 'dismal Situation' to be a place that urges 'torture without end' (1: 67), there is none. Given such an opportunity, surely Dante would have choked Mammon with moneybags, impaled Belial on a spit, loaded Satan with rocks and submerged him in a freezing river. Milton's contemporaries, however, generally accepted that there were two kinds of torture in Hell, physical pain and the pain of loss, of which the latter caused the greater agony. As Donne colourfully expressed it: 'The intensnesse of that fire, the ayre of that brimstone, the anguish of that worm, the discord of that howling, and gnashing of teeth, is no comparable, no considerable part of the torment, in respect of the privation of the sight of God, the banishment from the presence of God, an absolute hopelesnesse.'[68]

Milton retains the fire and brimstone, but banishes the physical torture to concentrate on exploring that state of privation. The 'lost happiness' and 'lasting pain' that torment Satan (1: 55–6) are one and the same, his alienation from God wracking him with 'deep despair' (126). The mournful words 'loss,' 'lost,' 'changed,' 'fallen' echo throughout Books 1 and 2, culminating in Satan's admission or renunciation, 'all Good to me is lost' (4: 109). C.A. Patrides concluded, 'Milton's Hell might well be described as the state wherein the fallen angels constantly lament their everlasting loss of Heaven.'[69] The human application takes the reader from the loss that is the poem's subject to the Book 3 dialogue with the Son's intercession, 'should Man finally be lost'? (150) and the Father's Arminian assurance, 'Man shall not quite be lost, but sav'd who will' (173).

After sensibly using the eruption of Mount Etna as a memory aid for Hell, Boncompagno could only throw up his hands with Heaven, conceding, 'Artificial memory gives no help to man for these ineffable things.' Nonetheless, doubting its existence was a damnable heresy: 'AND WE MUST ASSIDUOUSLY REMEMBER THE INVISIBLE JOYS OF PARADISE.'[70] The dilemma of describing a real, yet invisible, place had not changed when Milton grappled with it four centuries later. As with his Hell, Milton scrutinized carefully the scriptural sources – primarily Exodus for the Sinai revelation to Moses, Ezekiel's vision of the Temple, Revelation 4 and 21 – from which he might imagine something like Heaven.[71]

To begin with, when Satan emerges from Chaos, he can 'behold / Far off th' Empyreal Heav'n, extended wide / In circuit, undetermin'd square or round, / With Opal Tow'rs and Battlements adorn'd / Of living Sapphire' (2: 1046–50). Despite its original sense of 'fiery,' by the Middle Ages 'empyreal' had come to be accepted as pure light,[72] as it is here, an effective transition to the invocation of Book 3. Whereas Beelzebub speaks of Heaven's 'whole circumference' (2: 353) and Sin describes the 'Empyreal bounds' as 'His Quadrature' (10: 381), the poet leaves the question of shape, square or round, entirely open.[73] Yet squares and circles are known forms and thereby reassuring, as are the towers and battlements, a holdover from fortress-like medieval cities.[74] Then one hits an imaginative wall with 'living Sapphire.'

Milton reflects the description of the New Jerusalem in Revelation, which has a 'foursquare' city (19: 16) and a wall of which the second foundation is sapphire (19: 19). We know that everything in creation, even minerals, has a vegetative soul, but Milton reserves the refrain 'living Soul' for animal and human life in the fifth and sixth days of Creation, leaving 'living Sapphire' an oxymoron, as indeterminate a material as the shape of Heaven itself. On considering such descriptions, Jackson Cope once asserted that Heaven 'cannot be captured in any metaphors of substance.'[75] An exegete versed in architectural mnemonics might recall a Pauline text, 'as a wise masterbuilder, I have laid the foundation, and another buildeth thereon' (1 Cor. 3: 10); for Paul, as for Milton, that foundation is Jesus Christ. Following Paul's metaphor, Hugh of St Victor advised students to act as masons in recollecting scripture: 'You are about to construct the spiritual building. Already the foundations of the story have been laid in you.'[76] With his odd metaphor of 'living sapphire,' the poet points to the mosaic of biblical language, the living doctrine of scripture, through which he will construct by recollection God's habitation, thereby stimulating the reader's own biblical ruminations.

Walls with battlements require an entrance, and the poet devotes careful attention to Heaven's gate. Like the doors of a modern supermarket, 'the gate self-open'd wide' (5: 254); rather than electronics, this is 'as by work / Divine the sovran Architect had framed' (255–6). When the 'Golden Hinges' move they emit 'Harmonious sound' (7: 206–7). Although audible, the gate is not visually comprehensible:

> The work as of a Kingly Palace Gate
> With Frontispiece of Diamond and Gold
> Imbellisht: thick with sparkling orient Gems
> The Portal shone, inimitable on Earth
> By Model, or by shading Pencil drawn. (3: 505–9)

Much like the gilded portals and jewelled altars of a medieval church,[77] here as elsewhere in Heaven the imagery of gold and gems symbolizes the radiance and preciousness of holy presence. At the same time, the 'as' signals that this is only analogy and the reality is beyond representation by graphic or plastic art. The primary sense of 'Frontispiece,' whether façade or pediment, is architectural, reminding us whose work this is. Since the bibliographical term had been available all Milton's lifetime (see *OED*, s.v., 3), it also seems likely that the word obliquely alludes to the truth that the sacred book contains his only entrance to knowledge of Heaven.

Within the gate we encounter not city or castle but a great plain, 'wider far / Than all this globous Earth in Plain outspread' (5: 648–9). The landscape is modelled on the Exodus setting of the Sinai epiphany, a plain with the mountain at its edge. 'And once Raphael's hyperbole has been removed,' Michael Murrin remarks, 'we have a military camp in a desert oasis, with the tents set up among the trees.'[78] Yet this is a plain unlike any on earth. As well as an oasis with streams and trees, we find 'seated Hills' with 'Rocks, Waters, Woods' (6: 644–5) and mountains, all of which the loyal angels uproot to hurl at their opponents (6: 639–66); when order has been restored Heaven assumes 'his' customary face 'And with fresh Flow'rets Hill and Valley smil'd' (6: 784). An unbridgeable distance from the arid desert wilderness of Exodus and of Book 12: 215–26.

Mountains in particular seem to proliferate. Aside from those employed as natural defensive weapons, there are the 'two brazen Mountains' (adapted from Zech. 6: 1) that protectively flank God's armory (6: 200–1). Overshadowing these, at the centre of Heaven looms the holy mountain on which the Father sits enthroned; this most directly resembles the Sinai prototype when his wrath is aroused, darkening it with clouds, smoke, and flames (6: 56–9. Cf. Exod. 20: 18, 21). Even when he is in a good mood, its top is obscured, 'as from a flaming Mount, whose top / Brightness had made invisible' (5: 598–9). Milton conflates Sinai with Sion where, on the authority of Psalm 2, God has begotten and anointed his Son (5: 603–15).[79] Again, relying on Psalm 11, which mingles imagery of mountain and temple, he adds elements of the latter: the Son rides 'Triumphant through mid Heav'n, into the Courts / And Temple of his mighty Father Thron'd / On high' (6: 889–91), with still further details from Revelation 4. However persuasive the biblical warrant for these associations, they do not create an apprehensible topography – nor are they so intended. On examining the biblical sources and the language, Murrin concludes that 'like the prophet, [Milton] chose spectacular events for heaven . . . events which, however, a person theoretically could witness. He then transformed each representation verbally so as to suggest that no one actually could view it.'[80]

If Heaven is beyond visualization, so is the entity whose image is at the centre of this holy place. On scriptural warrant, God the Father is endowed with human emotions by both narrator and characters within the poem: thus, he laughs (2: 731, 8: 78), smiles (5: 737), and is wrathful (6: 58–9). There are references to his nostrils, ear, feet, and hand, all obviously figurative, not phantom body parts. But, as the angelic choir attests, the reality is ineffable: 'Fountain of Light, thyself invisible / Amidst the glorious brightness where thou sit'st / Thron'd inaccessible' (3: 375–7). Mammon had asserted that the Father sometimes obscures his radiance with clouds of darkness (2: 263–7), which the chorus confirms, but even then he so dazzles Heaven that seraphim must veil their eyes (3: 377–82). Only the Son, 'Divine Similitude,' can behold him; and the Son, visibly expresses his Father as unclouded light, which means mercy, compassion, love, and grace (3: 385–9, 134–42). Milton fuses echoes of Exodus 24: 15, Isaiah 6: 1–4, and – perhaps above all – the gospel of light in John and 1 John.[81] As Hell externalizes the confusion, disorder, and alienation burning within Satan, so the pure light of 'Empyreal' Heaven reflects the essential quality of the radiant memory image within it. If we pose the reductive question of what lesson that image prods us to remember, the answer might simply be what the newly awakened Adam reasons out from himself and his surroundings – that there is a creator 'In goodness and in power preeminent' (8: 279).

In contrast to Heaven and Hell, the Bible is tangibly specific on Paradise, tantalizingly so in that the identifiable names in Genesis 2 (Ethiopia, Assyria, Euphrates) convinced centuries of commentators and cartographers through Milton's own lifetime that they should be able to locate the actual place.[82] A Scots traveller to the Holy Land spoke of recording the sacred geography in 'the Map of my owne Memory.'[83] The poet responded in keeping with the specificity of Genesis, causing J.B. Broadbent to summarize approvingly: 'Milton distinguishes Paradise from Heaven by proliferation of detail, classical allusion, natural sunlight; he only hints at the emblematic motifs; and he asserts the garden's actuality by reference to topical geography.'[84] To be sure, the topography in its larger features is quite distinct. Adam's recollection of being transported to the Garden is precise, 'A woody mountain; whose high top was plain, / A circuit wide, enclos'd, with goodliest Trees / Planted, with walls, and bowers' (8: 303–5), and further corroborated by the narrator. To 'the East / Of Eden planted' (3: 209–10), the Garden is situated on a mesa, 'Crowns with her enclosure green, / As with a rural mound the champaign head / Of a steep wilderness' (4: 133–5). The 'enclosure green' suggests a spiritual place,[85] although, unlike the mysterious living sapphire of Heaven, the 'verdurous wall' here is living nature, a thicket of vegetation and ranked trees with a single gate to the east by a mountain of alabaster. An underground river feeds a fountain and four streams which water the garden.

This great plain, nevertheless, proves as infinitely varied as its heavenly counterpart, 'A happy rural seat of various view' (4: 247), with groves, lawns, downs, pastures, hillocks, valleys, grottoes, caves, lakes, waterfalls, and, under shady retreats, the bowers of Adam and Eve. As God has populated the chain of being with every imaginable living creature, literally 'numberless' (7: 492), so also the vegetation, fruits, and flora are varied and luxuriant, 'Nature boon / Pour'd forth profuse' (4: 242–3), figuring forth his plenitude, the bounty graciously conferred on 'this new-made World, another Heav'n / From Heaven Gate not far' (7: 617–18). Despite the much remarked 'vegetable Gold' of fruit, flowers, and even 'sands of Gold,' which remind us both that nature is God's art and this 'another Heav'n,' the more significant aspect of the Garden, it emerges, is its robust and unruly vitality. Eve's complaint that nature mocks their labours, growing 'Luxurious by restraint' and 'with wanton growth derides / Tending to wild' (9: 209, 211–12), may exaggerate, but Adam does not substantially disagree. Rather than static perfection, the Garden is a place of dynamic growth, which must be ordered, a lesson that Herbert expressed visually with his pruning poem, 'Paradise.'

The initial description of Adam and Eve, the lively images whom God quite literally places in this memory space, first emphasizes their natural nobility, 'Two of far nobler shape erect and tall, / Godlike erect, with native Honor clad / In naked Majesty seem'd Lords of all' (4: 288–90). The repeated 'erect' serves to separate them from the lesser creatures whom they are to govern and calls attention to the special gift of their rationality, symbolized by their mediate position between Heaven and Earth, 'Godlike erect.' Given the conspicuous splendour of the Stuarts, 'naked Majesty' has the force of an oxymoron – who could imagine Charles and Henrietta Maria naked? – reminding us that merit, not fine costumes, confers authority, 'with native Honor clad.' Here, no less than with later monarchs, it all depends on who one's father is: 'And worthy seem'd, for in thir looks Divine / The image of thir glorious Maker shone' (291–2). Attractively, from Milton's recalling the pronoun shift of Genesis 1: 27, the image of God has been invested in both. Because they are created in God's image, they are 'in true filial freedom *plac'd*' (294, my emphasis); their free will and rationality – granted, Arminius thought, to create humans as fit associates of the divinity – in fact make them, Satan despairingly attests, 'to heav'nly Spirits bright / Little inferior'(360–1).

Equally, the description embodies Milton's subtextual rumination of Genesis 1: 28, which Adam already has heard: 'Be fruitful, multiply, and fill the Earth, / Subdue it, and throughout Dominion hold' (7: 531–2). He had begun with their freely delegated authority to hold dominion over every living thing; he now considers 'Be fruitful and multiply.' As the vine and elm topos signals,[86] he looks at this within the institution of marriage. Nearly the entirety *of De Doctrina*'s chapter on the special providence governing man is devoted to marriage (*CPW* 6: 355–81), a sure measurement of its importance. Milton believed that innocent sex was one of the blessings God bestowed on humans; he also insisted '*marriage is not a meer carnall coition*'(*CPW* 2: 275). He, therefore, could not accept that the commandment simply meant to procreate; most probably, he accepted it as a statement of God's covenant, assuring his providence for humans, and inclined to the figurative interpretation of cultivating Christian virtues.[87] A prolegomenon (or fore play) to the 'Hail Wedded Love' hymn (4: 750–75), the passage illuminates the erotic attraction between the couple: 'coy submission,' 'sweet reluctant amorous delay,' the guiltless exposure of 'those mysterious parts' (4: 310–13). No wonder that, when they kiss, Satan feels like a voyeur: 'aside the Devil turn'd / For envy, yet with jealous leer malign / Ey'd them askance' (4: 502–4). Insisting that their innocence is as spotless as the rose is thornless, the poet pays tribute: 'So hand in hand they pass'd, the loveliest pair / That ever since in love's imbraces met, / *Adam* the goodliest man of men since born / His Sons, the fairest of her Daughters *Eve*' (4: 321–4). The three superlatives – 'loveliest,' 'goodliest,' 'fairest' – all convey both exterior and interior, appearances revealing moral qualities, which Satan recognizes: 'my thoughts pursue / With wonder, and could love, so lively shines / In them Divine resemblance' (4: 363–4).

Elaine Pagels has affirmed that, 'for nearly the first four hundred years of our era, Christians regarded *freedom* as the primary message of Genesis 1–3.'[88] Whether he arrived at it through Arminius or by his own meditation on Genesis, this accords with Milton's interpretation: 'when God gave [Adam] reason, he gave him freedom to choose . . . We our selves esteem not of that obedience, or love, or gift, which is of force: God therefore left him free . . . Wherefore did he creat passions within us, pleasures round about us, but that these rightly temper'd are the very ingredients of vertu?' (*CPW* 2: 527). Even more bluntly, 'No man who knows ought, can be so stupid to deny that all men naturally were borne free, being the image and resemblance of God himself' (*CPW* 3: 198). That freedom extends to the passions and pleasures of sexual desire, which, rightly tempered, are virtuous. Summarizing the debate between Augustine and Julian of Eclanum, who rejected the belief that sexual passion was a consequence of the Fall, Pagels writes,

'For Julian, sexual desire is innocent, divinely blessed, and . . . offers us the opportunity to exercise our capacity for moral choice,' a view that Milton shared with his belief in providential trial.[89]

As with both Heaven and Hell, the place of Paradise in the richness of its natural endowments, luxuriant growth and corresponding need for restraint, and the tending of the Garden resembles the vivid images of its inhabitants. If we entertain the possibility that the characters within the poem function as memory images allocated to a system of places, two other considerations are pertinent. First, 'Keep in mind that when we speak of "place" in memory, we refer not to a literal spot or space, but to *location within a network*, "memory" *distributed* through a web of associations, some of which may involve physical space . . . many of which are socially constructed and maintained conventions,' and others which may be entirely personal.[90] Particularly given the expanded allusiveness in Milton's poetry, this may help explain why, beyond certain constant values (e.g., God is good, Satan is not), readers legitimately can assert the diverse responses which the epic has evoked. Not postmodern indeterminacy, but traditional sacred meditation. Phillip Donnelly likewise contests 'the "New Milton Criticism," which emphasizes the role of "indeterminacy," "chaos," or "incertitude" in Milton's poetry,' arguing, 'The epic attempts instead to mimic biblical form in its very susceptibility to multiple interpretations.'[91] Second, since the poem is in no way a technical memory treatise but, I suggest, an adaptation of certain mnemonic principles, both as a compositional technique and as a means of engaging the reader's memory, characters in the narrative have the freedom or necessity to depart from their places, even to occupy new places, which takes us to the Last Things that are not themselves locations.

Mary Ann Radzinowicz finds in *Paradise Lost* 'an extended drama of the unfolding of the meaning of death,' certainly a matter of absorbing interest to its mortalist author.[92] Even before 'loss' is lamented and the Saviour celebrated, the keynotes sounded are sin and death, 'First Disobedience, and the Fruit / . . . whose mortal taste / Brought Death into the World, and all our woe' (1: 1–3). Rather like the Nativity Ode, in which Milton explains Christmas by the full compass of Christian time, so here he presents death as a process that begins with choice and extends to Doomsday. The Father states precisely, but abstractly, the consequences of disobedience: 'He with his whole posterity must die, / Die hee or Justice must' (3: 209–10); yet already this has been clothed with an unforgettable genealogy: Satan created Sin, together they generate Death, who punishes her in kind with the rape that produces the tormenting hell hounds. Not in this fable is death the mother of beauty.

Eve plucks the fruit and 'Greedily she ingorg'd without restraint / And knew not eating Death' (9: 791–2), whereas Adam, eyes wide open, makes a fatally wrong choice, 'if Death / Consort with thee, Death is to mee as life' (9: 953–4). The Son, passing judgment, confirms, 'For dust thou art, and shalt to dust return. / So judg'd he Man, both Judge and Savior sent, / And th' instant stroke of Death denounc'd that day / Remov'd far off' (10: 208–11). Adam needs first to understand 'That Death be not one stroke, as I suppos'd' (10: 809), for Milton conceives it as a process of several degrees: first, the 'guilty shame' that leaves Adam and Eve destitute of virtue; second, the impairment of reason that Adam exhibits in his long soliloquy (and Milton, 10: 611–13, carefully exempts animals from these stages); lastly, death of the body, 'dissolution' (11: 552), which yet takes such various forms as the murder of Abel, the disease-wracked bodies in the Lazar House, and the depopulation by Flood. The hardest to contemplate (and therefore abbreviated in presentation) is 'A shameful and accurst [death], nail'd to the Cross / By his own Nation, slain for bringing Life' (12: 413–14), which epitomizes the entire providential action of bringing good out of evil.

Judgment follows death as does the day the night; and, Gerald Hammond appositely comments, 'The effort of *Paradise Lost* is to turn memory into prophecy.'[93] Most English Protestants accepted belief in two judgments, particular and general. At the hour of one's death, God pronounces his sentence: 'The soule of every man accordingly is (by the power of God and the ministry of Angels) immediately conveyed into that state of happiness or misery wherein it shall remaine till the resurrection.' Last Judgment is 'The great day of assize for the whole world, wherein all mens lives that ever have been, are, or shall be, being duly examined, every one shall receive according to his works.'[94] Purgatory and prayers for the dead having been eliminated, some wondered why Ockham's razor should not be applied here as well. Elnathan Parr's catechism addressed this head on: 'If the soules of the elect goe presently after their death to heaven, and the soules of the reprobate to hell, what neede a general Iudgement?' His answer may not have allayed sceptics. A general judgment was necessary, Parr argued, 'both that the iustnesse of such particular Iudgement may bee made more manifest to the glorie of God, and that the whole man, consisting of body and soule, may receive the due reward.'[95] Because he was a mortalist, believing that body and soul died together, for Milton the question of redundancy did not arise. The Son confidently predicts to his Father:

Though now to Death I yield, and am his due
All that of me can die, yet that debt paid,
Thou wilt not leave me in the loathsome grave
His prey, nor suffer my unspotted Soul
For ever with corruption here to dwell. (3: 245–9)

Even with his reason impaired by the Fall, Adam can puzzle out that his 'Spirit' has sinned against God and concludes, 'All of me then shall die' (10: 792).

Nonetheless, Genesis 3 provided a particular judgment that could not be ignored. The Son passes judgment on Adam and Eve, confirming their mortality and defining the conditions of their fallen lives. Even before this, he judges the serpent amplifying Genesis to include Satan explicitly, 'To Satan first in sin his doom appli'd. / Though in mysterious terms' (10: 172–3), making the Protevangelium more direct: the Woman's 'Seed shall bruise thy head, thou bruise his heel' (181). Adam partially comes to grasp the sense of this (10: 1029–36) and later learns the full meaning from Michael:

The Woman's seed, obscurely then foretold,
Now amplier known thy Saviour and thy Lord,
Last in the Clouds from Heav'n to be reveal'd,
In glory of the Father, to dissolve
Satan with his perverted World. (12: 543–7)

Milton makes the Eden judgment into a prophecy of the Last Judgment. The Battle in Heaven had shown that Spirits 'Cannot but by annihilating die' (6: 347), and Moloch had bruited the possibility that God's ire will 'quite consume us, and reduce / To nothing this essential' (2: 96–7). Now Michael confirms that, at the end of time, Satan will be dissolved, annihilated – in mortal terms, dead without the possibility of resurrection. Milton presents the Son's first victory over Satan as a foreshadowing of their final encounter; consistent with this typology, the biblical echoes in the expulsion of the rebel angels from Heaven evoke overtones of the Last Judgment.[96] The expulsion effectively is an act of excommunication, driving the rebels down to Hell, 'thir prepar'd ill Mansion'; but no formal sentence is announced in Book 6. Milton's 'unfolding' of Genesis 3: 14–15 satisfies that lack. On the human side of the judgment, the Father had decreed that Adam's 'crime makes guilty all his Sons' (3: 290) and Genesis 3: 16 – which is directly restated, 'Thy sorrow I will greatly multiply / By the Conception; Children thou shalt bring / In sorrow forth' (10: 193–5) – had delivered the declaration, not simply the pain of childbirth but the sorrow of original sin.[97] In this respect, too, the particular judgment is general.

Death and judgment are the consequences of sin; sin is a matter of choice, and at important moments in the action choice begins with remembering or forgetting. The latter especially seems to be not a casual mental lapse, but an act of the will;[98] such acts ought to be understood as failed trials, wrong responses to individual providences. To Abdiel's reminder that the Son created 'All things, ev'n thee' (5: 837), Satan scoffs: 'remember'st thou? Thy making, while the Maker gave thee being? / We know no time when we were not as now' (857–9). Interceding to prevent either filicide or patricide, Sin must lament, 'Hast thou forgot me then, and do I seem / Now in thine eye so foul, once deem'd so fair' (2: 747–8). Satan hates the rays of the sun 'That bring to my remembrance from what state / I fell' (4: 38–9), forcing him to acknowledge that he was 'Forgetful what from [God] I still receiv'd' (54).

Forgetfulness doesn't necessarily arise from bad intentions, but invariably causes trouble. An almost comic demonstration occurs when Satan, immobilized and rendered 'Stupidly good' by Eve's virginal beauty, excoriates himself for forgetting his purpose as his 'Fierce hate he recollects' (9: 465, 471). In considering the differences between Eve's own creation story ('That day I oft remember') and the version Adam tells to Raphael, Joshua Scodel comments, 'Adam reveals himself too eager to forget that Eve ever was – and therefore could once more become . . . autonomous in her desires . . . and that his own authoritative intervention was necessary to redirect her desires to himself as her proper consort.'[99] Book 9 is an epic catalogue of tragic forgetfulness: Eve forgets the warnings that she heard from Adam and from Raphael (6: 912, 'remember and fear to transgress'); Adam forgets both God's 'Remember what I warn thee, shun to taste' (8: 327) and the proper authority Raphael had urged upon him. Although Adam had pledged, 'Yet that we never shall forget to love / Our maker, and obey him'

(5: 550–1), they do. The narrator comments objectively, 'For still they knew, and ought to have still remember'd / The high Injunction' (10: 12–13), thus identifying 'their wilful disjunction of knowledge from memory' as the crux of disobedience.[100]

Fortunately for us, they are capable of recollecting – remembering how to remember, one might say – and learning from their recovered memories; Regina Schwartz correctly observes, 'Memory plays a key role in their movement toward repentance.'[101] Eve, remembering her love and need for Adam (10: 914–24), implores forgiveness and reconciliation, 'by herself remembering' the Protevangelium, thereby 'undo[ing] the amnesia that caused the fall.'[102] Adam, disarmed of his bitterness and anger 'call[s] to mind with heed / Part of our sentence' (10: 1030–1) that implies a hopeful future; and, 'Remember[ing] with what mild / And gracious temper [God] heard and judg'd' them (1046–7), proposes that they 'confess / Humbly our faults, and pardon beg' (1088–9), the first step toward reconciliation. Reflecting hopefully on God's response to their prayer for forgiveness, Adam confides to Eve: 'peace return'd / Home to my Breast, and to my memory / His promise, that thy Seed shall bruise our Foe' (11: 153–5). Hugh MacCallum comments pertinently, 'The key is the promise that lies in memory. Here as elsewhere grace is seen as recalling what was known, yet unrecognized, enabling the mind to grasp its significance.'[103]

A consequence of the wilful forgetting that leads to sin is displacement; the characters whom I have been discussing as memory images must leave the places they once resembled. Satan, no longer compatible with Heaven, is exiled to Hell, the place that now mirrors him; Adam and Eve must leave Paradise for a fallen world; Sin and Death, now part of their being, are permitted to occupy that world. The Son, who does not forget, voluntarily leaves Heaven to become mortal. In the end, place ceases to matter, for there will be only one. Paradise, washed away in the Flood, will become 'The haunt of Seals and Orcs, and Sea-mews' clang, / To teach thee that God attributes to place / No sanctity' (11: 835–7). Hell, too, will be negated; the Son shall sling 'Both *Sin*, and *Death*, and yawning Grave at last / Through *Chaos* hurl'd, obstruct the mouth of Hell / For ever, and seal up his ravenous Jaws' (10: 635–7). Returned to his rightful place at the Judgment, the Son shall 'dissolve / *Satan* with his perverted World, then raise / From the conflagrant mass, purg'd and refin'd, / New Heav'ns, new Earth' (12: 546–9), 'wherein the just shall dwell' (11: 901). Remember, remember.

This chapter has looked broadly at the benevolence of Creation and the workings of providence, both generally in the ordering of the created world itself and in its special concern for angels and humans. Unavoidably, this has proceeded in tandem with the extraordinary providence the poet was granted, his inspiration to compose, recreate, a lost world from *sacra memoria,* his ruminations on scripture ordered by the art of memory, in the generous hope of renovating the reader's own such memories. During his lifetime many accepted the deficiency of memory to be itself a consequence of the Fall, concomitant with Adam's impaired reason: 'Our fraile and britle memory before / Did safely keep the whole conceptions store.'[104] All the more imperative, then, to renew memory in his poem and through his poem. Milton attempts to convert his own providence into the reader's through the trials of reading because, as Donnelly argues, 'he views regenerate reason's participation in the goodness and beauty of creation as continuous with its understanding of human texts.'[105] The poem's engagement of the reader's memory, renewing and reforming memories of the Bible if successful, thereby itself becomes an act of providence.

In the chapters that follow we shall look more closely at the lively memory images inhabiting this world, as well as the places they occupy, are exiled from, or voluntarily abandon. Following the order outlined above, these are, first, Satan; then the Son of God; next Eve and Adam. The themes of death and judgment become prominent in the later chapters as the poem itself shifts from the cosmic memory theatre of the created world to the progression of mortal time toward the Last Things.

Chapter 3 considers the disgraced angel who will become the first reprobate. Christian orthodoxy dismissed any possibility that Lucifer-turned-Satan could ever be forgiven, and probably most Miltonists, including those of the devil's own party, would agree that the epic excludes that possibility.[106] The Father's decree at the Son's begetting sounds conclusive: 'who disobeys' will be 'Cast out from God and blessed vision, falls / Into utter darkness, deep ingulft, his place / Ordain'd without redemption, without end' (5: 611, 613–15). Satan fails the temptation of the begetting; yet, as we know, God's permissive will leaves Satan 'at large to his own dark designs' (1: 213) and free to escape his ordained 'place.' The Father confirms that both humans and angels were created with free will, 'and free they must remain, / Till they enthrall themselves' (3: 124–5), implying that such a point has not been reached. His further clarification, 'Man falls deceiv'd / By th' other first: Man therefore shall find grace, / The other none' (3: 130–2) might seem to slam the door decisively. This would, I think, misunderstand the zeugma of the parallel clause – 'The other [shall find] none.' This declaration is, Diane McColley urged, 'prophecy, not decree,' causing Keith Stavely to assert audaciously 'that Milton, ruthlessly consistent in his Arminianism as in all else, refuses to take' the step of 'assuming that Satan *must* remain Satan.'[107] It is a provocative argument and, in its consistency with the free-will logic of the poem, plausible and well worth entertaining.

The subject of Satan's reprobation will be addressed in chapter 4; first, we need to consider just what Satan does with the freedom that God permits. Again the Father's foresight is instructive; observing Satan winging toward 'the new created World, / And Man there plac'd,' he comments, 'with purpose to assay / If him by force he can destroy, or worse, / By some false guile pervert; and shall pervert' (3: 89–92). In allowing Satan to 'assay' or try Adam and Eve, as he later will Job, the Father reveals that Satan's efforts to pervert providence (1: 162–4) will be absorbed into the design as providential temptations and trials. *De Doctrina* discusses temptation within the purview of general providence: 'God either tempts a man or allows him to be tempted by the devil or his agents. Temptation is either good or evil' (*CPW* 6: 338). The biblical citations permit no clear distinction between 'temptation' and 'trial' (*tentatio* and *exploratio*). The purposes of 'good temptations,' however, seem apposite for the seventeenth-century sense of 'trial.' These include proving men by 'exercis[ing] or demonstrat[ing] their faith or patience . . . lessen[ing] their self-confidence . . . so that they may become wiser, and others may be instructed.'

Next, the Father specifies the tactics Satan will employ, 'by force' and 'false guile,' as those identified with a particular kind of godlessness. Victoria Kahn comments perceptively on 'the resources of force and fraud': 'Milton begins *Paradise Lost* with Satan in order to show that rhetorical and political indeterminacy, which his contemporaries stigmatized as Machiavellian, is also the condition of free will.'[108] Chapter 3 will focus on his use of these two tactics.

Chapter Three

Satan's Machiavellian Enterprise: Force and Fraud

> You must expect that the militia of hell and the trained bands of Satan, those that have received the mark of Antichrist, shall be put into a posture of war.[1]
>
> Joseph Caryl

> *What providence deny'd to force,* he thought it might grant to fraud, which he stiles *Prudence:* But Providence was not couzen'd with disguises, neither outward nor inward.
>
> *Eikonoklastes* (*CPW* 3: 545)

Through the first ten books of the epic, chronologically from the rebellion in Heaven until his return to Hell after successfully tempting Eve, Satan motivates the action. Himself a paradigm of how not to respond to trial, he wilfully engages in a course of action that he acknowledges to be wrong; stubbornly persists in drawing mistaken lessons from each defeat; and unwittingly becomes an instrument of providence, 'a provoking object' (*CPW* 2: 527) to other characters in their own trials. This chapter considers Satan's conduct in continued pursuit of the war by force or fraud (*PL* 1: 645–9, 2: 40–1; 'force or guile,' 1: 121), following the devastating loss of the battle in Heaven. These tactics a seventeenth-century reader immediately would have identified with Machiavelli. Francis Cheynell urged Parliament to help Charles I recover 'that power which the antichristian faction by force or fraud hath wrested out of the King's hand.'[2] Defending Cromwell's policy, Michael Hawke argued that necessity required the Protector to operate like a Machiavellian prince, to 'participate of the fraude of the Fox as well as the force of the Lion.'[3] Nonetheless, Hawke's defence elides a correlative implied by Cheynell and, even earlier, stated directly by John Carpenter: 'Such an one was that *Macchiavile,* who perswaded men to governe in this world, partly by fraud, partly by force, and partly by fortune; and not by the divine providence, whereat hee jested.'[4]

The English stereotype of the godless Machiavel derived largely, if not entirely, from *The Prince,* for which as early as 1539 Cardinal Reginald Pole denounced the author as a 'finger of Satan.'[5] Edward Dacres, the first English translator of *Il principe,* acknowledged that the Florentine's 'maximes and tenents are condemnd of all, as pernicious to all Christian States, and hurtfull to all humane Societies.' Three of these tenets in particular were abhorrent: condoning the pragmatic use of cruelty to maintain power (chaps 7 and 8); the lion and fox tactics of force and fraud (chap. 18); and the notorious advice that men should control their own fortunes (chap. 25): 'because Fortune is a mistresse; and it is necessary, to keep her in obedience, to ruffle and force her.' This provokes Dacres's indignant rebuttal: 'Surely there is the finger of God . . . Surely this is a blessing proceeding from the divine providence.'[6] In *Paradise Lost* Satan's ambition means nothing less than driving a stake in the heart of God's grand, providential design – 'to pervert that end' (1: 164). Like Machiavelli, Satan wants to believe that he can control his own fortune by force. Here we will, first, focus upon force by looking at his battle strategy through the lens of contemporary military tactics; and, second, examine his use of disguise to show that this 'fraud or guile' reveals more than it ever conceals.[7] The Machiavel should know better than to jest at providence.

Force: The Forlorn Hope

In early modern military discourse, the phrase 'Forlorn Hope' designated a select body of troops ordered to attack, at high risk, in advance of an army. In Samuel Johnson's pithy definition, 'The soldiers who are sent first to the attack, and are therefore doomed to perish' (1755). It derives from the Dutch expression, *verloren hoop* or 'lost troop,' and the fanciful English substitution has been described as 'one of the best, or worst, examples of folk etymology recorded anywhere.'[8] The English usage is analogous to the French phrase, *enfants perdus,* which Randle Cotgrave defines as 'gentlemen of companies, reserved for, and exposed vnto, all desperate seruices.'[9] Robert Barret speaks of 'the forlorne hope, or *Enfans Perdus,* as the French doe terme them,' indicating that the phrases were coterminous.[10]

'Forlorn Hope' entered the English language in the sixteenth century. Although the *OED* dates the first military usage to 1579, this self-evidently is belated as examples of the figurative extension to encompass any desperate or doomed enterprise, surely a secondary development, are given for 1572. Elsewhere, in fact, it has been traced back to 1539.[11] By the end of the century, unquestionably the phrase had become firmly lodged in the soldier's vocabulary. Sir John Smythe, quixotically maintaining the superiority of the long bow to harquebus and musket, derided the adoption of 'Walloon and Dutch terms . . . as though our language were so barren that it were not able of itself or by derivation to afford convenient words to utter our minds in matters of that quality.'[12] Yet he describes the formation into 'squadrons with sleeves, wings, troops, or forlorn hopes,' apparently unaware that the last was a Dutch loan.[13]

The Civil Wars marked a turn from the theory of military manuals to practice recorded in letters, dispatches, memoirs, and histories. Both Royalist and Parliamentary armies employed the tactic of the Forlorn Hope. Joshua Sprigge's *Anglia Rediviva* (1647) celebrates the providential guidance of the New Model Army to victory: 'You will easily discern a thread of Divinity running through the whole proceeding of this Army' ([A3v]). His account of Fairfax's western campaigns from the Army's inception (4 April 1545) to the surrender of Raglan Castle (19 August 1546), gives us a sense of the regularity with which Forlorn Hopes were employed: the battles of Naseby, Langport, Dartmouth, Torrington, the siege of Bristol, and various lesser skirmishes.[14] In a set battle the task of the Forlorn was to begin the storm; if the unit was on the move, they reconnoitered ahead of the vanguard or, less frequently, protected the rearguard.[15] Once a storm was decided, the New Model Army positions were determined, at the front or in the reserves, by the drawing of lots, the results of which were determined not by chance but by providence,[16] appropriately since, more than with any other battle tactic, survival in the Forlorn required an act of extraordinary providence.

For a major engagement both foot and horse might be employed; at Langport, 'instantly the Army was ordered to be put to Battalia, the forlorne hope of horse and foot drew out' (Sprigge, *Anglia Rediviva,* 65). At Bristol on the Somerset side a brigade 'was ordered to storm in three places, *viz.* 200 men in the middle, 200 on each side, as forlorne hopes to begin the storm' (94). At Naseby, Sprigge reports that the Parliamentary army occupied 'the brow of the hill, having placed a Forlorn of Foot (musquetiers) consisting of about 300. down the steep of the hill towards the enemy, somewhat more than carbine shot from the main battail, who were ordered to retreat to the battail, whensoever they should be hard pressed' (35).[17] Since William Marshall engraved Sprigge's frontispiece of Fairfax on horseback before his troops, it seems highly probable that Marshall also made the engraving of the battle formations at Naseby, representing the placement of the Forlorn with more accuracy than he had achieved with his engraved portrait of John Milton two years earlier.[18]

Although battle reports tend to mention only the casualties to officers, there can be no doubt that the name of the duty was justified. In the storming of Shelford (3 November 1645), the Forlorn led by Colonel John Hutchinson

> . . . found many difficulties more then they expected, for after they had fill'd up the ditches with faggots, and pitcht the scaling ladders, they were twenty staves too short, and the enemie, from the top of the workes, threw downe loggs of wood, which would sweep of a whole ladder-full of men at once: the lieftenant-collonell himselfe was once or twice so beaten down.[19]

Engaging the Royalists near Berkeley Castle, a Parliamentary regiment 'kil'd the Captain of the forlorne hope' (Sprigge 64); at Langport 'some fourteen or sixteen of Major *Bethels* troop were hurt, and himself shot in the right hand' (66); and at Bristol, 'Captain Ireton, who led on the Forlorn hope at the storm, was shot with a brace of bullets in the arm (and it broken thereby)' (111). Sprigge describes a poignant late encounter between enemy Forlorns: 'when our Forlorne of Horse coming neer theirs . . . they did not endeavour to put themselves in order to receive us, nor did they make any resistance, but stood still: our men much wondring thereat' (213). The Royalists cried, '*A Cessation, a Cessation:* ours cryed, *No, no there was none:* and much adoe had Commissary-generall *Ireton* . . . to perswade them there was none'; but the Parliamentarians declined to take advantage of their defenceless opponents, effectively granting the cessation that they had denied.

If the New Model Army used Forlorn Hopes with deadly effectiveness, at an earlier stage of the war the tactic may have been more associated with the Royalists. Sir Richard Bulstrode, who rode in the Prince of Wales's Regiment of Horse, Northampton's troop, recalls that, at the Council of War on the evening preceding the Battle of Edgehill

(23 October 1642), 'a forlorn Hope of Six Hundred Horse were ordered . . . to descend before the Army.'[20] Edgehill ended inconclusively. In 1643, however, the king's armies took the offensive, implementing his plan of a three-pronged drive upon London with considerable success for much of the year. At Braddock Down (19 January), in defeating Colonel Ruthin's army, Sir Ralph Hopton used a 'forlorn of musketeers in little inclosures'; advancing on Stratton (15 May), Hopton's 'forlorn hope beate in a party of the Enymies,' gaining a passage over the river. At Chalgrove Field (18 June), where John Hampden received his death wound, Prince Rupert's raiding party featured a Forlorn of 100 horse and fifty dragoon. At Adwalton Moor (30 June) Fairfax reported, 'our Forlorn Hope gained [the hill] by beating theirs into their Main Body'; nevertheless, Newcastle's main force recovered and Fairfax could be grateful only for the 'happy Providence,' which 'brought us off without any great loss.'[21] Preceding the Battle of Lansdown (4 July), Hopton used a 'strong forlorn hope of horse' as a rearguard while moving his army into position; and in the victory at Roundway Down (13 July) the Royalists again mounted a Forlorn of horse against Waller's army.[22]

The standardized British military decorations that we now know are largely the product of the nineteenth century; until then, such awards were occasional and ad hoc. The tentative movement beyond recognition by battlefield knighthoods can be seen, not surprisingly, in the 1640s.[23] The question was raised in Parliament:

> What if the poor Souldier had some remembrance, though small, to leave as the acceptance of this service, which is already begun by a worthy Member of this House, who hath appointed some Medals to be made of gold to be bestowed upon those that ventured on the greatest difficulties. (Sprigge, *Anglia Rediviva*, 142)

This refers to the 1645 medal of Lord General Sir Thomas Fairfax, which Parliament had authorized. The medal was awarded sparingly for exceptional valour,[24] and the speaker rightly recognizes that 'the poor Souldier' was unlikely to view a gold medal even at a distance. The concept of a medal for general distribution was not realized until 1650 when Parliament lauded the victory at Dunbar with a resolution 'return[ing] their thanks also to the officers and soldiers of the army, and that a number of gold and silver medals be distributed amongst them,' although it is not certain that the intention was

CHARLES R.

CHARLES P.

TRUSTY and well-beloved We greet you well. Whereas We have received information that thoſe Souldiers which have been forward to ſerve Us in the Forlorn hope, are not looked upon according to their merited Valour and Loyall ſervice: We doe therefore require, that from hence-forward the Commanders in chiefe, both of Horſe and Foot, which lead up the Forlorne-hope, upon whom alſo We mean to beſtow ſpeciall tokens of Our Princely favour, doe ſignify in writing the names of thoſe ſouldiers whom they find moſt forward in ſerving Us their King, and Country, that care may be taken to reward their deſervings, and make them ſpecially known to all Our good Subjects; For which end we have thought fit to require Sir *William Parkhurſt*, Knight, and *Thomas Buſhell*, Eſquire, Wardens of Our Mint, to provide from time to time certain Badges of Silver, containing Our Royall Image, and that of Our deareſt ſonne Prince *Charles*, to be delivered to weare on the breaſt of every man who ſhall be certified under the hands of their Commanders in chiefe to have done us faithfull ſervice in the Forlorne-hope. And we doe therefore moſt ſtraitly command, That no Souldier at any time doe ſell, nor any of Our Subjects preſume to buy or weare any of theſe ſaid Badges, other then they, to whom we ſhall give the ſame, and that under ſuch paine and puniſhment as Our Councell of Warre ſhall think fit to inflict, if any ſhall preſume to offend againſt this Our Royall command. And We farther require the ſaid Commanders, and Wardens of Our Mint, to keep ſeverall Regiſters of the names of thoſe, and of their Country, for whom they ſhall give their Certificates. *Given at Our Court at* OXFORD, *the Eighteenth day of* May. 1643.

To Our Truſty and wellbeloved Sir WILLIAM PARKHURST *Knight, and* THOMAS BUSHELL *Eſquire, Wardens of Our Mint at* Oxford.

Figure 3. Royal warrant commissioning the wardens of the Oxford mint to produce silver badges honouring the Forlorn Hope. Issued at Oxford by Charles I, 18 May 1643. Heberden Coin Room, Ashmolean Museum, University of Oxford.

fulfilled.[25] The Royalists, however, already had anticipated Parliament with the first military reward for a category of participants, rather than for selected individuals.

In a warrant dated 18 May 1643 (fig. 3), Charles noted, 'We have received information that those Souldiers which have been forward to serve Us in the Forlorn hope, are not looked upon according to their merited Valour and Loyall service.' The King, therefore, ordered Sir William Parkhurst and Thomas Bushell, wardens of the Royal Mint at Oxford:

> . . . to provide from time to time certain Badges of Silver, containing Our Royall Image, and that of Our dearest sonne Prince *Charles,* to be delivered to weare on the breast of every man who shall be certified under the hands of their Commanders in chiefe to have done us faithfull service in the Forlorne-hope.

The printed warrant is headed by a woodcut representation of the badge: on an octagonal shell, pierced for it to be sewn on clothing, there is an oval with the jugate busts of king and prince.[26] Designed by Thomas Rawlins, the badges seem to have been created at the instigation of Bushell, who later claimed a £100 reimbursement for their cost. If Bushell's request was for the silver only, it has been estimated that 'a maximum of around three thousand badges might have been made,' somewhat fewer if the claim also covered production costs.[27] In either case, the numbers would suggest that the intention of a general distribution to honourable survivors of Royalist Forlorns was realized.

Attesting both to the promptness with which his warrant was implemented and to his own satisfaction with its effectiveness, on 12 June Charles wrote to commend Bushell for his services: 'your invention for our better knowing and rewarding the fforlorn hope with Badges of Silver at your owne chardge when the souldiers were readie to runne away through the instigacon of some disaffected persons.'[28] The mark of favour that the king had bestowed on his Forlorn Hopes surely instilled an esprit de corps in their members. Providence helps those who help themselves; following the victories at Adwalton Moor, Roundway Down, and the capture of Bristol, Charles was able to issue a declaration that God 'hath wonderfully manifested his care of us and his defense of his and our most just cause.'[29] The note of triumph is distinct in Abraham Cowley's inept poetic account of the Fairfaxes' defeat by the Earl of Newcastle at Adwalton Moor: 'I see him lead the *Pikes!* What will he doe? / Defend him *God!* Ah whether will he goe? / Up to the *Canon* Mouth he leads; in vaine, / They speake lowd *Death*, and threaten till they're t'ane.'[30] In the hard months before the tide turned at Marston Moor, the very phrase 'Forlorn Hope' must have taken on a bitter Royalist inflection for the Parliamentary faithful.

Satan and the Forlorn Hope

Expressing his admiration for Milton's literary daring, Macaulay reached to a military metaphor: 'He never came up in the rear when the outworks had been carried and the breach entered. He pressed into the forlorn hope.'[31] Had the compliment been literal, the poet would not have taken exception. In *Of Education* (registered 4 June 1644), Milton advised that students of his academy should learn

> . . . the rudiments of their Souldiership in all the skill of embattailing, marching, encamping, fortifying, beseiging and battering, with all the helps of ancient and modern stratagems, *Tactiks* and warlike maxims, they may as it were out of a long warre come forth renowned and perfect Commanders in the service of their country. (*CPW* 2: 411–12)

That he was quite capable of providing the instruction, there seems little doubt. Recalling the years when he had full vision, Milton proudly claimed, 'Girded with my sword, as I generally was, I thought myself equal to anyone' (*CPW* 4, pt. 1: 583). Although there has been sharp disagreement on the question of his attitude toward war, a chorus of voices has spoken to his interest and knowledge of the subject, providing documentation from a range of 'ancient and modern' sources.[32] When the Civil Wars were over, the military expertise became a fruitful source of metaphor, as in *The Tenure of Kings and Magistrates* (1649), when he elaborately compares the shifting beliefs of clergymen to close-order drill:

> Sometimes they seem furiously to march on, and presently march counter; by and by they stand, and then retreat; or if need be can face about, or wheele in a whole body, with that cunning and dexterity as is almost unperceavable; to winde themselves by shifting ground into places of more advantage. (*CPW* 2: 255)

If effective in prose, why not poetry?

The chronological narrative of *Paradise Lost* begins with rebellion and civil war, 'Intestine War in Heav'n' (6: 259), as the poet phrases it. Loyal and rebel angels alike are represented as disciplined and efficient soldiers, a conception that, for the rebels, 'effects a genuine revolution in angelology.'[33] Descriptions of equipment, behaviour, drill, and manoeuvers are saturated with military vocabulary; formations and tactics, down to that of using massed infantry to conceal an artillery placement (6: 550–78), have been matched in the manuals.[34] Even the 'great consult' in Pandaemonium, expressly convened to plan strategy 'Whether of open War or covert guile' (2: 41), before peace advocates disrupt the agenda, resembles the Councils of War that opponents routinely held before battles, as does the 'Council' Satan holds after the first day's battle in Heaven (6: 414–95). Milton differentiates bad from good angels chiefly by endowing the latter, 'inviolable Saints' (6: 398), with the spiritual discipline exemplified by the New Model Army.[35] So pervasive are the contemporary parallels that some critics have been tempted to read the War in Heaven as a roman à clef,[36] forgetting that this is the archetype from which all subsequent civil wars derive.

The same point needs to be repeated about the father of evil. In James Freeman's succinct summary:

> He is a general who has lost the opening battle of a war. Reacting to his defeat in the manner recommended by the martial manuals, he composes himself, musters his despondent legions, harangues them optimistically, consults with his staff, announces new strategy to the assembled troops, and sets off on a scouting expedition. His maneuvers in the no man's territory around Chaos and on the disputed fields of earth, like his reported behavior during the battle for Heaven, keep close dress and cover with tactics discussed in innumerable treatises.[37]

Although Charles I led his own army until the end, winning a respectable number of engagements during the first two years, Satan is the archetype of the tyrant general, Charles only the ectype.

The Forlorn Hope enters *Paradise Lost* in three ways that are largely sequential: the military tactic attaches to the fallen angels in Hell; then it shifts to Satan who is both general of the first Forlorn and himself a Forlorn Hope in single-handedly renewing the battle; last, in the figurative, rather than the military sense, it is associated with Adam and Eve in their newly fallen condition. Probably because the phrase was so familiar and laden with such powerful connotations of risk and loss from the Civil Wars, Milton never uses it directly; rather, he plays on it allusively. Hell, by definition, is the place where 'hope never comes / That comes to all' (1: 66–7); and the first description of land beyond the burning lake is of a 'dreary Plain, forlorn and wild' (1: 180). The word 'hope' echoes ironically through Books 1 and 2, sometimes pointed through linkage with an adjective or noun bearing an initial *f* consonant: 'our final hope / Is flat despair' (2: 142–3); 'what hope the never-ending flight / Of future days may bring' (2: 221–2); 'false presumptuous hope' (2: 522); 'Fallacious hope' (2: 569). The last two quotations record the raised expectations of the fallen angels after the council; these are dashed by the experience of the most military group, who go 'in Squadrons and gross Bands / On bold adventure to discover wide / That dismal World' (2: 570–2), only to end 'roving on / In confus'd march forlorn' (2: 614–15).[38] The first beings to enter the interior landscape of Hell, they are the Forlorn Hope of their own army, as well as the army of fallen humans to follow at Judgment Day.

Satan's role, not only as general of his army but leader of its Forlorn Hope, emerges even before they move from the burning lake. In response to his leader's question about the morale of his followers, Beëlzebub replies:

> If once they hear that voice, thir liveliest pledge
> Of hope in fears and dangers, heard so oft
> In worst extremes, and on the perilous edge
> Of battle when it rag'd, in all assaults
> Thir surest signal, they will soon resume
> New courage and revive. (1: 274–9)

The 'perilous edge / Of battle' is virtually a textbook description of the Forlorn Hope, whose assault properly would be directed by the 'signal' of their commanding officer's voice. When Satan is seated 'High on a Throne of Royal state' (2: 1), the clause 'and from despair / Thus high uplifted beyond hope' (2: 6–7) carries a dual meaning. Physically, the general is positioned above his Forlorn as psychologically he is committed to the desperate, renewed assault that will doom himself and his troops: 'insatiate to pursue / Vain War with Heav'n' (2: 8–9).

The council that follows presents the first challenge to Satan's leadership.[39] On hearing the 'open War or covert guile' alternatives that Satan presents for debate (2: 41), Moloch responds with scorn. Rather than endure the pain of Hell 'without hope of end' (2: 89), Moloch urges storming God's citadel, even if failure of the frontal assault means their annihilation: 'let us rather choose / Arm'd with Hell flames and fury all at once / O'er Heav'ns high Tow'rs to force resistless way' (2: 60–2).

The suicidal course Moloch advocates meets with a notable lack of enthusiasm, allowing Satan's own strategy to prevail. Absolutely as committed as Moloch to continuing the war, Satan differs in having a more flexible concept of the Forlorn's tactical resources. At the culmination of the council's debate, he volunteers to become a solitary Forlorn, 'our last hope' (2: 416).

As we have seen, in the major Civil War battles Forlorns regularly numbered their infantry or horse in the hundreds; it was possible, nonetheless, to so designate a single man. Fairfax describes both leading his Forlorn at Sherburn, 'I went to the head of my troops and presently charged them,' and acting as a solitary Forlorn at Wakefield; 'being advanced a good way single before my men,' he was cut off, but 'by a good Providence, got to my men again.'[40] In *The Theorike and Practike of Modern Warres,* Barret explains the manifold uses of light-armed horsemen:

> These and the other shot on horsebacke do serue principally for great *Caualgadas,* they serue to watch, to ward, to discouer, to scoute, to forage, to skirmith, for *Ambuscados,* for gaining of a straight, hilles, and ground of aduantage, to be put for a forlorne Sentinell, to discouer the enemies proceedings, to spoyle forrages, and to assaile troupes at their lodgings, either in villages, straights, or fields; and if occasion serue, they may alight and serue on foote, either to assaile a straight, to surprise a barrier, to performe an Ambuscado, and in such points of sudden seruice, doe the dutie of foote shot, wherein they may do many good peeces of seruice to the enemies annoyance. (143)

The points of resemblance to Satan's second battle plan – scouting, watching, discovering the enemy's proceedings, assailing them at their lodging, waiting in ambush – scarcely need emphasis. Indeed, Beëlzebub's job description for the volunteer suggests that he and Satan might have read the same manual before drafting it: 'what strength, what art can then / Suffice, or what evasion bear him safe / Through the strict Senteries and Stations thick / Of Angels watching round?' (2: 410–13). Even Satan's progression from flight to reptilian and serpentine locomotion parallels the more mundane movement from horse to foot. When Satan has his destination in sight, the narrator confirms his role of 'forlorne Sentinell': 'As when a Scout / Through dark and desert ways with some peril gone / All night; at last by break of cheerful dawn / Obtains the brow of some high-climbing Hill, / Which to his eye discovers unaware / The goodly prospect of some foreign land / First seen' (3: 543–9).

As Michael Lieb has commented, Satan's conquest of this New World is 'conceived as a battle,' 'portrayed appropriately through the language of war,' and 'Eden itself is an armed camp.'[41] Satan penetrates this closely guarded place by storming its wall, and then sets out 'with narrow search' to 'no corner leave unspi'd' (4: 528, 529). His first sight of the civilian inhabitants causes him briefly to consider the possibility of a military alliance: 'yet no purpos'd foe / To you whom I could pity forlorn / Though I unpitied: League with you I seek, / And mutual amity so strait' (4: 373–6). The construction allows 'forlorn' to refer either to the vulnerability of Adam and Eve or to his own military mission. Satan's thought passes, he perseveres, and, the narrator notes, 'with necessity, / The Tyrant's plea, excus'd his devilish deeds' (4: 393–4). Because the doctrine of necessity was a justification for both royal prerogative and Cromwellian policy, this may be a textual aperture encouraging the reader to superimpose the portraits of contemporary tyrants. Behind both Charles and Oliver, however, stands Niccolò Machiavelli.[42]

When Satan, making his initial assault on the enemy asleep in their field lodging, is discovered and seized by the watch, he starts up, 'As when a spark / Lights on a heap of nitrous Powder, laid / Fit for the Tun some Magazin to store / Against a rumor'd War, the Smutty grain / With sudden blaze diffus'd, inflames the Air' (4: 813–18). Beyond the familiar attribution of gunpowder to demonic origin, the simile draws precisely on military expertise. Soldiers who ran out of powder in battle had to replenish it from casks, which could be set afire from enemy marksmanship or by their own haste. Fairfax recorded a 'remarkable Providence' at Tadcaster: 'During this conflict, our Magazine was blown up: which struck such a terror in the Enemy, thinking we had cannon . . . that they instantly retreated.'[43] Confronted by the guardian angels, the Forlorn Satan similarly terrified, 'fled / Murmuring' (4: 1014–15).

After this humiliating retreat, Satan adopts more effective protective coloration and alters his tactic in the second attempt, switching from force to fraud. Victoria Kahn remarks, 'Satan appears in book 9 as the archetypal hypocrite, using fraud and malice (9.55) to wage war against Adam and Eve.'[44] Rather than a Royalist field commander, his 'sly assault' (Adam's words, 9: 256) is more reminiscent of Cavalier court poets, no improvement in Milton's view.[45] His luck in finding Eve alone stimulates a familiar verbal sequence: '*Eve* separate, he wish'd, but not with hope / . . . / Beyond his hope, *Eve* separate he spies' (9: 422, 424). In this encounter of solitary Forlorns, there is no cessation. Momentarily 'disarm'd' by her innocent beauty, he yet must put on the face of battle: 'What hither brought us, hate, not love, nor hope / Of Paradise for Hell, hope here to taste / Of pleasure, but all pleasure to destroy' (9: 475–7). As William Gerrard advised, although a general may be 'accounted most vicious,' he fulfils his duties 'if he know how to govern and guide his charge.'[46] At the brink of success, 'Hope elevates' Satan (9: 633), and, having achieved it, he reports to his army that he has 'return'd / Successful beyond hope' (10: 462–3), only to have that triumph transformed to shame. Satan had anticipated this outcome in his soliloquy to the Sun, first regretting that 'unbounded hope had rais'd / Ambition' to rebel (4: 60–1). But he recognizes that he is from 'All hope excluded thus' (4: 105); and, recanting his recantation, concludes, 'So farewell Hope, and with Hope farewell Fear, / Farewell Remorse: all Good to me is lost' (4: 108–9). His deliberation merges the two senses of Forlorn Hope, as both military tactic and doomed enterprise, before he sets off, in the narrator's geographical pun, 'Beyond the *Cape of Hope*' (4: 160). The Forlorn can hope to survive only by an act of extraordinary providence; some instead receive a judgment on their cause.

We have pursued the Forlorn Hope in narrative, not chronological, order, which has the advantage of allowing us to see that, although not yet so named, the tactic originated in Heaven. Reading Book 6 in isolation, one might dismiss the initial battle action – challenge to single combat, flyting, clash of opposing champions – as a remnant of the heroic 'Trappings' later dismissed (see 9: 27–36): 'Twixt Host and Host but narrow space was left, / A dreadful interval . . . before the cloudy Van, / On the rough edge of battle ere it join'd' (6: 104–5, 107–8). Satan alights from his idolatrous chariot and strides to the fore. An incensed Abdiel determines to 'try' his 'puissance, trusting in th' Almighty's aid' (119). Scoffing at Satan's vain 'hope' of surprising 'th' Omnipotent' who 'with solitary hand [i.e., an extraordinary providence] / Reaching beyond all limit, at one blow / Unaided could have finisht thee' (139–41). Following their exchange of accusations, with a 'noble stroke' Abdiel drives the apostate ten paces back, 'the tenth on bended knee' (194), neatly enforcing God's commandment (5: 607–8), after which the 'storming' begins. Satan acted as a single Forlorn here as he does in Eden, paying the expected penalty in humiliation, not death, angels being what they are.

Abdiel's position is rather more complex. On his return from the rebel camp, the Father had commended his valour: 'well hast thou fought /

The better fight, who single hast maintain'd / Against revolted multitudes the Cause / Of Truth, in word mightier than they in Arms' (6: 29–32). He has been a solitary Forlorn in the cause of 'Right Reason' – as Michael later will teach Adam, a higher calling and harder challenge than physical valour, to which Satan now is committed. Returning to that verbal encounter, we have to register that Abdiel is thrice defined by his 'zeal,' a quality to which *De Doctrina* assigns a brief chapter (bk. 2, chap. 6), citing among other scriptural places, 'My zeal hath consumed me, because mine enemies have forgotten thy words' (Ps. 119: 139). Satan forgets, Abdiel remembers. He correctly describes Satan's speech as an 'argument blasphemous.' The opposite of true zeal, talking about God in an 'impious and shameful way . . . is commonly called blasphemy' (*CPW* 6: 698). In reasoning with Satan, he formulated the chronologically first explicit statement of providence in the poem: 'by experience taught we know how good, / And of our good, and of our dignity / How provident he is, how far from thought / To make us less, bent rather to exalt' (5: 836–9). When Satan sophistically rejects the zealous angel's reasoning, identifying himself in another first with 'evil,' Abdiel knows that he is lost: 'I see thy fall / Determin'd' (5: 878–9), an Arminian self-determination, and so Abdiel turns back, passing through the gamut of 'hostile scorn' protected by his zeal: 'For he put on righteousness as a breastplate . . . and was clad with zeal as a cloak' (Is. 59: 17). When Satan declares his Machiavellian anti-providence (1: 162–4), implicitly he concedes the truth of Abdiel's reasoning; he was not 'self-begot' by his own 'quick'ning power' (5: 860–1) and the object of his resentment is God's goodness.[47]

From his initial assault on Eve, Satan's objective had been to instill 'Vain hopes' (4: 808) in her mind; when he achieves this, the hope / forlorn complex transfers to our 'Grand Parents.' Eve feels herself to have 'op'n'd Eyes, new Hopes, new Joys' (9: 985); Adam believes that, without Eve, he cannot 'live again in these wild Woods forlorn' (9: 910). The ambiguous referent of 'forlorn,' both Adam's state of mind and his new perception of Paradise, replicates the 'forlorn and wild' landscape of Hell (1: 180), sadly confirming Satan's boast that 'The mind is its own place' and can make 'a Hell of Heav'n' (1: 254–5) – or Paradise. Adam's delayed recognition of this results in his ineffectual wish to assume all the blame, which failure 'alike destroys all hope,' leaving him in Satan's condition, 'both crime and doom' (10: 838, 841). Fortunately, Eve has the strength to make the first act of reconciliation, confessing that she cannot live 'forlorn of thee' (10: 921) and offering to assume all responsibility. Her proposed remedies, which would be as suicidal as the most desperate of Forlorns, provoke Adam 'To better hopes' (10: 1011) by reflecting on the promise within the judgment.

This dawning awareness of the Protevangelium is confirmed and amplified by Michael's instruction in Book 12, still in the vocabulary of battle but shifting the meaning to spiritual warfare.[48] In the span of time from the Fall to human reconciliation, Adam and Eve have been in the situation of the pilot who, 'while Night / Invests the Sea, and wished Morn delays' (1: 207–8), mistakenly fixes his anchor on Leviathan's side. From the point of Adam's comprehension of the curse on the serpent through his understanding of the rainbow covenant to his acknowledgment of Christ as his Saviour (12: 572–3), the doomed, Satanic Forlorn Hope providentially comes to be replaced by the anchor of Christian hope (Heb. 6: 19). Mary Fenton says appositely, 'For Satan, hope is a form of power rather than a form of spirituality, and thus he materializes hope.'[49] Nonetheless, the consequences of the Fall remain for humans. The narrator laments that men, 'though under hope / Of heavenly Grace . . . / Yet live in hatred, enmity, and strife / Among themselves, and levy cruel wars, / Wasting the Earth, each other to destroy' (2: 498–502). Nor does he exempt himself, who in darkness risks falling 'Erroneous there to wander and forlorn' (7: 20). In Milton's book, we are not devoid of hope, but we all remain *enfants perdus* in need of providential guidance.

Fraud: Satan's Disguises

Life in a fallen world of deceptive appearances, Isabel MacCaffrey aptly commented, is 'not only a contest between good and evil, but an effort to see them clearly.' Appearance no longer conforms to truth, she noted, for 'after Satan's rebellion and man's sin, the two are no longer congruent.'[50] The space between angel's rebellion and human sin is the issue, however, for Milton's view of the Creation allows no impenetrable obscurity in truth until after the Fall. In 'this World,' he explains in *Aeropagitica,* 'the knowledge of good is so involv'd and interwoven with the knowledge of evill, and in so many cunning resemblance hardly to be discerned' (*CPW* 2: 514). But our world is a consequence of the Fall, not the original model. The significant instances of deceptive appearance before then occur with Satan's disguises; careful consideration of the disguises should reveal that providence is at work to counteract deception. God 'will not suffer you to be tempted above that ye are able; but will with the temptation also make a way to escape, that ye may be able to bear it' (I Cor. 10: 13, cited *CPW* 6: 339). At his creation, Adam was 'endowed with natural wisdom, holiness and righteousness,' not to mention 'very great intelligence' (6: 324). Then there are external safeguards. The tree of knowledge was not a sacrament, but a 'pledge or memorial of obedience' (6: 352, 'pignus et monumentum quoddam obedientiae'), a providential emblem. Only remember.

In Heaven before the rebellion, appearance conforms to reality; the angels are physically beautiful because they are beautiful in essence. When Abdiel encounters Satan on the battlefield, he is stunned and indignant at the disjunction: 'O Heav'n! that such resemblance of the Highest / Should yet remain, where faith and reality / Remain not' (6: 114–16). After the expulsion of the rebels, the same direct correspondence is restored in Hell. Satan acknowledges the external alteration in his appearance, but refuses to recognize the inward change that it reveals: 'Nor . . . / . . . do I repent or change, / Though chang'd in outward luster' (1: 95–7). Nonetheless, his inner nature already has changed as the battle in Heaven plainly indicates. Satan cannot admit that his appearance now is the inward reality, blustering indignantly, 'Know ye not mee?' when the guardian angels fail to identify him. Zephon answers bluntly:

> Think not, revolted Spirit, thy shape the same,
> Or undiminisht brightness, to be known
> As when thou stood'st in Heav'n upright and pure;
> That Glory then, when thou no more wast good,
> Departed from thee, and thou resembl'st now
> Thy sin and place of doom obscure and foul. (4: 835–40)

Only in his first soliloquy does he acknowledge to himself somewhat obliquely that the interior too has been transformed, conceding that his deceived followers are unaware 'Under what torments inwardly I groan,' that 'myself am Hell' (4: 88, 75). Even as he speaks, Satan's passions have 'marr'd his borrow'd visage, and betray'd / Him counterfeit' (4: 116–17) to the watchful eyes of Uriel. Although the 'Artificer of fraud' (120) immediately conceals his emotions, the defence has been alerted.

At the beginning of their encounter, Satan's first – and, briefly, only foolproof – fraud occurs when he assumes the guise of a 'stripling Cherub' (3: 636) to deceive Uriel and get the directions that he needs.[51]

He does succeed in avoiding immediate detection, and the reader may wonder both how Satan achieves this and why (putting Genesis out of mind for the moment) he does not consummate the temptation in the same shape. The narrator tells us quite explicitly: 'For neither Man nor Angel can discern / Hypocrisy, the only evil that walks / Invisible, except to God alone, / By his permissive will, through Heav'n and Earth' (3: 682–5). At one time the passage was misread as superfluous sermonizing,[52] but Milton is a more careful poet than that. The ready propensity to discount hypocrisy as only a venal sin can be weighed against the genealogy of evil embedded in the narrative. Satan's first trial occurred with the proclamation of another angel's elevation to Son of God; his hostile response set the pattern for the providences to follow: 'All seem'd well pleas'd, all seem'd, but were not all' (5: 617). Even before the birth of Sin, Satan acts on his displeasure, hypocritically pretending to honour 'our King / The great Messiah' (690–1). When captured in Eden, he presents himself as the self-sacrificing Forlorn, upon which Gabriel contemptuously denounces him, 'thou sly hypocrite, who now wouldst seem / Patron of liberty' (4: 957–8). A hypocrite is an actor (Lat. *hypocrita;* Gk. *hypokrites*), one who pretends to be something else, not only in appearance but in behaviour and speech. Gregory the Great concurred with Milton's estimate of the danger of hypocrisy, tracing its proliferation to Antichrist, 'the head of all hypocrites . . . who feign holiness to lead to sinfulness.'[53] Latterly the offence was thought to emanate from the Machiavelli's own city; William Bradshaw cautioned, 'Florentines can disguise and color any thing . . . so that in these days scant any thing is as it appears, or appears as it is.'[54] On Machiavellian discourse, Sir Thomas Browne admonishes, 'It is the Rhetorick of Satan, and may pervert a loose or prejudicate belief.'[55] Satan had invented hypocritical speech even before he needed to disguise himself (5: 685–91). His rhetoric will be considered more closely in chapter 5; here the focus is on physical appearance.

In the passage on hypocrisy Milton explains why Uriel, lacking the omniscience of divine providence, can be deceived. His mistake, inadvertently aiding Satan, involves no temptation and is therefore innocent. The deception is an evil act on Satan's part; however, 'God gives a good outcome to every evil deed, contrary to the intentions of the sinner' (*CPW* 6: 335). He converts the deception to a providence, a two-stage trial of Uriel to discover the truth. When Satan's passions subsequently mar his disguise, the 'sharpest-sighted Spirit' sees his mistake and corrects it. Uriel has learned from this trial how hypocrisy operates:

'oft though wisdom wake, suspicion sleeps / At wisdom's Gate, and to simplicity / Resigns her charge' (6: 686–8). Possibly suspicion was lulled to sleep by Satan's suspect flattery, 'The first art wont [God's] great authentic will / Interpreter' (656–7), but the implication is that 'now for once beguiled' (689) he will not be again.

Uriel's trial, thus, parallels that of Abdiel, innocently led astray by Satan's hypocrisy until he learns the true purpose of the northern assembly. Amusingly, Satan mimics Abdiel's zeal (4: 565, 'zealous, as he seem'd') in deceiving Uriel. The manoeuver is of a piece with his attributing to God the Machiavellianism that is his own.[56] God's announcement of the Son's begetting was for Satan an 'evil' temptation, as 'when God . . . throws opportunities for sin in his path . . . to unmask hypocrisy' (*CPW* 6: 338). Satan's response was remarkably like that predicted to religious compulsion in *A Treatise of Civil Power:* 'Since force neither instructs in religion nor begets repentance or amendment of life, but on the contrarie, hardness of heart, formalitie, hypocrisie, and . . . increase of sin' (*CPW* 7: 269). The differences, however, are significant in that the Book 5 'Decree' issues from God, not civil authority; it is predicated on angelic free will; and, as Abdiel perceives, it does honour to all angels. Still, as *De Doctrina* acknowledges, although 'absolutely just' on God's part, such a temptation will be perceived as 'evil' from the perspective of the one tempted (6: 338).

Because Eve will be subjected to a two-stage experience – first the trial of the dream, then the temptation itself – the Uriel episode functions to confirm that, within 'this system of providence' (*CPW* 6: 338), deception, whether by fraud or hypocrisy, cannot be a sufficient cause of the Fall, 'but rather,' Kahn says finely, 'that the possibility of deception means that appearances must be interpreted, and that the activity of interpretation is itself an occasion of free will.'[57]

The disguises that Satan does assume in Eden are both psychologically and dramatically appropriate. Within the garden it is natural that he would simulate the forms of various beasts, since they offer him a convenient way to approach Adam and Eve undetected. Beyond this, the animals are psychologically appropriate because each creature Satan enters is representative of a particular quality of his nature, revealing his dominant mood at that moment. Milton prepares the reader to accept the symbolism by a series of beast similes highlighting his predatory motives; successively he is compared to a 'Vultur' (3: 431), 'a prowling Wolf' (4: 183), and a 'Cormorant' (196). When, after this, he actually takes the shape of a lion, 'stalk[ing] with fiery glare' (401), the qualification divests manifold positive connotations from the king of beasts, leaving only warning of his ferocity and perhaps latent prophecy: 'Thou shall tread upon the lion and adder: / the young lion and the dragon shalt thou trample under feet' (Ps. 91: 13). The following, more naturalistic description of Satan become tiger, ready to pounce upon a brace of 'gentle Fauns at play' (404), emphasizes the savage cruelty foremost in his soul at this moment. Reputed to 'excel all other beasts' in swiftness and strength, 'Generally the nature of this beast, is according to the Epithetes of it, sharpe, vntamed, cruell, and rauenous.'[58] To be sure, the fallen natures of the beasts cannot be attributed to them at this time; only after Death is loosed in the world, 'Beast now with Beast gan war' and, abandoning herbivorousness, 'Devour'd each other; nor stood much in awe / Of Man' (10: 710, 712–13). As Milton uses pagan myth, classical epic, and post-Genesis scripture for lenses through which the Garden of Eden might be perceived, so he exploits the 'wild' nature of beasts to symbolize the changes in Satan's psychological state. The juxtaposition of original and fallen animal natures serves as another reminder that life in a state of innocence is not synonymous with a static perfection, for humans or lesser creatures.[59]

Neither lion nor tiger is fully representative of Satan's nature; for his first attempt upon Eve, Satan selects instead the guise of the toad. Milton assuredly was aware of the inseparable connotations of the word with that which is hateful, loathsome, or venomous; moreover he added a personal inflection, which would explain why this animal was selected for the initial disruption of the conjugal bed: 'although there bee not easily found such an *antipathy, as to hate one another like a toad or poison,* yet that there is oft such a dislike in both, or either, to conjugal love, as hinders all the comfort of Matrimony' (*CPW* 2: 739).[60] Because in contemporary usage the word 'toad' was applied to frogs (see *OED* s.v. 2), an association with Antichrist may be evoked: 'And I saw three unclean spirits like frogs *come* out of the mouth of the dragon, and out of the mouth of the beast, and out of the mouth of the false prophet' (Rev. 16: 13).[61] Alchemy, necromancy, and witchcraft had added connotations that certainly place the toad in Satan's camp. Milton plays upon the last when he pictures Satan as 'Squat like a Toad, close at the ear of *Eve,* / Assaying by his Devilish art to reach / The Organs of her Fancy, and with them forge / Illusions as he list' (4: 800–3). In the visual arts we find the toad allied with pride, vanity, and seduction,[62] a trinity of lures that Satan will deploy in the temptation. Hearing the hypnotic voice, Eve in her dream envisions the speaker not as toad but as angel (5: 53), foreshadowing her susceptibility to the Serpent's honeyed rhetoric in Book 9.

Satan next approaches Eden 'wrapt in mist / Of midnight vapor' (9: 158–9), which projects his 'dark intent' (162) and contrasts to Eve, 'Veil'd in a Cloud of Fragrance' (425), while anticipating the misty ambiguity of the world after the Fall. When he gets within range, Satan '*enters into the Serpent sleeping*' (bk. 9, 'The Argument'), even though he recognizes the humiliation in this disguise, 'constrain'd / Into a Beast, and mixt with bestial slime / This essence to incarnate and and imbrute / That to the highth of Deity aspir'd' (9: 164–7). Typically, Satan reasons away this unsettling thought with an argument that burlesques the concept of the Fortunate Fall: 'who aspires must down as low / As high he soar'd, obnoxious first or last / To basest things' (9: 169–71).

The serpent is the first disguise symbolically representative of Satan's entire perverted nature. Renaissance pseudoscience conceived of serpents as corrupt in origin, generated from excrement or the spinal marrow of corpses; like the toad, the serpent was believed poisonous and pernicious by nature.[63] Despite its classical and biblical associations with wisdom and prudence, the word 'serpent' seems to have had negative connotations whenever it was applied to any other living creature, particularly humans.[64] Much more important than this nexus of connotations, Milton explicitly represents the serpent as sufficiently wilful in his own right for Eve to be able to detect the threat, if she is alert. In striking contrast to the other creatures, even those destined to become predators – 'Sporting the Lion ramp'd, and in his paw / Dandl'd the Kid; Bears, Tigers, Ounces, Pards / Gamboll'd' (4: 343–5) – only one sets off warning flares at his first entrance: 'close the Serpent sly / Insinuating, wove with Gordian twine / His braided train, and of his fatal guile / Gave proof unheeded' (4: 347–50). The 'sin' hidden in 'insinuating' is perceptible only to the reader; however, his potentially revealing behaviour needs interpretation that it does not get. Like the 'Labyrinth' of the sleeping serpent (9: 183), 'wove with Gordian twine,' suggests a puzzle designed to baffle human wit, perhaps as with Alexander only solvable by destroying it. In the phrase 'Gave proof unheeded' the word 'proof' has the legal sense of evidence that determines a judgment, as well as the connotation of a trial or test (see *OED* s.v, B, 1, b and B, II, 4). Similar to Uriel's encounter with Satan, Adam and Eve are experiencing a providence that, unheeding, they do not recognize.

Both the narrator and Eve follow Genesis 3: 1 in describing the serpent as 'subtl'st Beast of all the field' (7: 495; 9: 86, 560). Renaissance biblical commentators carefully noted that the serpent's subtlety preceded his connection with Satan and predisposed Satan's choice of this, rather than another, creature. Edward Topsell, remarking 'the naturall disposition of this beast aboue other to subtiltie and policie,' avers:

> For I cannot approoue the saying of them, who thinke that the deuill at the beginning, might as well haue used the tonge of an Asse or a dogge to haue deceiued Man, as well as serpents; but surely the old Serpent knewe very well, (better then all they which speake the contrary) that he could not haue so fit a subiect in all the World, as the shape, wit, and cunning of a Serpent. And that this came not into the Serpent at that time when the deuill framed his tongue to speake . . . For if there had not beene naturally, some extraordinarie faculty of vnderstanding in this beast . . . his wisdome would neuer haue sent vs to a serpent possest with a deuill.[65]

Topsell's expansion of the Genesis 'subtle' to 'policie' credits the serpent with being a natural Machiavel. The affinity between these two politicians was reinforced by Genesis 49: 17, 'Dan shall be a serpent by the way, / an adder in the path, / that biteth the horse heels, / so that his rider shall fall backward,' which exegetes such as Rabanus Maurus understood as referring to Satan and Antichrist.[66] Milton in turn emphasizes the similarities of nature in Satan and serpent by repeatedly describing them in the same terms of subtlety and guile.[67]

Raphael, narrating the sixth day of Creation, catalogues the beasts of the earth, cattle, and creeping things, 'Insect or Worm,' ending with the serpent. Its antepenultimate position in the day's work, immediately before 'the Master Work' man, at least rhetorically assigns him a stature above all the other lesser creatures for his 'extraordinarie faculty of vnderstanding.' Yet Raphael's recital puzzles and concerns some readers; to Philip Gallagher, for example, the passage is 'a relevant afterthought arrived at by free association' that, contradictorily, both warns and reassures his listeners about the serpent: 'It is difficult for us not to construe Raphael's disarming of Adam and Eve . . . as at best a sardonic dramatic irony that implicates him – and God and Milton too – in the fall of man.'[68] Raphael's speech, however, is more coherent than this would suggest. It begins by reminding Adam that, in naming the serpent, he understood its nature (7: 493–5). The angel complements

Adam's interior perception by dwelling on appearances, the serpent's metamorphic capacity and threatening visage (496–7), before the 'disarming' conclusion: 'though to thee / Not noxious, but obedient at thy call' (497–8). Raphael speaks very precisely: the serpent is not harmful to humans; Satan is. What tends to get ignored in the passage is his last clause. Obedience, the angel already has taught Adam and Eve, is not a passive virtue, but a matter of reasoned choice. For both angels and humans 'voluntary service,' not 'necessitated,' is required; 'freely we serve, / Because we freely love' (5: 529–30, 538–9). Holding dominion over every living creature requires active firmness (5: 501–3), perseverance (5: 525), vigilance and resolution (6: 900–12). Even before Adam's own creation story is told, he learns from Raphael that obedience is a trial, a providence, lessons he will hear in the angel's Book 7 narration of God's commandments and warnings, which prompt his own Book 8 recollection of that day.

In contrast to Adam's heedlessness, Satan shows full awareness of the serpent's nature when he selects him as the truly appropriate disguise:

> and with inspection deep
> Consider'd every Creature, which of all
> Most opportune might serve his Wiles, and found
> The Serpent subtlest Beast of all the Field.
> Him after long debate, irresolute
> Of thoughts revolv'd, his final sentence chose
> Fit Vessel, fittest Imp of fraud, in whom
> To enter, and his dark suggestions hide
> From sharpest sight: for in the wily Snake,
> Whatever sleights none would suspicious mark,
> As from his wit and native subtlety
> Proceeding, which in other Beasts observ'd
> Doubt might beget of Diabolic pow'r
> Active within beyond the sense of brute. (9: 83–96)

Nicely, Satan's thoughts 'revolv'd' (Lat. *revolvere,* to roll back), a process imaged in the form of the sleeping serpent, 'many a round self-roll'd' (9: 183); the two will be united in the 'voluble' (436) approach to Eve. His irresolution after having accurately plumbed the serpent's character may arise from awareness that they are too alike, but human knowledge of the serpent alleviates that fear. Were Satan to inhabit any other creature, the suspicion of 'Diabolic pow'r' might be raised, but Adam and Eve are accustomed to the singularity of the serpent. A complex of meanings attaching to 'Imp of fraud' – grafting metaphor, small demon, child, witch's familiar[69] – conveys the fusion of identities, the confusion of Satan's mind, and validate his status as the father of all evil.

The serpent, then, consistently is described in ways that imply the superiority of his faculties among the creatures and that he was prone to abuse them, as Satan had done his. Milton's purpose seems clear: Eve should recognize the evil intent of the serpent by appearance and actions, unmistakably when he speaks, even if she cannot know that Satan is within the serpent. Armed with faith, grace, and reason, Eve, like any good Christian, should be able to withstand any such trial and detect the presence of evil.

Elizabeth Pope described the iconographic convention of portraying the disguised Satan always with a sign that reveals his identity – cloven hoof, horns, tail, or claws.[70] Although she attributed this only to the artists' desire to prevent confusion, this explanation hardly seems adequate when one reflects that the audience for whom this art was intended would have complete familiarity with the temptations of Jesus, as well as those of various saints. The graphic convention perhaps implies an accepted tradition: God's providence would not allow the devil to disguise himself so successfully that the deception cannot be perceived. Joseph Glanvill argued, 'But if there be a *Providence* that superviseth us, (as nothing is more certain) doubtless it will never suffer poor helpless Creatures to be *inevitably deceived* by the *craft* and *subtilty* of their mischievous Enemy, to their undoing.' Glanvill maintained that, if not '*visible Marks* and *Signatures*,' there will be '*Circumstances, Ends* and *Designs*, as shall discover whence they are, and sufficiently distinguish' the true from 'all *Impostures* and *Delusions*.'[71] In *Paradise Lost* Milton adopts the second option, the more challenging for the person experiencing trial; rather than tagging Satan with 'visible Marks and Signatures,' he provides him with a stolen identity that should resonate danger.

If the serpent is independently delinquent, the nature of his offence and its motivation needs to be considered. The most illuminating source of information is the preamble to God's curse:

> To Judgment he proceeded on th' accus'd
> Serpent though brute, unable to transfer
> The Guilt on him who made him instrument
> Of mischief, and polluted from the end
> Of his Creation; justly then accurst,
> As vitiated in Nature: more to know

Concern'd not Man (since he no further knew)
Nor alter'd his offense; yet God at last
To Satan first in sin his doom appli'd,
Though in mysterious terms, judg'd as then best:
And on the Serpent thus his curse let fall. (10: 164–74)

In describing the serpent as 'brute, unable to transfer the Guilt,' Milton certainly does not mean the serpent has received an unjust sentence because it is unable to plead his case. Most probably he intends us to believe that the serpent, could he speak without Satan's ventriloquism, would shift the blame to Satan, committing the same act of hypocrisy as did Adam in blaming Eve and God (10: 125–43).[72]

The phrasing 'instrument / Of mischief' may reflect the Geneva Bible's marginal note on Genesis 3: 1, 'God suffered Satan to make the serpent his instrument and to speake in him.'[73] 'Mischief' here means 'Harm or evil considered as the work of an agent' (*OED* s.v. 2). The phrase has been read to mean that, in conformity with the main line of biblical commentary, the serpent was merely a tool of Satan, 'polluted' and 'vitiated' in the sense of the sodomized beast who is condemned to death (Lev. 20: 15–16).[74] This postulates a form of mercy killing, which implicitly absolves the serpent of wilful or active sin. For the poem, the interpretation is unsatisfactory simply because other such instruments, most notably the toad, are not cursed, implying a difference in kind, nor is the serpent put to death in conformity to the Leviticus commandment for abused beasts. Milton's God, it would seem, is not a God who would either unjustly curse a creature or create a creature to curse. In Milton's 'relentlessly consistent' Arminianism (Keith Stavely's phrase), the serpent must be wilfully bad by choice. Possibly taking Matthew 10: 16 as licence and allowing the latitude of poetry, Milton comes very close to postulating a beast whose 'wit and native subtlety' operate near the reach of human rational intelligence, as if it had free will.

Another, more credible, reading of Milton's phrase arises from the discourse of Renaissance logic. Examining the causal structure of the Fall in these terms, John Steadman concluded that Satan was the external cause of the lapse, the serpent the instrumental cause, and Adam's free will the efficient cause:

> ... it seems certain that the serpent is really the instrumental cause. In the first place, this is the opinion of most of the theologians we have cited. Secondly, in Book X of *Paradise Lost* Milton explicitly states that Satan made the serpent an 'instrument Of mischief, and polluted from the end Of his

> Creation.' Thirdly, according to the *Artis Logicae*, instruments do not act of themselves; they merely assist some other cause, or are used by it.[75]

Milton's logic here leaves the door open. Instruments do not act independently, but assist the external or *procatarctic* cause, in this case Satan. Although the instrumental cause may only be 'used,' it may also 'assist' ('aguntur aut adjuvant'). Citing Aristotle's opinion that 'instruments are either animate or inanimate,' Milton observes, 'In this sense almost all helping and ministering causes can be called instrumental' (*CPW* 8: 225). Although subordinate to Satan's 'inciting' cause, the serpent is animate and ministering ('ministrae'), a willing, if limited, partner. *De Doctrina,* explaining that the Father creates through the Son, makes the same logical distinction: the Son 'is therefore the less principal cause' (6: 302 and n. 12). Satan and serpent act as an uncreating Father and Son.

Despite the several indications that the serpent's guilt warrants his independent punishment, the question of motivation for his behaviour receives no direct answer – 'more to know / Concern'd not Man.' Here 'Man' specifically refers to Adam, whose knowledge of the serpent's role is incomplete, and who at this moment of judgment should be concerned with his own guilt. Raphael first delivered the lesson to 'be lowly wise; / Think only what concerns thee and thy being' (8: 173–4). Moreover, the judgment on the serpent, which encompasses 'in mysterious terms' that on Satan, serves to remind us that God's judgments and the ways of his providence are never entirely knowable. Again Raphael is apt: 'Solicit not thy thoughts with matters hid, / Leave them to God above, him serve and fear' (8: 167–8). Yet the reader does know more than Adam, understanding how '*Jesus,* son of *Mary* second *Eve*' (10: 183) will verify the 'oracle' concealed in the curse on the serpent. And the reader knows how the unequal partnership of serpent with Satan effected the temptation. The omission of an explicit statement of the serpent's motives, combined with the assurance that he is 'justly then accurst' (168), may well mean that Milton could assume his reader to be familiar with them.

Most literary versions of the story did not dwell on this vexed question. In Joshua Sylvester's translation of Du Bartas's *Le Seconde Semaine,* Satan knows 'The knotty Serpents spotty generation / Are filled with infectious inflammation,' and for this reason: 'He crafty cloaks him in a Dragon skin / All bright-bespect; that, speaking so within / That hollow Sagbuts supple-wreathing plies, / The mover might with th' Organ sympathize.'[76] Sylvester (exhibiting a talent for rime equal to W.S. Gilbert's) implies that it is necessary for Satan to use a creature whose nature is hospitable to the deception, but leaves unexplained the question of how that nature came to be corrupt. Similarly, biblical commentators agree on the justice of the curse, but struggle in explaining just why the tool of Satan deserves that judgment.[77]

There is an alternative tradition that interprets the serpent not simply as a tool but as an active and voluntary participant in the deception. Gervase Babington explains:

> In considering the punishment of each one, marke how first the Serpent is proceeded against, because he was the cause and beginner of this fault: thereby teaching, that ring-leaders to anie mischiefe, are first to be dealt against as most worthy: then remember, how before was noted the gifts of God in the Serpent, in some respects aboue other creatures, which hee abusing, nowe is punished thereby.[78]

An explicit statement of the serpent's motive comes from Cornelius a Lapide; the devil chose the serpent because it had attempted to creep into friendship with humans:

> . . . right and just was this punishment of the serpent; certainly the snake made an effort to insinuate himself into the friendship and familiarity of man; therefore, to them he was odious and execrable: the devil raised up the snake that he could join with the woman in conversation; thus, he was commanded to crawl; he persuaded to eat the apple; therefore, he was damned to eat the earth: he contemplated the woman's face; therefore, now contemplates her heel, even in ambush.[79]

Accordingly, like Satan who 'thought one step higher / Would set me highest' (4: 50–1), the serpent violated his nature through pride in the desire to exceed his proper station. In the light of this tradition, Milton's initial description of the serpent as 'insinuating' (4: 348; cf. Lapide, 'in amicitiam & familiaritatem hominis conatus fuit anguis irrepere') takes on added significance.[80] As a literary antecedent Milton had Grotius's *Adam Exul,* which influenced *Paradise Lost* in other ways. Grotius's Satan decides, 'consili sapiens mei Serpens minister fiat' (let the wise serpent be a minister to me for planning), and in the curse his God judges serpent and Satan separately, implying independent guilt.[81] The first part of the curse, 'Upon thy Belly groveling thou shalt go / And dust shalt eat all the days of thy Life' (*PL* 10: 177–8), expressly strips the serpent of those natural gifts that raised him – perhaps literally – above his fellow animals and made him a fit ally for Satan.[82]

Although Milton does not specify the motivation of his serpent, at least one alternative to pride was available: the sexuality of serpents. In *The Living Librarie* Camerarius observes 'many Authors affirme, that Serpents have been noted to desire the companie of women,' and recites all of the pagan myths in which women have been impregnated by serpents.[83] This serpent, the narrator tells us, is lovelier than the ones that generated Alexander the Great and Scipio Africanus: 'Hee with *Olympias,* this with her who bore / *Scipio* the highth of *Rome*' (9: 509–10). Satan and the serpent, then, are closely paralleled in their motives. Both are ambitious; 'lifted up so high,' they think that 'one step higher / Would set me highest' (4: 49–51); both are sexually attracted to Eve and jealous of Adam.[84] Partners in crime, it would seem.

Whatever his particular sources, Milton could postulate a serpent complicit in evil and might expect his readers to recognize this as one traditional interpretation of a troublesome biblical crux. For the immediate consideration of appearances its relevance should be evident. The poem depicts a serpent acting in ways that reveal he has violated his nature. Eve does not need to know that Satan has entered the serpent. By using her knowledge and mental faculties properly, she would be able to detect danger in the appearance and behaviour of the serpent himself. Sir Thomas Browne wonders that the deception was 'not in an invisible insinuation, but an open and discoverable apparition, that is, in the form of a Serpent.' He notes that many have been 'empuzzled' how 'without fear or doubt she could discourse with such a creature, or hear a Serpent speak, without suspicion of Imposture.'[85] The narrator is exact when he describes humans as having been 'with strength entire, and free will arm'd, / Complete to have discover'd and repulst / Whatever wiles of Foe or seeming Friend' (10: 9–11). The 'seeming Friend' describes pointedly the serpent whom Eve should have 'discover'd and repulst.'

In *Eikonoklastes,* attacking the king's praise of treaties as more rational than fighting, Milton paradoxically argues that treaties have 'more bestialitie' than does force: 'from fighting to come to undermining, from violence to craft, and when they can no longer doe as Lions, to doe as Foxes' (*CPW* 3: 521). In this he subscribes to the belief of the Father, in whose view 'false guile' is worse than 'force' (3: 91–2). Whereas force only attacks the body, fraud can corrupt the inner being. Both Machiavellian tactics in Milton's view are reprehensible, but, as Satan's success with Eve demonstrates, fraud is the more pernicious. Even-handedly, the Son considers the impending fall as 'circumvented thus by fraud, though join'd / With [their] own folly' (3: 152–3).

Exultant at succeeding beyond expectation and in escaping immediate punishment, Satan expresses his triumph by journeying back to Hell in the form of an 'Angel bright' (10: 327), but, unlike the cherub disguise, this one immediately is penetrated. Sin and Death, perfectly attuned as they are to the presence of evil, 'Thir Parent soon discern'd, though in disguise' (331). Goodness can be oblivious to hypocrisy, but evil knows better. Milton builds a consistent irony through the repeated situation in which, whereas Satan thinks he disguises himself effectively, the fraudulence only reveals his nature more thoroughly, whether to the discerning character or only to the reader. Having returned to Hell, Satan in his oration to the fallen angels reveals that he can no longer distinguish himself from the serpent. He ignores the first part of the curse, which applies only to the serpent:

> True is, mee also he hath judg'd, or rather
> Mee not, but the brute Serpent in whose shape
> Man I deceiv'd: that which to mee belongs,
> Is enmity, which he will put between
> Mee and Mankind; I am to bruise his heel;
> His Seed, when is not set, shall bruise my head. (10: 494–9)

The initial attempt to separate their identities is abandoned as he unconsciously applies the curse to himself. In this confusion Satan is ironically correct, even though his comprehension of the judgment is only literal. Concluding his peroration, he awaits the 'high applause' of his audience and instead receives the appropriate judgment on his Machiavellian fraud: 'from innumerable tongues / A dismal universal hiss' (507–8), both the speech of the fallen serpent with whom he is now identified and the reward of a bad actor. Next, when both audience and speaker are transformed into serpents, he has immediate, existential confirmation that, in judging the serpent, God has judged him: 'punisht in the shape he sinn'd' (516). After Satan chose to assume the serpent's form, it becomes impossible to distinguish his nature from the serpent's nature and, in Book 10, Satan from serpent (10: 82–4, 171–4). With the transformation in Hell, appearance and reality again coincide for Satan, and so it is that in *Paradise Regained*, 'subtle Fiend' (1: 465; 2: 323) fuses the images of Satan and serpent.[86]

Satan's limited comprehension of how the curse applies to him – 'A World who would not purchase with a bruise, / Or much more grievous pain?' (500–1) – was not shared by the commentators who, Catholic and Protestant alike, universally understood it as 'a prophecy of the coming of Christ,' providence vindicated at the moment foreseen from the beginning of time and the poem.[87] The poet expresses his fervent agreement with the interpretation that Jesus, 'rising from his grave,' shall triumph over Satan 'Whom he shall tread at last under our feet, / Even he who now foretold his fatal bruise' (10: 185, 190–1).[88] Showing once again his failure to reason and learn from a trial, Satan misses the first announcement on earth of the grand providential design that will atone for the Fall.

Chapter 4 brings into conjunction the two beings who will war for the souls of the newly created humans. Although the entire narrative, from 'one greater Man' to the resumption of 'His Seat at God's right hand,' is predicated on the Son's eventual personhood, in the action he is a presence, not a personality. Despite his performance of physical actions in the garden – the first surgery, the first wound-dressing – and Adam's perhaps fanciful descriptions of a 'shape Divine' (8: 205) or 'vision bright' (367), to Eve he simply is a voice (4: 465), which the Son confirms, 'My voice thou oft hast heard' (10: 119). And so he is for the reader. In Heaven he also is a voice, but the meaning of that voice is amplified by a complex design of light, sight, and sun imagery: the poet's invocation to light; the sun as the eye of the world; the Father as the eye of heaven; the Son, future light of the world, as the shining visual expression of his father. All of these figure the providential agency to be embodied in the greater man.

Satan remains a spirit, albeit a fallen one whose physical descriptions are as varied as his disguises, and undeniably he has a personality. His soliloquies allow us more direct access to the quirks of his mind than we are granted with Adam and Eve. His *différance* notwithstanding, Satan has a perhaps unexpectedly parallel role in negative counterpart to the Son. He, too, commits himself to become mortal. After the dialogue in Heaven, the narrative returns to Satan's journey, following him through the Jacob's ladder episode, the flight to the Sun, the encounter with Uriel, and in Book 4, his soliloquy to the sun. All of these present him with providences, trials of reason and choice, while symbolizing Christ's mediatorial and providential roles. Satan's response in the soliloquy is to declare his undying opposition to the sun/Son, his future manifestation as Antichrist.

Chapter Four

Providence Working: The Son and the Adversary

> Next unto our Lord and Saviour Jesus Christ, there is nothing so necessary as the true and solid knowledge of Antichrist.[1]
>
> Thomas Beard

> Here comes the Sun.
> I say it's all right.
>
> George Harrison

In 1633 Charles I made a long-deferred journey north for his coronation as king of Scotland, arriving at Edinburgh 15 June to a splendid civic pageant with triumphal arches.[2] Among the royal entourage was the court medalist, the Frenchman Nicholas Briot, who had now become Chief Graver at the mint. Briot created a coronation medal of Charles crowned, wearing ermine robes with both the Garter and the Thistle, and a few pieces were struck in Scottish gold. Returning to London in late July, the king was greeted by cheering crowds, prompting another medal (fig. 4). The obverse depicts Charles on horseback, wearing armour but crowned; he holds upright his staff, above which is the eye of providence. Beneath a radiant sun, the reverse represents a view of London: the south bank in the foreground, the Thames busy with swans and row boats, old St Paul's across, London Bridge to the right. It is surrounded by the legend: SOL ORBEM REDIENS SIC REX ILLVMINAT VRBEM (As the sun returns to the world, so by returning the king illuminates the city).[3] The images by which Briot illustrated the king's providential guidance and government were by no means exclusively royalist property. Both eye and sun literally were commonplaces, the clay from which Milton moulded a complex metaphoric structure to

Figure 4. Nicolas Briot, medal of Charles I on horseback, returning from his coronation in Edinburgh, beneath the eye of providence. Reverse scene of the sun dispelling clouds to shine on London. Cast silver, 42 mm, 1633. Private collection. Photo by Charles Robb.

convey the essence of the Son who would become the incarnation of divine providence. It begins with light. Fiat lux.

The invocation to light (*PL* 3: 1–55) commences by collapsing distinctions between temporal and eternal, physical and spiritual, an unconfusing confusion since the former kind of light traditionally symbolizes the latter. Although the blind poet, entirely 'Cut off' (47) from created light, must himself directly seek the inward vision of 'Celestial light' (51), he fully deploys the metaphoric resources of light and sight imagery for his reader's imagination.[4] Shifting to narration, the poet presents God the Father beholding his creation, 'past, present, future' (78); as Sir Thomas Browne elegantly expressed it, 'in Eternity there is no distinction of Tenses.' From a mundane perspective, the Father's comprehensive vision itself proclaims him a prudent governor, maintaining providence.[5] He views 'Our two first Parents' working happily in the garden and, simultaneously, Satan approaching the world at the end of his voyage out of chaos. The Father explains to his Son the meaning of Satan's action and, looking to the future, predicts that man will fall, thereby initiating the divine dialogue of justice and mercy.

The synecdoche of God functioning as vision ('th' Almighty father . . . / . . . bent down his eye, / His own works and their works at once to view' [56, 58–9]), oddly, has lent ammunition to those critics who complain of the anthropomorphism of Milton's God. Leland

Ryken conceded that 'the most frequently mentioned of God's physical parts is his eye,' but defends the technique: 'The effect of the portrayal of God in human terms is not a composite human form but a series of anthropomorphic fragments, each describing concretely a function of the Deity or suggesting his whole being.'[6] Truthfully, the phrase 'anthropomorphic fragments' better fits Scott Fitzgerald's description of the oculist's giant billboard midway between West Egg and New York than it does Milton's presentation of divinity.[7]

In his practice, Milton may be acting upon the recommendation in *De Doctrina Christiana* (1: 2) that 'it is safest for us to form an image of God in our minds which corresponds to his representation and description of himself in the sacred writings. Admittedly, God is always described or outlined not as he really is but in such a way as will make him conceivable to us' (*CPW* 6: 133).[8] For this particular instance, he draws upon the frequent Old Testament epithet of 'the eye of the Lord' – for example, Psalm 33: 18, 'Behold, the eye of the Lord is upon them that fear him, upon them that hope in his mercy'; Psalm 11: 4, 'The Lord's throne is in heaven: his eyes behold, his eyelids try, the children of men'; or Proverbs 15: 3, 'The eyes of the Lord are in every place, beholding the evil and the good.' Such scriptural quotations serve in themselves to advance us a stage beyond Ryken's proposition; in them, as in Milton's description, one does not visualize an 'anthropomorphic fragment' but responds directly to the 'function of the Deity,' his omniscience, his eternal watchfulness. Rather than something that might quicken an optometrist's pulse, the Eye of God is as immediately figurative as an emblem.

When Milton chooses a representation of God with scriptural authority, such a 'correspondence' does not prevent him from drawing upon extrabiblical sources that accord with his conception, and he does so here. The image of God bending down his eye to view his creation deftly evokes a number of complexly interrelated, metaphoric traditions. First, there is the epithet 'the eye of the world,' which for two millennia had described the sun. The Orphic hymn 'To the Sun' begins: 'Hear golden Titan, whose eternal eye / With broad survey, illumines all the sky,' and the phrase echoes through the writings of the Platonic philosopher Secundus, the poet Ovid, St Ambrose, Macrobius, the astronomer Kepler, down to Milton's contemporaries Alexander Ross and John Swan, who asserts that 'the sunne may well be called Oculus mundi, The eye of the world. For he is indeed the chief fountain from whence the whole world receiveth luster.'[9] Milton's appositive 'Lordly eye' (3: 578) for 'The golden Sun' (3: 572) thus comes freighted with every sort of authority, and the morning prayer of Adam and Eve, 'Thou Sun, of this great World both Eye and Soul, / Acknowledge him thy Greater, sound his praise / In thy eternal course' (5: 171–3), recognizes both the similarity and the distinction that had exercised Ambrose:

> Do not, therefore, without due consideration put your trust in the sun. It is true that it is the eye of the world, the joy of the day, the beauty of the heavens, the charm of nature and the most conspicuous object in creation. When you behold it, reflect on its Author. When you admire it, give praise to its Creator.[10]

This pious and conventional distinction between the created and the Creator, the symbol and the reality symbolized, allows us to trace a splitting of our first figure into vehicle and tenor. On the one hand, the image of an eye frequently is reduced from synecdoche to an attribute of divinity – as it is in the hieroglyphics of Horapollo and Piero Valeriano or in the image of an eye mounted atop a sceptre. Leon Battista Alberti explains: 'The ancients likened God to an eye seeing all and everything. Thus we are admonished . . . to conceive of God as ever present, seeing all our deeds and thoughts.'[11] On the other hand, the sun itself metamorphoses from tenor to vehicle, for, as Hugo Rahner has remarked, 'Christian theologians have from the very beginning used the sun to express the fundamental truths of their revelation.'[12]

Reduplicating the same symbolic doubling which we observed in the invocation to 'Holy Light,' both the Bible and traditions of commentary permit the sun to symbolize interchangeably God the Father or the Trinity, and the Son. The germinal text for the latter is Malachi 4: 2, 'But unto you that fear my name shall the Sun of righteousness arise with healing in his wings,' an identification amplified by such commentators as Origen, for whom the sun is a symbol of grace, and Hilary of Poitiers, who compares the Logos to the sun. The Nativity Ode (st. 26) draws together such resonances with the antepenultimate image of the infant in the manger as the rising sun emerging from his bed of pillowy clouds.[13] But, as Christ is the created light emanating from the Father, so the Father is the source of all light. Psalm 84: 11 proclaims that 'the Lord God is a sun and shield'; and Marsilio Ficino muses in *De sole*: 'one should not attempt to grasp and state the hidden or occult light of God without noting its resemblance to the sensible light: namely, that of the Sun.'[14] Ficino concludes, 'nothing can be found in the world which resembles the divine Trinity more than the Sun,' a sentiment shared by Torquato Tasso, who begins *Il mondo creato* with an address to the

Trinity as 'triplicata Sole.'[15] Lest Italian Platonists seem too remote from God-fearing Englishmen, we might turn to Milton's respected antagonist Archbishop Ussher, who catechistically propounds:

> *What be those resemblances that are commonly brought to shadow out unto us the mystery of the Trinity?*
>
> First, the Sun begetteth his own beams, and from thence proceeds light and heat, and yet is none of them before another, otherwise then in consideration of order and relation, that is to say, that the beams are begotten of the body of the Sun, and the light and heat proceed from both.[16]

Ussher's succeeding points compare to the Trinity the interrelatedness of light and heat with fire, of spring and stream with fountainhead, and of understanding and will with the human soul.

Milton's image of the Eye of Heaven overseeing the creation, I would maintain, directly evokes Old Testament descriptions of 'th' Almighty Father,' but simultaneously suggests the *oculus mundi,* the sun of the physical world, a symbolic sun that potentially figures both the Holy Trinity and the Son of God.[17] The figural interplay, however, has an even more specific bent than this. John Steadman once contrasted the presentation of Milton's God to Dante's God of mystical contemplation, arguing that the concept in *Paradise Lost* of God as an active governor of the creation follows logically from Milton's expressed intention to 'assert Eternal Providence.'[18] Similarly, Isabel MacCaffrey found the highest illumination of that intention to occur in Book 3 – the assertion of 'the providential design for the future of mankind . . . by the only Being who has a right to do so,' an assertion dramatized as a 'great Argument.'[19] If God's providence is the aspect of his goodness with which Milton's epic at large is concerned and the specific purpose of Book 3 is to reveal the design of that providence, we would expect, as well, that the *Imago Dei* would present precisely that attribute of divinity. It does so, of course.

Both eye and sun traditionally have been used to symbolize God's providence, and the conjunction of symbols particularly underscores the motif. The point of significance in each case is the same: as his eternal vigilance permits him to foresee everything and therefore to order benevolently the course of the mundane world, so the all-seeing sun, source of light, heat, and life itself, orders the days and seasons of growth. To Ficino the sun alone 'is the illuminating Lord and Regulator of the Skies,' thereby declaring God's eternal power and divinity.[20] Boethius, explaining the workings of providence, uses the sun analogy, but – in a verse passage suggestively similar to Milton's – contrasts the limitations of the lesser sun's vision with that of the greater sun, his Creator:

> Not thus the Maker of this great universe:
> Him, viewing all things from his height,
> No mass of earth obstructs,
> No night with black clouds thwarts.
> What is, what has been, and what is to come,
> In one swift mental stab he sees;
> Him, since he only all things sees,
> The true sun could you call.[21]

Insofar as sun and eye can be said to carry differing connotations in Milton's usage, the distinction would be that between general and extraordinary providence. Whereas general providence is the orderly government of the entire creation (1: 8) – the kind of providence that George Herbert celebrates in his eponymous poem – extraordinary providence, as *De Doctrina Christiana* states, 'is that by which [God] produces some effect outside the normal order of nature or gives' such power 'to some chosen person' (*CPW* 6: 341). Contemporary religious discourse favoured two images for extraordinary providence; the 'Hand of Heaven,' in Henry Vaughan's phrase 'Sacred and secret hand' ('Providence'), represented God's omnipotence in direct intervention (see fig. 1). Cromwell attributed his victory in the battle of Preston (17–19 August 1648) to 'no thing but the hand of God'; Milton defended the king's execution as 'that impartiall and noble peece of Justice, wherein the hand of God appear'd so evidently on our side' (*CPW* 3: 311). To Michael's test of obedience, Adam responds, 'I follow thee, safe Guide, the path / Thou lead'st me, and to the hand of Heav'n submit, / However chast'ning' (11: 371–3). Prosaically, Arminius explained how 'the hand of the Providence of God' uses incitements to try ('exploret') whether a sinner will refrain or yield to them (1: 348).

Complementing the hand, the 'Eye of God' figured his omniscience, his eternal vigilance – in Elnathan Parr's phrase, 'Ocular Providence.' *De Doctrina* uses 'providence or foreknowledge' (providentia sive praescientia) as synonyms in denying that God's omniscience imposes necessity on human free will (*CPW* 6: 164). Confirming that the transgression of Adam and Eve immediately is known, the poet explains: 'for what can scape the Eye / Of God All-seeing, or deceive his Heart / Omniscient, who in all things wise and just, / Hinder'd not *Satan* to attempt the mind / Of man, with strength entire, and free will arm'd' (10: 5–9). One critic cogently finds compressed here the 'three main components' of Milton's justification, 'divine omniscience, divine permissiveness, and human freedom,'[22] to which one might add, a distinctly Arminian justification. Thus, whereas the sun aptly symbolizes the regulator of the world, the alternative image of the eye is the more appropriate one to register the action of Satan's rebellion:

> Meanwhile th' Eternal eye, whose sight discerns
> Abstrusest thoughts, from forth his holy Mount
> And from within the golden Lamps that burn
> Nightly before him, saw without thir light
> Rebellion rising, saw in whom, how spread
> Among the sons of Morn, what multitudes
> Were banded to oppose his high Decree. (5: 711–17)

The entire speech assumes divine permissiveness and angelic free will; the Father's joke, 'lest unawares we lose / This our high place' (731–2) only underscores his omniscience. The Son's response, 'thou thy foes / Justly hast in derision' (735–6), immediately evokes Psalm 2, his own begetting, and the grand providential design. Belial's rational, if self-serving, rebuttal of the Machiavellian 'force or guile' scheme was based on hard experience; the Almighty, 'whose eye / Views all things at one view . . . sees and derides' (2: 188–91). In Milton's poetry this image of 'th' Eternal eye' was established as early as Sonnet 7 in which 'my great task-Master's eye' expresses God's providential concern for the apprentice poet; it recurs in *A Maske* when the Lady, mistakenly trusting Comus, nonetheless appeals, 'Eye me blest Providence, and square my trial / To my proportion'd strength' (329–30), and it continues beyond *Paradise Lost* to *Samson Agonistes*.[23]

It may not be easy to draw a categorical line between special and extraordinary providence in the passage that we have been eying. In viewing 'His own works and their works,' God's attention is not focused on a review of the Book of Nature, as is the speaker of Herbert's poem; here actors and actions crowd the cosmic theatre before its watchful director:

About him all the Sanctities of Heaven
Stood thick as Stars, and from his sight receiv'd
Beatitude past utterance; on his right
The radiant image of his Glory sat,
His only Son; on Earth he first beheld
Our two first Parents, yet the only two
Of mankind, in the happy Garden plac't,
Reaping immortal fruits of joy and love,
Uninterrupted joy, unrivall'd love,
In blissful solitude; he then survey'd
Hell and the Gulf between, and *Satan* there
Coasting the wall of Heav'n on this side Night. (3: 60–71)

The loyal angels and the reminder that all of mankind will descend from 'Our two first Parents' identify the subjects of special providence, yet the introduction of 'His only Son' and the Forlorn Satan intimates that extraordinary providence is at work. The doubling possibly explains why the image of the eye is primary here and the sun latent or secondary. Those secondary connotations do, nonetheless, reverberate importantly, anticipating the very action that is to be the topic of the ensuing dialogue: the most extraordinary evidence of providence, which for Milton justifies the ways of God to man, the redemption of mankind through Jesus Christ, the 'greater Sun.'

Were one to postulate a specific poetic locus upon which Milton's imagination is playing, I might nominate Edward Fairfax's translation of the *Gerusalemme liberata.* Twice in the epic Tasso describes God as turning his eyes to scrutinize the affairs of men (see 1, st. 7–8; 9, st. 55–7). In both episodes the conception of deity is Trinitarian ('e de l' Eternita nel tron augusto / risplendea con tre lumi in una luce'),[24] and the context is providential intervention. Fairfax, perhaps himself influenced by Spenser's employment of 'the great eye of heauen' to symbolize 'heauenly grace' (*Faerie Queene* 1, cant. 3, st. 4), expands the descriptive usage to two apposite passages in later cantos (13, st. 72; 14, st. 2), modifying Tasso's plural 'gli occhi' to the singular and rendering 'turned' ('volse' or 'volgea') as 'bent.' Of the four instances, the most suggestive occurs at the beginning of canto 14: the watchful God sends down to the sleeping Goffredo a dream whereby he reveals his will. The dream descends from the east, via a crystalline gate (Tasso's addition to the Homeric gates of ivory and horn) located next to the golden gate through which the rising sun enters the world. Seemingly responding to the connotations activated by the sun image that follows, Fairfax replaces 'il Re del mondo' with God bending down his eye:

> But he, whose Godhead heaven and earth doth sway,
> In his eternal light did watch and wake,
> And bent on Godfrey down the gracious ray
> Of his bright eye, still ope for Godfrey's sake
>   To whom a silent dream the Lord down sent,
>   Which told his will, his pleasure, and intent.
>
> Far in the east, the golden gate beside
> Whence Phoebus comes, a crystal port there is,
> And ere the sun his broad doors open wide,
> The beam of springing day uncloseth this,
> Hence come the dreams, by which heaven's sacred Guide
> Reveals to man those high decrees of his. (14, st. 2, 3–8, st. 3, 1–6)

The poetic situation here – a God who is both a watchful eye and an eternal sun beaming rays of celestial light to shine inward and irradiate the mind of a mortal man – is very close to that of Milton's invocation.[25] Prompted by his own Christ-centred vision, he would need only to de-emphasize Tasso's Trinitarianism by bringing the Son into prominence – speaking imagistically, to make that golden gate of the rising sun not adjacent but consubstantial.

Milton's symbolic conception may be illuminated by comparison to the one we see in Jacopo Pontormo's painting *The Supper at Emmaus* (fig. 5). The artist takes out of time the moment at which the risen Jesus 'took the bread, and blessed *it*' (Luke 24: 30). The two disciples occupy the left and right foreground, sitting with their backs to us, still uncomprehendingly busy with their meal; dominating the centre and focal point is the Saviour, his right hand raised in benediction; on each side the white-robed figures of Carthusian monks crowd about him, both bearing silent witness to the miracle and taking the event out of historical time. Immediately above Jesus's head, at the upper centre, a conflation of symbols spells out the significance of the heightened but naturalistic scene beneath: at the centre of a globe of light is a triangle; at the centre of the triangle is an eye.[26] The eye within a triangle, surrounded by a radiating circle of light, is a familiar symbol of the Trinity;[27] however, the version here varies interestingly in two respects. The Eye of God is not an abstract icon, but a human eye, in shape and colour

Figure 5. Jacopo Pontormo (Jacopo Carucci), *The Supper at Emmaus*, 1525, with seventeenth-century overpainting of the eye of providence. Uffizi Museum, Florence. Erich Lessing / Art Resource, NY.

related to the eyes of the man-God below; and the globe is not a radiating circle but distinctly a sun, whose rays intersect with the nimbus of the risen Christ, connecting their identities. The providence of the Holy Trinity is manifested through the incarnation of the Son, a sacrificed god who now is the risen sun. Pontormo's choice of a New Testament subject, the bodily resurrection of Jesus Christ, allows the two natures of the Son to be conjoined visually, whereas the narrative logic of the epic determines the symbolic projection of eye and sun, his divine nature in its providential manifestation, reserving the human for *Paradise Regained*.[28]

Figure 6. Title-page engraving by Renold Elstrack to Sir Walter Ralegh, *The History of the World*, printed for Walter Burre, 1614. First edition, published anonymously. The William Andrews Clark Memorial Library, University of California, Los Angeles.

The assertive and schematic Trinitarianism of the triangle was a gesture from which English Protestants shied away. More congenial to them would have been the elaborate title-page of Sir Walter Ralegh's *The History of the World* (1614), engraved by Renold Elstrack with the design possibly by Ralegh himself (fig. 6). Within an architectural frame, the personification of History (MAGISTRA VITAE), flanked by Experience and Truth, treads on Death and Oblivion; she holds above her head a globe with a map of the world. Standing on a platform and helping to support the globe are figures of Good and Bad Fame. Watching over the world at top centre is a giant eye, radiating light as a sun emerging from clouds; the lines 'Curtain'd with cloudy red / Pillows his chin upon an Orient wave' (Nat. Ode, 230–1) seem appropriate. Above the eye is the inscription PROVIDENTIA.[29] The prominence assigned to the eye of God directly visualizes Ralegh's description of providence in the first chapter. Like Milton he begins with the three modes of time – 'Memorie of the past, Knowledge of the present, and Care of the future' – continues with scriptural citations 'proving' the existence of providence, and then gets to the heart of the matter:

> God therefore, who is euery where present, *who filleth the heauens and the earth, whose eyes are upon the righteous, and his countenance against them that doe euill*, was therefore by *Orpheus called oculus infinitus, an infinite eye*, beholding all things, and cannot therefore be esteemed as an idle looker on, as if he had transferred his pouer to any other: for it is contrary to his owne word. *Gloriam meam alteri non dabo: I will not give my glorie to another*.[30]

For Ralegh providence is characterized by 'absolute power,' 'euerywhere presence,' 'perfect goodnesse,' 'pure and diuine loue.' The marginal note suggests that the last holds primacy. His conception of a voluntarist God, no 'idle looker on' but eternally vigilant, omnipotent, yet more importantly benevolent and loving, is a suggestive forerunner to Milton's more complex conception. Particularly striking is Ralegh's contention that God's glory should be seen in his providence, a belief with which the poet certainly concurred.

Ben Jonson contributed to Ralegh's *History* a prefatory poem, 'The Minde of the Front' (unsigned, as was the book itself – i.e., published anonymously), explaining the design as a definition of history and concluding with her titles, 'The light of Truth, and life of Memorie' (18), epithets thoroughly apt for Milton's own illumination of biblical history through *sacra memoria* (chap. 2 above). Jonson obliquely hints at Ralegh's vindication 'to AEternity': 'High prouidence would so; that nor the good / Might be defrauded, nor the Great secur'd, / But both might know their wayes are vnderstood, / And the reward, and the punishment assur'd' (4–8). When Jonson prepared it for publication in *The Underwood* (no. 24), he prudently altered line 8 to the anodyne, 'When Vice alike in time with vertue dur'd.' By the time the volume was printed both he and Ralegh were dead and beyond further harm from 'the Great,' so it no longer mattered, except possibly to high providence.

Milton's descriptive emphasis upon the providential concern of the Godhead follows logically and poetically from the invocation to 'holy Light,' which – with its metaphors implicitly asserting the indivisibility of sun and ray, light and radiance, fountain and stream, eternal and temporal – seems, William B. Hunter and others have concluded, addressed to the Son of God as the manifestation through whom the deity may be approached.[31] The narrative bridge between the poet's direct speech in the invocation and the Father-Son speeches of the divine dialogue, this descriptive prelude foreshadows the discursive revelation of that dialogue. Remarking that 'Milton differentiates between the Father and the Son *only* during their verbal exchanges . . . but as soon as these councils end and the Godhead acts beyond the confines of heaven the distinction between the two persons is abruptly dropped,' C.A. Patrides argued that the entire distinction of Father and Son in the poem is a matter of accommodation to human understanding.[32]

It follows, therefore, that the dialogue itself is a ritual of accommodation, God talking to himself for the benefit of the overhearer, about which the only drama is the drama of apprehension taking place in the reader's mind.[33] As such, the dialogue spells out what already had been implicit in the imagery of invocation and description: the eye of providence, both *oculus divini* and *oculus mundi,* manifests its benevolent design for the redemption of mankind through the incarnation of the man who proclaimed himself 'the light of the world.' In his response to the Father's 'trial,' the Son's offer, 'Behold mee then, mee for him, life for life / I offer, on mee let thine anger fall; / Account mee man' (3: 236–8), verbally confirms the redemption, but throughout the scene he has presented a visual affirmation:[34]

Beyond compare the Son of God was seen
More glorious, in him all of his Father shone
Substantially express'd, and in his face,
Divine compassion visibly appear'd,
Love without end, and without measure Grace. (3: 138–42)

With the dialogue completed, the angelic choir mediates between invocation and dialogue by overtly applying the sun and light, fountain and stream imagery of the former to the persons of the latter.[35] The Father, 'Fountain of Light, thyself invisible / Amidst the glorious brightness' (3: 375–6), appears to his angels only when he shades 'The full blaze of [his] beams' in a cloud, permitting them to apprehend the adjuncts of his presence: 'Dark with excessive bright thy skirts appear' (380). Conversely, the immediately accessible Son presents not an image of himself but a mediated comprehension of the Father: 'Begotten Son, Divine Similitude, / In whose conspicuous count'nance, without cloud / Made visible, th' Almighty Father shines' (3: 384–6). In confirmation elsewhere the Father addresses the 'Son in whose face invisible is beheld / Visibly, what by Deity I am' (6: 681–2), at the end of which speech he 'on his Son with Rays direct / Shone full' (719–20), virtually making the Son / sun homonym explicit. In Book 3, even more pointedly, the entire episode returns in full circle to the invocation as, at the culmination of the choral hymn, the angelic voices ('Thus they in Heav'n') reduce to a solitary singer, who echoes the 'Hail holy Light' formula shorn of metaphor:

> Hail Son of God, Savior of Men, thy Name
> Shall be the copious matter of my Song
> Henceforth, and never shall my Harp thy praise
> Forget, nor from thy Father's praise disjoin. (3: 412–15)

Patently, image and theme are woven into a seamless whole through the first half of Book 3. But MacCaffrey's account of the thematic coherence of the entire book serves to alert us that we should respond to larger imagistic patterns, as well. The segment of Book 3 that we have been discussing is itself only the most conspicuous portion of a pattern of sun imagery constituting a symbolic structure extending through and beyond this book. After following Satan's journey from the utter darkness of Hell to the middle darkness of Chaos, Book 2 concludes with the 'glimmering dawn' of the natural sun, illuminating the created world. The Invocation of 'holy Light' transports us from sun to Son, defining the united natures, human and divine, of Jesus Christ (cf. *CPW* 6: 423–5), thereby presenting the providential agent. The subjects of his agency, the actions requiring his intervention, and the form that intervention shall take are clarified successively by the description of God's omniscient vision and by the dialogue. With the Limbo of Vanities episode we modulate back from metaphysical to physical sun, the 'gleam / Of dawning light' (3: 499–500), recapitulating the 'glimmering dawn' at the end of Book 2, but the symbolic overtones have become inescapable.

Satan, Antichrist

Orientating his course by that gleam of light 'from the walls of Heav'n' (2: 1035), Satan is drawn to Oriens himself; he 'hies' toward Heaven's gate, which is accessed by stairs 'such as whereon Jacob saw / Angels ascending and descending' (3: 510–11). The meaning of Jacob's dream was well understood: 'Christ is the ladder whereby God and man are ioyned together, and by whom the Angels minister vnto vs, & we by him ascende into heauen' (Geneva gloss). At the same time that understanding itself entailed a further recognition of the design. Andrew Willet reviewed and shunted aside competing interpretations of the ladder to proclaim that 'the proper and literal meaning of the ladder is, to set forth Gods prouidence, both in generall, wherby he gouerneth all things in heauen and in earth, Psal. 113.6.' So certain of this exegesis was Willet that he even composed on the subject a Latin emblem, titled 'Diuina prouidentia.'[36]

In Reformed circles, on the authority of Malachi and Paul, the story of Jacob and Esau was widely understood as a parable of predestination. The Geneva Bible annotates Romans 9 approvingly, 'The onelie wil & purpose of God is the chief cause of election & reprobation.' Arminius admitted that chapter 9 was obscure and difficult to interpret, but circumvented the difficulty to his satisfaction, explaining that Esau and Jacob should be understood as types, not individuals, the one seeking righteousness by works and the other by faith. For Arminius, Carl Bangs concludes, the message of Romans 9 is justification by faith: 'God has predestined to salvation all who believe in Christ.'[37] This interpretation, however dubious as a reading of Paul, anticipates Arminius's mature theology of free will and free acceptance of the offered grace. Keith Stavely perceptively comments on Milton's shaping of the Genesis narrative: 'Milton elides many details in order to convey the Arminian moment of faithful acceptance when Jacob judges and chooses correctly, believing that he has been dreaming the truth of God's mercy.'[38] Satan – like Jacob, a hypocrite who lies, disguises himself to get what he wants, and flees to another country – is given a providence. The stairs, 'drawn up to Heav'n sometimes,' 'were then let down' (3: 517, 523). Satan has a choice of alternatives, 'whether to dare' to accept the promise of 'easy ascent' or to 'aggravate / His sad exclusion' (523–5). In this trial he chooses wrongly, which aggravates (OED s.v. II. 6, 'To make worse') but does not yet determine his end. He still could learn from his experience.

Lingering at the foot of the mysterious stairs, beneath which opens a passage to Paradise, Satan glimpses something like the Father's view of his creation when he 'Looks down with wonder at the sudden view / Of all this World at once' (3: 542–3). The wonder, the *admiratio* appropriate to angelic witnesses (cf. 3: 271–3), is too soon replaced by Satan's stock response: 'but much more envy seiz'd / At sight of all this World beheld so fair' (3: 553–4). Plunging precipitously into this fair new world, Satan inevitably is drawn to its eye: 'above them all / The golden Sun in splendor likest Heaven / Allur'd his eye: Thither his course he bends' (571–3). Landing on the surface of the sun, the Devil gazes upon 'matter new' (613), including stones comparable 'to the Twelve that shone / In *Aaron's* Breastplate, and a stone besides / Imagin'd rather oft than elsewhere seen' (597–9), the fabled Philosopher's Stone. Aaron was accepted as a type of Christ in his priestly office, and, in the metaphor of spiritual alchemy, Christ is the Philosopher's Stone and the Great Elixir who transmutes the base metal of unredeemed souls to gold.[39] 'Th' Arch-chemic Sun,' like the vantage point from which Satan spotted it, symbolizes Christ the mediator.

Satan, A.B. Chambers observed, 'is surrounded with more light – both physical and metaphoric – than he will ever again be privileged to behold.'[40] He yet retains angelic power of vision which, the allusion to Galileo's telescope reminds us (588–90), exceeds that of humans even when enhanced by art; the optimal conditions permitted by God's will, 'all Sun-shine, as when his Beams at Noon / Culminate from th' *Equator*' (616–17), serve to sharpen his vision even further. In the description of how 'matter new to gaze the Devil met / Undazzl'd' (613–14), the adjective used as an adjunct is particularly suggestive. Literally, 'dazzle' means 'To lose the faculty of distinct and steady vision' (*OED*, s.v., 1); thus, 'undazzl'd' attests to Satan's power to withstand brightness 'beyond expression' (501). Figuratively, it is difficult to miss the connotation of his resistance to the grace now accessible through the Son, with the further suggestion that his eyes do not dazzle with tears of remorse.[41] Rather than Christ as the way to Heaven, Satan still chooses to follow – or, more accurately, forerun – the futile examples in the 'Paradise of Fools,' seeking to enter Heaven by force or fraud.

Having succeeded temporarily in defrauding Uriel, Satan reaches his destination, only to be plagued by despair with, in unconscious parody of the Father's omniscience, 'the bitter memory / Of what he was, what is, and what must be / Worse' (4: 24–6).[42] Vacillating between his present objective and his losses, he looks 'Sometimes toward Eden' and 'Sometimes toward Heav'n and the full-blazing Sun, / Which now sat high in his Meridian Tow'r' (27, 29–30). Satan begins his soliloquy by addressing the sun, 'O thou that with surpassing Glory crown'd, / Look'st from thy sole Dominion like the God / Of this new World' (4: 32–4), in terms that reveal both obsession and perception. He still wants to imagine himself as a Machiavellian locked in conflict over 'dominion' (see *OED* s.v. 3) of a new principality with the sort of rival whose weakness is truth to his word. This is bluster; his church Latin is sufficient to lead him through *dominio* to *dominus* and hence to the more realistic 'God / Of this new world.' Satan not only confesses the justness of his punishment and his inability to repent his sins, but intimates his undying enmity to the Son of God, foreshadowing his own assumption of the role of Antichrist: 'to thee I call, / But with no friendly voice, and add thy name / O Sun, to tell thee how I hate thy beams / That bring to my remembrance from what state / I fell' (4: 35–9).[43] As the Geneva Bible gloss to Revelation 20:1 comments, 'Iesus Christ, the Sunne of rightenouness, is persecuted of Antichrist.'

The myth of Antichrist was cobbled together from disparate scriptural texts. He is named only in the New Testament: 'it is the last time; and as ye have heard that antichrist shall come' (1 John 2: 18, 4: 3; 2 John 7). To these verses were linked the great 'beast' (Rev. 11, 13; Dan. 7: 7–8) and what became for the commentators the key 'place,' the 'man of sin' or 'son of perdition,' 'whose coming is after the working of Satan' (2 Thess. 2: 3, 9).[44] The myth, Bernard McGinn thinks, 'resulted logically from the opposition between good and evil implied in the acceptance of Jesus as divine Son of Man, Christ, and, later, Word of God.'[45] As Lieutenant Colonel John Jubbes confessed during the Putney Debates, 'Truly I do not know how to distinguish whether the spirit of God lives in me or no, but by mercy, love, and peace; and on the contrary whether the spirit of Antichrist lives in me, but by envy, malice, and war.'[46] Antichrist must derive from Satan, the progenitor of all evil, and sometimes was simply identified with Satan; yet several factors militated against such an identification.[47] Perhaps the strongest of these was the theological belief that only God has the power to assume human nature. For Origen Antichrist was the son of Satan; to others the 'man of sin' was a human possessed by Satan – as Jerome put it, 'the one man in whom Satan shall totally dwell in a corporeal way.' The predilection for symmetrical typology ensured that he was not only, like Cain, Nimrod, and Judas, a type of Satan but a Second Satan, corresponding to Jesus, the Second Adam, causing Gregory the Great to insist that Antichrist was the devil incarnate. 'Antichrist truly is the *opposite* of Christ, and as Christ is the "man assumed by God," so, too, Antichrist is the "man assumed by the devil."'[48] Beyond his nature, other questions about the Antichrist abounded. Was he already present or yet to come? Was he manifested as a collective or institutional evil (e.g., a particular people, the Roman Empire, the papacy) heralding the arrival of an individual, historical person, *the* Antichrist? With the alarming fall of Constantinople to Mehmet II in 1453, the Turks became a favoured candidate.[49] Martin Luther thought Antichrist might be the Turks or the papacy collectively before firmly settling on Leo X.[50] In England the choices could be domesticated.[51] 'If the splendor of *Gold* and *Silver* begin to Lord it once againe in the Church of *England*,' Milton declared, 'wee shall see *Antichrist* shortly wallow here, though his cheife Kennell be at *Rome*' (*CPW* 1: 590; also 850).[52] With the bishops removed, Milton could turn his attention to a higher target, accusing Charles I of attempting 'to inforce upon us an Antichristian tyranny in the Church' and intimating darkly that he was one of the worldly kings who fornicated with '*the great Whore*' (*CPW* 3: 442, 598).

Studies of Milton's millenarianism are not wanting, nor has an apocalyptic dimension of *Paradise Lost* been neglected; oddly, these turn a deaf ear to Howard Schultz's arguments for the presence of Antichrist in the two epics.[53] Nonetheless, his very brief comments on *Lost* are suggestive and deserve amplification. As Milton does with, say, Satan's animal disguises, he uses the more immediate, fallen world exemplar to elevate our understanding of its source. The poem thus exploits both the prevailing anti-Turkish and antipapal associations for Antichrist in the projection of Satan. The two stereotypes carried somewhat different connotations, dividing the Machiavellian dyad; whereas the papacy meant fraudulence and corruption, the Turks, as a scourge of God, embodied extreme force, savagery, and cruelty.[54] Satan is described as the 'great Sultan' in Hell (1: 348); Pandaemonium is furnished with 'the Soldan's chair' (764); as when the '*Bactrian* Sophi from the horns / Of *Turkish* Crescent' retreats (10: 433–4), Satan's council conducts a 'dark Divan' (457).[55] The narrator reminds us that Mehmed II occupied Byzantium, 'the Sultan in *Bizance, / Turchestan*-born' (11: 395–6); the expanding

Ottoman Empire had conquered Christian Constantinople. Conversely, it is a textbook commonplace to note that Pandaemonium may evoke St Peter's; its magnificence outdoes that of Babylon (1: 717–19), putative birthplace of Antichrist and, to many, a synonym for Rome.[56] When Satan passes through what will become the 'Paradise of Fools,' the anti-Catholic satire becomes overt. Its future inhabitants include 'eremites and friars / White, black and gray, with all their trumpery' (3: 474–5), 'Cowls, hoods, and habits with their wearers tossed / And fluttered into rags, then relics, beads, / Indulgences, dispenses, pardons, bulls, / The sport of winds' (490–3). Antichrist will reign in the last days preceding the Second Coming; in Michael's narrative the emphasis there shifts from clerical fraudulence and simony to institutional corruption and hypocrisy directed by an 'infallible' pope (12: 506–40, at 530), the claim that, for Milton, clinched his identification with Antichrist.[57]

The word 'Antichrist' (or *antichristos*) has several possible meanings, as commentators were quick to note: a false Christ who pretends to imitate him; an opponent to Christ; and one who appears before, or in place of, Christ, anticipating the Second Coming.[58] Milton's epic, understandably, develops most extensively the first two of these. Lambert Daneau charged that it was Antichrist's purpose to 'counterfaite as neere as was possible' Christ by 'craftie couzoning, and deceipt.'[59] In *Paradise Lost* we encounter the false Christ throughout the Hell books in which Satan's actions frequently parody those of Christ himself and of his Old Testament types, Moses and Noah.[60] The parody never allows confusion; the first physical description of Satan links him with Leviathan (1: 200–2), symbol of both Antichrist and the devil.[61] The role of false Christ is represented most pointedly when he commits himself to a mock Incarnation – 'This essence to incarnate and imbrute' (9: 166) – by possessing the serpent, just as later he would possess the 'son of perdition.'[62]

'The true birth of Antichrist,' McGinn writes, 'is inseparable from belief that Jesus of Nazareth, an itinerant Jewish preacher active around 30 C.E., was the messiah.'[63] Jesus becomes Jesus Christ (*Christos,* the anointed one), and the Adversary emerges. In *Paradise Lost* the oppositional role is clearly ordained following day two of the war in Heaven. The Father commands his Son:

> Pursue these sons of Darkness, drive them out
> From all Heav'n 's bounds into the utter Deep:

There let them learn, as likes them, to despise
God and *Messiah* his anointed King.
He said, and on his Son with Rays direct
Shone full; hee all his Father full exprest
Ineffably into his face receiv'd. (6: 715–21)

The ensuing third day's battle, accompanied by 'the great Ensign of *Messiah* blaz'd / Aloft by Angels borne, his Sign in Heav'n' (775–6), is the first public naming of the Messiah. But his future role had been known from the Father's proclamation of the Son's 'begetting,' his exaltation: 'on this holy Hill / Him have anointed, whom ye now behold / At my right hand' (5: 604–6). In constructing this speech from Psalm 2, Milton plainly is aware that Acts 4: 25–7 identifies the begotten Son as Christ, 'thy holy child Jesus,' and the Geneva translation directly substitutes 'Christ.' Milton's own translation of the psalm shifts 'anointed' from verse 2 to verse 6, replacing it with 'Messiah.' From the beginning, his conception of the Son is that of saviour, 'proclaim'd / Messiah King anointed' (5: 663–4), as the narrator tells us. Just what that means fully emerges in the Book 3 dialogue between Father and Son. The Father, good Arminian, reflecting on man's disobedience, gives priority to his love for justice: 'Die hee or Justice must; unless for him / Some other' volunteers to satisfy justice (3: 210–11). The 'Son of God, / In whom the fullness dwells of love divine' (224–5) determines that 'man shall find grace' (227). *Duplex amor Dei.*

Ironically Satan, 'fraught / With envy' (5: 661–2), first speaks aloud the Son's new name to Beelzebub in his equivocal invitation 'to prepare / Fit entertainment to receive our King / The great *Messiah*' (689–91). This is the rare occasion on which Satan directly acknowledges the Son's existence,[64] and that he does so by the epithet 'messiah' is not accidental. When confronted on his apostasy by Abdiel, who refers to the Son by the name 'Messiah' three times (5: 815, 835, 847), Satan scoffs at the notion that the angels were created 'by task transferr'd / From Father to his Son? strange point and new!' (854–5). Instead, in an argument that smacks of atheism, he retorts that they were 'self-begot' and taunts Abdiel to report the rebellion 'to th' anointed King' (870). When the Father anointed the Son, a second begetting occurred: Satan became the Antichrist. His imitation of the future 'greater Man' precedes the rebellion; Satan, 'High on a Hill,' holds court 'In imitation of that Mount whereon / *Messiah* was declar'd in sight of Heav'n' (757, 764–5). It continues in the battle itself, parodying in anticipation the Son's chariot: 'High in the midst exalted as a God, / Th' Apostate in his Sun-bright Chariot sat / Idol of Majesty Divine' (6: 99–101).

Only once can Satan bear to address the Son, and that mediated through the symbol of the sun, 'bright effluence of bright essence increate' (3: 6) or, as the Father says, 'Effulgence of my Glory, Son belov'd / Son in whose face invisible is beheld / Visibly, what by Deity I am' (6: 680–2). Despite his undoubtedly sincere expression of hatred for the sun, he nonetheless responds unconsciously to the priestly office of the Saviour. As Michael will inform Adam, 'to God is no access / Without Mediator' (12: 239–40, which here the Sun 'in figure bears' (241), enabling Satan's confession of guilt, a pointed question-and-answer self-catechism, and, lastly, recognition that his repentance would not be sincere. Before that recognition, however, the examination of his own conscience leads Satan to exhort, 'O then at last relent: is there no place / Left for Repentance, none for Pardon left?' (3: 79–80). Neil Forsyth believes that here Satan addresses not himself but God the Father, who (reprehensibly, it is implied) does not answer:

> As we watch Satan unable to get through to God, there is little question where our sympathies will go. And what is more, we know that God is responsible for Satan's plight . . . Ultimately, as most sensitive readers of the poem recognize, the problem of Satan leads beyond itself to the problem of God. An omniscient and omnipotent God is merely toying with this deviant devil.[65]

Granted, by the concept of God's 'middle knowledge' – his foreknowledge of possible choices of behaviour that will not occur – which Arminius and Milton accepted, the Father would foreknow both Satan's flirtation with a hypothetical repentance and his decision not to repent. Forsyth's rather 'presentist' view (envisioning a God who should be a counsellor or therapist?) still mistakes the meaning of God's Arminian self-limitation and concurrence. As Satan acknowledges, he had 'the same free Will and Power to stand' (66), 'Heav'n's free Love dealt equally to all' (68), and 'against his thy will / Chose freely what it now so justly rues' (71–2). Despite Forsyth's empathic response to the fictive character, free will places responsibility on the one given, not on the giver.

If, at the risk of exposing our insensitivity, we put aside the foreknowledge / predestination conundrum – to my mind, resoluble only by faith and not by reason – the focus of interest in the soliloquy might be the question of whether Satan cannot or will not repent. And, if the latter, why not? Certainly he retains free will; whether, as with humans, it is accompanied by the offer of grace is another matter. Historically, Patrides argued, 'The crucial issue was never whether Satan should be, or could be, redeemed, but whether Divine Love may be limited in any way, even to the extent of Satan's exclusion from Grace.'[66] Arminius, committed to the priority of God's love for justice over his love for his creatures, saw it differently. Angels who transgressed his law could not hope for forgiveness: 'For it was the good pleasure of God to act toward angels according to strict justice, and not [*explicare*] to display all his goodness in bringing them to salvation.' Nor is Christ the mediator for angels.[67] Making his case for universal atonement, John Goodwin first seems to allow an opening, stating that in dying for all men, Christ also died for the reprobates and devils, just not *as* reprobates and devils. Getting down to specifics, however, justice (called 'Honor') reemerges to prohibit 'the Salvation of the Devils'; moreover, their situation differs from that of humans in 'the Devils having desperately apostatized from a far greater light, from a far richer and more sensible experience of the Grace.'[68] George Rust comes closest to fulfilling Patrides's formulation, asserting the persistence of a 'wise and most gracious Providence' in motivating repentance, denying eternal punishment, and in posing the question, 'what difference is there in the distance betwixt a *devil* made an *angel* and an *angel* made a *devil?*'[69] *Paradise Lost* allows the possibility of Satan's redemption through his free choice of the grace providentially accessible through the Son; yet Milton stands with Arminius on the priority of justice and, like Goodwin, makes a sharp distinction between the two acts of apostasy, angelic and human. Only when Satan instigates the Fall is his self-enthralment complete. Then the implicit 'shall' of 'The other none'vanishes; future becomes past tense.

The spectre of a Calvinist God 'merely toying' with Satan rouses Empsonian indignation; however, as is evident, I stand with Stavely in maintaining that Milton's 'universe is not Calvinistic with respect to Satan and Arminian with respect to everyone else.'[70] Yet Satan's point of view does encourage Forsyth's response. John Stachniewski noticed that Milton 'retained important traits of the Calvinist-puritan imagination, in particular its theological and polarizing tendencies,' which Stachniewski saw projected into Satan's psychology.[71] And Satan's psychology, not God's, is the real issue in the soliloquy. Arminius thought the two dangers to assurance of salvation were *desperatio* or despair (no hope) and *securitas* (without care).[72] If the latter is Eve's failing, the former is Satan's. Acknowledging the pride and ambition that led him to rebel, he reasons that 'Heav'n's free love' (68) is now inaccessible and sees no escape from 'Infinite wrath and infinite despair' (74). Vacillating again in this 'Arminian moment of choice and truth,' he recognizes that continued wrong choices will only worsen his condition (76–8), reaches the point of considering repentance, but dismisses the possibility. Because his pride and sense of injured merit ('Disdain') prevent it, God would penetrate any feigned repentance; Satan 'deludes himself with the convenient fiction that God is a grim Calvinist "punisher."'[73] Arminius's comment on apostate angels may be pertinent: 'This fixed obstinacy in evil seems to derive its origin partly from an intuition of the wrath of God and from an evil conscience which springs out of that, and partly from their own wickedness.'[74] In opposition to the Arminian and Miltonic belief (3: 194–7) that it is possible to fall from grace, the Synod of Dort affirmed the irresistibility of grace and the perseverance of the saints: the elect cannot lose that status. In his 'fixed obstinacy,' his exclusion of 'All hope' (105), Satan concludes the soliloquy by shaping himself into a parody of the Calvinist doctrine – the perseverance of the reprobate. Despite his tactical adaptability with force and fraud, Satan's psychological rigidity even disqualifies him from being a Machiavellian prince.

Complacent at his easy deception of Uriel, Satan continues his journey with no inkling that the 'glorious Angel' with his head circled 'Of beaming sunny Rays, a golden tiara,' / 'The same whom *John* saw also in the Sun' (3: 622, 626, 623) offers a less amenable type of Christ and, for himself, a more threatening phase of the workings of providence. Revelation 19: 17 initiated John of Patmos's vision of the destruction of the wicked and the overthrow of the beast (understood to be Antichrist), preliminary to the binding of 'the dragon, that old serpent, which is the Devil, and Satan' (Rev. 20: 2). According to the Geneva Bible gloss, the sun 'signifieth [that] the day of iudgement shalbe cleare and euident so that none shal be hid: for the trumpet that blowe alowde & all that vnderstand it.' The commentators commonly linked the angel standing in the sun with the 'mighty angel' of Revelation 10, 'which was Jesus Christ [that] came to comfort his Church against furious assaltes of Satan and Antichrist.'[75] The angel's position standing in the sun makes 'a cleere token of the ensuing victory: and that the enemies should be destroyed in the sight of the Sun, as surely as we see the

Sun.'[76] Milton connects Satan's two solar episodes, the journey to the sun and the soliloquy to the sun, through a Johannine invocation:

> O for that warning voice, which he who saw
> Th' *Apocalypse*, heard cry to Heav'n aloud,
> Then when the Dragon, put to second rout,
> Came furious down to be reveng'd on men,
> Woe to the inhabitants on earth! (4: 1–5)

The passage echoes Revelation 12: 7–13, verses which not only warn the 'inhabiters of the earth' against the wrath of the devil now come among them, but where a voice from Heaven proclaims, 'Now is come salvation, and strength, and the kingdom of our God, and the power of his Christ.' The casting out of the dragon prophesies the ultimate victory of Christ over Satan, after he has served his purpose in testing the faithful and separating the wicked.[77] As 'a summe of those prophecies, which were written before, but should be fulfilled after the coming of Christ,' Revelation 'liuely set[s] forthe the Diuinitie of Christ, and the testimonies of our redemption . . . the prouidence of God for his elect, and of their glorie and consolation in the day of vengeance . . . [and] The liuelie description of Antichrist . . . whose time and power notwithstanding is limited.'[78] The rudiments of that great warfare have been laid down, and, in rejecting the 'greater Sun,' Satan should have full awareness of the consequences.

When he exits from the poem physically, if not psychically, Satan returns to Hell only to be transformed to a 'monstrous Serpent' (10: 514), 'Now Dragon grown' (529), foreshadowing the binding of the dragon prophesied in Revelation 20,[79] and the end of the reign permitted to both Antichrist and Satan. The imagery of the transformation scene has suggestive affinities with popular woodcuts such as 'The Popes Pyramides' (1624?), in which a giant serpent, poised in a rising spiral crowned with the tiara, supports an intertwined hatch of small snakes (cardinals and monks), 'This hatefull broode, of *Antichrist*' at Rome, as the setting of seven hills littered with ritual paraphernalia confirms.[80] With the end foretold, allusions to Antichrist, accordingly, shift from individual to institutional in Michael's recital of the last days (12: 506–40). Suggestively, on the death of Antichrist tradition divides as to whether he is dispatched by Christ himself or by his agent Michael. In the Protestant interpretation, 'the Lord shall consume with the spirit of his mouth'

(2 Thess. 2: 8) means that Antichrist will be defeated 'with his words' (Geneva gloss), the scripture that is the substance of Michael's narrative.[81]

Coda: Mattins

Happily, the first inhabitants of the earth are by no means such recalcitrant learners. A book later, in an action that significantly contrasts with Satan's abortive effort to repent, Adam and Eve, troubled by Eve's disturbing dream, offer their morning prayer, praising their Creator and petitioning him to disperse any evil, 'as now light dispels the dark' (5: 208). Complexly patterned upon Psalm 148 and the *Book of Common Prayer* themes for morning prayer, this hymn to the Creator seems addressed expressly to the Son of God. At first glance, the setting appears classical: 'Soon as they forth were come to open sight / Of day-spring, and the Sun, who scarse up risen / With wheels yet hov'ring o'er the Ocean brim, / Shot parallel to the earth his dewy ray' (5: 138–41). But the 'day-spring' is Luke's epithet for Jesus Christ – 'the dayspring from on high hath visited us, / to give light to them that sit in darkness' (1: 78–9) – a context that may associate the hovering chariot wheels as much with Ezekiel's vision and with the Son's ascension over the rebel angels as with the chariot of Phoebus Apollo.[82] Whereas Hughes annotates 'Fairest of Stars' (5: 166) with references to Venus, Lucifer, and Hesperus, Revelation 22: 16, 'I am the root and the offspring of David, *and* the bright and morning star,' seems equally relevant. The Geneva Bible comments: 'For Christ is the light [that] giveth light to euerie one [that] commeth into this worlde.' As a result of such thematic cues, Adam's and Eve's apostrophe to the sun,

> Thou Sun, of this great World both Eye and Soul,
> Acknowledge him thy Greater, sound his praise
> In thy eternal course, both when thou climb'st
> And when high Noon hast gain'd, and when thou fall'st (5: 171–4)

comes to encapsulate not only the pattern of providential order, the proper reading of the Book of Nature, and the end of knowledge, but to epitomize the action 'Of Man's First disobedience' and the effort of 'one greater Man' to 'Restore us.' While the bitter events of two high noons are yet to come, already the sun is on the rise.

Appropriately, the coda directs our attention to the subjects of the succeeding chapters. With protagonist and antagonist on stage, the rudiments of the great warfare over God's providence laid down, we progress to the humans over whom the struggle occurs. The poet's epithet, 'our Grand Parents,' captures in a fine pun our mingled response to the first humans: recognition of their original grandeur; the irony that they threw it away before earning a partial recovery; acknowledgment of lineal descent, relation. Chapter 5 begins by considering the relation between Adam and Eve as a pattern, itself expressive of providential design, of creation, separation, trial, and reunion by dialogue. It then examines that relationship through the framing story taken from the Book of Tobit, a germinal text for demonic possession, providential intervention, and chaste marriage. Milton uses the discourse and conventions of possession to inform Eve's dream and temptation; after the Fall, he similarly exploits the concept of exorcism in Eve's recovery. Effectively she performs a self-exorcism through repentance, and renews the broken dialogue with Adam, taking the initial steps to renew their marriage. Despite having chosen wrongly in crucial trials, she learns, perseveres, and responds admirably to the next in her sequence of providences, emerging as the hero of Book 10.

Chapter Five

Possessing Eve: Tobias and Sarah in Eden

> I hold that the Devil doth really possess some men.[1]
>
> Sir Thomas Browne

> The domestic arrangements of such a woman as filled the capacious mind of the poet, resemble, if I may say so without profaneness, those of Providence, whose under-agent she is.[2]
>
> Hannah More

Reflecting on the Book of Tobit, Søren Kierkegaard wrote: 'If a poet read this story and were to use it, I wager a hundred to one that he would make everything center on the young Tobias. The heroic courage to be willing to risk his life in such obvious danger . . . would be the subject. I venture to propose another . . . Sarah is the heroic character.'[3] His expectation is illustrated effectively by a sixteenth-century woodcut. Reversing the visual convention in which the angel leads Tobias, the artist's design has a resolute (if diminutive) Tobias, fish in hand, confidently leading Raphael (fig. 7).[4] But John Milton is the exceptional poet on whom Kierkegaard would have lost money. Possibly a common sense of scripture caused them to respond to Tobit in similar ways. The form of the story itself is instructive. It begins with Tobit's Job-like afflictions, gains narrative momentum with the preparation for Tobias's journey, and comes to life in the picaresque adventure of chapter 6, with the wedding preparations of chapter 7 building suspense for the impending climax. Were one to imagine a film adaptation of Tobit, chapter 6 would provide the nucleus for a road movie: the adventure of the giant fish, the young man learning about life from his good-

Figure 7. Tobias and the angel Raphael, woodcut printer's mark of Francesco Bindoni and Maffeo Pasini. This example from Bernardino Ochino, *Prediche predicate*, Venice, 1541. Photo by Charles Robb.

natured, older friend, always accompanied by the photogenic dog (much as Renaissance artists saw it); and then all stops out for the battle with the demon and satisfying romantic rescue of the haunted girl. Yet the Tobit narrative itself frustrates the expected climax. Asmodeus is efficiently expelled in the first three verses and chapter 8 is dominated by two prayers: in the first Tobias and Sarah pray that their marriage may be blessed (4–8) and in the second, on hearing that Tobias is alive, Sarah's father Raguel thanks God (15–17). As in Kierkegaard's analysis, and indeed in *Paradise Lost,* the struggle within matters more than the exterior battle.

Creating Souls: Separation and Reunion

Before we look at Milton's understanding of the Book of Tobit, it will be useful to consider more fundamentally the question of the relation between Adam and Eve. A pattern of action radically embedded in *Paradise Lost* as one of the poem's archetypes can be thus described:

a male being generates from his own material substance by physical separation, parthenogenesis, a new being who is either actually or by implication feminine. Following the separation into two persons, the new creature undergoes a period of trial, after which a reunion, spiritual rather than physical, is achieved through dialogue. This pattern of creation, separation, trial, and reunion through dialogue bears a distant but suggestive resemblance to the more general one envisioned by Arminius: God creates out of his goodness; humans separate spiritually by falling into sin; God's love makes reunion possible through belief and faith.[5] Both theologian and poet present a virtual blueprint of providential design.

The first of these actions occurs beyond the poem, before time, with the generation of the Son. Milton's commitment to a theory of creation *de Deo* has strict logical consequences: 'For Milton nothing can come from nothing, everything is made from matter produced from God . . . the Son, like all things, was created out of God.'[6] I am, of course, stretching a figurative point in implying that the Son is 'feminine.' Even before the Incarnation, however, he exemplifies all the qualities – patience, forgiveness, mercy, love, self-sacrifice – that characterize Christian values and which, in our culture, traditionally have been gendered as feminine.[7] In the purposefully advanced epic chronology, we enter the Son's story not at the beginning, but 'into the midst of things,' at the dialogue, where, in the last and greatest stage of trial, the Father asks, 'Which of ye will be mortal to redeem / Man's mortal crime'? (3: 214–15); and the Son replies, 'Behold mee then, mee for him, life for life, / I offer, on mee let thine anger fall; / Account mee man' (3: 236–8).[8] In honouring the perfect verbal harmony of Father and Son, the angelic choir summarizes the earlier acts, first celebrating the Son's origin, 'of all Creation first, / Begotten Son' (3: 383–4), and then his previously earned merit, the Father 'Heav'n of Heavens and all the Powers therein / By thee created, and by thee threw down / Th' aspiring Dominations' (3: 390–2).

The narrative technique and content of the dialogue in Heaven seem familiar because the reader already has encountered them darkly, as photographic negative precedes the glossy positive, in the demonic parody of the Sin and Death episode. Sin there tells the story of her own origin, the first creation of evil, during the assembly to plot rebellion in Heaven: 'thy head flames thick and fast / Threw forth, till on the left side op'ning wide, / Likest to thee in shape and count'nance bright, / Then shining heav'nly fair, a Goddess arm'd / Out of thy head I sprang' (2: 754–8). The shared substance of father and daughter is proclaimed by the likeness of Sin's appearance to Satan's, a similarity mimicking that of the Son to the Father: 'Divine Similitude, / In whose conspicuous count'nance, without cloud / Made visible, th' Almighty Father shines' (3: 384–6). Sin recounts her own deeds of demerit, the creation of Death and her participation in the 'loss and rout' of war, a trial process now completed by disobedience in her charge to keep the Gates of Hell closed. The dialogue concludes in perfect amity and unity of purpose between father and daughter.

The adduced parallels between Sin and the Son may seem specious because Sin is an allegorical being and the Son, at least for the Christian believer, is not, but, from creation through actions, Sin does not behave like a personified abstraction. Samuel Johnson long ago put his finger on the difficulty: 'To give [allegorical persons] any real employment, or to ascribe to them any material agency, is to make them allegorical no longer, but to shock the mind by ascribing effects to non-entity.'[9] Isabel MacCaffrey once answered Johnson by asserting, 'Milton's "abstractions" are always substances,'[10] which is exactly the point. As the Son 'Substantially express'd' in him 'all his Father' (3: 140, 139), so Sin substantially expresses Satan, thereby darkly rehearsing the revelation of Book 3. For the reader, at this stage in the poem, Sin and Death have the same ontological status as the other spirit entities.[11]

The third and central creation by separation also has occurred before the character enters the poem. Eve's first words acknowledge her relation to Adam, 'from whom I was form'd flesh of thy flesh' (4: 441). She recalls his plea when at first sight she turned away from him: 'of him thou art, / His flesh, his bone; to give thee being I lent / Out of my side to thee, nearest my heart / Substantial Life' (4: 482–5), an appeal climaxing with 'Part of my Soul I seek thee' (487). The last receives confirmation in Adam's grateful prediction to his Creator, 'And they shall be one Flesh, one Heart, one Soul' (8: 499). In Adam's speech Milton transforms Genesis 2: 23–4, which culminates 'and they shall be one flesh,' with his own generous addition of 'one Heart, one Soul.'[12] Rather than metaphor, Adam's 'one Soul' or, as 4: 487 more exactly states it, 'Part of my Soul' is a quite literal statement of Milton's traducianism.[13]

The heresy originated with Tertullian, who believed that the soul was material and, contrary to the orthodox 'creationist' view that God creates each soul individually, hypothesized that God created only one soul, Adam's, from whom all others descend. Tertullian 'allow[s] that there are two kinds of seed – that of the body and that of the soul' – while insisting that 'they are inseparable, and therefore contemporaneous and simultaneous in origin' through the generative act.[14] Reflecting on Eve's creation, he observes, 'her flesh was for a long time without specific form (such as she afterward assumed when taken out of Adam's side); but she was even then herself a living being, because I should regard her at that time in soul as even a portion of Adam.'[15] Martin Luther's sense of human sinfulness caused him to reject the church's creationist doctrine and embrace traducianism, investing it with important authority for a number of Protestants.[16] However much disputed, the Ockham's razor of traducianism neatly disposes of two thorny problems raised by the individual creation theory (the justice of original sin and the need for infant baptism),[17] and might be seen as spiritualizing the sex act, which Tertullian defends in a prosaic anticipation of Milton's 'Hail Wedded Love' (4: 750–70).[18]

The poet's interpretation effectively harmonizes the two Genesis accounts of Adam's and Eve's creations, the narrative of 2: 15–25 and the declarative of 1: 27, 'So God created man in his *own* image, in the image of God created he him; male and female created he them.' There is no contradiction or mystery between 'created he him' and 'created he them' because they are one and the same. Satan's reaction to his first sight of humans confirms this miracle; they are creatures 'whom my thoughts pursue / With wonder, and could love, so lively shines / *In them Divine resemblance*, and such grace / The hand that form'd them on thir shape hath pour'd' (4: 362–5, italics added). The testimony of the Adversary is difficult to refute.

The physical separation is compensated by the spiritual reunion through dialogue. The first human words that we hear in Eden are Adam's to Eve, which, in their easy command of complex rhetorical figures,[19] abundantly demonstrate the eloquence that is his birthright: 'Sole partner and sole part of all these joys, / Dearer thyself than all' (4: 411–12). Whether one understands 'Sole . . . sole' as paronomasia (pun) or as antanaclasis (repetition with a different meaning), the sole / soul homonym is activated; and the polyptoton (repetition in a different form) of 'partner . . . part' gives an expanded definition of their relationship: one soul. In contrast to the solipsism of Satan's preceding soliloquy with its sixteen first-person pronouns (I, mine, my, me), Adam's 'thyself' is the first of three second-person pronouns; the speech contains ten plurals (us, our), but no first-person singulars. Eve responds in kind: 'O thou for whom / And from whom I was form'd flesh of thy flesh, / And without whom am to no end' (4: 440–2).

Theirs is only the first of the many dialogues with which the Eden books abound. Dialogue was the preeminent humanist literary form during the Renaissance, and, despite Walter Ong's announcement of its decline, remained a vehicle for the expression of complex or disputable ideas well into the eighteenth century.[20] After the introduction of Raphael in Book 5, Milton presents speeches that evoke a virtual epic catalogue of dialogue types: philosophic, theological, political, scientific, astronomical, and amatory. At this initial stage the dialogue between the first humans is simply – to borrow a phrase from Stefano Guazzo – civil conversation, animating the poet's conviction that 'a meet and happy conversation' is 'the chiefest and the noblest end of marriage' (*CPW* 2: 246), but already the antiprovidential agent that will so try them has been introduced.

The Book of Tobit: Marriage and Possession

The innocent, spoken harmony of Adam and Eve must be tested, pro and con, by two speakers who are locked in absolute opposition and whom Milton wishes us to see through a particular lens. As Satan enters Eden, he responds to the 'Native perfumes' of the air:

> So entertain'd those odorous sweets the Fiend
> Who came thir bane, though with them better pleas'd
> Than *Asmodeus* with the fishy fume,
> That drove him, though enamor'd, from the Spouse
> Of *Tobit*'s Son, and with a vengeance sent
> From *Media* post to *Egypt*, there fast bound. (4: 166–71)

When God the Father responds 'With pity' to the morning prayer of the troubled couple, 'to him call'd / *Raphael*, the sociable Spirit, that deign'd / To travel with *Tobias*, and secur'd / His marriage with the seven-times-wedded Maid' (5: 220–3). The reader is prompted to understand the action of the Eden books through the prism of the Book of Tobit.[21] The stories of the righteous, but blinded, Tobit and the virgin Sarah, whose seven bridegrooms were murdered by the demon Asmodeus (Asmodai), are interwoven when they simultaneously pray to God for relief. The Lord responds with mercy and sends Raphael, who, in human guise, accompanies Tobias (Tobiah) on the journey to Media to collect a debt owed to his father. The picaresque adventures of the two travellers, to say nothing of the dog, begin with the giant fish that attacks Tobias and which he overcomes with the encouragement of Raphael, who then instructs him in its medicinal properties. The angel advises Tobias to visit his kinsman Raguel, Sarah's father, and claim her for his wife, explaining how to thwart the demon by burning the fish's entrails in the bridal chamber. All this is accomplished, the debt collected, and they bring Sarah home to Nineveh in triumph.

Both imaginatively engaging and exegetically inviting,[22] the tale enjoyed a long popular success. Jerome translated the Hebrew for the Vulgate; Caxton's translation of *The Golden Legend* (1484) made the story available in English;[23] Tobias and the Angel became a favourite subject for Renaissance painters, among them Botticelli, Titian, and, perhaps inevitably, the angel's namesake Raphael (*The Madonna of the Fish*). A number of Northern artists made series of illustrations; Rembrandt was sufficiently fascinated with Tobit that he drew, etched, or painted over fifty scenes from the story.[24] Milton undoubtedly first encountered Tobit in the family's Geneva Bible; later he may have studied the Hebrew text edited and translated into Latin by Paul Fagius, whom he cites approvingly as 'one so learned and so eminent in *England* once.'[25]

Tobias's dog and the fish easily became figures for faithfulness and baptism; the binding of the demon was understood as a type of Satan's binding at the end of the temporal order; the story established Raphael's identity as a guardian angel, healer, protector of travellers, pilgrims, and the innocent young.[26] His closing revelation that, although to Tobias he appeared to eat and drink, this was an illusion (chap. 12: 19) was accepted by many authorities as proof angels cannot eat and digest.[27] The materialist Milton appears to have considered this declaration and consciously reversed it, expressing his disdain through the narrator: 'to thir viands fell, not seemingly / The Angel, nor in mist, the common gloss / Of Theologians' (5: 434–6). To Adam's hesitant dinner invitation, *his* Raphael responds with a robust affirmation: 'Wonder not then, what God for you saw good / If I refuse not, but convert, as you, / To proper substance' (5: 491–3). The commentators read the story as a demonstration of divine providence from beginning to end – marvelling at the economy of the Lord's response to the simultaneous prayers of Tobit and Sarah in chapter 3 ('Nota hic miram Dei erga suos fideles providentiam') and the wisdom of the dying Tobit's advice to his son in chapter 14 ('Ubi nota miram Dei erga Tobiam providentiam').[28] Milton concentrated this perspective in Raphael, underscoring his role as an agent of extraordinary providence by making him a type of Jesus

Christ. 'A *Phoenix*, gaz'd by all' (5: 272),[29] who looks 'Like *Maia's* son' (285), born of a mortal mother and immortal father, he appears enveloped in the Son's solar brightness, 'another Morn / Ris'n on mid-noon' (310–11). The angel's greeting to Eve, '*Hail*,' used 'Long after to blest *Mary*, second *Eve*' (385, 387) anticipates the judgment on the serpent, 'this Oracle, then verified / When *Jesus*, son of *Mary* second *Eve*, / Saw Satan fall' (10: 182–4). Moreover, because the Son is the only other character to merit the salutation (3: 412), it foreshadows Eve's redemptive role, the heroic potential that Kierkegaard saw in Sarah.

Sarah is like Eve in her virginity, but the parallel would seem to falter on the circumstance of her seven marriages, however unconsummated. Here, nonetheless, might be evidence for inferring that Milton read the Hebrew text (or a faithful Latin translation). When Tobias first responds doubtfully to Raphael's matchmaking, the angel assures him, 'And do not *fear for she is appointed for you from the six days of creation*' (6: 16).[30] The numerical symmetry between the divine week of creation and the total of murdered consorts is hard to ignore. Asmodeus, like Satan, seeks to destroy the entire creation that was perfected only with the creation of humans.

The Book of Tobit overtly invites readers to accept Tobias and Sarah as a type of the first marriage ordained in Genesis. Having expelled the demon, Tobias asks his bride to join him in prayer to their God:

> And you created Adam first [and] gave to him Eve his wife. And so you established the way for the whole world in its entirety. And you said, 'It is not good for Adam to be alone; I shall make for him a helpmeet.' And now, O Lord my God, not because of lust do I take this young woman, but to establish your word which (is) true, merciful, and gracious. (chap. 8: 6–7)

Acting on this broad cue, a number of medieval marriage services direct the communicants to accept Tobias and Sarah as a model. The *Sarum Missal* (Salisbury), for example, appeals to God to bless and protect the young couple: 'sicut misisti sanctum angelum tuum raphaelem ad tobiam et saram filiam raguelis.'[31] The first *Book of Common Prayer* (1549) retains this prayer almost word for word: 'And as thou diddest sende thy Aungell Raphaell, to Thobie, and Sara the daughter of Raguel, to their great comfort: so vouchsafe to send thy blessing vpon these thy seruauntes.'[32] Tobias's denial that his desire to wed is motivated by lust led to the assumption that theirs particularly exemplified a chaste marriage. The Vulgate amplifies this with the specification that

Figure 8. Rembrandt Harmensz van Rijn, *The Wedding Night of Tobias and Sarah* (formerly called *Tobias and Sarah Praying*), drawing, 17.5 x 23.8 cm, ca. 1640–9. Asmodeus vanishes left as Raguel prays outside the door. The Metropolitan Museum of Art / Art Resource, NY.

the pair passed three nights of prayerful abstinence; in Caxton's version, Raphael advises Tobias to 'be thou continent by the space of three days from her, and thou shalt do nothing but be in prayers with her,' which restraint the couple duly observe.[33] In the standard marriage ritual established from the twelfth century, 'The ceremony at the church door was generally concluded with the prayer of Toby . . . Moreover, in certain liturgies the priest recommended that the couple practice the three nights of sexual abstinence attributed to Tobias.'[34] Rembrandt's drawing of Tobias and Sarah absorbed in devout prayer well captures the theme of 'conjugal chastity' (fig. 8).[35] To the left the demon vanishes 'unnoticed by the young couple,' now as irrelevant as Satan, who 'unminded slunk / Into the woods' (10: 332–3), although not until their own joint prayer will Eve and Adam renew their conjugal chastity.

It seems beyond question that Milton was aware that Tobias and Sarah were types of Adam and Eve in their marriage. The introduction of '*Raphael,* the sociable Spirit, that deign'd / To travel with *Tobias*' (5: 221–2) follows directly the description of Adam and Eve at work in the Garden: 'wed[ding]' Vine to Elm, 'she spous'd about him twines / Her marriageable arms, and with her brings / Her dow'r th' adopted Clusters' (5: 216–18). Their gardening is an image of their own relationship,[36] and in the recital of Raphael's credentials – 'secur'd / His marriage with the seven-times wedded Maid' (5: 222–3) – the primary sense of 'secure' (to render safe, protect, guard against danger) overtakes the ostensible, but secondary, sense (obtain, establish). Adam speculates accurately that Satan's 'first design' might be to 'disturb / Conjugal love,' which 'excites his envy' (9: 261–4). Whereas with Tobias and Sarah, Raphael's mission was both to protect and to institute their marriage on the model of the first couple, here it is to protect that marriage from danger without and within. *De Doctrina Christiana* (*CPW* 6: 355–81), one recalls, places marriage within the special providence governing humans, and the angelic embodiment of that providence fittingly appears in its defence. Raphael's salutation 'Hail' bestowed on Eve not only acknowledges her status as the 'first Mary' (5: 385–7; also 10: 183), but it reveals his awareness that the first marriage could be at risk by the sullying of her chastity.

Again, it is tempting to infer that Milton responds to details of the Hebrew, in which Tobias's 'soul fell in love with her, the young woman, before he saw her' (6: 18) and they meet and speak even before he enters her father's house. Both couples exemplify the concept that 'the purest and most sacred end of matrimony' is 'a cheerfull and agreeable conversation' (*CPW* 2: 248). By framing the Eden books with allusions to Tobit and by interposing Raphael as the guardian angel, Milton makes the stakes clear: not only does Satan want to disrupt the idyllic first marriage, but like Asmodeus 'enamor'd [with] the Spouse' (*PL* 4: 169), he intends to murder Adam and replace him. Satan is Eve's demon lover.[37]

Demonic possession, considered strictly, exists only within the fallen world, when the fallen angels became devils, 'wand'ring o'er the Earth, / Through God's high sufferance for the trial of man' (1: 365–6). With the exception of Saul, whose troublesome evil spirit was exorcised by David's music (1 Sam. 16, 14–23), the phenomenon of possession preoccupies the New Testament: 'Exorcism is, strikingly, among Jesus's favorite miracles in the synoptic accounts of Mark, Matthew, and Luke.'[38] Asmodeus himself was thought to be head of the fourth order of angels, 'a potent Throne,' who ingloriously loses his first encounter with Raphael (6: 361–8), eventually ending as a cautionary example in the

Malleus Maleficarum.[39] As with the allusions to classical mythology and to later biblical exemplars, Milton uses the postlapsarian type to illuminate its original for our fallen understanding.

We long have been aware that, in the episode of Eve's dream, Milton exploits the conventions of witchcraft and demonic dreams:

> The demonic attempt to corrupt the phantasy, the choice of woman as the weaker and more vulnerable instrument, the apparition as an angel of light, the diabolical illusion and the nocturnal flight 'up to the clouds' are all conventional features of witchcraft as Weyer and other demonologists had presented them.[40]

Milton certainly knew witchcraft, as also is made evident by the comparison of Sin, about to make an ungodly compact with her father-lover, to 'the Night-Hag, when call'd / In secret, riding through the Air she comes / Lur'd with the smell of infant blood, to dance / With *Lapland* witches' (2: 662–5). Yet these features of Eve's dream, equally, are characteristics of demonic possession, the conventions of which were so familiar that Shakespeare and Jonson found material for comic turns in them.[41]

The dream is presented both externally, in Satan's discovery by the guardian angels Ithuriel and Zephon, and internally, through Eve's narration of the experience. As William B. Hunter has noted, Satan's twofold purpose, 'to reach/ The Organs of her Fancy,' and 'forge / Illusions' or to 'taint / Th' animal spirits' and raise 'discontented thoughts,' has a single end, 'ingend'ring pride' (4: 801–9).[42] His image when found, 'Squat like a Toad, close at the ear of *Eve*' (4: 800) evokes, first, the toad's association as a demonic familiar, and, second, a perversion of the Annunciation, the representation of which, long conventional in religious art, has the Virgin impregnated with the words of the angel entering her ear.[43] Pride is Satan's own besetting sin and the anti-Word with which he attempts to impregnate Eve's mind. The process is represented in corporeal allegory by a fifteenth-century Italian fresco, in which Satan simultaneously devours one sinner and gives birth to another, who is labelled 'Superbia' (pride).[44] Most pertinently here, penetration through the ear was a familiar means by which demons entered the bodies of women.[45]

Eve's narration of her dream begins with a 'gentle voice' that she identifies as Adam's, calling her 'forth to walk' (5: 36, 37), not alarming in itself, except insofar as, after their discussion of moon and starlight

(4: 657–88), her reason might reject the claim that 'Heav'n wakes with all his eyes, / Whom to behold but thee' (5: 44–5). When she finds, not Adam, but 'One shap'd and wing'd like one of those from Heav'n / By us oft seen; his dewy locks distill'd / *Ambrosia*' (5: 55–7), it introduces a profoundly ambivalent dimension. One of Carlo Ginzburg's *benandanti,* Paolo Gasparutto, testified that he was visited by 'The angel of God': 'an angel appeared before me, all made of gold, like those on altars, and he called me, and my spirit went out.'[46] Although Gasparutto thought he was summoned to battle against the forces of darkness, his inquisitor was convinced that the herald was a demon.

Eve's angel tastes the forbidden fruit, then turns to persuade her to do the same. His speech is an incantation, a tissue of repeated words, phrases, and rhythms, designed to induce a state of trance.[47] Eve imagines that the angel 'Even to my mouth of that same fruit held part / Which he had pluckt' (5: 83–4). The construction suggests that Satan invites Eve to share, not just apples from the same branch, but the same fruit she has seen him taste, a blasphemous parody of her relationship to Adam; rather than a soul shared with her consort, Eve would, like Sin, become a part of Satan's substance. Absent reason, her appetite is aroused, and 'I, methought, / Could not but taste' (5: 85–6). The element of foreshadowing here suggests the power of prophecy, again a common attribute of demonic possession.[48]

What follows is literally an ecstasy, an out-of-body experience and a levitation – 'up to the Clouds / With him I flew . . . wond'ring at my flight and change / To this high exaltation' (5: 86–7, 89–90). Levitation was a phenomenon experienced by numerous saints both male and female, most famously by St Teresa of Avila, who referred to it as a 'rapture.' Eve's 'exaltation' conveys a similar sense of being uplifted, whether physically or by the soul's separation from body, as Teresa thought. Nonetheless, flying was not without its malign practitioners, notably Simon Magus, 'the messenger of the devil,' who astonished all Rome with his flights until Peter's appeal to Jesus Christ caused his fall.[49] Nor should we forget the aeronaut Satan, who similarly falls while Jesus is upborn by angels 'As on a floating couch through the blithe air' (*PR* 4: 541–91). Like these two, the exalted Eve suffers her inevitable fall: 'suddenly / My Guide was gone,' absent in more than one sense, the reader may add, 'and I, methought, sunk down / And fell asleep' (5: 90–2). The conclusion of her narrative conforms to the convention (modelled upon Mark 9: 26–7) of a possessed woman 'falling as if dead, [before] a return to consciousness.'[50] Eve's alarmed reaction to her dream is entirely justified. At the Last Supper Jesus identifies his betrayer by giving Judas Iscariot the sop of bread, 'And after the sop Satan entered into him' (John 13: 27), which the Geneva Bible annotates, 'Satan toke ful possession of him.' Providence can work in frightening ways to achieve its benevolent end.

With Eve, having read the framing account, we know the precise moment at which God's providence intervenes to arrest the spurious guide. When the guardian angels discovered Satan 'close at the ear of *Eve* / Assaying by his Devilish art to reach / Organs of her Fancy' (4: 800–2), Ithuriel touched him with his spear:

> up he starts,
> Discover'd and surpris'd. As when a spark
> Lights on a heap of nitrous Powder, laid
> Fit for the Tun some Magazin to store
> Against a rumor'd War, the Smutty grain
> With sudden blaze diffus'd, inflames the Air:
> So started up in his own shape the Fiend. (4: 813–19)

One gloss on the epic simile is provided by the exorcism of Nicole Tavenier of Reims (1590s):

> Tavenier and several priests were in a room together when a trail of gunpowder appeared on the floor before them, blowing up and leaving a foul odor. This they took to signify outwardly the departure of the devil from Tavenier's body in a sort of spontaneous exorcism, with the result that Tavenier was no longer able to speak in 'fine discourses and high conceptions.'[51]

Because, as Adam urges, Reason has retired 'Into her private Cell' (5: 109), leaving only Fancy awake, providence frustrates this first attempt to suborn Eve. In the next trial she must depend on her own resources.

The first and only literal act of possession in Milton's poetic history occurs when Satan selects the serpent as 'Fit Vessel, fittest Imp of fraud, in whom / To enter, and his dark suggestions hide' (9: 89–90). Lest there be any confusion, the narrator describes and names precisely the process: 'in at his Mouth / Th' Devil enter'd, and his brutal sense, / In heart or head, *possessing* soon inspir'd / With act intelligential' (9: 187–90, italics added). The mouth was the entrance to the victim's body most frequently used by demons.[52] Stuart Clark has observed,

'It was often argued that demonic possession was modeled on the incarnation, with the devil attempting to debase humanity, as much as Christ had elevated it, by clothing himself in its form.'[53] As he invents the act of possession, so Satan conceives the rationale, parodying the Son's sublime mercy: 'O foul descent! . . . now constrain'd / Into a Beast, and mixt with bestial slime, / This essence to incarnate and imbrute' (9: 163, 164–6).

In ironic juxtaposition, as Satan unites himself to serpent, Eve proposes to Adam, 'Let us divide our labors' (9: 214), raising the possibility that the dream successfully instilled in her mind the desire for individual perfection. Tantalizingly, she offers separation as 'what to my mind first thoughts present' (213). First thoughts that morning? First thoughts on the task of gardening? Or, possibly, first independent thoughts since the terrifying, yet exhilarating, experience of the dream? In the course of defining a character possessed with a single idea (like Eve at this point in the poem) as a 'demonic agent,' Angus Fletcher has reminded us that, etymologically, a demon is one who divides.[54] Eve's dismissal of human dialogue as 'casual discourse' (223) in its distance from the pre-dream ideal 'With thee conversing I forget all time' (4: 639) confirms that separation already has occurred. Addressing her as 'Sole *Eve*, Associate sole' (*ad*: join to, *socius*: companion, with the expected sole / soul homonym), Adam reminds her of the divinely ordained matrimonial imperative, but already it is too late. The discourse in this scene is 'casual' (*casualis*: by chance) because there is no real communication; they speak on two different tracks, as examination of their logic has shown.[55]

Arminius defined the two threats to perseverance in grace as *desperatio* and *securitas,* of which the latter, a false sense of security, is the greater danger. Adam learned enough about their enemy to diagnose his state of mind as 'Despairing' and 'Hopeless' (9: 255, 259), and rightly fears that Eve has fallen into the other trap of overconfidence or carelessness. God had instructed Raphael to 'warn [Adam] to beware / He swerve not too secure' (5: 237–8), and, increasingly concerned, Adam urges the lesson on Eve. Convinced she is impervious to fraud (9: 285), she scoffs at the possibility that they are not made 'secure to single or combin'd' (339). Adam corrects, explaining they are 'secure / Secure from outward force'; yet fraud is a different matter, for 'within [her]self / The danger lies' (347–9). She is not listening, so he concedes defeat. The failure of dialogue drives him to reluctant deference to her argument, 'But if thou think, trial unsought may find / Us both securer than thus warn'd thou seem'st' (370–1), and to the 'fervent' illogic of commanding her to 'Go' (372). As Keith Stanglin summarizes Arminius, 'To fail to have a care for something that deserves care is the essence of carelessness or *securitas*.'[56] In very different ways, both Adam and Eve now are guilty of being 'without care.' Although he cares passionately about Eve, abdicating his responsibility in response to her 'swerving' leaves her completely insecure.

It would be difficult to miss the signs that Satan's temptation of Eve is represented as a seduction, an enactment of the 'Serenate, which the starv'd Lover sings / To his proud fair' (4: 769–70); the question is one of assigning proper weight to them. Half a century ago, Arnold Stein conceded, 'The scattered hints of Satan's sexual rivalry for Eve seem deliberate enough, but they are never allowed to become more than hints, a useful small contribution to the drama.'[57] More recently, viewing the epic through the tradition of European Petrarchism, William Kerrigan and Gordon Braden give seduction a central place.[58] Certainly the angels express themselves through sexuality, whether unfallen as Raphael testifies (8: 620–9) or fallen as Satan's primal response to Sin reveals (2: 761–7). Satan's reproach to Belial in *Paradise Regained* confirms Milton shared the assumption that demons were capable of sex with women: 'thou with thy lusty crew / . . . / Cast wanton eyes on the daughters of men, / And coupl'd with them, and begot a race' (*PR* 2: 178, 180–1).[59] The erotically charged sight of how Eve, gazing at Adam 'with eyes / Of conjugal attraction unreprov'd, / And meek surrender, half imbracing lean'd / On our first Father, half her swelling Breast / Naked met his under the flowing Gold / Of her loose tresses hid' (4: 492–7) and how Adam responds with urgent 'kisses pure,' moves Satan expressly to sexual jealousy: 'fierce desire, / Among our other torments not the least, / Still unfulfill'd with pain of longing pines' (509–11). When he encounters Eve alone, 'Such Pleasure took the Serpent to behold / This Flow'ry Plat, the sweet recess of *Eve*' (9: 455–6), landscape and anatomy fuse in his open voyeurism.[60] 'The rebel angels,' Kerrigan and Braden aptly comment, 'have been cursed with the frustration of Petrarchan love.'[61]

If alleviation of that unfulfilled fierce desire is one of Satan's intentions, why does he not succeed? From rapt to rape is only a single letter, an impulse. Adam's immediate reaction, in fact, is to think (9: 901, 'deflow'r'd') that he has succeeded. In the short answer, Eve's prophylactic is her pure beauty, 'her Heav'nly form / Angelic, but more soft, and Feminine, / Her graceful Innocence' (9: 457–9), which 'overaw'd /

His Malice,' rendering him 'Stupidly good' (460–1, 464). Satan's awed and stunned (*stupidus*) reaction parallels, and makes more sympathetic, the transport that overthrows Adam's authority and reason (8: 529–59), as the direct verbal echo ('transported,' 9: 474) reminds us. Here the effect causes a neat reversal of motive – the ravisher ravished: 'with rapine sweet bereav'd / His fierceness of the fierce intent it brought' (461–2). The polyptoton of 'fierceness' and 'fierce' seems designed to recall that initial 'fierce desire,' implicitly defining the intention as sexual. When Satan recovers himself, this is redefined as 'Fierce hate' (471) and the possibility of sexual pleasure renounced: '[nor] hope here to taste / Of pleasure, but all pleasure to destroy, / Save what is in destroying, other joy / To me is lost' (476–9). Adam was wrong in thinking that Nature had bestowed too much 'outward show' upon Eve; her beauty serves a providential purpose, as the poet intimates by 'pleasure not for [Satan] ordain'd' (470). Like Asmodeus, Satan can murder, but he cannot satisfy his sexual desire.

Still, the bedrock of starved frustration invests his Petrarchan serenade, 'show of Love well feign'd' (492), with a convincing sincerity; rethinking his goals and tactics leads to a strategic sacrifice that is spectacularly successful, shifting the object of fascination from himself to the tree. Satan conducts Eve to a setting (626–30) that the classically minded reader will recognize as a *locus amoenus,* a pastoral site for erotic encounters;[62] here, by his bait-and-switch manoeuvre, the 'Tree / Of prohibition' becomes the seductive love object. Eve forgets the purpose of the tree, that 'pledge or memorial of obedience' (*CPW* 6: 352). The sophistry, rhetorical manipulation, and outright lies of Satan's speeches to Eve, 'his words replete with guile' (733), have been well analysed. More relevant is the way in which Eve's two soliloquies, the first nominally addressed to the fruit and the second an apostrophe to the tree, echo Satan's logic, language, and thoughts. Like Satan, she considers secondary, rather than primary, causes, omits or dismisses logical adjuncts, and relies on such devices as enthymeme, equivocation, and rhetorical question.[63]

Milton employs a distinctive device to show the isolation consequent on the act of separation – soliloquy in the presence of another being.[64] Eve's speech addressed to the 'best of Fruits' (9: 745–80), in which she decides to taste its delights, is spoken in the presence of the Serpent/ Satan, but clearly labelled soliloquy, 'thus to herself she mus'd' (744). Similarly, Adam's reaction to the news of Eve's transgression, although cast as direct address, 'O fairest of Creation,' and intimately personal (thou, thee, and thy throughout), causing the hasty reader to understand it as audible dialogue, nonetheless is an interior monologue: 'First to himself he inward silence broke' (9: 895). Only when he has made his own decision does he speak aloud, 'his Words to *Eve* he turn'd' (920). The speech act in each instance signals the spiritual isolation, reinforcing what we learn from the words themselves: each time the decision to disobey the prohibition is made for individual selfish reasons. Eve has absorbed Satan's spiritual isolation ('I perhaps am secret'), his ambition ('for inferior who is free?'), even his sexual jealousy ('A death to think'). In brief, she now speaks like Satan.[65]

One of the essential conventions of behaviour by which possession could be diagnosed was – like the Serpent possessed by Satan – speaking in an unfamiliar language or inappropriate voice. 'From [the demonic's] mouth would come the voices of demons, emitting obscene and blasphemous ravings, or talking fluently in foreign languages previously unknown to the victim'; the phenomenon of 'speaking in altered voices' most notably took the form of 'female demonics speaking as their male demons.'[66] Adam has not heard the voice of Satan, but can guess what has taken place: 'some cursed fraud / Of Enemy hath beguil'd thee, yet unknown' (9: 904–5). His immediate decision to join her, despite recognizing the sin, seems a debased expression of traducianism: 'Our State cannot be sever'd, for we are one, / One Flesh' (958–9). No longer one soul in his faulty perception, merely one flesh. Eve, feigning humility in the face of Adam's sacrifice, gives lip service to her subordination, lamenting, 'but short / Of thy perfection, how shall I attain' (963–4), and weeps tenderly at his 'ennobl'd' love. She is more accurate in the oblique recognition that 'One heart, one Soul in both' (967) has been transformed to 'one Guilt, one Crime' (971). At this point beyond any semblance of dialogue, they revert – as did Satan and Sin – to a parody of their original, material unity, coupling to become literally one flesh as 'in Lust they burn' (1015).

Exorcism

At this point it seems necessary to digress on the subject of exorcism, a matter of intense controversy in the early modern era. The Reformation created a number of litmus-test issues, of which this was one:

> Until well into the seventeenth century there was a predictable division along religious lines, for the mainline Protestants ... were generally hostile

> to the practice of exorcism. As time passed a number of sectarian groups, drawing on the biblical precedents for casting out devils, developed their own versions of these practices, but it was the Catholics who initially saw possession as an ideal opening to demonstrate that the heavenly force was with them. The corporeal power of relics, holy words, consecrated hosts and their like, exemplified in these dramatic circumstances, was to be a living refutation of Protestant claims that these were mere shams.[67]

Robin Briggs concludes, 'There were some unseemly contests in places where both confessions had a foothold.' Some such 'unseemly contests' occurred in Germany, where the Lutheran willingness to allow the exorcism rite to remain a part of baptism was bitterly opposed by Calvinists.[68] In France, over a sixty-year span, Catholic hardliners used exorcism as a political weapon against the Huguenots, staging as highly theatrical spectacles public exorcisms of possessed women, thereby demonstrating to the chagrin of Protestants the church's monopoly over miracles.[69] The extremism caused Jean Bodin to remonstrate, 'It is remarkable, the exorcisms which many resort to, since the holy prophets never practiced them: they abhorred questioning or asking anything of Satan, or doing anything he commanded . . . we read that people did nothing but pray to God to cast out demons.'[70] As Bodin's critics were quick to point out, such views placed him perilously near the Protestant position, which insisted on the efficacy of prayer and repentance. The extreme distance between these positions was moderated somewhat by the post-Tridentine reforms of the *Rituale Romanum* (1614), which set more stringent controls on exorcism, sensibly requiring that the exorcist carefully distinguish genuine possession from disease or mental disorder.[71]

In his musing on Tobit, Kierkegaard marvelled at the strength of Sarah's character: 'For what love for God it takes to be willing to let oneself be healed when from the very beginning one in all innocence has been botched . . . What faith in God that she would not in the very next moment hate the man to whom she owed everything!'[72] Milton, approaching Tobit as a foundational text on demonic possession, may have worked through a different set of preliminaries to arrive at a similar perception of character. How is a demon exorcised or, the preferred Protestant term, dispossessed? Melanchthon advised invoking the name of Christ and preaching on the Last Judgment; Pierre Viret affirmed that Jesus Christ is the only true exorcist.[73] Prayer and fasting, on the authority of Matthew 17: 20–1, were frequently urged remedies.

As keen as James I was on exposing fraudulent possessions, he still acknowledged that genuine cases existed and believed prayer was the appropriate response.[74] In other words, certainly no holy water, communion wafers, chrism, and priest performing magic. When Shakespeare's Lafew remarks, 'They say miracles are past' (*All's Well*, 2.iii.1), he speaks of Protestants. For them dispossession is achieved by prayer, repentance, and following the example of Christ. At the conclusion of *Paradise Regained*, the angelic choir celebrates the victorious Son of God and warns Satan:

> . . . hee all unarm'd
> Shall chase thee with the terror of his voice
> From thy Demoniac holds, possession foul,
> Thee and thy Legions, yelling they shall fly,
> And beg to hide them in a herd of Swine,
> Lest he command them down into the deep,
> Bound, and to torment sent before thir time. (*PR* 4: 626–32)

In *Paradise Lost* the only suggestion of an exorcism occurs following another physical separation so wrenching that Milton tactfully elides it. After the Book 10 judgment scene, Satan's return to Hell and the journey of Sin and Death to the world 'bridge' (in both senses) to the solitary Adam's despairing soliloquy. Eve, who is within sight but not voice, sitting 'Desolate' (*desolatus*: left alone, forsaken), beholds his affliction and approaches, only to be repulsed. His 'Out of my sight, thou Serpent' (10: 867) sounds very like a homespun version of a familiar ritual. The final exorcism of the *Rituale Romanum,* for example, begins: 'Therefore now depart, seducer depart. Your abode is the wilderness. Your habitation is the serpent, be humbled and prostrate.'[75] Undoubtedly Adam now does regard Eve as a demon: 'nothing wants, but that thy shape, / Like his, and color Serpentine may show / Thy inward fraud' (869–71). Here, in what might be her most severe trial, the temptation would be strongest for Eve to, in Kierkegaard's phrase, 'hate the man to whom she owed everything,' but she resists it.

Eve's superior strength of character had been twice demonstrated in Book 9, with the separation scene and again with the trial of love she set for Adam; now, however, that strength is directed positively. The situation inversely duplicates that in the separation scene. In both Adam commands her to 'go'; whereas in the first she obeys against his wishes, here she disobeys – also against his wishes, yet more truly obedient than Adam in his 'fierce passion' (865) can understand. Although Eve decided wrongly in the trial of the separation and in the temptation, nonetheless 'a failed effort is never the end of the story, but is another "providence" to be judged and incorporated into the plans for a next step.'[76] This time her gesture of repentance and humility speaks volumes: 'with Tears that ceas'd not flowing, / And tresses all disorder'd, at his feet / fell humble, and imbracing them, besought / His peace' (910–13). As with the tears of 'sweet remorse' that Eve shed and 'wip'd them with her hair' (5: 130–5) after her narration of the dream, unmistakably here the prototype is that of Mary Magdalene, the repentant sinner of Luke 7: 36–50, who 'stood at [Jesus's] feet behind *him* weeping, and began to wash his feet with tears, and did wipe *them* with the hairs of her head, and kissed his feet, and anointed *them* with the ointment' (7: 38). The image is an arresting one, made independently famous in religious art and in such baroque poetry as Crashaw's 'The Weeper,' which concludes with the tears' own assertion that 'we goe to meet a worthier object, *Our Lords* feet.'

Eve's immediate inspiration, however, can only be the example of the Son's humility and love. After passing judgment, he pitied them and 'disdain'd not to begin / Thenceforth the form of servant to assume, / As when he wash'd his servants' feet, so now' he clothed their nakedness (10: 213–15). Eve, then, expresses sincere contrition, which she has come to understand through a perception of Christian behaviour. Even more distinctly her verbal appeal reveals her spiritual strength in her offer to do what Adam confessed he could not (831–6) and bear all the guilt herself:

> And to the place of judgment will return,
> There with my cries importune Heaven, that all
> The sentence from thy head remov'd may light
> On me, sole cause to thee of all this woe,
> Mee mee only just object of his ire. (10: 932–6)

The repetitions of 'me' in both of their speeches evoke, for the reader, the Son's words (3: 236–41) when he volunteers to sacrifice himself that humans might be redeemed: 'Eve offers herself as a redeemer, and however inadequate she is to fulfil that role, her attempt mirrors the redemptive actions of the Son.'[77] More emphatically Joseph Wittreich declares: 'If before the Fall Adam gives life to Eve, after the Fall it is Eve who gives life to Adam, who redeems him and history and restores Paradise to both.'[78] As Kierkegaard intuited about Sarah, in Milton's rewriting of the Tobit story, Eve is 'the heroic character.'

Eve's heartfelt remorse and newly learned selflessness continue to parallel Mary Magdalene's conduct with the same result. Jesus commends 'this woman, [who] hath not ceased to kiss my feet,' proclaiming, 'Her sins, which are many, are forgiven, for she loved much.' To Mary herself he said, 'Thy faith hath saved thee; go in peace' (Luke 7: 45, 47, 50), an absolution echoed when Adam 'with peaceful words uprais'd her' (10: 946).[79] That the focus of the trial has shifted from Eve to Adam is indicated by textual, rather than scriptural, echo. The description 'as one disarm'd, his anger all he lost' (945) reprises Satan's stunned response to Eve's innocent beauty, 'of enmity disarm'd' (9: 465), gauging the depth of Adam's hostility. But, whereas Satan quickly resumes his fierce hatred, Adam does not. He, too, chooses rightly, groping toward the rudiments of Christian charity in renewing their marriage.

Luke, chapter 7, does not name Mary Magdalene; she is described only as 'a woman in the city, which was a sinner' (37); the traditional identification arises from plausible sequence.[80] The following chapter describes Jesus preaching in cities and villages, accompanied by his disciples 'and certain women, which had been healed of evil spirits and infirmities, Mary called Magdalene, out of whom went seven devils . . . and many others, which ministered unto him of their substance' (8: 2–3). The numerical symmetry of the seven devils irresistibly takes us back to Sarah's murdered bridegrooms. The image of the repentant Magdalene is that of a dispossessed woman, freed like Sarah of her demon lover, like Eve of the venom with which Satan had tainted her spirits. Unlike Sarah and Mary, Eve has managed to dispossess herself, and her altered style of speech suggests how. Armando Maggi insists, 'The ritual of exorcism is first and foremost a dialogic performance involving two idioms and two names, God's and the devil's.'[81] Eve no longer speaks in Satan's idiom, but, from the lesson of the judgment,[82] has taught herself the Son's idiom. She remembers. Later in the poem, after Michael's instruction, Adam comes to acknowledge Jesus Christ as 'my Redeemer ever blest' (12: 573); Eve has, in a sense, anticipated him.

With their reconciliation, the marriage resumes in mutual solace (10: 958–61),[83] as once again Adam and Eve speak in genuine dialogue. Eve's proposal of abstinence 'From Love's due Rites, Nuptial embraces sweet' (994) seems to imply a reversal; in her urgency to restore the first marriage, the chaste type of Tobias and Sarah becomes a model.

Whether this and her alternative suggestion of suicide mark the limits of her reason and faith or are 'brilliantly calculated' to lead Adam to a better understanding,[84] unquestionably they serve that end. A Renaissance rhetorician might recognize the process here as argument *in utramque partem* (on both sides of the question). Eve first proposed that she return to the place of judgment and pray to bear all the guilt (932–6); Adam had replied that he would do it, only it would not be granted (953–7). Now, prodded to reflect more deeply on the implications of the judgment, he perceives the right course of action, not solitary but dialogic prayer, and, in so doing, unknowingly echoes the divine dialogue (3: 191–5): 'How much more, if we pray him, will his ear / Be open, and his heart to pity incline, / And teach us further' (10: 1060–2). When both Adam and Eve shift their idioms from the devil's to God's, they communicate as one. The two voices are as distinct as their personalities, but unified in the divine idiom and in their recovered ability to reason together. Advancing from the trials of their individual providences, they again can act as one. They have fulfilled the pattern ordained by Father and Son in progressing from generation to separation, trial, and reunion through dialogue, thus becoming anew one soul.

In using the Book of Tobit as an implicit template for the central books of the poem and elaborating his conception through the rich lore of demonic possession and exorcism, Milton surely was aware that Tobit is itself framed by a narrative that he necessarily ignored: Tobit's affliction with blindness (chap. 2) and his miraculous cure when Tobias, at the instruction of Raphael, anoints his eyes with the fish's gall and his vision is restored (chap. 11). Good Protestant that he was, Milton knew that the age of miracles was past. He courteously provided a history of his symptoms to be given to a distinguished Parisian oculist, lest he seem to refuse providential aid, but was calmly resigned to accept that his was 'a case quite incurable':

> What should prevent one from resting likewise in the belief that his eyesight lies not in his eyes alone, but enough for all purposes in God's leading and providence? Verily, while only He looks out for me and provides for me, as He doth, leading me and leading me forth as with His hand through my whole life, I shall willingly, since it has seemed good to Him, have given my eyes their long holiday.[85]

Directed by his own providence, Milton therefore prays not for restored eyesight but for inward illumination, 'that I may see and tell /

Of things invisible to mortal sight' (3: 55–6). Who can doubt that he saw the children of his imagination as clearly as father Tobit saw Tobias and Sarah?[86]

In the poem's strategically rearranged presentation of the Last Things, the reader encounters in order Hell, Heaven, Judgment (the first foreshadowing the last) and, ever more insistently in the later books, death. Whereas Book 10 concludes with Adam and Eve abstractly puzzling out the relation between judgment and death, Book 11 confronts Adam with the reality of death for his offspring. Chapter 6 will examine in depth Adam's initial brief encounter with death in the vision of Abel's murder. Consideration of two oddities in the description, the weapon and the wound by which Cain dispatches his brother, leads into contemporary medical discourse and theory; the presentation of Abel and Cain as types of Jesus and Judas; and controversy over the soul in the blood. The last requires an account of Milton's mortalism, the 'heresy' complementing the traducianism discussed at the outset of this chapter 5.[87] The mortalism is consistent with the poem's conception of death as a gracious remedy for the human condition, a providential dispensation that Adam cannot yet comprehend. First he must resist his despairing reaction to the presence of death through a sequence of trials before he can learn its place in the larger providential design.

Chapter Six

Murder One: Blood, Soul, and Mortalism

> . . . if *Cain* were the first man born, with him entred not only the act, but the first power of murther; for before that time neither could the Serpent nor *Adam* destroy *Eve,* nor *Adam* and *Eve* each other.[1]
>
> Sir Thomas Browne

> These two Brothers did type out, or fore-run all the acting betweene man and man, from that time to this; being a plaine declaration of that darknesse, into which Mankind is falne.[2]
>
> Gerrard Winstanley

In the Book of Tobit after Tobias expels Asmodeus with the fishy fume, the demon flees to Egypt where he is bound by Raphael in a type of the binding of 'the dragon, that old serpent, which is the Devil, and Satan' (Rev. 20: 2). From the omniscient view of God the Father this is all one, but not so in human time. The human poet, lamenting the absence of the 'warning voice, which he who saw / Th' *Apocalypse,* heard cry in Heav'n aloud' (*PL* 4: 1–2; Rev. 12: 10–12), fills that void with *his* Raphael, still knowing that the Apocalypse presents the 'image of a high and stately Tragedy' (*CPW* 1: 815). Adam and Eve must face the consequences of their disobedience: 'From that day mortal, and this happy State / Shalt lose, expell'd from hence into a World / Of woe and sorrow' (8: 331–3). Before their expulsion and deaths, they must comprehend the 'woe and sorrow' that they bring into this world. It begins with the first instance of divine concurrence in the postlapsarian world; God limits himself from impinging on Cain's free will in his response to the trial of sacrifice.

At eighteen lines the first vision of that future 'woe and sorrow,' the death of Abel, is very concisely presented, yet powerfully evocative. Satan's motive of jealousy or envy has descended to the first-born human, causing a 'rage' not unlike the dragon's 'great wrath' (Rev. 12: 12); as the Geneva Bible notes, the dragon 'burneth with furie' (gloss on 20: 3). Cain's actions are equally and familiarly Satanic-cum-Machiavellian tactics, force and fraud. The Geneva gloss to Genesis 4: 5, following Calvin, highlights the fraud in his rejected sacrifice: 'Because he was an hypocrite and offered onely for an outwarde shew without sinceritie of heart.' The force, Sir Thomas Browne's 'power of murther,' is brutal, literally primitive. In one significant respect, however, Milton's account of that act is eccentric: 'Whereat hee inly rag'd, and as they talk'd, / Smote him into the Midriff with a stone / That beat out life; he fell, and deadly pale / Groan'd out his Soul with gushing blood effus'd' (11: 444–7).

Three decades ago, Roland M. Frye called attention to the crux: 'I cannot explain why Milton chose to describe the murder in terms that are at once so bizarre and so inherently improbable, but he did not haphazardly introduce such details and there must be a richness of meaning here which I have been unable to discover.'[3] Genesis 4: 8, 'Cain rose up against Abel, his brother and slew him,' specifies neither the murder weapon nor the fatal wound, but a well-defined iconographic tradition had supplied the deficiencies. Cain strikes Abel's head with a wooden club, an animal bone (most frequently the jaw-bone of an ass), or, more rarely, a farming implement.[4] Alternatively, the weapon of choice sometimes became a stone.

Golda Werman claims that 'Cain's use of a stone as a murder weapon is peculiar to Jewish sources,' pointing particularly to the Midrash *Pirkei de-Rabbi Eliezer,* which 'notes that Abel is hit in the forehead with a stone.'[5] She perhaps exaggerates in so narrowing the origins of this invention. Much more immediately pertinent would be the example of Cowley's *Davideis:* 'I saw him fling the *stone,* as if he meant, / At once his *Murder,* and his *Monument*' (I, st. 16, 3–4). What the couplet occludes, Cowley's textual note makes clear; on common-sense grounds, he has selected the same target as that favoured by the Midrashim. In the absence of scriptural directive, 'I had the Liberty to choose that which I thought most probable; which is, that he knockt him on the head with some great stone, which was one of the first ordinary and most natural weapons of *Anger.*'[6] The confluence of minority traditions in commentaries, art, and poetry argues that Milton surely was aware that Abel might have died by stoning, but his particular conception – a traumatic blow to the diaphragm with a stone, causing massive hemorrhage – is virtually unprecedented. Frye finds it puzzling on two counts: first, the impracticality ('It would be hard to find a less efficient method for killing a man'), and, second, the significance of the deviation from tradition.

The first point is the more easily discounted. Renaissance physicians and anatomists still viewed the body as a hierarchy; the diaphragm or 'midriff' performed a crucial division or linkage between lower and higher. In a 1616 lecture William Harvey asserted, 'In so far as it is the partition between the bellies its use is to divide the noble from the ignoble, the vital from the natural and the inferior from the superior parts of the body.'[7] In this Harvey is at one with such contemporaries as Helkiah Crooke, who attributes the value distinctions to Plato and Aristotle.[8] Like Harvey, who noted the 'very great sensitivity' of the diaphragm, most medical practitioners were conscious of its vulnerability. The *Treasury of Health* (1550?) advises that 'A wounde in the braynes, hert, midrife . . . or lyuer is deadly' (Aiii). John Woodall, Harvey's colleague at St Bartholomew's and Master of the Barber-Surgeons Company, defined a wound, broadly, as 'a recent solution of continuitie,'and then distinguished puncture wounds from contusions, 'when a weighty thing offending (as timber) falling downe or violently cast downe (as a stone), the flesh being bruised and broken.' In his experience,

> If the great Veynes and Arteries in the Breast be offended, an immoderate flux of blood, defection of virtue in all the faculties, a cold and an vnsaourie sweat doth ensue, and death within a few houres.
>
> The solution of continuitie in the sinowie parts of the *Diaphragma* causeth convulsion, difficile respiration, an acute feuor, rauing, and death.[9]

It appears unlikely, then, that Milton's contemporaries would have found an inherent improbability in the fatal wound that he describes. Indeed, in the first printed commentary on this episode, Patrick Hume observed, 'Our Author has followed the most probable Opinion, that Cain killed his Brother with a blow on the Breast with a great Stone . . . that beat the Breath out of his Body.'[10]

Allowing that a ruptured diaphragm and a cracked skull could render Abel equally dead still does not explain why Milton might have wanted to choose the former. Milton's retelling of sacred history is deeply informed by Augustine's vision of the temporal order and by a Protestant conception of typology, emphasizing Old Testament prefigurations of Jesus Christ; together these give shape and meaning to Books 11 and 12.[11] It seems reasonable, therefore, to consider Milton's handling of the Cain and Abel episode as the first movement in this scheme. Gilbert Cope remarked that 'Abel, the good shepherd who makes an acceptable sacrifice, and who is then put to death, clearly can be thought of as a type of the Shepherd-Priest who is also the Lamb of God: in the same way Cain can be thought of as pre-figuring Judas Iscariot.'[12] Browne, contemplating the alpha and omega of 'the holy line' culminating in Jesus Christ, explains that the Saviour 'was mystically slain in *Abel*.'[13] Gerrard Winstanley shared his belief in the typology, but gave it a less mystical, more immediate application: 'that Abel of old was but a type of Christ, that is now rising up to restore all things from bondage.'[14] The story appears to have taken on extraordinary emotional resonance during the 1640s. To the Ranter Abiezer Coppe it proved a direct continuity of shed blood, 'from the blood of righteous *Abell*, to the blood of the last Levellers that were shot to death.'[15] The very name Cain was a byword for political tyranny, class oppression, and the evil of primogeniture.[16] Millenarians were inclined to identify Cain with Antichrist; as one said, 'Antichrist was in Cain before Christ was in Abel.'[17]

The direct typology of figures paralleling Abel with Jesus and Cain with Judas was particularly strong in traditions of popular iconography – through the woodblock prints of the *biblia pauperum*, the *bibles moralisées*, and in manuscript illuminations of virtues and vices.[18] An illustration of temperance and wrath, for example, pairs Jesus, the Lamb of God, with Abel, struck dead by Cain.[19] One remarkably illuminated, moralized bible, Codex Vindobonensis 2554, although double-columned, follows the typical format of biblical text and image above and, immediately below, the commentary text and image. For Genesis 4: 8 the biblical text states, 'Here Cain kisses his brother in betrayal and says to him: Come play with me in the fields, and he does so, and kills him in betrayal.' The image (fig. 9), in simultaneous narrative, represents in the left background of the roundel the fraternal kiss as the two emerge from a portal; in the right foreground, Cain strikes down Abel with a grub hoe. Below, the commentary text explains, 'That Cain kissed his brother in betrayal signifies Judas who kissed Jesus Christ in betrayal and had Him delivered over to death on the Cross.'[20] The parallel commentary roundel illustrates the Judas kiss, left, and, right, two executioners on ladders, fastening Jesus to the cross.

In writing an episode that is presented as a vision, not surprisingly, Milton seems directly conscious of the visual tradition. Genesis 4: 4

Figure 9. Detail from Codex Vindobonensis 2554. In the upper roundel Cain kisses and kills Abel, the type of the lower roundel, in which Judas kisses Jesus, betraying him to death. Österreichische Nationalbibliothek, Vienna. Cod. 2554, fol. 2v.

does not say how the Lord indicated approval of Abel's sacrifice. 'His Offr'ing soon propitious Fire from Heav'n / Consum'd with nimble glance, and grateful stream' (11: 441–2), however, follows the pictorial convention of the descending fiery column.[21] Milton's Abel is a 'Shepherd . . . / More meek' (436–7), an obviously typological description; he sacrifices 'On the cleft Wood' (440), an altar evocative of the cross on which Jesus would die. Contrastingly, Cain's presentation as 'A sweaty Reaper' (434) both highlights his fallen condition (cf. Gen. 3: 19) and foreshadows, in Marvellian fashion, his role of death-bringer.[22] To account for the failure of Cain's sacrifice, Milton draws upon two lines of commentary.[23] Not only is the offering itself scant (435–6); in common with Protestant authorities – and probably marked by his childhood reading of the Geneva Bible – Milton finds Cain's motive suspect, 'for his was not sincere' (443). The presentations of both characters are entirely consistent with those in the tradition of the moralized and typological illustrations.

Interpreting Abel as a type of himself was authorized by Jesus, who cited Abel as the first prophet whose righteous blood has been shed upon the earth (Matt. 23: 34–5; Luke 11: 50–1). The Lord's rebuke to Cain, 'the voice of thy brother's blood crieth unto me from the ground' (Gen. 4: 10), thus becomes a prophecy of the Eucharist.[24] The New Testament offers two versions of the death of Judas. In Matthew 27: 5, he hangs himself, providing the exemplar for suicides who have despaired at their alienation from God,[25] but in Acts 1: 18, Judas 'purchased a field with the reward of iniquity; and falling headlong, he burst asunder in the midst, and all his bowels gushed out.'[26] Reading backwards, from truth to shadowy type, suggests that Milton has devised a parallel between the deaths to reinforce the typological relation. The manner of Judas's death, 'burst asunder in the midst,' becomes retribution for the fatal blow that Cain, the first Judas, inflicted on his brother, 'Sm[iting] him into the Midriff with a stone' (11: 445). The parallelism extends to the field, described by the commentators as barren,[27] into which Cain led Abel and from which God hears Abel's blood crying out, and the god-forsaken 'field of blood' (Acts 1: 19) where Judas died. Hyam Meccaby observes, 'The graphic picture of Judas's blood and entrails spilling on to the raw earth of an open field evokes the story of Cain and Abel.'[28] Within the poem this evocation is reversed. Nonetheless, the typology embedded in Milton's presentation of the first murder is thoroughly traditional, serving as a reassurance that even here providence is working. A more challenging aspect of the description takes us into the arena of contemporary biblical and providential science.

Blood and Soul

The linkage of Genesis and Acts by blood throws into relief another unconventional aspect of Milton's narrative: 'he fell, and deadly pale / Groan'd out his Soul with gushing blood effus'd' (11: 446–7).[29] As Abel groans, his soul departs in the effusion of blood; in other words, his soul is in the blood. Mosaic law forbade the eating of blood, 'For the life of the flesh *is* in the blood' (Lev. 17: 11), which in the Vulgate reads 'quia anima carnis in sanguine est.' *Anima* in this sense probably means no more than 'vital principle,' justifying the Geneva and King James translations as 'life,' but it was difficult for Latinate Englishmen not to see *anima* as 'soul,' as it had been in the Wycliffe and Coverdale translations. Expounding Colossians 1: 14, 'In whom we have redemption through his blood,' John Donne poses the question, 'Is effusion of bloud the way of peace?' He notes that 'bloud being ordinarily received to be *sedes animae,* the seat and residence of the soule; The soule, for which, that expiation was to be, could not be better represented, nor purified, then in the state, and seat of the soule, in bloud.' Donne reflects on the progression from Law, with the blood sacrifice of animals, to Grace, with the sacrifice of Christ's blood, concluding, 'So all bloud is his; no nor his, as the bloud of all the Martyrs was his bloud, (which is a neare relation and consanguinity) but his so, as it was the precious bloud of his body, the seat of his soule, the matter of his spirits, the knot of his life.'[30] For Donne, plainly *anima* means more than life force; blood is the location of the soul itself.

In Renaissance philosophy and physiology, to say the soul is in the blood meant something precise, stemming from the traditional faculty psychology of three souls – vegetative, sensitive (or organic), and intellective. The last, consisting of intellect, will, and conceptual memory, constituted the rational powers, whereas the sensitive soul encompassed the perceptual and motive faculties.[31] The entire body is animated by *spiritus,* a subtle vapour or exhalation generated from blood and distributed through the body by it. Marsilio Ficino, both physician and philosopher, described the indeterminacy of this 'first instrument' of the soul: 'Spirit is a very tenuous body, as if now it were soul and not body, and now body and not soul.'[32] Donne concisely summarized this doctrine of an infinitely refined intermediary between body and soul in a famous stanza of 'The Extasie': 'As our blood labours to beget / Spirits, as like soules as it can, / Because such fingers need to knit / That subtile knot, which makes us man' (61–4).[33] In philosophical and theological discourse, the argument that the sensitive soul existed throughout the human body, in each and every part thereof, was expressed in a venerable Latin tag – '*tota in toto et tota in qualibet parte corporis.*'[34] By the 1640s Richard Overton only could express his impatience with the ubiquitous topos, grumbling that, if we ask where the soul is, 'They *flap* us i'th mouth with a *Ridle, tota in toto, & tota in qualibet parte,* the whole in the whole, and the whole in every part.'[35]

During the sixteenth and seventeenth centuries both theology and natural philosophy tended to simplify explanations and to make them increasingly materialistic. Amid the general collapsing of distinctions, 'a small but growing number of philosophers . . . described the organic soul as material . . . and identified it with *spiritus*.'[36] Even more radically, one could simplify and materialize by eliminating the sensitive soul and identifying the intellective soul with *spiritus*. *Paradise Lost* goes far in this direction with Raphael's tutorial speeches,[37] explaining to Adam and Eve that 'Your bodies may at last turn all to spirit' (5: 497) and describing the sexual embrace of angels in language that plays allusively on the Latin formula: 'Total they mix' (8: 627), *tota in toto;* 'and obstacle find none / Of membrane, joint, or limb' (8: 624–5), *tota in qualibet parte corporis.*[38] But, if Milton could imagine bodies of spirit, Thomas Hobbes went in the opposite direction. In *Leviathan* (1651), he restored the suspect translation of *anima*, '*Eate not the Bloud, for the Bloud is the Soule,* that is, *the Life*' (Deut. 12: 23), using it to maintain that the soul cannot be a '*Substance Incorporeall*.'[39]

As John Henry has commented, 'By the seventeenth century, there was a tradition, well established in spite of its potentially heretical nature, which tended to identify souls with medical concepts of "spirit." '[40] The confused assessments of *spiritus* or 'soul' in the blood provide the background to contemporary controversies over Harvey's discovery of the circulation of the blood. In the mid-1960s, Christopher Hill argued that this event generated a number of radical political and religious consequences, for Harvey and others, aligning circulation of the blood with both mortalism and republicanism. His essay provoked a furious rebuttal from Gweneth Whitteridge, defending Harvey's consistent royalism, itself leading to a more measured, but unabashed, response from Hill.[41] One historian of science, in conversation, characterized the debate as 'proving that Hill knows nothing about Harvey, and that Whitteridge has no imagination.' Initially, Hill had argued that *De motu cordis* (1628) celebrates the heart in expressly monarchial terms, but *De circulatione sanguinis* (1649) and *De generatione animalium* (1651) 'dethrone the heart,' instead bearing an implication that 'can only be described as republican.'[42] In the face of Whitteridge's strictures, Hill gives some ground, and specifies that the central issue is less what Harvey thought than the reception of his discovery by contemporaries.

The drive to simplify concepts of the soul was not restricted to theology and philosophy but affected medical theory, as well:

> The rejection by many Protestants of the learned tradition, now seen as Catholic, the emphasis on personal reading of the scriptures, which so

> often led to personal interpretation, the preference for the Old Testament in place of the *ethnicae* authorities, led [Robert] Fludd, as it seems to have led his Protestant contemporary Daniel Sennert (at Wittenberg), to abandon the complex of Greek philosophical ideas about soul, *anima,* or *psyche* . . . In place of the Platonic or Aristotelian *psyche,* Fludd and Sennert saw the soul in Old Testament terms as the blood.[43]

Accordingly, Fludd, in the heat of the weapon-salve controversy, reviewed all the biblical texts pertaining to blood, concluding in an echo of Donne's sermon a decade before, 'The Blood is the seate of the Soule or vitall Spirit.'[44] So also Jean Baptiste van Helmont, who asserts, 'We therefore who have the like humanity, its no wonder if we contain Blood and a Spirit of a co-like Unity; and that the action of the Blood is merely spiritual: Yea therefore in *Genesis,* it is not called by the Etymology of *Blood* but is made remarkable by the name of a *Red Spirit.*'[45] Fludd, a member of the College of Physicians who heard Harvey's lectures and witnessed his demonstrations, was the first person to approve in print Harvey's theory of circulation with his *Medicina catholica* (Frankfurt, 1629). Five years before Harvey, he had reached the same concept from his reading of Psalm 19: 4–6, 'he set a tabernacle for the sun, / which *is* as a bridegroom coming out of his chamber, *and* rejoiceth as a strong man to run a race. / His going forth *is* from the end of the heaven, and his circuit unto the ends of it.'[46] In the microcosm of man, the sun is the heart; Fludd, however, focuses not on the organ per se, but on its function, the activity of running a circuit from end to end. Allen Debus explains, 'As early as 1617, we find that Fludd's primary concern is not with an anatomical study of the heart, but rather with the blood which has the all-important function of carrying the spirit of the Lord to all parts of the body.'[47] Van Helmont's similar understanding of scriptural authority for the soul in the blood caused him to oppose Harvey on the practice of blood-letting because of its deleterious consequences to the soul.[48]

Roger French has insisted that people in the mid-seventeenth century tended to accept or reject Harvey's doctrines, not on some objective standard of verification, but by whether they could be used to confirm their own visions of reality.[49] This can be demonstrated strikingly by two poems, both of which celebrate the circulation of the blood. Henry More, the Cambridge Platonist, was a determined opponent of mortalism, having written *Antipsychopannychia, or . . . a Confutation of the Sleep of the Soul after Death,* as the third book of his Spenserian *Psychozoia, or the Life of the Soul* (1642). In principle an avowed dualist, More's own pneumatology, expressed both in the poems and in his philosophical treatises, including *The Immortality of the Soul* (1659), contains inconsistencies and confusions resulting from his positions in controversies with, on the one hand, Descartes and, on the other, Hobbes.[50] On mortalism, however, he does not waver. A necessary correlative of his opposition to mortalism can be seen in his contemptuous dismissal of the belief that he calls 'Holenmerian':

> The other Mound of Darkness laid upon the nature of a *Spirit*, is by those who willingly indeed acknowledge that *Spirits* are *somewhere;* but add further, that they are not only entirely or totally in their whole *Ubi* or place, (in the most general sense of the word) but are totally in every part or point thereof, and describe the peculiar nature of a *Spirit* to be such, that it must be *Totus in toto & totus in qualibet sui parte.*[51]

More's Latin poem, CIRCULATIO SANGUINIS, *Ad celeberrimum Medicum G. HARVAEUM Inventorem,* although not published until 1679, may have been written as early as 1651.[52] So closely does the poem follow a sequence of proofs from *De motu cordis,* that More must have had it before him as he wrote. He describes the effect of blood-letting (*De motu cordis,* chap. 11), significantly, with no adverse comment on the procedure (ll. 59–62). In the most telling omission, the poem is completely devoid of biblical allusion. More celebrates Harvey's achievement, first through the time-honoured analogy of microcosm to macrocosm: as our ancestors have charted the orbits of the heavens, so Harvey teaches us the circuits of blood in silent dance throughout the body (ll. 1–15). The second verse paragraph shifts from macrocosm to geocosm: the course of blood through the body to the heart is like the subterranean rivers of the world leading to the ocean (1l. 16–32).[53] More carefully has avoided any possible association of blood with the soul, thereby purifying Harvey's work from the taint of mortalism.

John Collop, the quirky and highly independent physician, published his *Poesis Rediviva* in 1655, revealing a lively interest in his colleagues and in the state of his profession. There are two dozen poems praising or blaming individual doctors, on aspects of physiology, and disapproving various practices. Collop's admiration for Harvey is unstinting: 'Thou set'st up sail, swim'st through the purple flood, / Which blush'd before, 'cause never understood. / Thou circlest through our *Microcosm,* and we / Learn more then th' world, our selvs, new worlds by thee' ('On Doctor Harvey,' 13–16); and he responds immediately to the publication of *De generatione animalium* (1651), but through his own vision. Although he satirizes van Helmont and his disciple Noah Biggs, Collop shares their biblical belief that the soul is in the blood, and he 'borrows phrases' from Biggs's *The Vanity of the Craft of Physick* (1651) 'in almost every one of the medical poems.'[54] Thus, Collop's 'Of the Blood,' standing in sharp contrast to More's poem, presents a curious amalgam of Harvey and Biggs:

> Sure in these purple streams the Sun doth glide,
> And in his Crimson Chariot blushing ride,
> While he doth circle through the lesser world,
> Through veins of earth in strange *Meanders* curl'd.
> Now in a full tide channels doth disdain,
> Flows into flesh, and then ebbs back again.
> Thus blood, Sun-like, gives motion, life and sense,
> Spirit, and innate heat are nought from hence.
> Distinct from Blood, who can the Soul ought call;
> 'Tis all in every part, and all in all. (3–12)

The soul-in-body topos, which Collop also quotes in 'On the Soul' (l. 29: 'Th' soul's all in all, and all in every part'), probably comes directly from Harvey's *De generatione animalium*:

> And lastly, the *blood* doth so surround, and pierce into the whole body, and impart *heat* and *life* to all its *parts,* that the *soul* may justly be counted resident in it, and for his sake, *Tota in tota & tota in qualibet parte,* to be all in *all,* and all in every *part* (as the old saying is).[55]

The beginning of Collop's poem echoes Biggs, 'According to Scripture, the *soul* or *vital* strength, rides in the Chariot of the bloud' (*Vanity,* 139–40), whereas the ending, 'Gods Tabernacle thus plac'd in the Sun, / That Giant races must with th' whole world run' (ll. 39–40), envelopes Harvey in the mystically medical reading of Psalm 19, with the 'tabernacle for the sun' and the 'strong man to run a race.'[56] Consistent with this, in two poems against phlebotomy, he sides with Biggs, who follows van Helmont in denouncing blood-letting on the biblical authority that blood is 'the seat . . . chamber and magazine of life' and, consequently, phlebotomy will result in 'the fall or losse to the whole ocean of strength' (*Vanity,* 162).

However selective his understanding, Collop could well have taken the value assigned to blood directly from Harvey, who wrote that blood '*like a Tutelar Deity, is the very soul in the body.*'[57] D.P. Walker once observed that 'by the time we have finished reading the *De Generatione Animalium,* we realize that something very odd has happened. The spirits are indeed gone; but blood has not only taken their place, it has also taken over all their functions, including sensation, and has acquired their divine and celestial nature.'[58] Christopher Hill may have been right in maintaining that, even with Harvey, the distinction between 'the soul is in the blood' and 'the soul is the blood' is not always as clear as it might be. Contrary to what Browne conceded was 'the general scandal of my Profession,' pious physicians and haematologists turned from Genesis to the anatomy table and found only evidence of divine providence.

Descending from this heady mixture of scripture and physiology to biblical legend, we might pause at the apocryphal *Life of Adam and Eve.* The first couple are well settled in postlapsarian domestic life when the author attributes to Eve a dream more horrific than the one she has in Milton's epic: 'And Eve said to Adam, My lord, while I was asleep I saw a vision. The blood of our son Abel was in Cain's hand, and he was gulping it down with his mouth. I am worried by it.'[59] The implication of the dream is clear; the Satanic Cain drinks his brother's soul.

In *Areopagitica,* Milton boldly adapted the idea of the soul in the blood to the body politic: 'For as in a body, when the blood is fresh, the spirits pure and vigorous, not only to vital, but to rationall faculties, and those in the acutest, and the pertest operations of wit and suttlety, it argues in what good plight and constitution the body is' (*CPW* 2: 557). The free circulation of ideas through books and pamphlets, 'as in a body,' is the life-blood of the body politic.[60] Before thus defending the commonwealth of readers, in what may be the most celebrated passage of prose he ever crafted, Milton gave book-burning a mortalist interpretation: 'a goode Booke is the pretious life-blood of a master spirit, imbalm'd and treasur'd up on purpose to a life beyond life.' Killing it 'slaies an immortality rather than a life' (2: 493). In light of the extensively printed medical-theological controversy on the soul in the blood, and the knowledge of it implied by *Areopagitica,* I find it difficult not to accept that Milton consciously evoked the belief when he described Abel 'Groan[ing] out his Soul with gushing blood effused.' Thomas Corns has commented that 'Groan'd out his Soul' is 'a curious phrase for a mortalist';[61] but the converse is true. An awareness of seventeenth-century discourse on blood and soul serves to confirm its mortalism. The mortalist stamp of the passage further is emphasized by Milton's elision of Genesis 4: 10, 'the voice of thy brother's blood crieth unto me from the ground.' Here, avoiding the possible implication that the spirit in the blood does not die with the body, only the voice of Adam, reacting to the vision, cries out in protest.

Mortalism

Norman Burns importantly traced to Milton a tradition of mortalism in English theology.[62] Christopher Hill's 1964 article on Harvey mentioned Milton's mortalism in passing, returning to the subject more seriously in a subsequent book, in which the circulation of the blood and Milton's mortalism are cited as parallel, not connected, beliefs.[63] Hill presents a Milton in constant dialogue with Interregnum radicals, 'both emotionally and intellectually very close to the enthusiastic activists of the Revolution,'[64] from whom he ingested mortalist ideas. Burns emphasizes more Milton's indebtedness to the longer tradition, but allows the possibility that he had read Overton on *Man's Mortalitie* (1643). Like Hill, Burns remarks on the contemporary circulation of mortalist thought: 'The more one knows of the currency of mortalist ideas in Interregnum England, the more hesitant one becomes to suggest that Milton was stimulated by any particular person or book to examine the Scriptures for proof of soul sleeping.'[65] Whether Milton's interest in mortalism first was sparked by an Overton or, as seems more likely, by his own study of Lucretius,[66] is, one might say, immaterial. By the time that he wrote *Paradise Lost*, indisputably mortalism had engaged his mind.

Until more recently no one had discerned mortalist beliefs in Milton's poetry earlier than *Paradise Lost*; now the sonnets of the 1640s have become a locus of interest.[67] William Kerrigan examined Milton's early attraction to assumption – i.e., immediate translation of both soul and body, which Enoch and Elijah experienced – shrewdly commenting on the point of connection with mortalism: 'neither . . . permits the body to be severed from the soul in time or in eternity.'[68] Hill cited four mortalist loci in *Paradise Lost*. First, the Son of God predicting that 'Though now to Death I yield,' the Father 'wilt not leave me in the loathsome grave / His prey, nor suffer my unspotted Soul / For ever with corruption there to dwell' (3: 245, 247–9). Second, Adam, struggling to understand the penalty of death, considers and rejects the dreadful possibility that 'the Spirit of Man / Which God inspir'd, cannot together perish / With this corporeal Clod,' concluding 'All of me then shall die' (10: 784–6, 792). Third, the Father's own explanation that immortality is forfeit: 'Death becomes / His final remedy' until man is 'to second Life, / Wak't in the renovation of the just' (11: 61–2, 64–5). Fourth, Michael's description of Christ's victory over Sin and Death, redeeming humans from temporal death, 'a death like sleep, / A gentle wafting to immortal Life' (12: 434–5).[69] To these now must be added the death of Abel.

Yet mortalism is only half of the equation. *De Doctrina Christiana* clinches the case for mortalism by reviewing scriptural evidence to conclude that there is 'not a word about any intermediate state' of the soul between death of the body and the general resurrection – rather, 'the whole man dies' (*CPW* 6: 403). The next chapter begins, revealingly, by marking the transition, 'We have seen how God's providence operated in man's fall: now let us see how it operates in his redemption' (415). In its rejection of intermediate states the treatise exemplifies the Protestant drive to restore the biblical integrity it found in early Christianity. There was, as Burns notes, a close alliance between mortalism and traducianism,[70] and, though not himself a mortalist, Tertullian the originator of traducianism, importantly fuelled a third element of materialist belief, the resurrection of the body. Mortalists emphasized this 'because the unscriptural doctrine of the soul's immortality pushed the scriptural doctrine of the resurrection of the whole man into a minor, if not irrelevant position.'[71] In *De carne Christi* Tertullian insists that Christ lived and died in human flesh, excepting only the absence of sin, exactly like any other human. As for Thomas, who would believe in Christ's resurrection only when thrusting his hand into the wound (John 20: 24–9), the evidence of the flesh is crucial. In *De resurrectione carnis* Tertullian considers the situation of those ordinary mortals at the general resurrection: 'our flesh shall remain even after the resurrection – so far indeed susceptible of suffering, as it is the flesh, and the same flesh too, but at the same time impassible, inasmuch as it has been liberated by the Lord.'[72] The Apostles' Creed later would phrase it as '*resurrectio carnis* not *mortuorum* or *corporum*.'[73]

Paradise Lost faithfully reflects this emphasis. Michael instructs Adam, 'thy punishment / He shall endure by coming in the Flesh / To a reproachful life and cursed death' (12: 404–6); and the Father had assured the Son, 'thy Humiliation shall exalt / With thee thy Manhood also to this Throne; / Here shalt thou sit incarnate' (3: 313–15). After reviewing biblical evidence for the general resurrection, *De Doctrina* concludes with a thoroughly Arminian argument that, without it, the righteous would suffer and the wicked thrive, a situation 'quite irreconcilable with God's providence and justice' (*CPW* 6: 620). Given the indisputable logic of resurrection, then 'It appears indicated in Scripture that every man will rise numerically one and the same person' ('Videtur idem numero quisque homo resurrecturus').[74] God's justice requires death for disobedience (*PL* 3: 210), but through the Son's sacrifice humans providentially shall 'Receive new life' (3: 294). For mortalists death is a condition than not only fulfills justice; it is in itself an act of providence. As Adam reasoned out (10: 782–92), his spirit sinned, not his body, and therefore deserves punishment;[75] moreover, if his spirit were not to perish with his body, he would endure a 'living Death,' a thought too horrid to contemplate. The Father quite accurately describes death as 'His final remedy' (11: 62), to alleviate an unending state of misery – 'final' meaning in this life, to be succeeded by 'second Life, / Wak'd in the renovation of the just' (64–5).

Although Abel's violent death is unnatural and undeserved, Jesus's own endorsement of him as a prophet who has shed 'righteous blood' (Matt. 23: 35) and the firm acceptance that he is a type of Christ, sacrificed for his faith, abundantly confirm that his 'new life' is assured. The Son's prediction that the Father will not suffer his soul 'with corruption' to dwell in the grave (3: 247–9) is in one sense puzzling. 'Corruption' only can refer to the body, but his body is incorrupt, arising 'fresh as the dawning light' (12: 423). The subtext might be: '[resurrection] is sown in corruption, it is raised in incorruption' (I Cor. 15: 42). Indeed, the Father's description of sin's effect, 'of incorrupt / Corrupted' (11: 56–7) seems deliberately to evoke this verse. Paul's celebrated chapter made the seed metaphor (15: 35–8, 42–4) the most familiar image for resurrection of the body.[76] Even before he judges the serpent, the future 'woman's seed' speaks as representative of all mankind. When Abel is resurrected – the reward for faith Michael foretells – he, like Jesus Christ, will be numerically identical to his earthly, but now glorified, body. What greater reward could one ask of a beneficent providence?

Conversely, Cain's future life confirms the accuracy of Adam's guess about the horror of 'living Death.' Condemned to life in exile as a fugitive, Cain fears that he himself will be murdered, 'And the Lord set a mark upon Cain, lest any should kill him' (Gen. 4: 15). Ambrose thought that the Lord had protected Cain's life to give him ample time for repentance 'under the providence of God'; less charitably Jerome concluded: 'God protects Cain only so that he can be more severely punished, and the protection is achieved by the Lord's threatening sevenfold punishments on anyone who might try to release Cain from the torments he must suffer – seven-generations-worth of trials and tribulations.'[77] The transference of Cain's 'mark' to the legend of the undying Wandering

Jew suggests the popularity of this interpretation. The exegetical accretions to the cryptic verses of Genesis 4: 23–4 explain how Cain's life did end. While hunting, Lamech, a man of the fifth generation, mistakes the hidden Cain for a wild animal and unwittingly kills him.[78] Cain, therefore, was not slain for vengeance, and his death might well be seen as a merciful providence, rescuing him from unending sorrow and woe.

Mortalism tells us a great deal about the significance to Milton of Abel 'Groan[ing] out his Soul with gushing blood effus'd' (447); what it means for Adam is another question. He had passed one important trial in tortuously using his reduced rational faculty to understand what the Son knew immediately, that both body and soul die together. The vision confirms the correctness of his conclusion, but understandably, if ironically, Adam is so horrified by the physical brutality of the 'violent stroke' that initially he does not recognize he is witnessing death. Michael's commentary, with 'bloody Fact' (457) and the 'dust and gore' (460), which evoke the dust and soul of Adam's creation, gently nudges him to consider the significance of the gushing blood. But not until he learns of the Messiah's triumph over death, 'ris[ing] / Out of his grave, fresh as the dawning light, / Thy ransom paid, which Man from death redeems' (12: 422–4) will Adam entirely comprehend the meanings of death and of resurrection.

In other ways Adam's response to the vision is not imperceptive. He recognizes that Abel has sacrificed well and cuts to the essential question of God's justice: 'Is Piety thus and pure Devotion paid?' (11: 452). This gropes toward an inchoate awareness of the covenant of grace extrapolated from the curse on the serpent.[79] *De Doctrina* defines the covenant from Genesis 3: 15, then explains: 'From man's point of view the covenant may be said to have existed from the time when the worship of God by man is first recorded.'[80] Abel's sacrifice is the first post-exilic record of such worship. Although the Protevangelium remains obscure to him, Adam grasps that the 'meek man' has worshipped properly and intuits that there should be divine reciprocity. He is correct on both counts; the presentation of his sons as types of Jesus and Judas intimates both the righteousness of Abel's sacrifice and the providential design of turning evil to good. The last of the Father's charges to Michael before the expulsion itself had been to 'intermix / My Cov'nant in the woman's seed renew'd' (11: 115–16). The angel's reply to Adam's question begins that process of progressive revelation until he can affirm the identity of 'The Woman's seed, obscurely then foretold, / Now amplier known thy Saviour and thy Lord' (12: 543–4).[81] For now assurance that the murder 'Will be aveng'd, and th' other's Faith approv'd /

Lose no reward, though here thou see him die' (458–9) may be more than Adam can take in. The meanings of covenant and reward must be earned.

In this and in the succeeding visions the trial is a test of Adam's faith, by which alone he can be justified. His initial reaction had been – like that of the fallen angels when asked to encounter the unknown (2: 422) – dismay (11: 449), a loss of moral courage or resolution. With a fuller understanding of the vision, Adam's concern for Abel is commendable, but still only a limited response. His preoccupation with himself, 'Is this the way / I must return to native dust?' (462–3), obstructs him from making more than a minimal acknowledgment of his responsibility. In Adam's Book 10 soliloquy comprehension of his guilt overwhelmed him to the point of despair, from which state Eve's intervention aroused him. Now the physical reality of Abel's death threatens to bring it back. An unstated question then looms: when Adam does fully comprehend what he has done to his children, which example of behaviour will he follow, Abel's or Cain's? Dying for his faith or living in despair?

For the latter the interpretation of Genesis 4: 13 becomes relevant. Whereas the Geneva and King James Bibles translate this 'My punishment is greater than I can bear,' the Septuagint and the Vulgate (Maior iniquitas mea quam ut veniam merear) both have Cain asserting that his guilt is too great to be forgiven.[82] Commentators took this as an expression of Cain's pride and despair, the very faults Satan exhibited in the soliloquy to the sun; as Susan Snyder summarizes, Cain 'refuse[d] to acknowledge insufficiency of self and ask for God's help.' Milton's emphasis on Cain as a type of Judas, the despairing sinner who (in the alternative version of his death) hangs himself, would indicate the poet's sensitivity to this shared state of mind. Michael's lesson, 'many are the ways that lead / to [Death's] grim Cave, all dismal' (11: 468–9) possibly further alludes to the temptation to despair. The image of the 'grim Cave' has been annotated with Virgil's cave to the underworld (*Aeneid* 6: 237); more immediately relevant may be the corpse-strewn 'hollow' and 'darksome' cave in which Despair persuades Red Cross Knight to kill himself (*Faerie Queene* 1: 9, 28–54).

In the allegorical interpretations of the Cain and Abel story, Cain's inability to seek God's forgiveness was taken to signify the limitation of the Old Testament law. To Ambrose and Augustine this meant equating Cain with the Jews; for Luther and Calvin the Roman Church took their place.[83] Abel, as Ambrose stated it, symbolized the Christian who remains true to God (bk. 1, chap. 2: 'per Abel autem intellegitur Christianus adhaerens deo'), and, as Michael assures Adam, will be rewarded for his faith. Still reeling from his first sight of death, Adam at this point is only able to express the terror and horror of the immediate experience before Michael moves on to the vision of death in the Lazar house. It can be instructive to reflect on just what Milton passes over in his streamlined and telescoped visions from Genesis. He omits this, for example: 'And Adam knew his wife again; and she bare a son, and called his name Seth: For God, *said she,* hath appointed me another seed instead of Abel, whom Cain slew' (Gen. 4: 25). Seth becomes the stay and comfort of Adam's old age. The father confides to his son his final conversation with God, as well as the 'secrets' and 'mysteries' revealed by Michael. When Adam commences to fail, he sends Seth with Eve to the gates of Paradise, hoping to obtain the oil of life from the tree of mercy.[84] The poet does not afford Adam the heartsease of a surrogate Abel; instead he invents an extrabiblical vision, forcing Adam's concentration on the consequences of his disobedience, 'Death . . . and all our woe.' Rather than the often expansive treatment of the earlier providences, the visions of Book 11 beat down on Adam like the waves of a storm; only at their conclusion does it become clear that he has the strength of character not to succumb to despair. And only then can he commence to understand that, beyond punishment, death is a providential 'remedy.' Providences are a means to an end, seldom the end itself.

The final books of *Paradise Lost* engage the sweep of biblical history from Genesis to the Last Judgment, 'the Race of time, / Till time stands fixt' (12: 554–5), as Adam marvels. Chapter 7 argues that Milton's presentation of Christian time is both cyclical through typological recurrence and linear, advancing steadily to its ordained end. The large design of providential history is conveyed by Milton's poetic design, an implicit structure paralleling the six visions in Book 11, which comprise the first 'day' in the week of sacred history, to the succeeding six days narrated in Book 12. Juxtaposed to this grand design is the activity of providence, a sequence of trials through which Adam learns from what he sees and hears. By the end of Book 11 his responses to these providences have taken him through a symbolic death and baptism; Book 12 then concentrates on the religious instruction of Adam. Together they constitute a conversion story, at the end of which Adam professes his faith in Christ the Redeemer, a faith that Eve shares. They depart from Eden impelled by this faith, determined to persevere, and still guided by providence.

Chapter Seven

Providential Design: The Death and Conversion of Adam

> Since the Providence of God hath cast this upon us, I cannot but submit to Providence.[1]
>
> Oliver Cromwell

> In this light of eternity alone, is the Work of God seen aright, in the entire piece, in the whole design, from the beginning to the end.[2]
>
> Peter Sterry

In the final books of *Paradise Lost* Milton's complex and subtle design of interrelated visions and ages enables him to blazon the grand providential design of Christian history, while simultaneously showing how the first Adam comes to model himself on the second. In the extraordinary providence granted to Adam, like no other mortal, he experiences the future before moving back in time to apply that knowledge to his own future. Joseph Addison, who was responsive to so many of the poem's riches, has been abused for his censure of Milton's strategy here: 'To give my Opinion freely, I think that the exhibiting part of the History of Mankind in Vision, and part in Narrative, is as if an History-Painter should put in Colours one Half of his Subject, and write down the remaining part of it.'[3] To my mind, Addison's analogy quite accurately strikes the quality of affective response that the shift elicits from the reader. He needed only to consider more searchingly the 'very handsome Reason' for which the poet devised it.

Eve and Adam descend from their respective dreams and speculation, enlightened about the providential design that in time will result in 'great good' and a 'happy end' (12: 612, 605), and now reconciled to the decreed departure from Paradise, their last trial of obedience in the narrative present. As the Bible gives two accounts of human origin, an abstract proclamation (Gen. 1: 26–7) and an individualized story (Gen. 2: 7–25), so the Father gives two explanations for the expulsion, corresponding negatively to these. The first is, to borrow Abdiel's word (5: 895), an uncreation. Sin, having 'dissolution wrought . . . / . . . and of incorrupt / Corrupted' (11: 55–7), the Law of Nature forbids their presence, causing the pure elements to eject them. Milton's radical rewriting of Genesis 2, attributing to Adam free will and agency in arguing for Eve's creation, has its negative counterpart in God's second explanation for expulsion: 'Lest therefore his now bolder hand / Reach also of the Tree of Life, and eat, / And live for ever, dream at least to live / For ever' (11: 93–6). Protestants largely understood the tree of life to symbolize 'the pledge / Of immortality' (4: 200–1) attained through Christ by obedience.[4] Were he to eat this fruit Adam would be emulating the force-or-fraud tactics of the desperate sinners lodged in the Paradise of Fools, rather than the model of Christian behaviour revealed by Michael. 'Greatly instructed,' however, Adam can affirm 'I shall hence depart, / Greatly in peace of thought,' having learned that 'to obey is best' (12: 557–8, 561). Eve, too, can say, 'In mee is no delay' (615), having learned the lesson of the 'paradise within.' So they depart, dropping 'Some natural tears' (645) as Paradise becomes for them, as it is for us, a memory place.

The beautifully balanced ambivalences of the epic's final verse paragraph have disconcerted some readers, beginning with Richard Bentley who composed his own up-beat ending: 'THEN hand in hand with SOCIAL steps their Way / Through *Eden* took, WITH HEAV'NLY COMFORT CHEER'D.'[5] Many more have been moved by the poet's delicate perception of this liminal moment in which the felt loss of everything known and familiar tugs against entrance to a future not without considerable blessings: 'The World was all before them, where to choose / Thir place of rest and Providence thir guide' (646–7). Or have we gotten it wrong? A contemporary scholar, John Rogers, informs us:

> Although generations of readers have taken solace in the continued guidance of Adam and Eve by what is assumed to be the controlling force of an extraordinary providence, such interpretative assumptions have failed to register the complex transformations Milton has wrought on providential theology, and on the entire range of politically consequential organizational philosophies that that theology so often subtends.[6]

Surely no critical feat could be more pleasing than proving generations of readers mistaken, but, if the corrector needs correction, he runs the risk of becoming a new Bentley, as I think is the case here. In his broad and stimulating study Rogers imaginatively and plausibly relates Milton's projection of nature to the mid-century 'Vitalist Movement' of science, which in extreme instances endowed matter with agency and something like free will. For Milton the law of God and the law of nature were one, manifested as general providence. In extending his thesis to the Expulsion, Rogers seems to misunderstand the implications of Milton's Arminianism – for example, in taking God's 'self-limitation' as abdication: 'When Abdiel explains to Satan that "God and Nature bid the same," he can be construed to identify God, in effect, with the rules of the self-regulating natural universe that constitute ordinary providence.'[7] Even with the cautious qualifiers, this is untenable; Milton was not a pantheist. Rogers misidentifies Milton's concept of extraordinary providence as 'Calvinist' (i.e., the seventeenth-century English brand of Calvinism represented by Cromwell); in his reading, extraordinary providence disappears from the poem with the angel Michael, leaving only the redefined general providence. Reversing the syntactic elements in the description of cherubim 'Gliding meteorous, as the Ev'ning Mist / . . . glides / And gathers ground fast at the Laborer's heel, / Homeward returning' (629–32) and divesting the simile of religious connotations, Rogers argues that the mist becomes the expulsive force which 'reasserts the vitalist world of ordinary providence.' All of this is good because 'by liberating providence from the tyrannical bonds of an authoritarian logic' [Calvinism], the poem allows us to perceive 'the birth of the individual with her seemingly autonomous subjectivity.'[8] Not as brisk as Bentley's distich perhaps, but equally up-beat in a thoroughly postmodern vein.

Would Milton have thought that extraordinary providence disappears from his poem? It seems unlikely, given his belief that his entire life was guided by the hand of heaven, 'God's leading and providence' (Dei ductu ac providentia), as he told Leonard Philaris. Within the poem Adam's, and by implication Eve's, acceptance of Christ as their redeemer surely grants them an extraordinary providence extending beyond the narrative, a large point that Rogers simply elides. Moreover, does the linguistic texture of the poem enable what Rogers calls 'the poetics of agency' or 'the poem's attempt to engender a discourse of liberal individualism'?[9] We might consider as one index the word 'guide,' which appears eighteen times in the epic with four variants (guided / guides). Only once does the poem describe animate nature as guiding;[10] in Eve's apostrophe to the forbidden tree she lauds it as 'Best guide' (9: 808), a fatal misjudgment. Not unexpectedly, the most frequent usages of the term accrue to the Son of God and to the angel Michael. The Father instructs the Son to guide his chariot against the rebels (6: 711); as Creator the Son guides Adam to the Garden and to Eve (8: 298, 312, 486); as Judge – in a construction suggestively paralleling 'thy God' with 'thy guide' – he reproaches Adam, 'was shee made thy guide' (10: 146)? Throughout Book 11 Adam accepts Michael as his guide (371, 674, 785). In Book 12 Adam, remembering Michael's account of God's sending an angel to guide the Israelites (204), anxiously wonders who will guide the faithful when the Messiah ascends to Heaven (482), a situation paralleling his and Eve's. Michael, the Saviour's avatar, assures Adam that from Heaven the Son will send to dwell

> His Spirit within them, and the Law of Faith
> Working through love, upon thir hearts shall write,
> To guide them in all truth, and also arm
> With spiritual Armor, able to resist
> Satan's assaults. (12: 488–92)

The internal guide is 'The promise of the Father' (487), made in the divine dialogue: 'And I will place within them as a guide / My Umpire *Conscience*' (3: 194–5). This will give them a principle of decision-making to compensate for the impairment of fallen reason, while not impinging on their freedom of choice (3: 195–202). Far from being a 'mysterious term,' the phrase 'Providence thir guide' completes a sequence threaded through the poem and culminates an unfolding process within it. Michael, the embodiment of extraordinary providence in guiding Adam to a comprehension of the full design of Christian history, does disappear, but, like the 'paradise within' (12: 587), providence itself now becomes an internal principle of guidance throughout a 'Life / Tried in sharp tribulation, and refin'd / By Faith, and faithful works' (11: 62–4). The providences will not cease. The final image of the epic complexly compensates loss by bringing together in the 'solitary' action of Eve's and Adam's departure justice, obedience, and love.

This pattern of language, I realize, will convince no critic committed to finding fissures, inconsistencies, conflicting ideological imperatives and discourses within the poem. Admittedly, *Paradise Lost* has a share of these, and the more fully we understand their role in the poem the better; however, many of them arise from Milton's commitment, like most of his contemporaries including scientists,[11] to belief that the Bible is literally true, a coherent and progressive revelation of God's providence. It would be another two centuries before biblical scholarship, applying the principles of classical textual criticism, demolished this belief (and in many quarters word still has not gotten out). Milton found in Arminianism a theology that liberated him from the constraints of English Calvinism; the *duplex amor Dei,* God's twofold love of justice and humanity, appears to have facilitated the conception of his great epic as a vindication of providence. To show just how fully providence and providences pervade the activity of the poem, let us return to the structure or, preferably, design of the last books. Addison, commenting on Book 12, writes, 'the principal Design of this *Episode* was to give *Adam* an Idea of the Holy Person, who was to reinstate Humane Nature in that Happiness and Perfection from which it had fallen.'[12] His comment suggests the virtue of the contemporary term 'design' in conveying the multiple senses that are relevant here: God's plan or final purpose for humans; its implementation over time, which is to say through providence; and its representation in the form of an artistic or literary work.

The Design of Christian History

We know on good authority that Christian history is linear, not cyclical. C.A. Patrides summarizes, 'Using the traditional terms employed by Renaissance expositors, we may state that there is a "streight and perfect line from *Adam* vnto *Christ,*" "a golden vaine, a golden chaine, consisting of many linkes, from the first *Adam* to the *second.*" '[13] Richard Emmerson concurs, 'The Christian understanding of history is based on three acts of Christ: his work as Creator, as Savior, and as Judge,' but with the reminder that the line runs both ways: apocalypticism 'looks backward to the beginning of history as well as forward to the end of history.'[14] I nonetheless support Edward Tayler's stubborn insistence that for the poem the straight line is 'an oversimple model, limited in its usefulness.' He concedes the obvious truth of the linear paradigm, 'but to think exclusively in this way will not help very much in trying to understand the structure of *Paradise Lost.*'[15] Milton was an excellent classicist who would not have rejected out of hand the Greek and Roman acceptance of temporal recurrence. As Frances Yates once declared, 'The great forward movements of the Renaissance all derive

Table 1. Chronological sequence and narrative sequence

Sequence of Events		Narrative Sequence
1	Begetting of the Son	6
2	Battle in Heaven	7
3	Creation of the World	8
4	Adam's Creation Story	9
5	Eve's Creation Story	5
6	Satan in Hell	1
7	Satan's Voyage	2
8	Dialogue in Heaven	3
9	Satan in Eden	4

their vigour, their emotional impulse, from looking backwards.'[16] After all, with Ecclesiastes the cyclical vision makes a powerful incursion to scripture; what greater example of recurrence could there be than the Second Coming? Milton's responsiveness to both models, and his successful reconciliation of them, was exhibited early with the Nativity Ode, 'defining the eternal significance of an occurrence in time, measuring its meaning in respect to the past and future of scriptural history, seeing the event as a "shadowy Type" to be fulfilled according to the dictates of Eternal Providence.'[17]

Chapter 2 above proposed that the poet constructed *Paradise Lost* on two large organizational schemes: spatial, the structure of cosmic memory places; and temporal, the inverse progression through the Last Things, which effectively unites both since places are also destinations. Like Giotto demonstrating his draftsmanship, Milton rather flamboyantly signals the suspension of what we might normally call 'chronology' by having the first six books describe a perfect narrative circle, ending where the poem began. Somewhat less obviously, visualizing the narrative through memory places and images gave him the freedom to deconstruct or reorganize it, as he certainly does. Looking at key events in the story makes this more evident (Table 1).[18]

The begetting of the Son sparks Satan's rebellion, setting the entire sequence in motion, and the week of Creation occurs during the nine-day span that the rebel angels lie on the burning lake (1: 50–3). Milton has inverted the two halves of the sequence with Eve's recollection of her creation as a pivot between them. To be sure, there are thematic rationales for the displacement; however, the dislocations do reinforce the sense that, like the orator rearranging his memory places, this poet envisions his narrative units rather like pieces on a cosmic chessboard. Whereas Marvell more traditionally symbolizes the eternal with space, 'deserts of vast eternity,' Milton spatializes time: 'Nine times the Space that measures Day and Night' (1: 50). This distinctive characteristic has long been noticed, and causal explanations range from Milton's responsiveness to a universe expanded by the telescope to the effect of a visual epistemology fostered by Ramism.[19] I would contend that an older tradition, the palimpsest of classical mnemonics reinterpreted as *sacra memoria,* also deserves credit.

The Eden books carefully mark times and the passage of days, during which rampant natural growth occurs, but, rather than time as we experience it, this suggests an eternal present, evocative of Plato's 'Great Year' in the *Timaeus,* thus establishing a rhythm of recurrence.[20] Although the times of day at which trials occur have symbolic implications, the literal effect of prelapsarian time is close to the principle of aesthetic variation in Heaven. 'For wee have also our Ev'ning and our Morn, / Wee ours for change delectable, not need' (5: 628–9), Raphael explains. Very different is the mortal time that Sin calls 'The Scythe of Time' (10: 606) and that poets were fond of symbolizing by mechanical clocks. Whether Milton's 'lazy leaden-stepping hours, / Whose speed is but the heavy Plummet's pace' ('On Time,' 2–3) or Edward Herbert's apostrophe to his watch's 'Uncessant minutes, whilst you move you tell / The time that tells our life,' this time is linear in one direction, progressing to death and judgment.[21] So it is in an obvious way with the last three books of the epic.

Book 10 does narrate events in sequence, but the Sin, Death, and Satan episodes after the judgment and the prominent role Eve takes in the reconciliation give it a variety akin to the preceding books. With Books 11 and 12, the linearity is unmistakable. Few readers now would echo C.S. Lewis's condemnation of the concluding books as 'an untransmuted lump of futurity.'[22] Lewis's phrasing acknowledges a failure to perceive structure; in the era of literary structuralism a host of scholar-critics laboured to demonstrate that, as in *Paradise Regained* where the design also is subtle and complex, structure and function are very firmly controlled by the poet.[23] The most influential readings have been typological, expounding the presence of the three temptations, the stages of the Covenant, and the correspondence between the six ages of the world and the six days of Creation.[24]

The litmus test for all the defences of these books continues to be their ability to explain the shift from vision to narration that disconcerted Addison. Proceeding from awareness that this question is the crux, Joseph Summers made several useful contributions, and his suggestion that the division of materials in these books corresponds to the pattern of destruction followed by greater creation in Books 6 and 7 is especially valid. Indeed, the poet foreshadows the likeness: 'but the evil soon / Driv'n back redounded as a flood on those / From whom it sprung, impossible to mix / With Blessedness' (7: 56–9). This perception leads to the further recognition that Michael's narrative technique is itself an internal mimesis of the poet's narrative strategy revealed in the invocation to Holy Light: 'that I may see and tell / Of things invisible to mortal sight' (3: 54–5).[25] Finally, Summers realized that the chief significance of Book 11 is moral and of Book 12 typological, that 11 shows the horrors of Sin and Death whereas 12 grants a revelation of future redemption by 'inward rather than physical vision,' insights satisfyingly corroborated by other scholars.[26]

In their expositions of Books 11 and 12 through the 'week' of sacred history, perhaps because of their tendency to minimize the division and narrative distinction between the books, George Whiting and Hugh MacCallum failed to convince other critics that the six 'days' provide a primary structural pattern. Balachandra Rajan, for example, objects that 'the six ages are not decisively marked in *Paradise Lost* and do not form the basis for any clear structure of interpretation or of emphasis . . . The right conclusion seems to be that the six ages are used evocatively, rather than as a rigorous scheme of analysis.'[27] One might qualify that it is not the poem's imperfect reflection of the age divisions which causes the difficulty. The tradition, as Whiting and MacCallum describe it, blurs with the fifth age, largely for lack of an exemplary historical figure – an Adam, Noah, Abraham, or David – to nominate it, and the poem faithfully represents the tradition in this respect. Moreover, the apparent imbalance between book division and temporal division creates a disparity between the first age and the subsequent five, forcing us to seek multiple structural patterns. Only if Milton had chosen to leave the poem in the ten-book form, presenting the temporal episodes of the six days in one narrative unit, might we have been able to see the week of history as the primary configuration. In the final version of the poem, as in *Paradise Regained,* where the temporal units of the three days and the formal units of the four books conflict, the historical episodes comprising the six days are countered by the book division. This effectively gives the first age a thematic emphasis equal to all the subsequent ages (as it is given roughly equal spatial emphasis in allocation of lines), bringing us once again to the dichotomous perception of a 'world destroy'd and world restor'd.'

In the strict sense biblical typology understands historical persons and events within the Old Testament as foreshadowing, usually in a carefully limited way, events of the Christian era and particularly Jesus Christ himself. As such, it is a form of progressive revelation, 'From shadowy Types to Truth' in the frequently quoted phrase (12: 303), and therefore linear. Because the types cannot be understood fully until the Advent, the revelation is retrospective; only in looking back does one glimpse the providential design of history. Erich Auerbach once explained, with admirable clarity, that typology connects 'two events that are linked neither temporally nor causally'; the connection 'can be established only if both occurrences are vertically linked to Divine Providence, which alone is able to devise such a plan of history.'[28] With the completion of Michael's history tutorial the poem thus creates a somewhat disconcerting effect; for once Adam has the same perspective as the reader. Temporarily sharing the vantage point of the sixth age, he looks forward while we look back. The typological scheme that dominates the concluding books is accordingly that of the two Adams. Milton prepares us to respond to Michael's revelations within the framework of this symbolic perspective by pointedly comparing the hill that Adam ascends in Paradise to the hill 'Whereon for different cause the Tempter set / Our second *Adam* in the Wilderness, / To show him all Earth's Kingdoms and thir Glory' (11: 382–4), and by prefacing the vision proper with a bitterly ironic catalogue: the 'progress,' temporal, geographic, directional, of worldly glory, actually sin and corruption.[29] The only overt reference in the poem to the 'second Adam' concept serves to anticipate both the end of the cycle of action, which the first Adam has set in motion, and the full consequences of his sin, 'the Fruit / Of that Forbidden Tree,' that must be played out before 'one greater Man / Restore us.'[30] The figural scheme of world destroyed and restored thus overlays the temporal patterning with Book 11 dominated by the sins of the Old Adam and Book 12 with the prophecies of the second Adam.

Book 11 does contain three exemplary figures of the 'one just man' who anticipates Christ – Abel, Enoch, and Noah – yet within the main narrative the only prototype available at this point has to be Abdiel. The typological connotations of Abel and Cain discussed in the preceding chapter cannot yet be understood by Adam. In Book 12 Moses and Joshua are explained overtly as types of Christ; both Abraham and David are directly linked to the 'Woman's Seed.' Only with the retrospective knowledge from the final book, however, can Adam recognize the full significance of Abel and Cain or the three Genesis worthies as Christ types. The more immediate source for the presentation of the worthies in Book 11, several readers have noticed, appears to be the heroes of faith in Hebrews 11: 1–7.[31] These faithful few serve to keep before us the paradox of good emerging from evil and to hold forth the possibility of redemption, even while the dominant imagistic and thematic movements of Book 11 are downward: descent into evil, progress in the proliferation of sin.[32] In all five negative visions, the continuing disfigurement of the Maker's image holds a mirror to Adam's own face.

There is, nevertheless, the suggestion of another pattern controlling the structure of visions in Book 11, a symmetrical design offsetting or at least largely compensating for the asymmetry that the book division imposes on the week of sacred history. It should be remembered that Milton includes in his account the full week, six 'days' of history followed by the Son's return to preside over the day of judgment, the dissolution of the old world, and the raising

> From the conflagrant mass, purg'd and refin'd,
> New Heav'ns, new Earth, Ages of endless date
> Founded in righteousness and peace and love,
> To bring forth fruits Joy and eternal Bliss. (12: 548–51)

Book 11 encompasses the first age of history, presented in the form of six visions; Book 12 narrates history from the Flood to the Last Judgment in the structure of six 'days' or five ages succeeded by the end of the temporal order, the eternal Sabbath of rest. Within the two sequences one finds a design of correspondence between vision and age, which, for the sake of clarity, may be shown in a table (Table 2). Between each vision and age pair, I shall attempt to demonstrate, there are similarities in themes, episodes, and persons. This relationship between the larger sequences is not procrusteanly strict, but there are sufficient parallels and contrasts within each pairing to ensure that the correspondence of visions to days cannot be accidental.

Table 2. Visions and ages in Books 11–12

First Adam – Age 1 Bk. 11: 429–901	Second Adam – Ages 2–7 Bk. 12: 1–551
Vision 1 Abel and Cain	Age 2 Nimrod and tower
Vision 2 Lazar-house	Age 3 Abraham
Vision 3 Sons of God	Age 4 Sons of Abraham
Vision 4 Cities of the plain	Age 5 Captivity of Babylon
Vision 5 Flood	Age 6 Incarnation of Christ
Vision 6 Recession of Flood and rainbow	Age 7 Transcendence of temporal order

The first vision corresponds to the second age, and the obvious relationship occurs in the sinister figures of Cain, first killer, and Nimrod, hunter of men, both of whom were thought to be types of Antichrist.[33] Adam's response to the narrative keys on the tyranny of Nimrod, the putative first king, and linking him firmly to Cain whose fratricide was the original act of tyranny. By exploiting the extrabiblical character of Nimrod as builder of cities and creator of the original high-rise, the tower of Babel, Milton further strengthens the genetic linkage to Cain, first builder of cities (Gen. 4: 17).[34] Babel itself was noticed initially as an inferior imitation of Pandaemonium, the ur-city of Hell (1: 692–9). Throughout, the poem reminds us that such Satan-inspired 'mortal things' and the urban life they are designed to sustain are fallen, sadly vulnerable, and imperfect (cf. the similes at 4: 188–91 and 9: 445–51).

The vision of the Lazar-house and the third age (Abraham's) share some discreet parallels; the catalogue of diseases echoes faintly in the plagues endured by Pharaoh and his people (12: 177–81). Yet this pairing functions largely in contrastive terms because the motif of death as the fruit of the Fall, overt in Michael's Ciceronian simile (11: 535–7), is balanced in the Abraham episode by the promise of deliverance from death through the Seed of Woman (12: 125–6, 147–51, 232–5, 259–60, 271–3). The promise is later manifested in the laws revealed to Moses:

> . . . part such as appertain
> To civil Justice, part religious Rites

Of sacrifice, informing them, by types
And shadows, of that destin'd Seed to bruise
The Serpent, by what means he shall achieve
Mankind's deliverance. (12: 230–5)

Before that time the horrors of the Lazar-house are caused by 'ungovern'd appetite' (11: 517), and Michael teaches Adam to 'well observe / The rule of not too much, by temperance taught, / In what thou eat'st and drink'st' (11: 530–2). Gluttons 'pervert pure Nature's healthful rules' (11: 523), and, according to *De Doctrina* (*CPW* 6: 516), the unwritten law of God is the law of Nature originally given to Adam. The law itself provides an inward discipline, corresponding to the natural 'rule' of temperance, through which humans can be led to accept the better covenant of grace.[35] The dialectic of these two episodes turns on the antithesis of intemperance as the way of death, the fruit of original sin, and temperance in the law, whether natural or Mosaic, as the way of life.

The third vision matches the Sons of God (Gen. 6: 2–4) with the Sons of Abraham in the fourth age of the world (12: 324–43). Whereas the Sons of God lose righteousness through their lust for the daughters of Cain, the Sons of Abraham lose the righteousness attained through the building of the Temple by committing 'foul Idolatries' (337), so incensing God that he leaves them in captivity to Babylonia. The logic of the poem makes both offences parallel, as well as their consequences; Adam's infatuation with Eve, like that of Satan for Sin, had been represented as self-love and therefore a form of idolatry that the Sons of God reenact.[36] In another closely related pairing, the fourth vision juxtaposes the cities of the plain to the Babylonian captivity, quarrelling elders (11: 660–4) with quarreling priests (12: 353–8); the former would have 'seiz'd with violent hands' Enoch, 'that Just Man' (11: 669, 681), and the latter 'seize / The Scepter, and regard not *David's* Sons' (12: 356–7).

Though Adam at this time cannot comprehend it, the fifth vision, through the exemplary figure of Noah, powerfully counters the dismal universal decline into corruption. The ark traditionally prefigures both Christ and church; Milton accepted the Flood as a type of baptism, which sacrament he considered to symbolize Christ's death, burial, and resurrection. MacCallum concluded, 'Noah in the flood suggests both Christ's act of atonement and the baptismal rite whereby the Christian commemorates that act.'[37] A typological relationship between Adam and Abraham, 'one faithful man' (12: 113), has been argued persuasively, suggesting that Abraham's obedience to God's call provides the proper model for Adam's exile from Paradise.[38] Noah, too, fits this pattern. The fulfilment of the types of wayfarer, pilgrim, and exile should be seen, as *Paradise Regained* reminds us, in the desert temptations of Jesus. The phrase, 'Wand'ring that wat'ry Desert' (11: 779) evokes his forty days in the wilderness as much as it does the exile of Abraham.[39] Through these implications Milton's audience could associate the fifth vision with the coming of the Messiah, the rite of baptism, and the founding of the church.

Although one of the purposes of the structural parallels is to teach Adam to see history in similitudes, he does not learn to interpret typologically until the sixth vision, as Stanley Fish once aptly remarked.[40] The meaning of the fifth vision thus does not become fully apparent to Adam until the narration of the parallel sixth age of the world. In that episode Michael foretells the nativity of the Saviour, patiently explaining the fulfilment of the prophesy through Christ's love and obedience to the law of God. The angel describes the crucifixion, traditionally equated with the founding of the church:[41]

> . . . this God-like act
> Annuls thy doom, the death thou shouldst have di'd,
> In sin for ever lost from life; this act
> Shall bruise the head of *Satan*, crush his strength
> Defeating Sin and Death, his two main arms. (12: 427–31)

He further explains the priestly role of the disciples, dwelling on the administration of baptism: 'the sign / Of washing them from guilt of sin to Life / Pure' (12: 442–4).

What really needs no explication is the connection between the sixth vision, the recession of the Flood and the sign of the rainbow covenant, with the seventh 'day' of history, the Sabbath of everlasting rest. The traces of Creation imagery, which anticipate the 'New Heav'ns, new Earth, Ages of endless date' (12: 549) have been well noted; Michael explicitly connects the purgation by water with the final purgation by fire (11: 885–901; 12: 546–51).[42] The baptismal implications may require more discussion. The Creation, as well as the Flood, is a traditional type of baptism, 'an eschatological typology in which the first creation is presented as the type of the new creation . . . to be accomplished at the end of time.'[43] Relevant to the 'pacific sign' is the assumption in *De Doctrina Christiana* (*CPW* 6: 545) that baptism is a covenant of grace.

Perhaps because in the preceding five visions modern readers lack the aid of Adam's typological interpretation, they have commented systematically only on the final set of parallels. No doubt the similarities do stand out most sharply at the beginning and end. Cain and Nimrod, Noah and Christ, ark and church give us a pattern of repetition with progression: from individual evil to individual salvation, institutional evil to institutional salvation. Although the above recital of thematic, episodic, and figural correspondences may exaggerate the degree of symmetry and firmness of design by ignoring differences in length, emphasis, and mode of presentation, it describes one of the implicit design principles, the skeleton decently clad with flesh, which helps to create a sense of inevitability in movement through the final books and which justifies the parallel redemptive revelations at the conclusion of Book 11 and the climax of Book 12.

Moreover, to return to a thesis of chapter 2, the discrete sequence of six visions is the most conspicuous example of literal memory loci. Mary Carruthers has shown that in late Roman and medieval rhetoric verbal and visual held equal importance, with the topos of *pictura,* whether actual or descriptive, a prominent resource of the latter. Paradoxical as it may seem, Aeneas weeping at the painful memories activated by the ekphrases of Troy's destruction (*Aeneid* 1: 446–97) is the direct ancestor of Adam weeping at the destruction of his world. During the monastic ages the purposes of such pictures were twofold, instruction and meditation, literary compositions deploying the topos 'address[ed] the memory of both the fictional onlooker and the reader/hearer.'[44] Whereas Adam, the novice onlooker, is instructed through the visions, the poet intends the more knowledgeable reader to meditate on them. Carruthers adduces the example of a twelfth-century dream vision poem, in which tapestries, covering the walls of a chamber, are elaborately described. Woven into them are 'the stories of Genesis (through Noah), and then, splitting into two currents, the history of the Jews from Abraham through Solomon, and, on the opposite wall, the fables of the Greeks.'[45] Each tapestry is designed to be a 'memorable' locus. The scheme of corresponding images was far from unique and in later times easily adaptable to, for example, the walls of the Sistine Chapel with six frescoes from the life of Moses on the south wall, typologically paralleled to six from the life of Jesus on the north wall.[46] Or to Milton's mnemonic scheme of six Genesis visions and six ages of history.

In effect, I have attempted to reinforce the argument for the structural importance of the 'week' of sacred history by showing Milton's unconventional complication of that scheme, a reconfiguration that emphasizes recurrence or circularity within the providential design of history and poem. What, then, of the question with which we began, the relation to structure of the shift from vision to narration?

Several plausible and satisfactory thematic rationales for this have been offered.[47] Still another avenue of explanation appears from the insight of some readers that Milton marks the limits of Adam's own horizon. Barbara K. Lewalski commented on Book 11, 'Adam appropriately sees with physical sight that form of the Covenant which is part of his own experience'; and George Williamson once said of Book 12, 'Such matter is beyond Adam's ken and so it is narrated.'[48] These statements hover on the verge of a very simple recognition: Adam cannot be permitted to see the events beyond Genesis 9 because he is dead. Just what I mean by Adam's 'death' will become somewhat clearer after an examination first of Milton's preparation for this event, and then of the historical problem of Adam's death as explained by commentators who evolved a set of assumptions upon which Milton implicitly relies.

The Death of Adam

A major preoccupation of the poem from the Fall until the end of Book 11 is the theme of death. Adam knows that he must die on the day that he eats the forbidden fruit (8: 323–30). His immediate response to Eve's fall articulates the certainty of death; while he can speciously hope that God will not make good his threat, Adam accepts this penalty for disobedience in words that parody Christian paradox, 'Death is to mee as Life' (9: 954). Book 10 presents the ascendance of Sin and Death – both from their own point of view and from God's, in which they are subsumed to providence[49] – as a prelude to Adam's soliloquy, where we find him wishing for immediate death (771–9) and speculating that both body and soul must die (782–92). Having concluded 'That Death be not one stroke, as I suppos'd,' he fears an 'endless misery' in which 'both Death and I / Am found Eternal' (10: 809, 810, 815–16). To Eve's proposal that they thwart the heritage of death, Adam responds by recollecting the curse on the serpent and reasoning that to circumvent their children's punishment would only release their enemy from his. Book 10 establishes Adam's and Eve's need for and potential responsiveness to divine revelation and guidance; further, it at once suspends the very future of humanity on an accommodation to the existence of death and underscores the inevitability of Adam's own encounter with death.

Book 11 opens with God explaining the 'remedy' of death to his Son (11: 57–66), and the visions granted to Adam are preceded by Michael's brusque announcement that the death sentence has been postponed (11: 251–8). Of the first five visions, four contain direct scenes of death in quantitative progression: first, Cain's primal act of murder; in the second, the many shapes of delayed death in the Lazar-house; third, the slaughter from primitive warfare (vision 4); and, finally, the annihilation of Adam's offspring in the Flood (vision 5). Adam's anguished question, 'But have I now seen Death?' (11: 462) sets the keynote for this sequence.

I wish here to pose a question that the poem seems to demand of the reader by this point. With all of this emphasis on the fulfilment and comprehension of the punishment, on coming to know the meaning of death and the fate of humanity, why is there nothing about the issue presumably of greatest importance to Adam, the event of his own death?

Genesis 5: 5 supplies his obituary: 'and all the days that Adam lived were nine hundred and thirty years: and he died.'[50] An abundance of 'biographies' in many languages attests to the compulsion to fill out the details of his post-exilic life. In the Latin, Christian-influenced *Life of Adam and Eve*, the dying Adam experiences weakness and great pain, causing him to send Seth and Eve for the oil of mercy to relieve the pain.[51] The imaginative hold this event had for ordinary Christians might be seen through Piero della Francesca's fresco of *The Death of Adam* (Arezzo, ca. 1457).[52] Part of a sequence illustrating the legend of the Holy Cross from *The Golden Legend*, this fresco represents on the left a young couple, possibly Adam and Eve still in Paradise; on the right the dying Adam, white-haired and bearded, dispatches Seth to the gates of Paradise to seek the medicinal oil. A frail Eve, supported by a stick, helps the semi-recumbent Adam rise enough to speak (fig. 10). In the (severely damaged) central scene we see his prone body surrounded by his grieving and wailing descendents.

For the commentators the problem that Adam's very ripe age presented was the same one with which Adam wrestled in the garden after the Fall: how to reconcile this leisurely departure with Genesis 2: 17, 'for in the day that thou eatest thereof thou shalt surely die.' Their conclusion, that God's day must mean something other than the twenty-four-hour day of human time, does not advance signally on Adam's; and his phrase 'A long day's dying' (10: 964) may reflect the conventional solution to the dilemma: 'According to the rabbis, Adam died in strict accordance with God's threat on the same day as his transgression,

Figure 10. Piero della Francesca, *Legend of the True Cross: Death of Adam*, fresco, 390 x 747 cm, ca. 1450–65. At the right the dying Adam dispatches Seth for the oil of mercy; in the damaged centre scene Adam's descendants lament his death; at the far left are a young couple, possibly Adam and Eve in Paradise. S. Francisco, Arezzo. Scala / Ministero per i Beni e le Attività culturali / Art Resource, NY.

though, to give him time for repentance, he was allowed one of God's days, which, according to Psalm 90: 4, consists of one thousand years.'[53] The actual total of 930 is accounted for variously by subtracting from 1,000 the seventy of the life-span allotted to Adam's descendants; by the tradition which had Adam bequeath seventy years of his own life to David; or by the mode of computation that added to the Genesis figure whatever number of years God was supposed to have given him at birth thus bringing the total closer to one thousand.[54]

The idea of the thousand-year day of the Lord, setting the absolute limit of human duration, not unnaturally tended to conflate with the division of world history into six days, tempting chronologers to nudge Adam's death to the very boundary of the first day. Irenaeus commented, 'And there are some, again, who relegate the death of Adam to the thousandth year; for since "a day of the Lord is as a thousand years" he did not overstep the thousand years, but died within them, thus bearing out the sentence of his sin.'[55] Despite the undisputed gap between Adam's death in 930 and the Flood in the year 1656, almost all commentators tend to extend Adam's life, figuratively if not literally, nearer to the end of his own day.[56] Sir Thomas Browne writes, 'So by compute of Scripture *Adam* lived unto the ninth generation, unto the days of *Lamech* the Father of *Noah; Methuselah* unto the year of the flood; and *Noah* was the contemporary unto all from *Enoch* unto *Abraham*.'[57] By living into the lifetime of Noah's father, the insinuation might be, Adam becomes a virtual contemporary of Noah. Henry Ainsworth explains, 'By this computation it appeareth, that *Adam* lived to see *Lamech* the ninth generation, in the 56. yere of whose life he dyed first of al these patriarchs.'[58] If one considers that Noah, by surviving the Flood, really becomes a man of the second age, Adam indeed has spanned the first age by living into the lifetime of Lamech, who completes another cycle as the legendary slayer of Cain.[59] Adam, the patriarch of patriarchs and the first man of the first age, dominates his own day with his presence.

Whiting correctly reminded us that the precise detail matters less to Milton than the traditional, Augustinian pattern that he employs as a design.[60] For poetic purposes, Milton willingly presents a highly stylized version of history from the Fall to the Flood. Only four of the first men – Abel, Cain, Enoch, and Noah – are introduced by name; the figures against whose existence Adam's life-span ordinarily would be measured (i.e., Seth, Lamech, and Methuselah) are silently omitted from the visions. Moreover, Milton's poetic view of the first age is latitudinarian enough to permit him to incorporate wholly extrabiblical material (the vision of the Lazar-house, the 'Bevy of fair Women' in vision 3) for thematic purposes.[61] Fittingly, in Milton's symbolic visions of the first age, which thematically anatomize the sins of the Old Adam and lead him to comprehend death – 'For Death from Sin no power can separate' (10: 251) – Adam again lives to the end of his day.

Milton's handling of the two Flood visions that conclude Book 11 may be illuminated by the symbolism of the baptismal rite itself: 'Baptism is a new creating of man to the image of God, following the destruction of the old Adam.' The two-stage rite, which Jean Daniélou describes as 'essentially constituted by the immersion and emersion,'[62] corresponds exactly to Milton's division between the annihilation by the Flood proper (vision 5) and the recession of the Flood with a sign of the renewed covenant between man and God, amid echoes of Creation and anticipations of the millennium (vision 6).

Thematically and, by courtesy of commentary and legend, figuratively as well, the appropriate point at which to represent Adam's death would be prior to the recession of the Flood and therefore within the context of the fifth vision. After the sight of the waters overwhelming all mankind, save those in the ark, Adam collapses under his burden of knowledge:

> How didst thou grieve then, *Adam*, to behold
> The end of all thy Offspring, end so sad,
> Depopulation; thee another Flood,
> Of tears and sorrow a Flood thee also drown'd.
> And sunk thee as thy Sons; till gently rear'd
> By th' Angel, on thy feet thou stood'st at last,
> Though comfortless, as when a Father mourns
> His Children, all in view destroy'd at once. (11: 754–61)

Here Milton appears to draw on the popular belief that one's state of mind in the final moment before death can determine the disposition of one's soul.[63] Adam has progressed from the self-centred reaction to Abel's death (462–5) to a heart-felt desolation at the catastrophic loss of his children, tormented by his responsibility but responding to the trial of this providence with no suggestion of the earlier selfishness. Comprehension of just what his sin has wrought brings Adam to a state of contrition and repentance, symbolized here as elsewhere in the poem (5: 130–5, 10: 909–18, 1100–4) by tears of remorse, now a necessary preliminary to the sacrament of baptism.

The symbolism of the Flood as a type of the reality fulfilled in the antitype of baptism establishes the microcosmic relationship in the 'Flood' of Adam's tears. Daniélou explains:

> As sinful humanity in the time of Noe was destroyed by a judgement of God in the midst of water, and one just man was saved to be the first-born of a new human race, so in Baptism the old man is annihilated by means of the sacrament of water, and the man who comes out of the baptismal pool belongs to the new creation . . . Baptism, as St. Paul tells us, is a sacramental imitation of the death and the resurrection of Christ.[64]

In the vision of the Flood, having watched the progression of his own sin to a state of universality, Adam now has an answer to the questions of his soliloquy in Book 10; he experiences not the death he thought he saw in Abel's, but the death of his own sinfulness in a baptismal flood of remorse, a death which in reality will be achieved through the death of Jesus as described in the matching episode (12: 404–14). Expounding on the meaning of the Saviour's death and resurrection, Michael makes an almost inevitable connection to this rebirth through the mission of the disciples:

> . . . them who shall believe
> Baptizing in the profluent stream, the sign
> Of washing them from guilt of sin to Life
> Pure, and in mind prepar'd, if so befall,
> For death, like that which the redeemer di'd. (12: 441–5)

With the 'old man' (Eph. 4: 22–4, Col. 3: 9–10) put to death, Adam is symbolically purified of his sins and the birth of the 'new man' by the restoration of God's image becomes possible. That Adam has struggled through education, repentance, and purification to spiritual renewal in this succession of providences is suggested by his success at interpreting the spiritual implications of the final vision.

The two visions of the Flood and its recession, then, show Adam making a recovery which itself foreshadows the larger recovery of mankind through Christ's mediation. The imagery used by the narrator to describe Adam's collapse thematically relates the episode to the central issues of the entire poem by recourse to the fall-and-rise pattern ('drown'd,' 'sunk,' 'rear'd,' 'stoods't') that some critics have associated with the *felix culpa.*[65] As Milton wrote in another poem about the meaning of death by water, 'So *Lycidas,* sunk low, but mounted high, / Through the dear might of him that walk'd the waves' (172–3), which serves to emphasize that here Adam does *drown.* The passage alludes tactfully and gracefully (in both senses), I think, to the physical death of Adam. Again the pairing of the fifth vision with the sixth age holds a thematic significance within the design. The reader does not yet know this, but when his mortal life actually ceases Adam will die a Christian.[66] Following his collapse, the phrase 'gently rear'd' describes the literal action of the angel in raising the disconsolate Adam to his feet, but it typologically anticipates his eventual bodily resurrection when 'long Eternity shall greet our bliss / With an individual kiss; / And Joy shall overtake us as a flood' ('On Time,' 12–14).[67] In his personal sequence of providential trials, Adam has learned from each, sometimes backwardly, often painfully, but has come to reason and choose rightly.

The likelihood seems strong that Milton got from Du Bartas the ideas for both Adam's collapse and the shift from vision to narration.[68] The only structural principle of Du Bartas's epic is the parallel week pattern; in the incomplete second week, there are four days, those of Adam, Noah, Abraham, and David, each divided into four parts. Near the end of the fourth part of Adam's day, he is questioned by Seth concerning the fate of the world, and Adam answers by projecting himself into a visionary state, 'by a cleere and certaine pre-science / As *Seer* and *Agent* of all accidents' (605–6). Adam gives Seth a quick overview of the six ages and 'the very *Resting-Day*' (667) before concentrating on the first, bringing this day to a conclusion with the Flood and Adam's reaction to his vision:

> O sonne-les father! o too fruitful haunches!
> O wretched root! o hurtfull hateful branches!
> O gulphes unknowne! o dungeons deepe and blacke!
> O worlds decay! o universall wracke!
> O heav'ns! o seas! o earth! (now earth no more)
> O flesh! o bloud! Heere sorrow stopt the doore
> Of his sad voice, and almost dead for woe,
> The prophetizing spirit forsooke him so.[69]

As is usual with Milton's sources, the differences are more instructive than the similarities. He retains the concept of Adam as visionary, but by placing Adam, rather than Du Bartas's Seth, in the tutorial role, he makes Adam's education and spiritual regeneration the focal point. Whereas by concluding the book with the vision of the world's destruction Du Bartas emphasized the wrath of God, Milton ends with the positive vision of divine love and mercy through the recession of the Flood and renewal of the covenant. Since Du Bartas's Adam begins by summarizing the import of the entire week of history, the failure of the 'prophetizing spirit' clearly has nothing to do with the proper limits of his knowledge; conveying no more than conventional hyperbolic grief, 'almost dead for woe' has no discernible thematic relation to the Flood or to Adam's actual death. The Adam-Seth colloquy simply terminates abruptly at this point, the structure of the ages taking precedence over verisimilitude in dramatic narrative. The second day commences with the poet narrating the story of Noah and makes no mention of the uncompleted recital to Seth.

Milton's reasons for having Michael withdraw the gift of vision and continue in narration would seem, simultaneously, simpler and more complex. First, as Adam's response to the fifth vision served to remind us, there is the fact that his own life must end during the first age. Michael very nearly states it directly:

> Much thou hast yet to see, but I perceive
> Thy mortal sight to fail; objects divine
> Must needs impair and weary human sense:
> Henceforth what is to come I will relate,
> Thou therefore give due audience, and attend. (12: 8–12)

'I perceive / Thy mortal sight to fail' may be understood literally; the point in the revelation of the future has been reached at which the life of the historical Adam has ended. The narrator has covertly described this historical death in the flood-of-tears passage. Michael grants to Adam's purified eyes one glimpse of the renewed world, then terminates the entire visionary process with this speech, succinctly but undeniably linking the two phenomena – mortality and the limits of prophetic vision.

The poetic motive for suppressing any explicit reference to the death of Adam appears to be twofold. On the one hand, the thematic emphasis of the last books on the conversion of Adam dictates that the symbolic death of baptismal purification is the more important. On the other, there is what, for want of a more adequate vocabulary, one is forced to call the angel's humanity. Michael may not be as 'sociably mild' as Raphael, but neither is he fearsome (11: 233–7). As the narrator notes, Michael is himself moved by the death of Abel; moreover, he scrupulously heeds the Father's admonition: 'Yet lest they faint / At the sad Sentence rigorously urg'd, / For I behold them soft'nd and with tears / Bewailing thir excess, all terror hide' (11: 108–11). The stipulation, in retrospect, is an interesting one to ponder, suggesting as it does an index to Adam's strength as well as his weakness.

Consider that at the announcement of his impending exile from the Garden, Adam 'Heart-strook with chilling gripe of sorrow stood' (11: 264); with the vision of the Lazar-house '*Adam* could not, but wept, / Though not of Woman born' (11: 495–6). The cities of the plain (vision 4) again reduce him to tears; finally, the tears culminate with his collapse in a 'flood' at the fifth vision. All of these powerfully affecting revelations are, in Michael's judgment, within Adam's capacity of assimilation. We may well ask, then, what 'terror' does Michael 'hide'? The answer only can be the one revelation that Adam expects and dreads: 'Is this the way / I must return to native dust? O sight / Of terror, foul and ugly to behold, / Horrid to think, how horrible to feel!' (11: 462–5). This must be what Michael deems him incapable of bearing, and he withholds this particular 'sight / Of terror.' Adam's death is a providence granted by the Father as 'His final remedy' (11: 62), allowing him to escape the nightmare of 'endless misery' (10: 810). But the blessing cannot be appreciated until Adam comprehends the 'second Life' (11: 64) to succeed this one. The angel therefore humanely palliates the blunt truth of 'I perceive / Thy mortal sight to fail' with the pretence that he refers only to Adam's present physical state – 'objects divine / Must needs impair and weary human sense' – and not to Adam's situation as an actor in the historical progression.

MacCallum argued that Milton's 'concern with decorum' shapes the proportions of the story, reversing 'normal perspective': 'Events farthest from us are those closest to Adam: they stand in the foreground of his vision, and are correspondingly large. Events which come late in time, even though of great magnitude, are foreshortened.'[70] I would suggest that a related principle of decorum governs the shift in narrative technique: Adam may see directly the events to be lived in his own day, but it is inappropriate for him to see into other ages, which are to be lived by other men. As Arthur Barker put it, Adam can be instructed in the Law and Gospel 'only by prophecy since the dispensation under which Adam lives will end with the many-coloured post-deluvian covenant.'[71]

More significantly, however, the Old Adam is dead. The symbolic baptism that Adam has undergone implies purification by the death of his fallen nature, regeneration of the spirit, and movement toward union with Christ. The thematic division between first Adam and second Adam, a transition that Michael underscores (12: 7, 'Man as from a second stock proceed'; 13, 'This second source of Men'), dictates a shift from the technique associated for Adam with knowledge of evil. Adam must turn from this deadly fruit to the seed of new life growing within, to faith and love as he strives to recreate his spirit in the successive images of the 'one greater Man.'

The Conversion of Adam

The two Adams connect when the first, now taught by Michael how 'joins the Son / Manhood to Godhead' (12: 388–9), acknowledges the second Adam as 'my Redeemer ever blest.' Whereas the secularized reader, committed to the 'autonomous subjectivity' of the individual, may not register the significance of this moment, for Milton, as Addison recognized, it was the narrative climax of the final book, the point at which the epic's dual themes of personal trial and providential design conspicuously merge.[72] For this reason, I would suggest, Books 11 and 12 should be understood as a conversion story. Speculating as to how the Jews might be converted to Christianity, Moses Wall concluded that 'it will be Gods worke, and not mans, as much as Pauls conversion was wholly of God, which himselfe makes the type, or patterne of the conversion of his Country men.'[73] The poet's commitment to the essential roles of human free will and choice, however, ruled out the dramatic model of the sudden conversion, Saul become Paul on the road to Damascus. Nor for Adam's pre-literate stage was conversion through reading, whether Augustine's sudden illumination or Luther's dogged wrestling with the text of Romans, an option, turning the poet instead to another 'type or patterne.'[74] Rather than the immediate transformation, he adopted the model of gradual conversion through instruction. Possibly his use of Augustine's version of the six ages implies an oblique tribute to a famous convert, but, for the actual process of Adam's conversion, Milton looked to a contemporary situation, the conversion of Native Americans.

After their fallen descent to lust, Adam proposes to Eve that they conceal their shame by gathering broad leaves from the banyan fig tree, 'such as at this day to *Indians* known' (9: 1102), and sewing them into a primitive cache-sexe. In one of the poem's rare evocations of a modern man the narrator comments: 'Such of late / *Columbus* found th' *American* so girt / With feather'd Cincture, naked else and wild / Among the Trees on Isles and woody Shores' (9:1115–18). In a nice sleight of hand the sequence begins with a tree from the East Indies, where Columbus had intended to go, and ends with his actual 'discovery' of the West Indies, accurately evoking the attire of the Tainos on Hispaniola.[75] The nature of the Amerindians was a much-vexed controversy throughout the sixteenth and seventeenth centuries. More carefully than most, Martin Evans has considered the implications of Milton's comparison and convincingly maintains that Milton's view, reflected through Adam and Eve, most closely parallels that of the great advocate of Indian rights, Bartolomé de las Casas (1484–1566).[76]

To opponents who justified land seizure, massacres, and enslavement on the grounds that Indians were not human or that they exemplified

Aristotle's theory of natural slaves, las Casas stoutly insisted all races were equal. He conceded that the Indians were at an earlier stage of cultural development, but argued they were in some respects nobler than their Spanish oppressors who had corrupted them. His beliefs were shaped by the first defender of Indian rights, his fellow Dominican, Antonio de Montesinos, who in 1511 delivered a fiery sermon to the settlers at Santo Domingo: 'Are they not men? Do they not have rational souls? Are you not bound to love them as you love yourselves? How can you live in such profound and lethargic slumber? Be sure that in your present state you can no more be saved than the Moors or Turks.'[77] Montesinos's comparison makes an implicit distinction: Indians are heathens, ignorant of Christianity but capable of learning, whereas the Turks, with whom the Spanish are allied by their unchristian behaviour, are infidels, who know but reject it.

With varying degrees of sincerity, the New World colonists from all nations were intent on converting the natives to Christianity; James I praised the Virginia colony for 'so Noble a worke, which may by the providence of Almightie God hereafter tend to the glorie of His Divine Majestie, in the propagating of Christian Religion to such people as yet live in darknesse.'[78] The practices of the Spanish, nonetheless, were distinct. Las Casas and his fellow Dominicans believed Indians must be led to Christianity by Christ's own method of loving and gentle persuasion without coercion, but were hampered by the opposition of both the military and lay settlers. The rival Franciscans, full of millenary fervour, were willing to condone moderate force and, eager to fulfil conditions for the Second Coming, baptized before preaching. Mass baptisms were not uncommon, with one lay brother claiming to have baptized 100,000 Indians in a day.[79] In contrast, profiting from the cautionary examples of the Spanish and of their own earlier blunders, by the 1640s and 1650s both the French Jesuits in Canada and the English Protestants in the New England colonies had evolved more rigorous, yet non-coercive, procedures. Both 'held the Indians to a high standard for baptism and church admission, indeed higher than that set for their own countrymen,' but the process could be much slower in the New England colonies. Whereas the Jesuits held probationers to at least three years preparation for baptism, English missionaries insisted on 'civilizing' the Indians before even beginning religious instruction. In 1654 John Eliot examined eight postulants before his congregation: 'Although their answers to 101 questions on Scripture, Protestant belief, and the conversion experience were entirely satisfactory, Eliot weighted their knowledge and behavior for another six years' before fully admitting them to the church.[80]

In 1713 the fourth-generation missionary Experience Mayhew set off from Martha's Vineyard to the wilds of Connecticut. At Stonington, finding an Indian interpreter, he preached to a group of Pequots: 'Through the interpreter, Mayhew gave the assembly a two-hour history of the world from Creation to the Crucifixion.'[81] I have no doubt that the hard-pressed translator's Pequot was less euphonious than Milton's verse; otherwise, this sounds not unlike the instruction Adam received from two guardian angels. The preparatory stages of religious conversion were fairly consistent: exposition of the scripture to arouse a sense of personal sinfulness and contrition; catechizing to teach the essentials of doctrine and knowledge of Christ's redemptive sacrifice for those who truly repent and accept grace.[82] 'J.F.' [J. Fotherby] summarizes the process: 'If any heathen man desired to be received into the fellowship of the Church, he was first catechized in the principles of Religion, and then hearing further in the Word of God . . . confessed that hee did believe . . . whereupon he was baptized.'[83]

Adam and Eve are like the 'heathen' Amerindians in their fallen condition, their ability to reason, possession of free will, and capacity to learn, expressed both by intellectual curiosity and practical skills.[84] Yet in other ways they clearly are not constrained to the light of nature: they have spoken to their maker; they have been told about Heaven and Hell; and they have heard the Protevangelium, over which Adam searches with his 'steadiest thoughts' (12: 377). If anything, they more nearly are in the situation of the neophyte 'praying Indians,' with some glimmerings of religious knowledge incompletely understood. It would be futile to expect the process of Indian conversion to supply a template for the final books; rather, it may help us to comprehend movements and nuances in the design. In the first positive step Adam's memory focuses on the mysterious curse, 'calling to mind with heed / Part of our Sentence, that thy Seed shall bruise / Th' Serpent's head' (10: 1030–2). Adam does not know that he is aided by the 'Prevenient Grace' that 'remov'd / The stony from thir hearts' (11: 3–4), since he cannot hear the Son remark approvingly, 'See Father, what first fruits on Earth are sprung / From thy implanted Grace in Man' (11: 22–3). Adam's recollection prompts the resolution to 'confess / Humbly our faults, and pardon beg, with tears' and, echoing David's penitential psalm (51: 17), sighs 'sent from hearts contrite' (10: 1088–9, 1091).[85] Reciprocally, the prayer evokes the Son's compassionate promise of redemption and the Father's charge to Michael. Some readers, encountering the acknowledgment of 'implanted' grace, have felt that this robs the prayer of significance. The concept of prevenient grace presented in the poem, however, is distinctly Arminian – universal, necessary, but not sufficient, and resistible.[86] This Arminian moment of free responsiveness to resistible grace, human will colleague with divine mercy, initiates a process of trial and learning that is completed with justification by faith alone, Christ's 'obedience / Imputed becomes theirs by Faith' (12: 408–9).

Nonetheless their first confession is imperfect. Adam and Eve at this point know they have been disobedient, but have no adequate comprehension of the evil they have loosed in the world. The visions that follow, as we have seen, bring home by brutal shock and by incremental expansion what it means to have 'Brought Death into the World, and all our woe' (1: 3). Michael's technique of instruction through the power of vision is here like that employed by the Jesuits, who, in contrast to the Protestant missionaries' heavy reliance on the catechism, used a panoply of visual devices – painted cards, engravings, illustrated books, hand-drawn pictures. Father Jean Pierron wrote, 'Our Indians see a graphic representation of what I teach them, by which they are powerfully moved.'[87] Each in his own way, Pierron and Milton seemingly draw on the medieval tradition of *sacra memoria*, adapting the visual rhetoric once expressed in illuminated Bibles, carved friezes, murals, and 'storied Windows richly dight' ('Il Penseroso,' 159). As powerfully as any of his Indian descendants, Adam is moved by the visions, which reach their wrenching nadir, first, in massacre (vision 4), then in what Adam fears is genocide by a wrathful God (vision 5): 'The end of all thy Offspring, end so sad, / Depopulation' (11: 755–6). At this moment Adam, with a heightened sense of sinfulness and remorse, undergoes his symbolic baptism, drowned in 'another Flood / Of tears and sorrow' (756–7).

Because catechizing is fundamental preparation for baptism,[88] we may wonder at its apparent omission; this query again brings into relief the differences between Books 11 and 12, the former being more dialogic and the latter expository. Although Adam addresses Michael as 'guide,' 'teacher,' and 'instructor,' in Book 11 there is a role reversal in that he is (to borrow George Herbert's terms) the 'Questionist' and the angel the 'Answerer.' To five of the six visions Adam responds with questions; only with the third, exhibiting his particular vulnerability, does he react to the 'Bevy of fair Women' with the mistaken confidence of flat declaration. This unorthodox process implicitly concedes the historical situation in the first age – no Ten Commandments, Apostles' Creed or Lord's Prayer – while evoking a sense of catechistic instruction through Adam's earnest effort and Michael's patient responses. The baptismal 'death' following vision 5 indicates that Adam now understands the meaning of original sin with full remorse for what he has done to his descendants. With the sixth vision, the recession of the Flood, his questions cease to be appeals for information. Confirming his augmented knowledge, he seeks his teacher's approval of cautiously ventured interpretations and receives it: 'Dext'rously thou aim'st; / So willingly doth God remit his ire' . . . 'And makes a Cov'nant' (11: 884–5, 892). The 'skill' of catechizing, Herbert advised, resides first in having in mind 'an aim and mark of the whole discourse.'[89] The angel's approval effaces his own skill, while commending Adam's in hitting that mark.

Baptism, 'being the first step in their great and glorious calling,'[90] is a significant advance, not an end, and so the process continues. With the shift from vision to extended narration in Book 12 the questions become sparse. As Herbert explains, catechistical instruction has its limitation and must be supplemented by sermons, 'For questions cannot inflame or ravish, that must be done by a set, and labored, and continued speech.'[91] What follows is 'labored' in more than one sense. Not only must Michael work hard to achieve his end; Adam must labour to comprehend the strange, rather disjunctive narrative. His responses sometimes expose both a novice's eagerness to please and an incomplete grasp, which the angel patiently corrects and advances.[92] When Michael's sermon reaches the New Testament and he tells the Nativity story, 'discerning *Adam* with such joy / Surcharg'd, as had like grief been dew'd in tears' (12: 372–3), he pauses for Adam's interjection, 'O prophet of glad tidings, finisher / Of utmost hope!' (375–6). The angel continues his account of the Son's life to the Four Last Things, and again pauses for Adam, 'Replete with joy and wonder,' to exclaim, 'O goodness infinite, goodness immense!' (468, 469). Addison commented appreciatively on this speech:

> The Poet has very finely represented the Joy and Gladness of Heart which rises in *Adam* upon his Discovery of the *Messiah.* As he sees his Day at a Distance through Types and Shadows, he rejoices in it; but when he finds

> the Rede[m]ption of Man compleated, and *Paradise* again renewed, he breaks forth in Rapture and Transport.[93]

Like Herbert, Addison apprehends the power of a good sermon to 'enflame or ravish.'

Michael's perception that the intensity of Adam's present joy, 'dew'd in tears,' equals the intensity of his tearful 'like grief' at the Flood, reminds us of the parallel between vision 5 and the sixth age, a reminder made more overt with the angel's explanation of the meaning of baptism: the cleansing of guilt and preparation 'For death, like that which the redeemer di'd' (12: 445). As with the judgment on the serpent, baptism is a mystery, the meaning of which gradually exfoliates over the final books. *De Doctrina* presents baptism as signifying spiritual regeneration and 'a kind of symbol of our death, burial and resurrection with Christ' (*CPW* 6: 552), supported by a cluster of citations from the Pauline epistles, perhaps most pertinently Romans 6: 3, 'Know ye not, that so many of us as were baptized into Jesus Christ were baptized into his death?' and Colossians 2: 12, 'buried with him in baptism, wherein also ye are risen with *him* through the faith.' The Crucifixion slays both the old Law and Adam's sins; although Christ dies, he rises incorrupt, 'Out of his grave, fresh as the dawning light' (12: 423). Adam, 'Greatly instructed' (12: 557), has come to understand that through faith his death, in the narrative past but temporal future, can be 'the Gate of Life; / Taught this by his example whom I now / Acknowledge my Redeemer ever blest' (571–3). Whereas he correctly reasoned, 'All of me then shall die' (10: 792), he now knows that, through his redeemer, all of him shall rise again.

In this response to extraordinary providence, the crucial trial for which Books 11 and 12 have prepared him, not only does Adam become the first Christian and the first Protestant justified by faith,[94] he also converts his 'baptism' from symbol to reality, to a true covenant of grace. The usual objections marshalled against the baptism of such 'heathens' as Indians or of infants – their lack of instruction and understanding, their inability to undertake a covenant or make a vow (see *CPW* 6: 544–5) – have been obviated. On hearing the contrite prayer of Adam and Eve, the Son urged his Father to peaceful reconciliation with mankind until death 'To better life shall yield him, where with mee / All my redeem'd may dwell in joy and bliss, / Made one with me as I with thee am one' (11: 42–4). The first Adam and second Adam are to become one, a promise that will guide Adam's future life, 'to walk /

As in his presence, ever to observe / His providence, and on him sole depend' (12: 562–4).[95]

Milton's attraction to the Amerindian model for conversion may well have been an outgrowth of political circumstances in the 1650s, during England's war with Spain (1655–9). 'Providence' had been nudging the Protector into hatching his ambitious 'Western Design' with its multiple objectives of challenging Spain's imperial dominance and thereby striking a blow at the papacy, gaining a share of the New World treasure and, not least, converting the Indians. In 1654 Thomas Gage advised Cromwell that a military strike would lead to the 'ruining and utter fall of Romish Babylon, and to the conversion of those poore and simple Indians.'[96] Milton's role, if any, in Cromwell's *Declaration* of the cause against Spain has been much disputed. The English *Declaration* was printed in October 1655, followed in November by a Latin translation; during the eighteenth century the Latin was attributed to Milton and the additional claim was made that it preceded the English text, thus implying that the English was the translation.[97] The fact that Milton's nephew John Phillips translated las Casas's *Brevíssima relación de la destruición de las Indias* (1542) has not seemed relevant, given the legend of Phillips's estrangement from his uncle.

Recently, however, John Shawcross has discredited that legend and indicated, in their shared opposition to the papacy and the Spanish, the 'probable positive connection' between the kinsmen and the works printed a year apart.[98] Phillips's translation, *The Tears of the Indians being An Historical and True Account Of the Cruel Massacres and Slaughters of above Twenty Millions of innocent people; Committed by the Spaniards* (1656), is dedicated to the Lord Protector, urging him to 'arm for their Revenge,' and to 'all true English-men.' Phillips describes the Indians as 'poor innocent Heathens . . . having onely the light of Nature, not knowing their Saviour Jesus Christ.' He praises the *Declaration* set forth 'as if Providence had so ordain'd it,' and asserts the rights of the English to the West Indies, 'seeing that by Divine Providence the cruelties and Barbarian Massacres of the Spanish have been so apparently presented to you.'[99] Phillips's projection of a providence that creates optimal conditions for Englishmen to smite God's enemies seems more suited to Oliver Cromwell than to John Milton with the possible exception of one provocation – genocide. Urging 'just Revenge,' the *Declaration* asserts, '*God hath made of one blood, all Nations of men, for to dwell on all the face of the Earth,*' and 'will have an accompt of the Innocent Blood of so many Millions of Indians so barbarously Butchered by the Spaniards.' At the end of the *Declaration* the author links Spanish barbarity in the West Indies with 'that sad Tragedy which was lately acted upon Our Brethren in the Valleys of Piedmont.'[100] Milton's Sonnet 18 called on the Lord to avenge the Waldensians, whom he had praised for practising the most ancient reformed Christianity (see *CPW* 3: 513–14; 7: 291–2 and n. 34); in the *Declaration* the English are called upon to exact the Lord's will.

Bartolomé de las Casas's career particularly was associated with Hispaniola (now Haiti and the Dominican Republic), his first post in the Indies and the place that remained his base. Although the *Brevíssima relación* ranges from the Indies to the mainland Americas, it begins with the atrocities committed on Hispaniola. John Phillips's translation may have been timed to foment support for Cromwell's ambitious but risky 'Western Design' in the Caribbean. Answering John Lambert's strenuous objections to the plan, the Protector replied, 'Now Providence seemed to lead us hither, having 160 ships swimminge,' causing him to dispatch thirty-eight of those ships and over 8,000 soldiers to capture Hispaniola.[101] The mismanaged assault failed (April 1655); the lesser prize of Jamaica was captured instead (May); and, when the commanders, Admiral William Penn and Colonel Robert Venables, returned to England without permission (September), they were imprisoned briefly for their incompetence. Never again could Cromwell assume that his judgment and providence were one; instead, he became haunted by the sin of Achan (see chap. 1). Phillips's translation was in press at the very end of the year (Thomason's copy is dated 9 January 1656), but plausibly begun before the failure of the Hispaniola expedition was known. If Cromwell ever read the dedication, it must have been ashes in his mouth.

John Phillips may have been more credulous, or simply pragmatic, than his uncle, but, given the probability of Milton's participation in the state correspondence concerning the Piedmont massacre (25 May–31 July 1655) and the personal reaction expressed in Sonnet 18,[102] there is no reason to think he would not have been equally appalled by the far more extensive massacre of the Amerindians. Nor that he would not have held the 'Triple Tyrant,' in thrall to Antichrist, responsible for both. In his official capacity Milton wrote for the Protector to the king of Sweden (August 1656): 'Who does not know that the counsels of the Spaniards and the Roman Pontiff have for these two years thrown all these places into confusion by the burning, the massacre [*cladibus*] and the harassment of the orthodox?' (*CPW* 5, pt. 2: 755). Solicitude over Spanish depredations rises to the surface of the epic when the narrator speculates that, ascended to the visionary height, 'in Spirit perhaps [Adam] also saw' the riches of the New World 'yet unspoil'd' (11: 406, 410). Adam soon learns that the crime of massacre, too, was in his heritage (vision 4); and the lesson he draws from it, 'all in tears,' is the same one espoused by Montesinos, las Casas, and by the author of Cromwell's *Declaration:*

> O what are these,
> Death's Ministers, not Men, who thus deal Death
> Inhumanely to men, and multiply
> Ten thousandfold the sin of him who slew
> His Brother; for of whom such massacre
> Make they but of thir Brethren, men of men? (*PL* 11: 675–80)

The poet expands Genesis 6: 5 into a 'bloody fray' and 'slaughter' that Adam can recognize as massacre in words coming close to Phillips's vision of the Spanish killing Indians 'not as if they had been their Fellow-Mortals, but like Death itself.' It seems unlikely, therefore, that Milton did not respond to the plight of the Amerindians, nor that he did not consider the concomitant problem of their conversion, for here, having only the 'light of Nature,' they part company with the Waldensians.[103]

Amerindian conversion itself, moreover, was part of a larger phenomenon. By the beginning of the century the origin of the Indians had become a subject of debate, one theory being that they descended from the ten lost tribes of Israel. The debate intensified in the 1640s when the Marrano Antonio de Montezinos (Aaron ha-Levi) 'proved' the theory, convincing the Amsterdam Rabbi Menasseh ben Israel that he had found, in the interior of Quito Province (Ecuador), a secret kingdom of Israelites. At the request of John Dury, who in 1652 would translate *Eikonoklastes* into French, Menasseh sent an account of this to London; it was translated and printed in Thomas Thorowgood's *Ievvs in America* (1650) with an 'Epistolary Discourse' by Dury. This rapidly was followed by Menasseh's own book, *The Hope of Israel* (1650; 2nd ed., 1651, corrected 1652), translated by Moses Wall, a figure in the Dury-Hartlib circle and an astute correspondent with Milton.[104] Menasseh's preface offers the judgment that 'no opinion [is] more probable, nor agreeable to reason, than that . . . the first inhabitants of American were the Ten Tribes of the Israelites'; and Montezinos's 'Relation' concludes with the assurance that the secret Israelites will lead the Indians to expel the Spanish oppressors and release all Jews from their bondage.[105]

Reading *The Hope of Israel*, Ralph Josselin prayed, 'lord my heart questions not the calling home the nation of the Jewes thou wilt hasten in its season, oh my god, oh thou god of the ends of the whole earth, hasten it Amen.'[106] His reaction was not unique. With the 'discovery' of the lost tribes in the Americas, only one condition remained to be fulfilled before the Second Coming. Andrew Marvell, in a lyric probably composed in the early fifties, wittily exploited the climate of millenary excitement over 'the conversion of the Jews.'[107] Dury announced enthusiastically, 'The palpable and present acts of providence, doe more than hint the approach of Jesus Christ. And the Generall consent of many judicious, and godly Divines, doth induce *considering minds* to beleeve, that the conversion of the Jewes is at hand.'[108] Menasseh came to England in 1655, appearing before the Council of State to petition for Jewish readmission and remaining two years as a dependent of Cromwell's government. The Whitehall Conference of December 1655 debated the readmission question through four sessions without reaching a conclusion.

Milton remained silent on the whole matter, a reticence entirely to his credit; nonetheless, he could not have been ignorant of the weight with which religious conversion of both Jews and Indians had been freighted.[109] Although by January of that year the elder poet may have had misgivings about the millenarian expectations for Cromwell's leadership in Marvell's 'The First Anniversary,' nonetheless he may well have shared his friend's view of the Protector's foreign opponents, 'Unhappy princes, ignorantly bred, / By malice some, by errour more misled' (117–18). '[M]ad with reason, so miscalled, of state,' they 'sing hosanna to the whore / And her whom they should massacre adore: / But Indians whom they should convert, subdue; / Nor teach, but traffic with, or burn the Jew' (111, 113–16). Neatly turning the massacre trope against Catholic Spain, the lines concisely present the religious motives impelling the 'Western Design.' The spiritual situations of Jews, disbelievers in the divinity of Jesus Christ, and 'heathen' Indians obviously were dissimilar. Even so, in popular imagination the myths associating Native Americans with the ten lost tribes firmly linked their conversions as among the 'great designs kept for the latter days' (110).

Milton was motivated, I suggest, by his own and by contemporary English revulsion at the massacres of innocent peoples to use this crime for Adam's anguished comprehension with vision 4 of the evil that his legacy of original sin entails. This awareness is compounded by the crushing recognition of his own responsibility for an even greater massacre, the world's 'depopulation' in the Flood (vision 5), moving him to full contrition. The angel Michael complements this tormenting awareness in the stern but benevolent sermon, leading Adam to become, like the 'praying Indians' of New England, a Christian.

When Michael commands Adam to 'Ascend / This Hill' in order to learn the future from Genesis to Revelation, the first man 'gratefully' replies, 'Ascend, I follow thee, safe Guide, the path / Thou lead'st me, and to the hand of Heav'n submit, / However chast'ning' (11: 371–3), intuiting that he will see providence working. Christian history is by definition providential, informed by the Son's voluntary incarnation and sacrifice to redeem fallen humanity, thereby fulfilling the 'Law of God,' 'Both by obedience and by love' (12: 403). The Christocentrism of *Paradise Lost* now has become an accepted truism, although not all of its ramifications have been considered. Indulge me by entertaining for a moment this scenario. A printer, desirous of publishing a poetry anthology – a Restoration *Norton Anthology,* if you will – approaches our poet with an agonizing choice. Given the necessity of including ample selections from Dryden, Waller, Rochester, and others, there is space for only a single book of the epic. Which will it be, Mr. Milton? I think he might have offered the final book as the most important in the poem. In Books 11 and 12 the subtle juxtaposition of visions to ages most directly manifests the large design of providence while presenting a sequence of trials, providences, to which Adam must respond and from which he learns obedience, faith, and love, 'the Soul / Of all the rest' (12: 584–5). His baptism and the Book 12 conversion are effective warrants of his renovation; yet, even with providential guidance, the trials will continue, 'Tri'd in sharp tribulation, and refin'd / By Faith and faithful works' (11: 63–4), as perseverance becomes the issue (3: 194–7). Nor will Satan be the only tempter. The forlorn fallen angels, under new names, will wander the world, 'Through God's high sufferance for the trial of man' (1: 366).[110] In a popular advice manual for ministers, Richard Bernard addressed the problem of how to frame the 'reasons of Comforts and Encouragements.' These come 'generally from Gods prouidence,' and prominent among the specifics are 'the benefits of tryall.'[111] Michael's sermon has made Adam understand that he is blessed in both.

Providentially for Adam, he has Eve with her strength of character, commitment to their marriage and to their redeemer: 'Both in one Faith unanimous' (12: 603). In the last spoken words of the epic, her assurance that 'In mee is no delay; with thee to go / Is to stay here; without thee here to stay, / Is to go hence unwilling' (615–17) paraphrases

Ruth 1: 16 in figures of repetition that emphasize the renewal of their marriage, but also her own perseverance in her commitment to their Saviour. The Calvinist annotators of the Geneva Bible interpreted Ruth's declaration to exemplify irresistible grace,[112] but Milton gave it a different inflection. Eve is 'secure' (620) not in her own salvation, but in the consolation that through her others will be saved. As Ruth's decision results in the house of David, so Eve's will eventuate in Jesus. Countermanding the Satanically inspired clairvoyance of Eve's earlier dream, the God-sent sleep has endowed her with understanding and acceptance of the Protevangelium that her consort so racked his mind to comprehend: 'Such favor I unworthy am voutsaf't / By mee the Promis'd Seed shall all restore' (622–3).[113] Sometimes the workings of providence are not mysterious. Eve's *all* affirms what is not stated in Genesis 3: 15, nor explicit in 10: 179–81 of the epic;[114] in Milton's Arminian vision, Christ died, not just for the elect or the 'saints,' but for all of us, 'that whosoever believeth in him should not perish, but have everlasting life' (John 3: 16).

When the Father dispatched his 'Vicegerent Son' to judge Adam and Eve, he characterized him as 'Man's Friend, his Mediator, his design'd / Both Ransom and Redeemer voluntary, / And destin'd Man himself' (10: 60–2). The concise description brings together at once God's love for justice and for humans ('Ransom and Redeemer'), angelic and human free will ('voluntary'), and his providence ('design'd' and 'destin'd'). The angelic emissaries of extraordinary providence do vanish with the expulsion, Michael's direct guidance now replaced 'within them as a guide' by God's 'Umpire *Conscience*.' It would be a mistake, however, to conclude that 'Providence thir guide' encompasses only 'special,' ordinary human providence in the fallen world. Like no other, this couple, their marriage now secure, bear in memory Michael's revelation of the future Redeemer, whom they have embraced as their own. In the poet's view, Adam and Eve truly have received an extraordinary dispensation of providence, perhaps the most extraordinary imaginable. And providence is not just 'thir guide'; one might well say, as Milton himself apparently believed, that in imagining and completing the composition of *Paradise Lost*, providence was *his* guide.

Afterword

> But even the faithful are sometimes insufficiently aware of all these methods of divine providence, until they examine the subject more deeply and become better informed about the word of God.
>
> (*CPW* 6: 339)

In the preceding chapters I have attempted to 'examine the subject more deeply,' thereby shedding some light on the manifold 'methods' of providence that inform Milton's poem. Doubtless there are poetic simulations and evocations of providence that I have not discussed, and not everything I have argued will be equally convincing to readers. Milton scholars and critics all are Protestants, fiercely guarding their individual right to pore over the sacred text and decide each for him or herself what it means. This is as it should be, in accordance with the universal free will asserted by the poem, for to do other against one's own judgment, the author argued, would be heresy. Nonetheless, some limitations and difficulties have to be acknowledged. Brian Cummings adamantly maintains, 'Without reference to religion, the study of early modern writing is incomprehensible.' One senses the tone of frustration in his complaint: 'Writing was produced in the context of a religious crisis which overwhelmed political and social culture. Only by an odd prejudice of literary history can such matters be regarded as peripheral to literary production.'[1] This disinclination to take religion seriously as a motive in literary texts may well be a reflex of the secularization that has created, in John Rogers's phrase, the 'autonomous subjectivity' of the individual or what Charles Taylor defines as a 'self "buffered" by a sense of confidence in its own powers of control.'[2]

In Milton scholarship the problem is not so much that religion is neglected, but that frequently it tends to focus on ecclesiology, sacramentalism, and on rather abstruse theological questions, which perhaps have the appeal of intellectual puzzles and constructs. Much of this has little relevance to *Paradise Lost*. By contrast seventeenth-century providentialism was the most quotidian of religious beliefs, a felt connection with the omnipresence of God in everyday life – popular, rather than elite religion, one might say. Yet by 'popular,' as the first chapter will have made clear, I do not endorse Christopher Hill's now often challenged thesis of a Milton ingesting ideas from radical sectarians. This is neither to deny Milton's engaged knowledge of theology nor his immersion in current events, but only to insist that for him, as much as for Cromwell or Charles I, providence was a vital, direct force in his life, crucial to the production and understanding of much of his writing.

The lack of sustained attention to providence in *Paradise Lost* quite possibly results from the assumptions of a secularism that make it difficult to give credence to the assumptions of – in Peter Laslett's celebrated title – 'the world we have lost.' Discussing eighteenth-century deism as the intermediate step to modern secularism, Taylor notes that extraordinary providence had been the first casualty, leaving only a remote general providence: '[God's] Providence consists simply in his plans for us, which we understand. "Particular providences," unforeseeable interventions in specific cases, have no more place in the scheme than miracles.'[3] This particular 'disenchantment' obviously did not occur overnight; in a more nuanced account we have the irony that deists saluted Milton as an ancestor for his writings on religious toleration.[4] Nonetheless, by 1674, the year in which two long providential trials were completed – the twelve-book edition of *Paradise Lost* and the poet's own life – already there were straws in the wind. Shortly thereafter the Earl of Rochester, atheist until his death-bed conversion (1680), wrote dismissively of a providence 'that never made a thing in vain, / But does each Insect, to some end ordain.' So much for the provident Emmet.[5] Indeed, Cartesian mechanism brought even general providence under threat, causing English philosophers to worry that 'the banishment of Providence from the present world would lead men to believe that the world had always been without Providence.' In response to such concerns Newton projected an 'unwinding' cosmos that required periodic providential governance to reform the system.[6] Genevieve Lloyd concurs with Taylor's account of the path to secularism, observing that 'For us . . . providence is akin to those evocative but ghostly ideas Wittgenstein describes as wheels that turn without moving any part of the conceptual mechanism.'[7]

Rather than only turning ghostly wheels, I hope to have succeeded in reading the epic in the spirit of the idealized contemporaries whom the poet praised as 'a Nation not slow and dull, but of a quick, ingenious, and piercing spirit, acute to invent, suttle and sinewy to discours . . . reading, trying all things, assenting to the force of reason and convincement' (*CPW* 2: 551, 554). If so, readers may have become 'better informed' about the centrality of providence to seventeenth-century life, and to Milton's great poem.

Notes

Introduction

1 For a concise summary of Milton's prose comments on the subject, see John M. Steadman, 'Providence,' in Hunter, *A Milton Encyclopedia*.
2 See Gerald Hammond's provocative reading in *Fleeting Things*; quotation, 192.
3 Burden, *The Logical Epic*, is an exception, but his emphasis on a neoclassical epic of order, rationality, and clarification makes his exposition distinct from my own.
4 See, e.g., McGrath, *Iustitia Dei*. Recently Michael Bryson has stated with commendable lucidity: 'What Milton says he will "justify" is not God itself – God as an ontological essence – but the "ways of God": the observable, conceivable, categorizable aspects and actions of God in the world.' See *The Tyranny of Heaven*, 122.
5 Lieb, *Theological Milton*, discusses the concept of the 'hidden' God, *deus absconditus*, at length; see 73–6 for Reformed thought on the matter; see also Bryson, 'The Mysterious Darkness of Unknowing.'
6 Summers, *The Muse's Method*, 113. J.R. Watson, 'Divine Providence,' similarly urged that these books are 'the expression of a Divine Providence which is outside time and not subject to the laws of cause and effect' (154).
7 Shawcross, *With Mortal Voice*, 21–32.
8 See Bennett, *Reviving Liberty*, 83–92, 109–18; quotation, 89. 'This view of providential history,' she writes, 'looks at events not as discrete manifestations of God's intervention in human affairs, but as a complex, ultimately unified, network of passages comprising God's universal government' (84). In a later article she states, 'In Milton's poetic conception,

before the fall, Providence appeared to humans as a Person, but after the fall, that Person appeared more commonly in "providences" and "signs."' See 'Asserting Eternal Providence,' 223. The earlier definition sounds like ordinary providence; the later an extraordinary providence seemingly indistinguishable from that discounted in the earlier quotation. Fleming, *Milton's Secrecy and Philosophical Hermeneutics*, 167, explains, '"Special" providence designates direct and targeted divine intervention,' without noticing that *DDC* would term this 'extraordinary.'

9 See Rogers, *The Matter of Revolution*, 144–7, 154–66; 170–6; quotations in order, 157, 159, 160.

10 Evans, *Milton's Imperial Epic*, 138. See 135–9 for a discussion of providence at odds with what will follow here. In sharp criticism of Evans, Paul Stevens objects, 'Over and again Milton is credited with the views of the most extravagantly idealizing of propagandists.' See 'Milton and the New World,' 91.

11 See Paul Stevens, 'Milton's "Renunciation" of Cromwell,' who argues that 'nationalism' is a more appropriate rubric than 'republicanism'; he extends this view in 'How Milton's Nationalism Works.' Robert Fallon, '*A Second Defence*,' denies that Cromwell is criticized; Knoppers, *Constructing Cromwell*, 93, mediates, 'But too strict a focus on republicanism underestimates the shared Protestant ideals.' Holberton, *Poetry and the Cromwellian Protectorate*, 2, also cautions that 'the impress of republican thought on mid-century writing might be exaggerated.' In a frontal attack William Walker, Paradise Lost *and Republican Tradition*, argues that republican tradition has been misrepresented and challenges political readings of the epic.

12 Stephen M. Fallon, *Milton's Peculiar Grace* 38, x, 30. Though he would disagree thoroughly with the denial that Milton is religious, the title emphasis of Lieb's *Theological Milton* unwittingly may lend support. In a review, *MP* 108 (2011): 177–82, Paul Stevens astutely notes that, in denying Milton has an authentic religious sensibility, Fallon revives a commonplace of mid-twentieth century criticism. Milton's Puritanism is an unquestioned assumption of Fallon's book (see, e.g., 21). That assumption is contested by Martin, *Milton among the Puritans*.

13 As will be seen, my concern with the multiplicity of designs distinguishes the usage from that by Crump, *The Mystical Design of* Paradise Lost, who finds circles and circularity everywhere in the poem.

14 Letter to Robert Hammond, 25 November 1648, quoted from Paul, *The Lord Protector*, 408.

1. Providence and Providences

1 Worden, 'Providence and Politics,' 55. More recently see Walsham, *Providence in Early Modern England*. Still valuable are Thomas, *Religion and the Decline of Magic*, chap. 4, 'Providence,' 78–112; and Christopher Hill, *God's Englishman*, chap. 9, 'Providence and Oliver Cromwell,' 219–50.

2 Walsham, *Providence*, 2–3.

3 See Worden, 'Providence and Politics,' 60–1; Walsham, *Providence*, 12.

4 *DDC*, bk. 1, chap. 8 (*CPW* 6: 326); chap. 9 addresses the special providence governing angels and chap. 10 humans. For the attribution controversy set off in 1991 by William B. Hunter, see Campbell, Corns, Hale, and Tweedie, *Milton and the Manuscript of* De Doctrina Christiana, v, 1–4, and bibliography. With the addition of David L. Holmes, this team published an inconclusive preliminary report, 'The Provenance of *De Doctrina Christiana*.' There the stylometric analysis confirmed Milton's involvement, but suggested possible collective authorship or adaptation of other texts. Now, somewhat more firmly, they state that, 'if one adopts a nuanced sense of what constitutes authorship' in the genre of systematic theology, 'then Milton may be said to be the author of the treatise' (3, and see 139). Although the extent of his authorship is open to question, for the sake of simplicity I cite it as 'Milton's.'

5 'Providence,' 1–4, 8, quoted from *The Works of George Herbert*, ed. F.E. Hutchinson. Text quoted hereafter.

6 For the popularity of the text, see Worden, 'Providence and Politics,' 60, 80; and Walsham, *Providence*, 10–11. For the particularly Protestant filiation of Shakespeare's play, see Waddington, 'Lutheran Hamlet.'

7 Patrides, *The Grand Design of God*, 7.

8 Letter of 2 April 1650, quoted from Paul, *The Lord Protector*, 28. Providential design is the guiding principle of Ralegh's *History of the World* (1614).

9 Quoted from Worden, 'Providence and Politics,' 63. He cites *The Works of Francis Bacon*, ed. J. Spedding, R.L. Ellis, and D.D. Heath, 14 vols (London, 1857–74), 6: 413. I have been unable to verify the reference.

10 Thomas, *Religion*, 80.

11 See John Henry, 'Henry More versus Robert Boyle,' 67, from Boyle's *Considerations about the Reconcileableness of Reason and Religion* (1675). For Boyle's conviction of his own providential deliverance from death, see Worden, 'Providence and Politics,' 64.

12 Sibbes, 'Of the Providence of God,' quoted from Walsham, *Providence*, 10.

13 *A Priest to the Temple, Or, The Country Parson*, chap. 30, *The Works*, 270.

14 See Corbett and Norton, *Engraving in England*, 146, no. 149. Early in the treatise (pt. 1, sec. 17) Browne expatiates on extraordinary providence: 'Surely there are in every mans Life certain rubs, doublings and wrenches, which pass a while under the effects of chance, but at the last well examined, prove the meer hand of God.' Quoted from *Religio Medici* (7th ed. 1672), 13 (bound with *Pseudodoxia Epidemica*, 6th ed. 1672). Texts cited hereafter.

15 For the constant activity of reading judgments and mercies in daily life, see Seaver, *Wallington's World*, 46–66, 152–6.

16 Donne, *Devotions upon Emergent Occasions*, Meditation XVII, p. 109. For the best account of affliction, see McGee, *The Godly Man in Stuart England*, chap. 2, 'The Rhetoric of Suffering.' See also Walsham, *Providence*, 15–17; and Harley, 'Spiritual Physic, Providence and English Medicine, 1560–1640,' who concentrates on the afflictions of illness and plague.

17 *Advice to Sufferers*. In *The Complete Works of John Bunyan*, 2: 273.

18 See Thomas, *Religion*, 82.

19 Ibid., 79.

20 Worden, 'Providence and Politics,' 88, n. 157.

21 See Cust, 'Charles I and Providence,' 198. See also the prison verses attributed to Charles, which begin: 'In all things here Gods providence / and will alone commands.' *The Kings last Farewell to the World* (1648), quoted from John Wallace, *Destiny His Choice* (Cambridge, 1968), 80.

22 See Dzelzainis, '"Undoubted Realities": Clarendon and Sacrilege,' and Finlayson, 'Clarendon, Providence and the Historical Revolution.'

23 Walsham, *Providence*, 2, 5.

24 Quoted from Chandos, *In God's Name*, 427.

25 I quote the Geneva Bible translation. The King James version, 'Prove all things; hold fast that which is good,' may underlie Herbert's struggle with the burden of providence in 'The Holdfast.'

26 Quoted from Christopher Hill, *God's Englishman*, 225. His discussion treats this activism as a particularly Puritan phenomenon, but, following Walsham, I would suggest it is simply Protestant.

27 See Smith, *Perfection Proclaimed*, 157–9.

28 See Christopher Hill, *God's Englishman*, 227–8, 234–5, quotation, 228; Worden, 'Providence and Politics,' 65–6; and Paul, *The Lord Protector*, 114–15.

29 For the biblical context, see Lieb, *Poetics of the Holy*, 297–301; and Haskin, *Milton's Burden of Interpretation*, 91–109, on 'talent.'

30 See Tyacke, 'Appendix: Defining Arminianism,' in his *Aspects of English Protestantism, c. 1530–1700*, 156–9; quotation, 156. His use of the term does not imply a direct line of influence; 'what comes to be called Arminianism

is virtually indistinguishable from the Melanchthonian brand of Lutheranism' (156). A similar doctrine of conditional election was developed by Peter Baro (Pierre Baron), Lady Margaret Professor of Divinity at Cambridge (1574–96). For a comparison, see Stanglin, '"Arminius *avant la letter*."' For the influence of Melanchthon and Hemmingsen on Arminius, see also Stanglin, *Arminius on the Assurance of Salvation*, 84 and n. 47.

31 It was in the debates of the synod that the five points of Calvinist doctrine summarized by the acronym TULIP (Total depravity, Unconditional election, Limited atonement, Irresistible grace, the Perseverance of the saints) were set in stone. On the respective positions, see, e.g., Tyacke, 'Defining Arminianism'; also Stephen Fallon, 'Milton's Arminianism and the Authorship of *De doctrina Christiana*,' 104–6; and Kendall, *Calvin and English Calvinism to 1649*, 149–50.

32 Anthony Farindon, letter of 27 September 1657, in Hales, *Golden Remains*, A4v. Hales attended as chaplain of the ambassador, Dudley Carleton, to whom he reported in letters. For a documentary history of the British delegation, see Anthony Milton, *The British Delegation and the Synod of Dort (1618–1619)*. Godfrey maintains that Hales's apostasy is more myth than truth, but concedes that Farindon's prefatory comment, 'He has often told me,' remains difficult to explain. See 'John Hales' Good-Night to John Calvin.' Campbell and Corns, *John Milton*, 104, follow David Masson in speculating that Hales may have been 'Mr H,' the 'learned friend' who introduced Milton to Sir Henry Wotton.

33 Tyacke's published work began with a celebrated article, 'Puritanism, Arminianism and Counter-Revolution' (1973), reprinted in *Aspects of English Protestantism*, 132–55, expanded and extended with his book *Anti-Calvinists*, and with further articles. For qualifications to and refinements of his position, see his introduction to *Aspects*, 1–36. For an appraisal of its significance, see Peter Lake, 'Introduction: Puritanism, Arminianism and Nicholas Tyacke.' I allude, obviously, to Christopher Hill's *The World Turned Upside Down*. In *Milton and the English Revolution*, 268–78, Hill distinguishes between 'sacramental' (Laudian) and 'radical' Arminians, but construes the latter too broadly and imprecisely, placing Milton 'in the company of John Goodwin, General Baptists, Quakers, Ranters and other radicals' (275).

34 See Lamont, 'Comment: the Rise of Arminianism Reconsidered,' 229. Coffey, *John Goodwin and the Puritan Revolution*, 202, places his full 'conversion' to Arminianism late in 1647; see his entire chapter, 198–232. Lamont, following More, 'John Goodwin and the Origins of the New Arminianism,' dates it to the early 40s. Goodwin's most notable defence

of Arminianism, *Redemption Redeemed*, appeared in 1651. Campbell and Corns, *John Milton*, 194, describe Goodwin as moving toward 'convergence' with Milton's position 'over the 1640s.' See also Dewey Wallace, Jr, *Puritans and Predestination*, 79–111, on Arminian controversies.

35 See Lamont, 'Arminianism: The Controversy That Never Was,' 59. Lamont argues here that Hugo Grotius (whom Milton met in 1638) was the Dutch Arminian who most engaged Baxter. On the Arminian bishops, see Leo F. Solt's appendix, *CPW* 1: 1009–12.

36 See Lamont, *Puritanism and Historical Controversy*, 47–8, 89–90; quotation, 90.

37 See Muller, *God, Creation, and Providence in the Thought of Jacob Arminius*, 236. In this paragraph I am indebted to his chapter, 'The Doctrine of Providence,' 235–68. Dekker, 'Was Arminius a Molinist?' argues that the concept of 'middle knowledge' (*scientia media*) developed by the Jesuit theologian Luis de Molina enabled Arminius's views of providence and free will. For Molina's explanation of how middle knowledge relates to providence, see his *On Divine Foreknowledge (Part IV of the* Concordia*)*, 248–53.

38 *The Writings of James Arminius*, 2: 68. Cited hereafter.

39 Muller, *God, Creation, and Providence*, 267; and see 258–9.

40 See ibid., 193–5; quotation, 194. Cf. Milton's stated theme, *PL* 1: 25–6.

41 See den Boer, 'Jacobus Arminius.' I am grateful to Dr. den Boer for sending me this in manuscript. See now his important book, *God's Twofold Love*, first published in Dutch, *Duplex Amor Dei* (Apeldoorn, 2008). On providence, see particularly 90–8.

42 Stanglin, *Arminius on the Assurance of Salvation*, 239. They differ, however, on the crucial place that the *duplex amor* holds; see den Boer, *God's Twofold Love*, 168–77.

43 Thomas N. Corns, arguing from *A Mask*, offers the 'hypothesis' that in the 1630s Milton 'already had arrived at a theory of salvation' consistent with Arminianism. See 'Milton's Antiprelatical Tracts and the Marginality of Doctrine,' 43.

44 Compare, e.g., 'I place in subjection to Divine Providence both *the free-will* and even *the actions of a rational creature*, so that nothing can be done without the will of God, not even any of those things which are done in opposition to it' (1: 251). Maurice Kelley notes that Arminius deliberately eschewed rhetorical flourishes (*CPW* 6: 246, n. 112). He concludes from the Delft allusion that by 1644 'Milton was familiar with the *Opera* of Arminius' and in *Areopagitica* 'at least tacitly accepted the Arminian posi-

tion on free will,' taking 'a position that would logically develop into' Arminianism (*CPW* 6: 82).

45 John T. Shawcross denies that Milton is an Arminian because 'the view of reprobation accepted by Arminius is rejected.' See *The Development of Milton's Thought*, 68–70; quotation, 69; also his earlier comments in *John Milton*, 138–40. This is puzzling since their positions on reprobation are quite similar. Paul R. Sellin argues that, because they present God's decrees in differing orders, 'the gulf between Arminius and *Paradise Lost* becomes unbridgeable.' Sellin here seems to demand the strict correspondence between a treatise and the poem that he denies exists between *DDC* and *PL*. See his 'John Milton's *Paradise Lost* and *De Doctrina Christiana* on Predestination,' 54.

46 See Kelley, *This Great Argument*, 14–20; this was preceded by his article, 'The Theological Dogma of *Paradise Lost* III, 173–202.' More recently, see Danielson, *Milton's Good God*, 75–82; and Stephen Fallon, 'Milton's Arminianism.' I am more in sympathy with Hamilton, 'Milton's Defensive God,' who situates the poem's Arminianism in contemporary religious controversy with sparing use of *DDC*.

47 *CPW* 6: 155–6, 164. On divine permission as an act of providence, see den Boer, *God's Twofold Love*, 90–8.

48 Stephen Fallon, '"Elect above the Rest": Theology as Self-Representation in Milton,' revised as chap. 7 of *Milton's Peculiar Grace*, 182–202; quotation, 193. In this he follows Danielson, *Milton's Good God*, 82–3. Fallon, 187, criticizes Kelley's book for being 'uncharacteristically inadequate' on *PL* 3: 183–4, unaware that Kelley later flatly denied that 'peculiar grace' was a 'Calvinist term because it posits freedom of man's will.' Kelley instead traced the 'technical theological term' *gratia peculiaris* to Erasmus. He cites *De Libero Arbitrio*, for which see *Collected Works of Erasmus*, vol. 76, 31–2. Erasmus states 'the opinion that this second kind of grace . . . is, through God's goodness, never lacking to any mortal being' (32). See Kelley in 'Letter to the Editor.' Calvin once uses the word 'peculiar': 'sed quibus peculiariter è caelo datum sit' (*Institutes* 2: 8, 42). This describes the power to castrate oneself for chastity as a special gift from Heaven. Peculiar, indeed. I thank David Whitford for this information.

49 See *The Writings of James Arminius*, 3: 481–2; quotation, 481. Stephen Fallon, *Milton's Peculiar Grace*, 200–1, misunderstanding Arminius's rhetorical ploy, reads this as a 'momentary and anomalous' inconsistency (201). Carl Bangs states succinctly, 'Arminius . . . rejects Perkins's distinction between common grace and peculiar grace, which in turn rested back

on Calvin's distinction between a universal call and a special call.' See 'Arminius and the Reformation,' 169; also his *Arminius*, 212–15; and den Boer, *God's Twofold Love*, 183.

50 Admittedly, without close attention to the Arminius-Perkins agon, the 'Trojan Horse,' as I have called it, invites misunderstanding. For Hamilton, 'Milton's Defensive God,' 97–8, it is a rhetorical reassurance that God's sovereignty is not limited, without detracting from universal grace; Christopher Hill, *Milton and the English Revolution*, 276 and n. 9, similarly sees it as 'apparently Calvinist' without implying predestination; Danielson, *Milton's Good God*, suggests a category that is a 'compromise solution.' Donnelly, *Milton's Scriptural Reasoning*, 95, dismisses Calvinism, but thinks this refers to individuals with a special vocation. Even Kelly's resolute denial of a special category relies on a somewhat facile definition of 'as' and does not mention 'some' (*TLS* letter).

51 Fuller, *The Holy State*, bk. 2, chap. 10, 'The Life of Mr. Perkins,' 82. Fuller concedes, 'Some object that his Doctrine, referring all to an absolute decree, hamstrings all industry, and cuts off the sinews of men's endeavours towards salvation' (83).

52 Corns, *Regaining 'Paradise Lost,'* 83. Campbell and Corns, *John Milton*, 338, comment that the language 'resonates with English Calvinist discourse.'

53 Goodwin, [*Apolytrosis Apolytroseos*] *Redemption Redeemed* (1651), 64; available as an electronic resource. On this major work, see Coffey, *John Goodwin*, 214–28.

54 Resbury, *Some Stop to the Gangrene of Arminianism, Lately Promoted by Mr. John Goodwin in his Book entituled Redemption Redeemed* (1651), A2r–v; available as an electronic resource. Resbury's refutation consists of six sermons that he happened to have on hand. The first, on election and reprobation, is an exposition of Romans 1: 2–7, in which one finds 'meer grace and peculiar, favor' (p. 3).

55 See also Exod. 19: 6; Deut. 14: 2 and 26: 18 (which the Geneva Bible glosses as a covenant); Ps. 135: 4; and 1 Pet. 2: 9.

56 On the ubiquitous trope of the English as the new Israelites, see, e.g., Walsham, *Providence*, 287–325. On 'Peculiar People,' see further Rufus Jones in *Encyclopedia of Religion and Ethics*. Christopher Hill, *The English Bible and the Seventeenth-Century Revolution*, 269–70 comments on 'peculiar people' as an alternative phrase to 'chosen people.' McLeod, 'The "Lordly eye,"' 49, assumes that *PL* 3: 183–4 alludes to England as an elect nation. See also Sauer, 'Milton's Peculiar Nation,' esp. 51 (although the several references to Moses Wall as 'Hall' do not inspire confidence).

57 Campbell et al., *Milton and the Manuscript*, 117, state that this doctrine of reprobation has 'no antecedents' in the Dutch Arminians who 'took

a quasi-Calvinist line that resembles double predestination.' Campbell and Corns repeat the point in *John Milton*, 275; thus also Shawcross (n. 45 above) and John Spencer Hill, *John Milton Poet, Priest and Prophet*, 12–13. This interpretation of Arminius, I believe, is simply wrong. The confusion may arise from Kelley, who states: 'In the matter of reprobation, however, Milton parts company with the Arminians, who generally accepted Calvin's doctrine of double predestination' (*CPW* 6: 84). He supports this with a 'brief and irenical' quotation from Arminius (83, n. 45), which he then conflates with the Remonstrants and with Philip Limborch's belief. For a more accurate statement of Arminius's own position on reprobation, see the *Declaration of Sentiments*, 1: 247 (quoted above). Arminius can be said to espouse double predestination only in the sense that God elects believers in Christ and disbelievers reprobate themselves; he rejects supralapsarian, absolute predestination. Since potentially everyone could accept the offered grace, there is no necessity for any reprobation. I am grateful to William den Boer for advice on this subject.

58 Quoted from Patrick Collinson who comments, 'The binary distinction between the better part and the worse part was instinctive to Protestantism, together with the conventional wisdom that the worse part would always constitute the greater part, the better the smaller.' See 'Biblical Rhetoric,' quotations, 34.

59 Shawcross, *With Mortal Voice*, 32.

60 Augustine's signal contribution to providential theory was to coordinate justice with love. See Lloyd, *Providence Lost*, 131–52, particularly 138–9. Despite her evocative title, Lloyd does not mention Milton's poem.

61 Stanglin, *Arminius on the Assurance*, 221–2.

62 See Muller, *God, Creation, and Providence*, 247–8. On providential trial ('exploret'), see *The Writings* 1: 348, 503; and den Boer, *God's Twofold Love*, 95.

63 I owe this quotation to Campbell et al., *Milton and the Manuscript*, 116.

64 H.D., *Historie & Policie Re-viewed, in the Heroick Transactions of his Most Serene Highnesse, Oliver, Late Lord Protector* (1659), 107–8. Available as an electronic resource; quoted by Knoppers, *Constructing Cromwell*, 156.

65 Quoted from McGee, *The Godly Man*, 35. Whichcote's writings were published posthumously, largely in the next century.

66 For a somewhat different interpretation, see Fixler, *Milton and the Kingdoms of God*, 164–5. Possibly also in the category of official opinion would be the rescue of liberty in Holland by 'the most providential death of that headstrong youth' William II (*Defensio*, *CPW* 4, pt. 1: 312).

67 For Beard's role in this development, see, e.g., Vander Molen, 'Providence as Mystery, Providence as Revelation.' Walsham, *Providence*, 65–75,

assesses *The Theatre* as part of a longer and more eclectic tradition. John Morrill disputes the assumption that Cromwell and Beard were close personally. See 'The Making of Oliver Cromwell,' 27–35.

68 See Worden, 'Providence and Politics,' 68–70, 81–8; Cust, 'Charles I and Providence,' 199, states 'There seems little doubt . . . that [Charles] believed that one of the clearest and most conspicuous signs of God's approval was victory in battle.' Randall, 'Providence, Fortune, and the Experience of Combat,' discusses news reports of 'battlefield providences,' which he finds (questionably) particularly Puritan in tenor.

69 Calamy, *Cromwell's Soldier's Bible*, title-page. This compilation was culled from the Geneva Bible.

70 Sprigge, *Anglia Rediviva,* [B3v], 205, 210.

71 Letter of August 1645, quoted from Cust, 'Charles I,' 196.

72 Letter of consolation, 5 July 1644, to Col. Valentine Walton on the death of his son in the battle. Quoted from Paul, *The Lord Protector*, 413, who notes Psalm 83: 13.

73 See 'A Short Memorial of the Northern Actions,' in *Stuart Tracts, 1603–1693*, 380, 395–6.

74 Sprigge, *Anglia Rediviva*, 11. Previous quotation, Davis, 'Cromwell's Religion,' 199; see 186–91, 199–203 particularly on his providentialism.

75 As quoted by Worden, 'Oliver Cromwell and the Sin of Achan,' 145.

76 Quoted from Kahn, *Machiavellian Rhetoric*, 161; see her entire discussion, 156–65. The fundamental study is that by John Wallace, *Destiny His Choice*, 43–68; see also Worden, 'Providence and Politics,' 80–1.

77 *A Letter to a Gentleman in the Country*, quoted from Masson, *The Life of John Milton*, 4: 521, 520. Masson follows George Thomason's misattribution to Milton. The possibility that Thomason was correct has been floated by Worden, *Literature and Politics in Cromwellian England*, 283–5. I thank John Shawcross for advice on the authorship.

78 McGee, *The Godly Man*, 33.

79 This paragraph is conspicuously indebted to Worden, 'Oliver Cromwell and the Sin of Achan'; quotations in order, 135, 137, 140. For Milton's own use of the Achan analogy (*CPW* 7: 328–9), see Worden, *Literature and Politics*, 342.

80 'A Poem upon the Death of his Late Highness the Lord Protector,' 1–6.

81 As Austin Woolrych has pointed out, 'Milton and Cromwell,' particularly 187–8. I here am indebted to his discussion, and to that by Worden, 'John Milton and Oliver Cromwell'; also *Literature and Politics*, 41–2.

82 See Honigmann, *Milton's Sonnets*, 144, whose commentary is the most helpful on this sonnet.

83 See *The Racovian Catechism*, sect. 5, chap. 10, 'Of Free Will,' which asserts, 'For it is certain that the first man was so created by God as to be endowed with free will; and there was no reason why God should deprive him of it after his fall' (325). On the falsity of predestination, see 332–46; chap. 11 explains justification by faith. Gary Hamilton notes that the commission to examine orthodoxy 'refused to allow anyone to preach who would not publicly denounce Arminian views.' See 'Milton's Defensive God,' 91. For recent considerations of the *Racovian Catechism* incident, see Lieb, *Theological Milton*, 218–22, 233–4; and Worden, *Literature and Politics*, 200–1, 242–3. For Owen's dispute with John Goodwin, see Knapp, 'John Owen's Interpretation of Hebrews 6: 4–6.' Also on Owen, see Christopher Hill, *The Experience of Defeat*, 170–8.

84 In J.C. Davis's analysis, Cromwell's toleration seems a reflex of his lack of interest in the forms of religion; his complete trust in providence accompanied distrust in humans and their institutions. See Davis, 'Cromwell's Religion,' especially 201–7; also Worden, *Literature and Politics*, 247–9, 252–4, on 'Owen's scheme.'

85 First quotation, Parnham, *Sir Henry Vane, Theologian*, 265; second, Rowe, *Sir Henry Vane the Younger*, 200.

86 See Rowe, *Sir Henry Vane the Younger*, 202–8; quotations, 205, 208. Worden, *Literature and Politics*, 243–5, comments on the sonnet and proposes Vane as a model for Milton's Samson (363–5).

87 Worden, *Literature and Politics*, quotations 266, 294; see the entire discussion, 262–88, 289–305, and Appendix B, 405–9.

88 See Worden, 'John Milton and Oliver Cromwell,' 260; *Literature and Politics*, 326–34; and Taft, '"They that pursew perfaction on earth . . ."' In 1655 Overton was imprisoned, without charge or trial, until his release by the restored Rump after the Protector's death.

89 On Bradshaw see Worden, *Literature and Politics*, 45–7, 196–9. Bradshaw left Milton £10 in his will.

90 Kahn, *Machiavellian Rhetoric*, 155, sees the implication that providential empowerment already is in the past; regrettably, she relies on an inaccurate translation.

91 More, *Fides Publica* (October 1654), 'Against the Calumnies of John Milton,' quoted from *CPW* 4, pt. 2: 1109. Milton mistakenly believed More was the author of the *Clamor.* I am not persuaded by Robert Fallon's case for an entirely positive treatment of Cromwell, but his argument is a reminder that rhetorically Milton walks a fine line. See his '*A Second Defence*: Milton's Critique of Cromwell?' Campbell and Corns, *John Milton*, 262, similarly assert, 'We find no hint of criticism of Cromwell in this

tract,' although they do allow that the praises of Fairfax, Bradshaw, and Overton are surprising. Chernaik, 'Victory's Crest,' comments on the admonitory address, 'Cromwell, as presented, has the potential for becoming the patron of liberty or its destroyer' (98).

92 In a rather subtle argument Martin Dzelzainis maintains that Milton implied his opposition to the Protectorate in 1658 in his edition of *The Cabinet-Council*, attributed to Walter Ralegh, and with the revised first *Defense*. See his 'Milton and the Protectorate in 1658.' Paul Stevens, 'Milton's 'Renunciation' of Cromwell,' 364–89, has made a trenchant refutation. Worden, *Literature and Politics*, 323–5, sides with Dzelzainis. Stevens notes that the 1658 revision of the first *Defense* retains the reference to 'Cromwell, the brave leader of our army' (*CPW* 4, pt. 1: 458), but Milton had no quarrel with Cromwell's generalship.

93 Letter to Samuel Hartlib (9 January 1659), quoted from Popkin, 'A Note on Moses Wall,' 168.

94 I rely here on the lucid discussion by Partee, 'Calvin on Universal and Particular Providence,' quotations, pp. 86, 84, 74 (Commentary on Isaiah). Calvin uses 'special' and 'particular' for what *DDC* terms 'extraordinary.' See also Helm, 'Calvin (and Zwingli) on Divine Providence,' 389–90.

95 Quoted from Worden, 'Providence and Politics,' 69–70. As early as 1649 Marchamont Nedham, cloaked by the anonymity of the *Mercuius Pragmaticus*, commented witheringly on Cromwell's invocations of providence, 'By which speech you may see, they entitle God's providence to all their villainies.' See Worden, *Literature and Politics*, 87.

96 Commentary on 2 Cor. 5:19; quoted from Helm, *John Calvin's Ideas*, 395. As Calvin expresses it elsewhere, 'Thus in a marvelous and divine way he loved us even when he hated us.' Trans. Ford Lewis Battles, *Calvin: Institutes of the Christian Religion*, 1: 507 (bk. 2, chap. 16, 4).

97 Quoted from McAdoo, *The Spirit of Anglicanism*, 37. Bouwsma, *John Calvin*, 173, famously stated, 'God, for Calvin, is identified with power.' Subsequently, Calvin scholars have laboured to demonstrate this is an oversimplification, but Englishmen such as Sanderson would not have disagreed. Helm, *John Calvin's Ideas*, 123, concedes, 'Calvin's views of providence (and of course of predestination) clearly tend toward determinism.'

98 Quoted from Worden, *Literature and Politics*, 379.

99 See the standard study by Hoopes, *Right Reason in the Renaissance*). *DDC* equates right reason with conscience (see *CPW* 6: 132). Donnelly, *Milton's Scriptural Reasoning*, 13–15 (and see index), identifies *recta ratio*

('ethico-cognitive' reason in his definition) as the image of God in man. Kahn, *Machiavellian Rhetoric*, 144–5, enters a caveat on 'the infinite regress' of appeals to right reason. She quotes Lord Brooke (praised highly in *Areopagitica*): 'But who shall tell us what is *Recta Ratio*? I answer, *Recta Ratio*' (145).

100 See Worden, 'Oliver Cromwell and the Sin of Achan,' 138–9; quotation, 139.

101 Norbrook, *Writing the English Republic*, 338.

102 I owe the idea of an implicit dialogue between writers to Richard S. Ide, *Possessed with Greatness*.

103 See John Wallace, *Destiny His Choice*, 69–105; and Worden, 'Andrew Marvell, Oliver Cromwell, and the Horatian Ode.' Norbrook, *Writing the English Republic*, thickly contextualizes this and his other political poems in contemporary political discourse. His concern with the classical and secular, however, leaves the religious dimension largely undeveloped.

104 On the possible dates of his stay at Appleton House, see Worden, *Literature and Politics*, 216–17 and n. 94.

105 *The Rehearsal Transpros'd*, quoted from *The Prose Works of Andrew Marvell*, 1: 192.

106 See his letter to Cromwell (28 July 1653), in *The Poems and Letters of Andrew Marvell*, 2: 291–3 and preceding facsimile. John Dixon Hunt speculates that the position was obtained through Oliver St John, who was connected to both Cromwell and Oxenbridge by marriages. See *Andrew Marvell*, 116. Worden, *Literature and Politics*, 116–30 and Appendix A, 399–404, presents the 'hypothesis' that Marvell was a member of St John's 1651 embassy to Holland.

107 *The Rehearsal Transpros'd*, in *Prose Works*, 1: 130. Parliament had deprived Hales of his fellowship at Eton and his position as canon at Windsor; he was living in reduced circumstances when Marvell met him.

108 See Lamont, 'The Religion of Andrew Marvell,' 151. For a recent refinement of Lamont's argument, see von Maltzahn, 'Milton, Marvell and Toleration,' 91–6. Pertinently, Nigel Smith has reported finding a holograph copy of the *Racovian Catechism* in the hand of Marvell's father (MLA meeting, Los Angeles, 2011).

109 The quoted phrases are from the lives of Milton by Edward Phillips and by John Aubrey in Hughes, 1035, 1023.

110 *Poems and Letters*, 2: 293; also *CPW* 4, pt. 2: 864. On 'Overton's business,' see Worden, *Literature and Politics*, 331–2.

111 See *Filarete's Treatise on Architecture*, 314.

112 Chernaik, *The Poet's Time*, 46; and see 51–2. For the poem's indebtedness to the *Second Defense*, see also Patterson, *Marvell and the Civic Crown*, 71–3; Hirst, '"That Sober Liberty,"' 24; and Smith, *The Poems*, 283.

113 Wortham, 'Marvell's Cromwell Poems,' 42. I disagree with Hirst's purely eulogistic reading, and Worden's contention that it is an 'unquestioning poem,' marking Marvell's conversion into 'a Cromwellian monarchist' (*Literature and Politics*, 152, 153). Smith, 283, cautiously allows, 'Although M. does not so obviously qualify his praise of the Protector as Milton did . . . it may be that' he remained 'privately worried.' Raymond, 'Framing Liberty,' finds an equivocal commitment to Cromwell; Holberton, *Poetry and the Cromwellian Protectorate*, 101–18, emphasizes concern about the fragility of the government and uncertainty of the succession.

114 Smith demotes the poem to an appendix; see his discussion of the attribution, 425. Margoliouth, *Poems and Letters*, 1: 255, notes that, although Cromwell is not named, 'there can be no doubt' the quoted lines are addressed to him.

115 Campbell and Corns, *John Milton*, 255, note that, as his blindness increased, Milton's position was shifted from the Council to the Secretary of State's office; however, they describe Marvell as only a 'clerical assistant' (257).

116 For a contextual discussion, see Holberton, *Poetry and the Cromwellian Protectorate*, 153–62.

117 William Riley Parker writes: 'In the elaborate order of procession for Oliver's funeral on 23 November there was a place for Milton along with the other "Secretaries of the French and Latin tongues" – Marvell, Sterry, Dryden, and Hartlib. Although proof is lacking, it is probable that the blind man actually walked (the guiding hand Marvell's?) with the many mourners from Somerset House to Westminster Abbey, where an effigy of the protector was solemnly deposited in the Chapel of Henry VII.' *Milton*, 1: 518–19. Campbell and Corns, *John Milton*, 277, note that they received a grant to purchase mourning cloth. For an account of the procession, effigy, and hearse, see Knoppers, *Constructing Cromwell*, 139–46. She emphasizes the monarchial qualities of the spectacle, adapted from the funeral of James I (133–6, 144). Another relevant precedent would be the memorable 1612 funeral for the lost Protestant hope, Prince Henry. See particularly William Hole's engraving of the effigy and catafalque, first published in Chapman's *An Epicede* (1612); the folded engraving is illustrated by Hind, *Engraving in England in the Sixteenth and Seventeenth Centuries II*, 322, no. 10 and pl. 200; and Strong, *Henry, Prince of Wales and England's Lost Renaissance*, fig. 90.

118 See Martin, 'The Enclosed Garden and the Apocalyptic Moment versus Transcendent Time in Milton and Marvell,' 150; also her companion article, 'Rewriting Cromwell.' Von Maltzahn, 'Milton, Marvell and Toleration,' similarly discriminates their positions on religious toleration: 'Where Marvell favoured a more comprehensive but still national church, Milton early and late decried the very institution' (89).

119 Quoted from Christopher Hill, *God's Englishman*, 248, 249.

120 'He began about 2 years before the K. came in, and finished about 3 years after the K.'s restoration' (Hughes, 1024). This approximate span generally has been accepted by scholars.

121 Smith, 182, comments on the indications that Marvell read the first edition in the fifth issue (with arguments and note on the verse added), as well as the later additions to the twelve-book edition. McWilliams, 'Marvell and Milton's Literary Friendship Reconsidered,' quite possibly exaggerates in concluding that Marvell praises the epic 'uneasily and warily.'

122 Kerrigan, *The Prophetic Milton*, considered a major dimension; John Spencer Hill, *John Milton Poet, Priest and Prophet*, provided a brisk tour with useful references; more recently Haskin, *Milton's Burden of Interpretation*, chaps 2 and 4, offers a nuanced discussion; Stephen Fallon, *Milton's Peculiar Grace*, gives a highly tendentious account of 'self-representation.' The notion that literary talent is a providential gift to be used appropriately was not uncommon. Adrian VI urged Erasmus 'to employ in an attack on these new heresies the literary skill with which a generous providence has endowed you so effectually.' Quoted from *Collected Works of Erasmus*, vol. 76, introduction, liii.

123 Rosen, 'Return to Paradise,' 74.

2. Memory and the Art of Composition

1 *Religio Medici*, 1, sect. 14, p. 11.

2 Ellmann, *James Joyce*, 649. I exaggerate slightly; Joyce was nearly, but not totally, blind.

3 The composition of *Paradise Lost* is a fundamental, but surprisingly neglected, subject. Sixty years ago Allan H. Gilbert published *On the Composition of* Paradise Lost. Reviewing 'The Dates of Composition' twenty-five years ago, John T. Shawcross noted, 'The two major conclusions which should be drawn from Gilbert's study . . . are the very logical realization that the poem was not written as we have it from first to last and, second, the development of the poem was extended over some time.' See *With Mortal Voice*, 174–5; also on the dating, see Shawcross, *John Milton*, 145–8,

173, and 'Appendix C: Dating of the Plans,' 289–94. Campbell and Corns, *John Milton*, 345–6, note that the early biographers offer a (probably self-mythologized) Virgilian composition model, but this yields few specifics. Gilbert acknowledged, 'We know little of his procedure when he was composing freely' (7), speculating: 'Much work on small units, and that greatly interrupted, would take the poet's attention from the larger matters of his plan' (8). That plan and procedure are the subjects here.

4 *Novum Organon* 2.26: 'Item carmina facilius haerent et discuntur memoriter quam prosa.'

5 The practical efficacy of this ancient technique has received very recent confirmation from Judt, *The Memory Chalet*, and Foer, *Moonwalking with Einstein*.

6 For Milton's own references to these works, see Boswell, *Milton's Library*, nos. 348, 361, 1200. For the classical tradition, see the valuable study by Caplan, 'Memoria.'

7 Donald Lemon Clark, *John Milton at St. Paul's School*, 12. For the correctives, see Paolo Rossi, *Logic and the Art of Memory;* Yates, *The Art of Memory;* Bolzoni, *The Gallery of Memory*. See also William West's article, 'Memory.'

8 Ong, *Ramus, Method and the Decay of Dialogue*, 194–5, 280–1; quotation, 280; Yates, *The Art of Memory*, 231–42, emphasizes Quintilian's influence on Ramus. Donnelly, *Milton's Scriptural Reasoning*, 45, comments, 'Despite the consequences of Ramism' Milton 'obviously shared in the residual belief that the extensive cultivation of memory was part of education,' but does not elaborate on that cultivation.

9 Campbell et al., *Milton and the Manuscript*, 156. They comment, 'Milton broke the intellectual structure down into sections in which a combination of his good memory and his support network . . . could allow him to work on it, chapter by chapter.'

10 Quoted from Merritt Y. Hughes, editor of *John Milton: Complete Poems and Major Prose*, 1035 (Phillips), 1022 (Aubrey), and 1043–4 (anon.). The author of the last has been identified as Cyriack Skinner, the friend to whom Milton addressed two sonnets (21 and 22); see, e.g., Shawcross, *The Arms of the Family*, 85.

11 See Carruthers, *The Book of Memory*, 165. Petrarch's letter to Boccaccio is quoted at 219. For Donne, see Holy Sonnet 11, 'Wilt thou love God, as he thee!'

12 Bacon, *The Wisdome of the Ancients*, 129. Lemmi, *The Classical Deities in Bacon*, 199, documents the indebtedness to Natale Conti's *Mythologiae sive explicationum fabularun*.

13 Although Martz made some forays into Protestant meditation, Barbara Lewalski much more extensively documented that development, and, less persuasively, argued for a recognizably Protestant form of meditation. See Lewalski, *Protestant Poetics and the Seventeenth-Century Religious Lyric*, 147–78. Low, *Love's Architecture*, 81, n. 32, comments that what Lewalski identifies as a distinctly Protestant form, combining meditation and sermon, actually is a mixed form used by Catholics as well. See also the response by Martz, 'Meditation as Poetic Strategy,' and Young, *Doctrine and Devotion in Seventeenth-Century Poetry*, 85–9.

14 Martz does briefly acknowledge that 'these methods of meditation are in themselves adaptations of ancient principles of logic and rhetoric,' but the awareness is fleeting, as are the nods toward the longer meditative tradition. Quotation, *The Poetry of Meditation*, 38.

15 Martz, *Poetry of Meditation*, xxiv. He argues that, from the late sixteenth century onward, the concept of meditation 'took on a more sharply delimited significance' (14); for his exposition of the Ignatian method, see 25–39.

16 Ibid., 156; and see 164–8. On the inapplicability of 'Calvinist' to Milton, see chap. 1 above.

17 Martz, *The Paradise Within*, 178.

18 Ibid., 23. For a tactful but stringent account of the book's shortcomings on Milton, see the review article by Stein, 'The Paradise Within and Without.' See also Sloane, 'Rhetoric, "Logic" and Poetry,' 332–3.

19 For Augustine, see Carruthers, *The Craft of Thought*, 80, 95–6. Donne's indebtedness to Augustine on memory has been well discussed. See, e.g., Donald Friedman, 'Memory and the Art of Salvation in Donne's Good Friday Poem,' and Guibbory, 'John Donne and Memory as "the Art of Salvation."'

20 Carruthers, *Book of Memory*, 146.

21 For the custom of seeking out scriptural 'places,' I am indebted to Haskin, *Milton's Burden of Interpretation*, xiii–xvi, 1–28, 245 n. 20. On the multiple senses of *place*, including places in a book, with which memory places conflate, see Bolzoni, *The Gallery of Memory*, 188–91.

22 In *Remembering and Repeating*, Regina M. Schwartz has discussed the title concepts, but does not consider the intermediary of artificial memory. Regarding the subject, Anne Davidson Ferry once stated a basic truth that sometimes gets forgotten: 'We are meant to remember that the events of the poem have already occurred.' See *Milton's Epic Voice*, 44.

23 Carruthers, *Craft of Thought*, 9. The description just provided is more accurate for her earlier, broader study; in the later she discriminates the

early medieval tradition from the influence of classical mnemonics, maintaining that the common features are parallel developments. *The Craft of Thought* terminates at 1200, and the *Ad Herennium* underwent a revival in the thirteenth century (see *Book of Memory,* 122). In what follows I have used both as they seem relevant.

24 *De oratore* I. xxxi. 142, p. 99.

25 Trans. quoted from Carruthers, *Craft of Thought,* 99. See also her discussion of Anselm of Bec, whose 'entire composition is woven from remembered texts and common images, from Job, the Psalms, Apocalypse, and the Gospels, together with their accrued commentary, including . . . programs of meditational pictures' (104).

26 'Hic autem non novum quicquam docetur, sed memoriae tantummodo consulitur; ut quae sparsim sacris in libris leguntur, commode velut in unum corpus redacta, perque certos digesta locos, ad manum sint.' *The Works of John Milton,* 14: 20. I here quote the Charles Sumner translation, *Works* 14: 21, in preference to John Carey's (*CPW* 6: 127).

27 Aristotle distinguished recollection, an association of ideas requiring rational thought, from memory. See *De memoria et reminiscentia,* in *Parva naturalia,* 451.a18–453.a25. I owe this citation to Rhodri Lewis. In the tradition of *sacra memoria,* wherein the meditator would have memorized much of scripture, the distinction is less clear. One might describe this recollection as a sorting of memories.

28 Schwartz, *Remembering and Repeating,* 4, calls attention to the 'composition history, imagining some editorial patchwork by Moses' in this passage.

29 See Stanley Stewart's important chapter, 'Herbert and the "Harmonies" of Little Gidding,' in his *George Herbert,* 56–82.

30 *A Priest to the Temple,* in *The Works,* 228, 229.

31 Quotation, Carruthers, *Craft of Thought,* 70; and see *Book of Memory,* 167–8 (Petrarch's *Secretum*), 66–7 (Aquinas), also 178–82 (on florilegia).

32 See Carruthers, *Book of Memory,* 80–5 and 262–3.

33 On the last, see particularly a pair of articles by Shawcross, 'The Balanced Structure of "Paradise Lost,"' and 'The Son in His Ascendance.' See also his *With Mortal Voice,* where these appear in revised form.

34 *Institutio oratoria* XI. ii. 21; and see Yates, *Art of Memory,* 21–6. For the currency of the Simonides story, see, e.g., Langley, in Vergil, *An Abridgement of the Works of the most Learned Polidore Virgil,* 87: 'By that fact, both he perceived the order of the Art of Memory, and what commodity came to the remembrance of man by such an Art.'

35 See *The Sermons of John Donne,* ed. Potter and Simpson, 2, no. 11, 235–49 (on Eccles, 12.1, 'Remember now thy creator in the dayes of thy youth');

and 5, no. 12, 231–44. There is a brief discussion by Guibbory, 'John Donne and Memory,' 265–6, 270. The suggestion has been made for Herbert; see Plett, 'Topik und Memoria.'

36 Carruthers and Ziolkowski, *The Medieval Craft of Memory,* 20.

37 See Ong, 'Logic and the Epic Muse,' 253.

38 *Heptaplus,* Proem to the Second Book, trans. Douglas Carmichael, in Pico della Mirandola, *On the Dignity of Man, On Being and the One, Heptaplus,* 95. See further Waddington, 'The Sun at the Center.'

39 Quoted from Carruthers and Ziolkowski, *The Medieval Craft of Memory,* 6.

40 For the topos of 'God as Maker,' see Curtius, *European Literature and the Latin Middle Ages,* 544–6. On the visual traditions, see the learned article by John Friedman, 'The Architect's Compass in Creation Miniatures of the Later Middle Ages,' and Tachau, 'God's Compass and *Vana Curiositas.*'

41 See a pair of articles by Røstvig, 'Structure as Prophecy,' particularly 33–6; and '*Ars Aeterna*'; also Waddington, 'The Sun at the Center'; and Michael Allen, *Nuptial Arithmetic,* 138–9, 260–2. For commentaries on Wisdom 11:21 see Lapide (Cornelissen van den Steen), *Commentarii in Scrituram Sacram*4: 936–58.

42 Quoted from Christopher Hill, *God's Englishman,* 247. In *Tetrachordon* Milton refers to 'the perfet scales of [God's] justice and providence' (*CPW* 2: 658).

43 See Caplan, 'Memoria,' and Carruthers, *Book of Memory,* 33–45. The alternative metaphor of the mark on a wax tablet was limited by the shift in writing technology: wax tablets were replaced by erasable tablets of paper or parchment coated with a mixture of gesso and glue. See Stallybrass, Chartier, Mowery, and Wolfe, 'Hamlet's Tables and the Technologies of Writing in Renaissance England.'

44 Carruthers, *Book of Memory,* 44.

45 See Yates, *Art of Memory,* 23–4.

46 For Bradwardine, see Carruthers, *Book of Memory,* 133–4, 283–4; and Yates, *Art of Memory,* 115–17 for Romberch; 122 for Rosselli; 212–15 for Bruno; 329–31, 333–4, for Fludd. Camillo's memory theatre uses the seven planets as its basic system of places with the planetary gods for images. See Yates, 136–56, and the fold-out diagram following p. 144.

47 On 'argument,' see Sloane, 'Rhetoric, "Logic" and Poetry,' 307–11; for 'cause,' see Steadman, '"Man's First Disobedience."' I am indebted to John Shawcross for the point that the connective between *providence* and *justify* is causal, having the force of 'and thereby' (see *OED* s.v. II.8, 'Introducing a consequence.'). Donnelly, *Milton's Scriptural Reasoning,* 82,

sensibly describes the 'two-fold purpose' as 'distinct, and yet logically connected.' Poole, *Milton and the Idea of the Fall,* 147, frets, '*all* those ways? Or is it a more modest project: to justify the ways of God inasmuch, and *only* inasmuch as they apply to, and can be understood by, men?' The latter (special and extraordinary providence).

48 See *A Letter of Resolution Concerning Origen,* 'To the Reader,' [A4]. Marjorie Hope Nicolson's attribution to George Rust ('Bibliographical Note') has been questioned, but see Rhodri Lewis, 'Of "Origenian Platonisme,"' 274–6. I owe the quotation to Stachniewski, *The Persecutory Imagination,* 333. He argues that Milton's declaration is Arminian in rejecting Calvinism while retaining the Lutheran *sola fide* (see 332–6).

49 The *OED,* s.v. 8, gives 1671 as the first written example, which means that in printers' vocabulary 'justifying' type would have been in use earlier. For George Hakewill, printing was a benefit of providence. See *An Apologie of the Power and Providence of God in the Government of the World* (1627), bk. 3, chap. 16, sec. 2.

50 *The Writings of James Arminius,* 3: 499.

51 I adapt den Boer's summary of how, for Arminius, providence precedes and enables predestination. See *God's Twofold Love,* 118.

52 Ralegh, *The History of the World* (1614), 'The Preface,' D2 (original in italics). For the influence of Ralegh's providentialism on Milton, see Paul Stevens, 'Milton's 'Renunciation' of Cromwell,' 376–7 and n. 30.

53 See Kelley's introduction, *CPW* 6: 87–90. For Arminius, see *The Writings* 2: 54; and Muller, *God, Creation, and Providence,* 213–17.

54 Considering the prohibited tree, Patricia M. Howison sensibly differentiates from a classical memory image: 'It is . . . both an object of memory and a mnemonic device; it both provokes memory in Adam and Eve, and itself has a particular meaning which must be remembered.' The reader's memory adds another dimension. See 'Memory and Will,' 527.

55 John Shawcross remarks (in correspondence) that the running title of the first edition (1667) and the surviving manuscript of bk.1 did not capitalize 'lost.' Seemingly place is more important than the human act of disobedience. See Moyles, *The Text of* Paradise Lost, figs 1–7, who illustrates title-pages of all five issues and two variants.

56 On the Gunpowder Plot (aside from Milton's own juvenilia), see Cressy, *Bonfires and Bells,* 141–55.

57 There is some discussion of *Paradisus Amissus* by Hale, 'Early Translations of *Paradise Lost,*' 32, 35–7. *Thoughts Upon the Four Last Things* is available as an electronic resource. For Trapp, I am indebted to John Shawcross's encyclopedic knowledge of Miltoniana.

58 See Yates, *Art of Memory,* 16. This feature of mnemonic composition seems pertinent to the presumption that *Paradise Lost* was not composed in the printed narrative sequence. See Gilbert, *On the Composition of Paradise Lost,* esp. 152–5, his table suggesting a sequence of composition.
59 As D.P. Walker has shown in *The Decline of Hell;* see 23–6, 40–2 on the deterrent effect. The scriptural sources are collected in *DDC (CPW* 6: 629–30). For the strength of the popular tradition, see Patrides, 'Renaissance and Modern Views on Hell'; also Watt, *Cheap Print and Popular Piety, 1560–1640,* 110–12, 171, 238–9, 312.
60 See Roland Frye, *Milton's Imagery,* 127–33. Yates, *The Art of Memory,* 94–6, 163–5, suggested that Dante's poem may have been used as a memory system. In one confirmation Massimiliano Rossi discusses the woodcut illustrations to *La Comedia di Dante Aligieri* (Venice, 1544) as memory places. See 'Alessandro Vellutello e Giovanni Britto che "per sé fuoror." Sul corredo grafico della "Nove esposizione"' (1544).
61 See Marshall, '"The Map of God's Word,"' 113–14.
62 See Dewey Wallace, Jr, 'Puritan and Anglican.' As a mortalist, Milton did not believe in the descent to Hell. *DDC* (*CPW* 6: 439) dismisses this 'peevish controversy,' citing Matt. 27: 46 and I Cor. 15: 4.
63 On this topic, see Roland Frye, *Milton's Imagery,* 139–40. Later in the poem (10: 288), 'the mouth of Hell' becomes overt.
64 Roland Frye, *Milton's Imagery,* 130, n. 16, provides an extensive bibliography.
65 Trans. Yates, *Art of Memory,* 59. On this writer, see Witt, 'Boncompagno and the Defense of Rhetoric.'
66 Edwards, *Milton and the Natural World,* 85–98, discusses the transformation as an image of the error Satan embodies.
67 Yates, *Art of Memory,* 10.
68 *Sermons of John Donne,* 4: 86 (no. 2, Easter 1622). See also *DDC* 1, 33, for 'the punishment of loss' and 'the punishment of sense' (*CPW* 6: 628)
69 See Patrides, 'Renaissance and Modern Views on Hell,' 220–6; quotation, 225.
70 Trans. Yates, *Art of Memory,* 59.
71 For discussion of the biblical sources, see particularly Murrin, *The Allegorical Epic,* 153–71; and Lieb, *Poetics of the Holy,* 119–70.
72 See McDannell and Lang, *Heaven,* 82–8. This is perhaps the most helpful of the several such 'histories.'
73 Roland Frye, *Milton's Imagery,* 195–6, dismissing the 'or,' argues for a 'blending,' the circle squared; for Lieb, *Poetics of the Holy,* 348, n. 20, Sin's square Heaven is 'conclusive.'

74 See McDannell and Lang, *Heaven*, 72–8.

75 Jackson Cope, *The Metaphoric Structure of* Paradise Lost, 54. The phrase 'living sapphires' reappears as an apt metaphor for stars (4: 605), connoting brightness and motion, but this sheds no light on the construction material.

76 Trans. quoted from Carruthers, *Craft of Thought*, 20; see her entire discussion of this metaphor, 16–21. See also the passage in *Areopagitica* on building 'the Temple of the Lord,' which concludes: 'Let us therefore be more considerate builders, more wise in spiritual architecture, when great reformation is expected' (*CPW* 2: 555 and n. 244).

77 See, e.g., Panofsky's classic essay, 'Abbot Suger of St.-Denis,' reprinted in his *Meaning in the Visual Arts*, 108–45; particularly, 122–33.

78 Murrin, *The Allegorical Epic*, 156, commenting on 5: 650–5. I am indebted to his admirable chapter, 'The Language of Milton's Heaven.'

79 See Milton's translation of Psalm 2, and, for his extended use of this text in bks 5 and 6, see the fine article by William Hunter, 'The War in Heaven,' 114–30; also Donnelly, *Milton's Scriptural Reasoning*, 107–23.

80 Murrin, *The Allegorical Epic*, 171. On the holy mountain, see also Lieb, *Poetics of the Holy*, 140–52.

81 For useful commentary, see Roland Frye, *Milton's Imagery*, 149–54; Lieb, *Poetics*, 185–210; and Murrin, *Allegorical Epic*, 156–7, 164–70.

82 See Arnold Williams, *The Common Expositor*, 94–102, and the wonderful book by Scafi, *Mapping Paradise*.

83 Lithgow, *A Most Delectable and Trve Discovrse of an Admired and Painfull Peregrination from Scotland* . . . A2r (available as an electronic resource).

84 Broadbent, *Some Graver Subject*, 173. For the tradition that he both uses and deviates from, see Duncan, *Milton's Earthly Paradise;* also see Almond, *Adam and Eve in Seventeenth-Century Thought*, 65–82. Roland Frye, *Milton's Imagery*, 235–55, is helpful in visualizing Eden.

85 See Stewart, *The Enclosed Garden;* Almond, *Adam and Eve*, 94–6; and on dressing and keeping the garden (Gen. 2: 15), 98–101.

86 For this, see Demetz, 'The Elm and the Vine.'

87 See Jeremy Cohen, *'Be Fertile and Increase, Fill the Earth and Master It.'*

88 See Pagels, *Adam, Eve, and the Serpent*, xxv.

89 Ibid., 141. I owe this quotation to Catherine Gimelli Martin.

90 Carruthers, *Craft of Thought*, 54.

91 Donnelly, *Milton's Scriptural Reasoning*, 5, 98. Donnelly's promising concept that the reader is educated through a process of 'triall . . . by what is contrary' (28, 33–9) needs sustained development, both textual and

historical. His belief that Milton 'expects . . . a second reading of the poem' (185, also 48) is welcome; but why limit it? The poem requires and rewards as many readings as does Genesis.

92 See Radzinowicz, *Milton's Epics and the Book of Psalms* (Princeton, 1989), 174–87, for a succinct account of death in the poem; quotation, 174. For the commentators on death, see Arnold Williams, *The Common Expositor,* 131–4. On mortalism, see chap. 6 following.

93 Hammond, *Fleeting Things,* 216.

94 Ussher, *A Body of Divinitie,* 446. Ussher later disclaimed authorship of this 'hyper-Calvinistic' work, stating that the manuscript was a commonplace book of opinions culled from Protestant writers, but it continued to be printed under his name. See *The Encyclopedia Britannica* (11th ed.): 27: 810.

95 Parr, *The Grounds of Divinitie* (1614), 237; quoted from Marshall, *Beliefs and the Dead in Reformation England,* 221.

96 See Hunter, 'The War in Heaven,' 125–9; and Lieb, *Poetics,* 291–7.

97 Poole, *Milton and the Idea of the Fall,* chap. 3, reconstructs contemporary controversy on original sin. Harrison, *The Fall of Man and the Foundations of Science,* presents these discussions as one motivation for the development of experimental science.

98 Grant Williams and Christopher Ivic find this determined by both biblical authority and philosophy. See their useful introduction to *Forgetting in Early Modern English Literature and Culture.* Carruthers and Ziolkowski, *The Medieval Craft of Memory,* 21, remark, 'For a Christian to forget was one way to end up offending God and suffering oblivion as a consequence.'

99 Scodel, *Excess and the Mean in Early Modern English Literature,* 276.

100 Howison, 'Memory and Will,' 523.

101 Schwartz, *Remembering and Repeating,* 106.

102 Gallagher, *Milton, the Bible, and Misogyny* 128; also Howison, 'Memory and Will,' on 'selective amnesia.'

103 MacCallum, *Milton and the Sons of God,* 187–8.

104 Farley, *The Kalendar of Mans Life* (1638), quoted from Harrison, *The Fall of Man,* 157.

105 Donnelly, *Milton's Scriptural Reasoning,* 48.

106 For the orthodox position and the minority tradition, see Patrides, '"*A Principle of Infinite Love*": The Salvation of Satan,' in his *Premises and Motifs in Renaissance Thought and Literature,* 200–17. About the epic he remarks noncommittally, 'the dramatic context demands that Satan's redemption should at least be entertained as a possibility' (208).

107 Diane Kelsey McColley, *Milton's Eve,* quotation, 190; Stavely, 'Satan and Arminianism in *Paradise Lost,*' quotations, 125. A recent *advocatus diaboli* disputes Stavely's reading. See Forsyth, *The Satanic Epic,* 156, n. 15.

108 Kahn, *Machiavellian Rhetoric,* 210.

3. Satan's Machiavellian Enterprise: Force and Fraud

1 Caryl, *The Saints Thankfull Acclamation* (1644), 37.

2 Cheynell, *Sions Momento and Gods Alarm* (1643), A3, p. 6; quoted by Christopher Hill, *Antichrist in Seventeenth-Century England,* 85. Stuart Clark, *Vanities of the Eye,* 179, comments: 'Traditionally, the power of the Antichrist was twofold; it was upheld by tyranny and cruelty but also sustained by false appearance.' In other words, force and fraud; the next chapter discusses Satan's relation to Antichrist.

3 Hawke, *Killing is Murder* (1657), 20; quoted from Raab, *The English Face of Machiavelli,* 143; see the entire discussion, 137–44. Cromwell's Machiavellianism probably is a book-length subject in itself; for recent discussion see Kahn, *Machiavellian Rhetoric,* 3–4, 153–5; Knoppers, *Constructing Cromwell,* 15–18, 21–30, 158–66; and Worden, *Literature and Politics,* 86–102.

4 Carpenter, *A Preparative to Contentation* (1597). I owe the quotation to Kahn, *Machiavellian Rhetoric,* 209. Hers is the most sophisticated account of Machiavellianism in *Paradise Lost* (see 209–35). See also Riebling, 'Milton on Machiavelli.'

5 See Anglo, *Machiavelli – The First Century,* 115–42; quotation, 126. Milton's commonplace book demonstrates his careful study of the *Discourses* (see *CPW* 1: 414, n. 2), which most scholars agree influenced his political thought. For a minority opinion see Rahe, *Against Throne and Altar,* 103, who contends it would be a 'grave mistake to believe that [Milton] ever embraced the novel republican teachings' in the *Discourses,* and he asserts, 118, 'Milton very much regretted the influence that Machiavelli exercised over his compatriots.'

6 *Nicholas Machiavel's Prince,* A4, 209, 211. The classic study is Pitkin, *Fortune is a Woman.*

7 Fleming, *Milton's Secrecy,* 9–10, accurately states, 'Satan reveals himself, he does not hide himself, by hiding.' His exaggeration of the 'comically self-defeating' and 'grotesque' aspects, however, travesties the poet's subtlety.

8 Hendrickson, *The Facts on File Encyclopedia of Word and Phrase Origin,* s.v.

9 Cotgrave, *A Dictionarie of the French and English Tongues.* The German *verloren kinder* parallels the French phrase.

10 Barret, *The Theorike and Practike of Moderne Warres,* 32. See also Sutcliffe, *The Practice, Proceedings, and Lawes of Armes,* 174. For these books, see Cockle, *A Bibliography of Military Books up to 1642.* There is a helpful survey in Freeman, *Milton and the Martial Muse,* 25–43.
11 See Hyamson, *A Dictionary of English Phrases,* s.v.
12 Smythe, *Certain Discourses Military,* 41–2.
13 Ibid., 48; see also 49 and xvi (a 1587 letter to Lord Burghley).
14 See Sprigge, *Anglia Rediviva (1647),* 35, 64, 65, 70, 94, 106, 111, 115, 167, 168, 185, 186, 190, 198, 213. Sprigge's important book is placed in context by Smith, *Literature and Revolution in England,* 50–3. See also Fairfax's laconic account of the battle at Winceby (11 October 1643), in *Stuart Tracts,* 389.
15 For a fuller account of tactics, see Webb, *Elizabethan Military Science,* 100–2, 121, and fig. 21. Barret, *The Theorike and Practice,* 198 and 211, also diagrams battle formations illustrating placements of the Forlorn.
16 See Calvin, *Institutes,* 1: 16, 6, commenting on Proverbs 16: 33.
17 For another contemporary description of the Forlorn, see the letter to William Lenthall, Speaker of the House of Commons, from Har. Leighton and Tho. Herbert in Ellis, *Original Letters, Illustrative of English History,* no. 367.
18 On Marshall, see Corbett and Norton, *Engraving in England, Part III,* 102–3. The unsigned battle plan is not mentioned, but similarities between the depiction of troop formations here and on the signed frontispiece (catalogue no. 35) make the attribution virtually certain.
19 Hutchinson, *Memoirs of the Life of Colonel Hutchinson,* 183. The predicament she describes was not uncommon. Cf. Cowley's versified account of Prince Rupert's storming of Lichfield (21 April 1643): 'Some whilst the walls (bold men!) they'attempt to scale, / Drop downe by'a leaden storme of deadly haile. / Some with huge stones are crusht to dust beneath, / And from their hasty *Tombes* receive their *Death.*' Cowley, *The Civil War,* bk. 2: 107–10. Undeterred by the failure of his Forlorn, Rupert mined the walls and blew open a breach (2:115–21).
20 Bulstrode, *Memoirs and Reflections upon the Reign and Government of King Charles the Ist and Charles the IId,* 1: 77.
21 *Stuart Tracts,* 379, 381.
22 This set of examples and quotations is taken from Besly, ' "To Reward Their Deservings," ' 25.
23 The badges and medals of the Civil Wars 'may be considered as the inauguration of the custom of granting military and naval decorations, so

general in the present century.' Hawkins, *Medallic Illustrations of the History of Great Britain and Ireland*, 1, xiv.

24 The British Museum now possesses a rare survival, both the gold medal presented to John Sharpe in 1645 and the accompanying warrants signed by Fairfax. For a photograph of these, see *The Medal*, no. 47 (autumn 2005), 99. On the Fairfax medal itself, see *Medallic Illustrations*, 1: 317–18.

25 Quotation, *Medallic Illustrations*, 1: 391.

26 The printed warrant, intended for distribution to field commanders, is illustrated by Besly, '"To Reward Their Deservings,"' fig. 2, to whom I am indebted for the factual account. Hawkins, *Medallic Illustrations*, 1: 301–2, misidentified the Forlorn Hope badge. The mistake was corrected in 1930 by Helen Farquhar, but no complete example was known until Besly published the one in the National Museum of Wales (his fig. 5). The British Museum has an example lacking the surrounding shell (Besly, fig. 3). Its scarcity would indicate that the badges were, indeed, worn in battle.

27 Besly, '"To Reward Their Deservings,"' 25.

28 Quoted from Besly, '"To Reward Their Deservings,"' 23.

29 Quoted from Cust, 'Charles I and Providence,' 199.

30 Cowley, *The Civil War*, 1: 531–4. The belated (1679) publication spared Milton, who admired Cowley's *Davideis*, the necessity of revising his opinion.

31 Macaulay, 'Milton,' in *Literary Essays Contributed to the Edinburgh Review*, 48 (first pub. August, 1825).

32 See, particularly, Hanford, 'Milton and the Art of War' (1921), reprinted in *John Milton, Poet and Humanist*, 185–223; Freeman, *Milton and the Martial Muse;* Lieb, *Poetics of the Holy*, 246–312; and Robert Fallon, *Captain or Colonel.* Campbell and Corns, *John Milton*, 156, comment, 'He knew nothing of practical soldiering,' Iago's complaint about Cassio, one recalls, and true also of Cromwell before 1642. For Norbrook, *Writing the English Republic*, 438–67, the war rhetoric of the poem echoes the contemporary political co-optation of Lucan's *Pharsalia.*

33 Freeman, *Milton and the Martial Muse*, 63; for the following paragraph, see his chapter, 63–112.

34 On the hidden cannon, see Hanford, 'Milton and the Art of War,' 211–14; and Scudder, 'Satan's Artillery.'

35 Lieb, *Poetics of the Holy*, 298–308, is suggestive here; see also Berry, *Process of Speech*, 171–85.

36 See, e.g., Christopher Hill, *Milton and the English Revolution*, 371–5.

37 Freeman, *Milton and the Martial Muse*, 112. His chapter again stresses the originality of Milton's conception.

38 Freeman, *Milton and the Martial Muse*, 107–8, remarks, 'The last phrase reminds us of . . . "the forlorne hope."'
39 Armitage, 'John Milton: Poet against Empire,' 217–19, detects Machiavellian discourse in the council scene.
40 *Stuart Tracts*, 373, 377.
41 Lieb, *Poetics of the Holy*, 304, 305.
42 On necessity see, e.g., Kahn, *Machiavellian Rhetoric*, 154–5; and John Bernard, *Why Machiavelli Matters*, 66–7. On Cromwell, see Beaumont's *Psyche* (1648): 'When this more than brutish General once / In lawless gulfs himself had plunged, he / Prints on his mad adventure's exigence / The specious title of Necessity' (11, st. 32). Quoted by Christopher Hill, *God's Englishman*, 234. Rahe, *Against Throne and Altar*, 131, argues that Satan is modelled on Cromwell. For royal prerogative, see Kevin Sharpe, *The Personal Rule of Charles I.*
43 Fairfax, *Stuart Tracts*, 367. For an earlier example, see Webb, *Elizabethan Military Science*, 102.
44 Kahn, *Machiavellian Rhetoric*, 228.
45 See the excellent essay by Kerrigan and Braden, 'Milton's Coy Eve: *Paradise Lost* and Renaissance Love Poetry,' *ELH* 53 (1986): 27–51, which considers the love chase and Satan as a hunter. In revised form it appears in their book, *The Idea of the Renaissance*, chap. 10.
46 Gerrard, *The Arte of Warre* (1591), quoted from Webb, *Elizabethan Military Science*, 56.
47 Donnelly, *Milton's Scriptural Reasoning*, 117–22, 129–33, discusses Abdiel's dialogue intelligently; also Kahn, *Machiavellian Rhetoric*, 213. Fish, *Surprised by Sin*, 180–90, deserves credit for first giving the Abdiel episode serious attention.
48 See Lieb, *Poetics of the Holy*, 308–12.
49 See Fenton, 'Hope, Land Ownership, and Milton's "Paradise Within,"' 151; now revised as chap. 2 in *Milton's Places of Hope.*
50 MacCaffrey, Paradise Lost *as 'Myth,'* 34.
51 This episode causes MacCaffrey to assume that a world of duplicity exists before the Fall.
52 Balachandra Rajan saw Milton 'using the occasion for a sermon on hypocrisy,' in Paradise Lost *and the Seventeenth-Century Reader*, 98. Martin, *The Ruins of Allegory*, 257–8, rightly calls this incident a 'trial' for Uriel. Milton's God is economical; a providence for the angel will serve the same purpose for Eve.
53 *Moralia in Job*, 25. 15. 34; quoted from McGinn, *Antichrist*, 81.
54 Bradshaw, *A Treatise of Things Indifferent* (1605), quoted by Kahn, *Machiavellian Rhetoric*, 143.

55 *Religio Medici,* 1, sect. 20, p. 17. Kahn, *Machiavellian Rhetoric,* 232, comments, 'Satan's rhetoric plays with the unreliability of appearances.'
56 On this see Kahn, *Machiavellian Rhetoric,* 211, 228, 230.
57 Ibid., 231.
58 Topsell, *The Historie of Foure-Footed Beastes* (1607), 708. This and the companion volume on serpents (1608; combined ed. 1658) largely are translations of Konrad Gesner's *Historia Animalium* (1551–87).
59 See, e.g., Ogden, 'The Crisis of *Paradise Lost* Reconsidered'; Stein, *Answerable Style,* 75–108; and, the ultimate authority, Raphael: 'God made thee perfet, not immutable' (*PL* 5: 524).
60 See also *OED* s.v. 1b, 'As a type of anything hateful and loathsome.' The always unsavoury reputation of the toad has been traced by Boll, *Autour du couple ambigu crapard-grenouille.*
61 The Geneva Bible identifies these as the pope's ambassadors, which 'come out of Antichrists mouth.' See further Emmerson, *Antichrist in the Middle Ages,* 22–4.
62 Bosch's *Table of the Seven Deadly Sins* (ca. 1480–5, Prado), roundel at lower left, shows Superbia approached by a naked lover as a witch holds a mirror before her; a toad covers her mons veneris.
63 See Rabanus Maurus in Migne, *Patrologia Latina,* 111: 230.
64 The *OED* cites examples of a serpent as proverbially representing guile, treachery, malignancy; a symbol of envy, jealousy, malice, wiliness.
65 Topsell, *The Historie of Serpents* (1608), 18. Milton expressed his distaste for Machiavellian policy, 'the masterpiece of a modern politician,' in *Of Reformation:* 'There is no art that hath bin more canker'd in her principles, more soyl'd, and slubber'd with aphorisming pedantry then the art of policie' (*CPW* 1: 571).
66 See Emmerson, *Antichrist in the Middle Ages,* 80.
67 Describing Satan we find 'subtle' (9: 307, 324) and 'subtle Fiend' (2: 815, 10: 20). In the encounter with Sin and Death, Satan, finding force will not work, switches to subtlety or guile, just as he will in the later assault against Adam and Eve.
68 Gallagher, *Milton, the Bible, and Misogyny,* 20, 21.
69 See *OED* s.v., and Forsyth, *The Satanic Epic,* 273–4.
70 Pope, '*Paradise Regained*', 47.
71 See Glanvill, *Saducismus Triumphatus,* pt. 1, 'Some Considerations about Witchcraft,' section 14, p. 51. Increase Mather gratefully adopted Glanvill's position, 'divine providence has taken care that the greatest part of mankind shall not be left in unavoidable deception,' quoted by Stuart Clark, *Vanities of the Eye,* 149.

72 Gallagher, *Milton, the Bible, and Misogyny,* 23 and n. 24, bizarrely reads ll. 165–7 to mean 'the Lord God Almighty is unable to transfer the guilt onto Satan.' Although syntactically possible, theologically this is nonsense, and it ignores the context of Adam's preceding attempt to transfer guilt. Gallagher labels the explanation 'finespun sophistry'; to Forsyth, in *The Satanic Epic,* 275, the serpent's punishment is self-evidently unfair and Milton's version of it 'patently unsatisfactory.'

73 On the Geneva Bible and its importance, see e.g. Berry's introduction to the cited facsimile, Greaves, 'Traditionalism and the Seeds of Revolution in the Social Principles of the Geneva Bible'; and Betteridge, 'The Bitter Notes.'

74 See Williams, *The Common Expositor,* 127–8.

75 Steadman, '"Man's First Disobedience": The Causal Structure of the Fall,' in *Milton's Epic Characters,* 149. As Steadman notes, 141, Arminius also regards Satan as the external cause and the serpent as the instrumental cause, but his comment, 'whose tongue the devil abused to propose what arguments he chose,' seems to dismiss the serpent as only a tool. See *The Writings of James Arminius,* 2: 74.

76 Kirkconnell, *The Celestial Cycle,* 67. 'Dragon' here may reflect the Vulgate (*draco*) or the native English usage for 'large snake' (see *OED,* s.v., 1). Again in Vondel's *Adam in Ballingschap* the serpent guise is chosen because of the beast's character: 'Slyness is born inherent in this beast, / And daring likewise' (Kirkconnell, 451).

77 See Williams, *The Common Expositor,* 127–8.

78 Babington, *Certaine Plaine, briefe, and comfortable Notes, vpon euery Chapter of Genesis,* 39.

79 Cornelius a Lapide, *Commentaria in Pentateuchun Mosis* (1616), in *Commentarii in Scripturam Sacram,* 1: 90. The commentary had eleven editions before *Paradise Lost* was published. Lapide cites as his source Martin Del Rio's *Pharus sacrae sapientiae* (Lyon, 1608). In several of Kirkconnell's analogues, the serpent is described as being Eve's pet before Satan's intervention. This would suggest a merging of traditions.

80 Gallagher, *Milton, the Bible, and Misogyny,* 24, notes the meaning of 'insinuating,' but, probably because be believes the serpent is 'quite innocent,' shifts his attention to 'fatal guile,' which he misreads as '"God-willed" or "God-destined,"' rather than 'lethal guile.'

81 Kirkconnell, *The Celestial Cycle,* 111, 211. See also Ziegierus's *Protoplastus, Drama comico tragicum* (552–3), in which the serpent alone tempts Eve with Lucifer watching in the background. In Ruff's *Adam und Heva* (559–60) Lucifer persuades the serpent to tempt Eve, and the serpent again acts independently.

82 Topsell, *Historie of Serpents*, A3v, expresses doubt on Josephus's theory that God, punishing the serpent for 'false friendship,' 'tooke away from him his legges, & maketh him creepe vppon the earth.' While it would be reasonable to assume that, as with the power of speech, his erect posture and progression are animated by Satan, the poem leaves the matter open: 'not with indented wave, / Prone on the ground, as since, but on his rear, / Circular base of rising folds, that towr'd / Fold above fold a surging Maze, his Head / Crested aloft . . . / . . . erect' (9: 496–501). The phrase 'as since' might imply that he was upright in Eden. In the first description, 'Wove . . . / His braided train' (4: 348–9) can mean either prone or erect; however, 'others on the grass / Coucht' (350–1) does seem contrastive. On this question, see also Edwards, *Milton and the Natural World*, 40–1.

83 See Svendsen, *Milton and Science*, 165–70; quotation, 169. The specified myths were also available in Topsell's *Historie of Serpents*. Harris Fletcher, *Milton's Rabbinical Readings*, 184–6, notes a rabbinical tradition that the serpent envied Man's conjugal bliss.

84 Satan's presentation as a jealous demon lover will be discussed in chap. 5 below.

85 Browne, *Pseudodoxia Epidemica*, I, chap. 1, pp. 1–2.

86 See Jackson Cope, 'Satan's Disguises.'

87 Arnold Williams, *The Common Expositor*, 128; on the Protevangelium, see further Patrides, '"The first promise made to man": The Edenic Origins of Protestantism,' in his *Premises and Motifs*, 90–104; and Duncan, *Milton's Earthly Paradise*, 128–47.

88 Milton's commentary on 'this Oracle' (10: 182–91) is a tissue of New Testament echoes. Flannagan, *The Riverside Milton*, cites Luke 10: 18, Eph. 2: 2, Col. 2: 14, Eph. 4: 8, Rom. 16: 20 (see 629, nn. 71–5).

4. Providence Working: The Son and the Adversary

1 Beard, *Antichrist the Pope of Rome* (1625), preface, A4r; quoted by Christopher Hill, *Antichrist in Seventeenth-Century England*, 2.

2 On the coronation, see Kevin Sharpe, *The Personal Rule of Charles I*, 775–83; and Brown, 'The Vanishing Empire,' 66, 78–80.

3 See Mark Jones, *A Catalogue of the French Medals in the British Museum*, nos. 154–6 (Scottish coronation); 157–9 (return to London); and pp. 143–6 on Briot.

4 For my purposes the most helpful studies of the invocation have been those by Chambers, 'Wisdom at One Entrance Quite Shut Out,' and Cirillo, '"Hail Holy Light" and Divine Time in *Paradise Lost*.'

5 Browne continues, 'for to his Eternity which is indivisible, and all together, the last Trump is already sounded, the reprobates in the flame, and the blessed in *Abrahams* bosome.' *Religio Medici*, I, sect. 11, p. 8.
6 Ryken, *The Apocalyptic Vision in 'Paradise Lost,'* 131, 132. Roland Frye, *Milton's Imagery*, 151, follows Ryken in responding too literally to the image. To James Fleming, *Milton's Secrecy*, 10, it bespeaks the poet's 'psychological imperative': 'Milton is quite obsessed with the idea of divine surveillance.'
7 'The eyes of Doctor J.J. Eckleburg are blue and gigantic – their retinas are one yard high. They look out of no face but, instead, from a pair of enormous yellow spectacles which pass over a non-existent nose.' *The Great Gatsby*, chap. 2, second par.
8 Milton's view of scriptural anthropomorphism (and anthropopathism) as an accommodation to the capacities of human understanding is orthodox. See, e.g., Ussher, *A Body of Divinitie*, 33: '*Why then doth the Scripture attribute unto him hands, feet, &c?* / The Scripture so speaketh of him as we are able to conceive thereof, and therefore in these and such like speeches humbleth it self to our capacity, attributing members unto God to signifie the like actions in him.' For Milton's fidelity to scriptural precedent in narrating the ineffable, see Murrin, *The Allegorical Epic*, chap. 6, 'The Language of Milton's Heaven.' On the dialogue in Heaven, see Parish, 'Milton and an Anthropomorphic God'; Hughes, 'The Filiations of Milton's Celestial Dialogue'; and Lieb, '*Paradise Lost*, Book III: The Dialogue in Heaven Reconsidered.'
9 *The Hymns of Orpheus*, trans. *Thomas Taylor, the Platonist*, ed. Kathleen Raine and G.M. Harper (Princeton, 1969), 281. For Secundus, see Rahner, *Greek Myths and Christian Mysteries*, 91; Ovid, *Metamorphoses* 4: 197, 228; Macrobius, *Saturnalia* 1: 21; Johannes Kepler, *Harmonices mundi* 5: 10; Ross, *Mystagogus poeticus*, 342–3; Swan, *Speculum mundi*, 322, as quoted by Svendsen, *Milton and Science*, 68. A variant formula is 'the eye of heaven' as in Donne's *Metempsychosis* 2: 1 and Shakespeare's Sonnet 18.
10 Ambrose, *Hexameron*, 4: 1.2, p. 127.
11 See Horapollo, *Hieroglyphica*, 222; Valeriano, *Hieroglyphica*, no. 33, fol. 234. For the 'oculus in sceptro,' see Claude Mignault, 'Syntagma de Symbolis,' commentary to Andrea Alciati, *Emblemata*, xlvii; and Cartari, *Imagini delli Dei de gl' antichi*, 35. Alberti's dialogue *Anuli* is quoted from Wind, *Pagan Mysteries in the Renaissance*, 234; see also plates 84 (Horapollo, 'Quo modo Deum') and 86 (winged-eye reverse of Alberti's portrait medal).
12 Rahner, *Greek Myths*, 99.

13 See Origen, *Commentaria in genesin,* and Hillary, *Tractatus in psalmum 118,* both in Rahner, *Greek Myths,* 97; see also 103–29 for the symbolism of the Easter Sun. The Christian implications of the sun imagery in the Nativity Ode have been most thoroughly explored by Pecheux, 'The Image of the Sun in Milton's "Nativity Ode."'

14 Ficino, *De sole,* 119. On the 'preoccupation with the sun . . . typical of all Ficino's works,' see D.P. Walker, *Spiritual and Demonic Magic from Ficino to Campanella,* 18. For the medieval tradition, see two essays by Mazzeo: 'Dante's Sun Symbolism and the Visions of the Blessed,' in *Structure and Thought in the 'Paradiso,'* 141–60; and 'The Light-Metaphysics Tradition,' in *Medieval Cultural Tradition in Dante,* 56–90.

15 Ficino, *De sole,* 136; *Il mondo creato* 1: 12; and see Cirillo, 'Tasso's *Il mondo creato.*'

16 Ussher, *A Body of Divinitie,* 76.

17 Cf. 'Lycidas' 168–71, in which, as Norford notes, 'the rising sun is both head and eye.' See 'The Sacred Head,' 43.

18 Steadman, 'The God of *Paradise Lost* and the *Divina Commedia.*'

19 MacCaffrey, 'The Theme of *Paradise Lost,* Book III,' 84–5.

20 Ficino, *De sole,* 121.

21 Boethius, *The Consolation of Philosophy,* 5, met. 2, 393–5; see also 5, prosa 6. MacCaffrey, 'The Theme of *Paradise Lost,* Book III,' 62, cites these passages in relation to the Father's dialogue, but does not note the relevance to the preliminary description.

22 Evans, *Milton's Imperial Epic,* 139. He spoils the effect by arguing that this is the narrator's 'authoritarian' attempt to silence any 'potential objections' to the providential thesis, seemingly forgetting that God's knowledge is *fore*knowledge, known to the reader since bk. 3.

23 *SA,* ll. 1172–3, '[His] ear is ever open; and his eye / Gracious to re-admit the suppliant,' virtually echo *PL* 3: 191–3. Samson describes himself as growing up 'Under [God's] special eye' (636) – i.e., *DDC*'s 'extraordinary' providence. In *Animadversions* Milton asserts that God has 'ever had this Iland under the special indulgent eye of his providence' (*CPW* 1: 704).

24 Tasso, *Gerusalemme liberata* 9, st. 56, 5–56. For the Fairfax translation (by the uncle of Thomas, the Lord General), I quote from *Jerusalem Delivered,* ed. Henry Morley. Milton admired Tasso's poem as a model of the 'diffuse' epic (*CPW* 1: 813–14).

25 The dialogue within the dream also suggests a possible imaginative refraction. Transported to Heaven by his vision, Godfrey there is addressed by the spirit of his friend Hugo (Ugone). They look down on the world below and discuss the mission God has ordained for Godfrey, the

completion of which is dependent on the return of a man from exile. It emerges that, to recover this man (Rinaldo), a volunteer will be necessary; but God will inspire the volunteer (Guelpho) to act. The licence to read such episodes in that manner I am suggesting is granted by Tasso's own commentary on the allegory: 'The Army wherein Rinaldo and the other worthies by the grace of God and advice of Man, are returned and obedient to their Chieftain, signifieth Man brought again into the state of natural justice and heavenly obedience' (*Jerusalem Delivered,* 442–3). Such a response would not have been remote from Milton.

26 X-rays have revealed that the triangular *occhio divino* is an overpainting of Pontormo's original symbol of a three-faced head, apparently done in response to Urban VIII's 11 August 1628 decree banning anthropomorphic representation of the Trinity. See Monica Bietti in the catalogue, *da Pontormo & per Pontormo,* 87–93. The overpainting nonetheless integrates skillfully with Pontormo's repeated disegno of triangles.

27 For a mid-seventeenth-century example, see the title-page of Athanasius Kircher, *Arithmologia* (Rome, 1665): 'At the top the beneficent deity is depicted as the eye of providence watching over creation from the center of a triangle symbolizing the trinity.' Heninger, Jr, *Touches of Sweet Harmony,* pl. 43; quotation, 209. The best-known example will be the Great Seal on the reverse of the US one-dollar bill, featuring a pyramid, the top of which has a radiant eye with the Virgilian motto 'Annuit Coeptis' above. The description approved by Congress (20 June 1782) states: 'The Eye over it & the Motto allude to the many signal interpositions of providence in favour of the American cause.' A nineteenth-century example of the symbolic complex may be seen at the Mission San Miguel Arcángel (San Miguel, CA). In the 1820s, the reredos was decorated with a mural, designed by the Catalonian artist Esteban Munras and executed by Salinan Indians; the eye of God within a triangle looks out from a fluffy cloud, behind which a surrounding burst of sun rays emanate.

28 Even so, the Son insists on the corporeality of his future resurrection (3: 241–50); see chap. 6 below.

29 For a full commentary, see Corbett and Lightbown, *The Comely Frontispiece,* 129–35. Their description differs from mine in seeing, rather than a sun, only 'a lighted circle of billowing cloud.' See also Bosch's *Table of the Seven Deadly Sins* on which at the centre of a sinful world is an enormous eye; within the pupil Christ rises from his sarcophagus. Beneath at the edge of the iris an inscription warns sinners, 'Cave, cave d[e]us videt' (Beware, beware God sees). The golden iris unmistakably evokes a radiant sun. Again providence is figured by both eye and sun.

30 Ralegh, *History of the World* (1614), bk. 1, chap. 1, sec. 13, 'Of Providence,' p. 18. He cites Isa, 42: 8. In sec. 14, 'Predestination,' he reserves his opinion of Calvin, possibly indicating a lack of sympathy with English Calvinism.

31 See, particularly, Hunter, 'Milton's Muse,' in *Bright Essence,* 149–56; and 'Holy Light in Paradise Lost.' See also Cirillo, '"Hail Holy Light,"' and J.H. Adamson, 'Milton's Arianism,' in *Bright Essence,* 53–61.

32 Patrides, 'Milton on the Trinity,' and 'The Godhead in Paradise Lost: Dogma or Drama?' in *Bright Essence,* 3–13, 71–7, especially 12.

33 See Jackson Cope, *The Metaphoric Structure of* Paradise Lost, 167–76. Fleming, *Milton's Secrecy,* 157, remarks that God has no need for dialogue, 'What is notable, rather, is that *God sees fit to use dialogue anyway.*' For the 'drama' reading, see Samuel, 'The Dialogue in Heaven,' and Revard, 'The Dramatic Function of the Son in *Paradise Lost.*'

34 As Jackson Cope, *Metaphoric Structure,* 170, has pointed out.

35 Michael Fixler's comment on the function of the angelic choruses is apposite: 'They mark with climactic devotion crucial phases in the unfolding of the scheme of Providence.' See 'The Apocalypse within *Paradise Lost,*' 142.

36 See Willet, *Hexapla in Genesin* (Cambridge, 1605), 300; quoted by Patrides, *Premises and Motifs,* 37–8. For the (unillustrated) emblem, see Willet, *Sacrorum Emblematum Centuria Una,* C4v. Lapide, *Commentarii in Scripturam Sacram,* 1: 238, explains that the ladder is a symbol of providence and divine governance; the angels ascending and descending are God's ministers and executors of providence. On the typology of the ladder, see further Patrides, 38–51; and MacCaffrey, 'The Theme . . . of Book III,' 78–9.

37 Bangs, *Arminius,* 198. For the commentary (written 1596, published 1612), see *The Writings of James Arminius,* 3: 527–65. Goodwin, presumably drawing directly on Arminius, makes the same argument in *An Exposition of the Ninth Chapter of the Epistle to the Romans* (1653). See Coffey, *John Goodwin,* 231–2.

38 Stavely, 'Satan and Arminianism,' 130.

39 On Aaron, see Chambers, 'Milton's Proteus,' and Herbert's poem, 'Aaron.' For Christ as the Philosopher's Stone, see Waddington, 'Melancholy against Melancholy,' 280–1. The twelve stones of Aaron's breastplate (Exod. 28: 17–21) further are related to the vision of the New Jerusalem, in which the foundations of the wall are ornamented with twelve precious stones (Rev. 21: 19–21). The allusion prepares for the association of Uriel with the angel of Rev. 19: 17.

40 Chambers, 'Milton's Proteus,' 287.

41 Cf. Ferdinand in *The Duchess of Malfi:* 'Cover her face. Mine eyes dazzle. She died young' (5.2.263).

42 In theological terms despair is caused by alienation from God. Susan Snyder writes, 'Pride and despair are linked in the refusal to acknowledge insufficiency of self and ask for God's help.' See 'The Left Hand of God,' 32.

43 Sims, *The Bible in Milton's Epics,* 227–8, commented that Satan 'express[es] his hatred for the Son as the Sun of Righteousness.' Stephen Wigler plausibly suggested a parodic relationship between the Book 4 soliloquy to the sun and the Book 3 invocation to light. See 'The Poet and Satan before the Light.'

44 See Hughes, *Constructing Antichrist,* and Roldan-Figueroa, '*Filius Perditionis.*'

45 McGinn, *Antichrist,* 33.

46 Quoted from Woodhouse, *Puritanism and Liberty,* 99.

47 In the following summary I rely mainly on the work of Emmerson, *Antichrist in the Middle Ages,* and McGinn, *Antichrist.*

48 Hughes, quoting Gregory in *Constructing Antichrist,* 109.

49 See Emmerson, *Antichrist in the Middle Ages,* 67–8; Christopher Hill, *Antichrist,* 181–2; and McGinn, *Antichrist,* 85–7.

50 See Russell, 'Martin Luther's Understanding of the Pope as the Antichrist,' and Whitford, 'The Papal Antichrist.' In his *Table Talk* Luther said, 'Antichrist is at the same time the pope and the Turk . . . The spirit of Antichrist is the pope, his flesh the Turk. One attacks the Church physically, the other spiritually.' Quoted from Setton, *Europe and the Levant in the Middle Ages and the Renaissance,* chap. 10, 'Lutheranism and the Turkish Peril,' 151.

51 On the *fortuna* of Antichrist in England, see Christopher Hill, *Antichrist in Seventeenth-Century England;* McGinn, *Antichrist,* 218–26; and, as part of a larger phenomenon, Peter Lake, 'Anti-popery.' See also Lake's earlier article, 'The Significance of the Elizabethan Identification of the Pope as Antichrist.'

52 Howard Schultz, possibly underestimating the depth of Milton's anti-popery and the complexity of the tradition, maintained, 'Milton was too good a scripturalist to call the Pope Antichrist, whose identity would not be known before the Last Things.' *Milton and Forbidden Knowledge,* 125. For the stubborn persistence of the papal Antichrist, see Anthony Milton, *Catholic and Reformed,* 93–127. Lawrence P. Buck is undertaking a history of the idea; see his article, '*Anatomia Antichristi.*'

53 A commendable exception is the essay by Simpson, 'The Apocalypse in *Paradise Regained.*' For Schultz on *PR,* see 'Christ and Antichrist in *Paradise Regained,*' and *Milton and Forbidden Knowledge,* passim; for *PL,* 126–7.
54 See, e.g., Patrides, '"*The bloody and cruell Turks*": The Judgments of God in History,' in *Premises and Motifs,* 137–51; for the drumbeat of rhetoric on 'the Roman Antichrist,' see Christopher Hill, *Antichrist,* 1–40; Anthony Milton, *Catholic and Reformed,* traces the Laudian repression of the myth, but does not consider the Interregnum.
55 MacLean, 'Milton, Islam and the Ottomans,' offers very general parallels between Satan and Iblis, the Satan-figure in the Koran; however, he does not descend to the textual level.
56 On the birthplace, see Emmerson, *Antichrist in the Middle Ages,* 80–1; as Rome, 70, 267, n. 16.
57 In *A Treatise of Civil Power* (1659), Milton used the papal Antichrist as a stalking horse for his authoritarian opponents: 'all true protestants account the pope antichrist, for that he assumes to himself this infallibilitie over both the conscience and the scripture' (CPW 7: 244). His real target is a Protestant state church that would enforce its interpretation of the Bible, which is 'no less antichrist in this main point of antichristianism, no less a pope or popedom than he at *Rome,* if not much more' (7: 244).
58 See Emmerson, *Antichrist in the Middle Ages,* 76; McGinn, *Antichrist,* 56.
59 Daneau, *A treatise, touching antichrist* (1589), 145; quoted by Stuart Clark, *Vanities of the Eye,* 179.
60 See, for exampleLabriola, 'Christus Patiens,' and 'The Medieval View of Christian History in *Paradise Lost.*'
61 See Emmerson, *Antichrist in the Middle* Ages, 21, 46, 217–18.
62 In the view of some commentators; see Hughes, *Constructing Antichrist,* 70, 160–1.
63 McGinn, *Antichrist,* 33.
64 C.A. Patrides, 'The Godhead in Paradise Lost: Dogma or Drama?' (1965), in *Bright Essence,* ed. Hunter, Patrides, and Adamson, 74–7, noted Satan's refusal to acknowledge by name the Son's existence. Hunter, 'The Heresies of Satan' (1967), in *The Descent of Urania,* 56–62, interpreted this as the heresy of dynamic monarchianism. Neither mentions Satan's single use of 'messiah.'
65 Forsyth, *The Satanic Epic,* 156, 157.
66 Patrides, '"*A Principle of infinite Love*": The Salvation of Satan,' in *Premises and Motifs,* 200–17; quotation, 201.
67 See Arminius, 'Private Disputations,' in *The Writings,* 2: 60–62; quotation 60–1.

68 Goodwin, *Redemption Redeemed*, 96, 484–6; quotations, 484, 485.
69 Rust, *A Letter of Resolution Concerning Origen*, quotations, 73, 131; and see Patrides, *Premises and Motifs*, 212–16.
70 Stavely, 'Satan and Arminianism,' 125.
71 Stachniewski, *The Persecutory Imagination*, 354.
72 See Stanglin, *Arminius on the Assurance of Salvation*, particularly 145–93.
73 Quotations, Stavely, 'Satan and Arminianism,' 135.
74 Arminius, *The Writings*, 2: 61–2.
75 Geneva gloss. Cf. Cornelius a Lapide on Rev. 19: 17: 'Angelus hic stat in sole, ut significet quod in oculis totius mundi fiet haec Antichristianorum per Christum ultio' (The angel standing in the sun indicates that, fixed in the entire eye of the world, this Antichrist will be punished by Christ). *Commentarii in Scripturam Sacrum*, 10: 1302. See also Dent, *The Ruine of Rome*, 104, and Burton, *The Seven Vials*, 86.
76 *The Dutch Annotations Upon the Whole Bible*, trans. Theodore Haak, 2 vols. (London, 1657) as quoted by Stavely, 'Satan and Arminianism,' 133.
77 Fixler, 'Apocalypse Within,' 159–60, relates the passage to Rev. 8: 13, which is echoed in 12: 12; but that ignores the clear indebtedness of Milton's lines to Rev. 12: 7–13. Hunter finds that Milton builds his conception of Book 6 on Rev. 12. See 'The War in Heaven,' in *Bright Essence*, ed. Hunter, Patrides, and Adamson, 125–6.
78 Geneva Bible, 'Argument' to Revelation. For a brief account of Revelation, emphasizing both its providential thrust and Milton's understanding of it, see Fixler, 'Apocalypse Within,' 132–51.
79 For this, see Labriola, '"Thy Humiliation Shall Exalt,"' 39–41.
80 See Watt, *Cheap Print and Popular Piety*, 154, 156 (fig. 15).
81 See Emmerson, *Antichrist in the Middle Ages*, 102–3, 229.
82 Cf. the commentary on Luke in Diodati, *Pious and Learned Annotations upon the Holy Bible;* and see Milton's adaptation of Ezekiel's vision to the battle in Heaven (6: 750–9, 827–34). Diodati describes Ezekiel's chariot (Ezek. 1: 15–21) as a 'figure of the consonant harmony, which is in all the works of God's providence.' Roland Frye, *Milton's Imagery*, 156–8, finds strong precedent in the visual arts for Milton's association of the chariot with Christ; see further Lieb, *Poetics of the Holy*, 291–7.

5. Possessing Eve: Tobias and Sarah in Eden

1 *Religio Medici*, 1, sect. 30, p. 24.
2 *Coelebs in Search of a Wife* (1808), quoted from Wittreich, *Feminist Milton*, Appendix D, 164.

3 Kierkegaard, *Fear and Trembling, Repetition, Problema* III, 103–4. Tanner, *Anxiety in Eden,* does not mention Tobit.

4 For the conventional ordering, see Gombrich, *Symbolic Images,* 'Tobias and the Angel,' 26–30, and figs 23–7.

5 See Stanglin, *Arminius on the Assurance of Salvation,* 223, who finds this stated most distinctly in the commentary on Perkins.

6 MacCallum, *Milton and the Sons of God,* 42–3. The term 'created' here, in fact, is imprecise; *DDC* (bk. 1, chap. 5) consistently describes the Son of God as 'generated': 'GENERATIO est qua Filium ex decreto suo genuit Deus unicum. unde et Pater primario dicitur' (*Works* 14: 178). 'By GENERATION God begot his only Son, in accordance with his decree' (*CPW* 6: 205). The distinction matters because *generatio* more immediately suggests creation from the same substance. On Milton's materialism, see Stephen Fallon, *Milton among the Philosophers,* and Rogers, *The Matter of Revolution.* Sugimura, '"*Matter of Glorious Triall,*"' 'challenges the prevailing scholarly consensus that "Milton's poetry supports monist materialism"' (ix) – unsuccessfully, I believe. See my review in *MQ* 45 (2011): 3–6.

7 As others have noted. For example, Shawcross, *The Development of Milton's Thought,* 117, comments that 'the merciful and loving nature of the Son' is one 'often associated with women.'

8 Campbell and Corns, *John Milton,* 345, collapsing the distinction between trial and temptation, comment: 'Milton's poem offers a series of temptations, to the angels, to Adam and Eve, perhaps in a sense to the Son as he accepts the challenge of atoning for fallen humankind.'

9 Johnson, 'Life of Milton,' here quoted from Shawcross, *Milton 1732–1801: The Critical Heritage,* 306.

10 MacCaffrey, Paradise Lost *as 'Myth,'* 198.

11 In focusing on the archetype described above, I risk simplifying the matter. Stephen Fallon, *Milton among the Philosophers,* 183–90, denies that Sin and Death are substances; for the opposite view, see Gallagher, '"Real or Allegoric."' Recently Catherine Gimelli Martin has advanced a more sophisticated version of Gallagher's 'minority view.' See *The Ruins of Allegory,* particularly 165–9. She elaborates on her argument in 'Eliding Absence and Regaining Presence.' I thank Professor Martin for allowing me to read her essay in manuscript.

12 Augustine concurred with Milton's sentiment: 'How much more tender and loving it would have been if he had said, "and soul of my soul."' See *The Literal Meaning of Genesis,* vol. 2, bk. 10, chap. 1; quotation 97.

13 I am grateful to Timothy Burbery for conversation and for his paper at the International Milton Congress (Duquesne University, 2004), which caused

me to think seriously about traducianism. See now his essay, 'From Orthodoxy to Heresy,' which argues that Milton's attraction to mortalism and traducianism in the 1640s can be discerned in these sonnets.

14 Tertullian, 'A Treatise on the Soul' (*De anima*) chap. 27, 3: 208. On *De anima*, see Quasten, *Patrology*, 287–90. The Renaissance *editio princeps* by Beatus Rhenanus was printed in 1521, with *De anima* added in 1545.

15 Tertullian, 'Treatise on the Soul,' chap. 36, 217.

16 See George Huntston Williams, *The Radical Reformation*, 788–98. As he notes, Calvin and Melanchthon disagreed, staying with a modified creationism.

17 Augustine disliked the theory, conceded he could not disprove it, and vacillated between creationism and a spiritualized traducianism. See O'Connell, *The Origin of the Soul in St. Augustine's Later Works*, and Mendelson, 'The "Business of Those Absent."' Jerome, with whom Augustine corresponded on the question (see *Epistula* 166), thought that most Western writers were traducians: 'au certe ex traduce, ut Tertullianus, Apollinaris et maxima pars occidentalium autumat' (*Epistula* 126, cited in *CPW* 6: 319, n. 63).

18 For Milton's traducianism, see Hunter, 'The Origin and Destiny of the Soul' (1946), in *The Descent of Urania*, 115–17; Patrides, *Milton and Christian Tradition*, 97–108; and Burns, *Christian Mortalism from Tyndale to Milton*, 172–4; also *DDC* (*CPW* 6: 319–24). Poole, *Milton and the Idea*, 23, 44, 47, 52–3, touches on traducianism, but curiously does not mention Milton's belief.

19 For advice on the figures discussed here, I am indebted to my consultant rhetor, Thomas O. Sloane.

20 Among many studies, one might mention these: Cox, *The Renaissance Dialogue*; Jon Snyder, *Writing the Scene of Speaking*; Heitsch and Vallee, *Printed Voices*; and Smarr, *Joining the Conversation*. Fleming, *Milton's Secrecy*, 123–58, discusses dialogue in *PL* from the perspective of Hans-Georg Gadamer's hermeneutics. For the premature announcement (which, to be fair, concerns an epistemological shift, not the literary form), see Ong, *Ramus, Method, and the Decay of Dialogue*.

21 There have been three studies focused on the role of Raphael. The most helpful is Beverley Sherry's suggestive appreciation, 'Milton's Raphael and the Legend of Tobias.' Wollaeger, 'Apocryphal Narration,' is concerned with narrative authority, which causes him to emphasize difference: 'Through Raphael . . . Milton's counternarrative asserts a critical distance from the story of the Fall' (137). Some of the argument I find strained or simply incorrect: the Book 4 prayer is not, as implied, on

Adam's and Eve's wedding night (142); Asmodeus does not have 'sexual possession of Sara in Tobit' (143); Adam does not 'accuse Eve of being wedded to the serpent' (143). Farris, 'Angelic Visitations,' largely is a review of previous criticism.

22 For a summary of commentaries on Tobit, see Lapide, *Commentarii in Scripturam Sacram,* 2: 835–76, 'Commentaria in Tobiam.' For Milton's use of the Apocrypha, see Mollenkott, 'The Pervasive Influence of the Apocrypha in Milton's Thought and Art'; on Tobit, see 29–30.

23 See *The Golden Legend or Lives of the Saints as Englished by William Caxton,* 2: 57–77. Milton may follow Caxton in his use of 'fume' to describe the odour of the burning fish heart and liver. On the popularity of the story in England, see Watt, *Cheap Print and Popular Piety,* 118–19 (broadside ballads) and 209–10 (wall paintings and hangings, woodcuts); and Sherry, 'Milton's Raphael,' 234–6 (ballads, religious writings). Parish, 'Milton and the Well-Fed Angel,' 90, called attention to the Tobias windows of King's College Chapel, Cambridge.

24 See Held, 'Rembrandt and the Book of Tobit.' For the wide attraction of artists to the subject, see the impressively thorough study by Lugt, 'Man and Angel, II,' and Sherry, 'Milton's Raphael,' 236–9. To their listings one can add J.M.W. Turner (Tate Gallery, London).

25 *CPW* 2: 239; also 243, 246, 344. Fagius (1504–49) was invited to England by Archbishop Cranmer and appointed reader in Hebrew at Cambridge, only months before his death. The text and translation from Fagius's *Sententiae Morales Ben Syrae vetustissimi authoris Hebraei* (1542) were reprinted in Brian Walton's *Biblia Polyglotta,* 6 vols (London, 1653–7), 4: 15–63. Loren T. Stuckenbruck very generously sent me in manuscript his translation, 'The "Fagius" Hebrew Version of Tobit: An English Translation Based on the Constantinople Text of 1519' (translation quoted hereafter).

26 On Raphael, see Ferguson, *Signs and Symbols in Christian Art,* 99–100; also Gombrich, 'Tobias and the Angel,' who comments that the story was understood as 'the epic of the Archangel Raphael' (27). Gallagher, *Milton, the Bible, and Misogyny,* 147, calls Milton's Raphael an agent of 'special providence'; although 'extraordinary' might be more accurate, the description applies equally well to Raphael in the Book of Tobit.

27 See Robert West, *Milton and the Angels,* 45–6, 164–9; and, on the materiality of Milton's angels, see Stephen Fallon, *Milton among the Philosophers,* 141–7.

28 Lapide, *Commentarii in Scripturam Sacram,* 2: 846, 876.

29 For the phoenix as a symbol of Christ, see, e.g., Ferguson, *Signs and Symbols,* 23; and Waddington, 'Melancholy Against Melancholy,' 280–1.

30 By comparison, the Geneva Bible less precisely states, 'for she is appointed vnto thee from the beginning.'

31 Quoted from *The Sarum Missal,* 415.

32 *The First Prayer Book of King Edward VI,* 331.

33 Caxton, *The Golden Legend,* quotation, 66; 68.

34 Elliott, *Spiritual Marriage,* 171.

35 Held, *Rembrandt Studies,* quotations, 126.

36 The classic exposition is that by Lewalski, 'Innocence and Experience in Milton's Eden,' especially 92–5. See also the fine essay by Yu, 'Life in the Garden,' and Joshua Scodel's learned account 'Pleasurable Restraint, and the Mean of Self-Respect.'

37 Here I am anticipated by Sherry, 'Milton's Raphael,' 232, who comments, 'Satan . . . proves a kind of demon lover.'

38 Caciola, *Discerning Spirits,* 36. See Matt. 8: 28–34, 17: 14–21; Mark 1: 23–8, 34, 3: 10–12, 5: 1–20, 9: 14–29; Luke 8: 26–39, 9: 37–42. Only John does not recount exorcisms. Acts 8: 5–8 describes Philip preaching Christ and expelling 'unclean spirits.' For a reliable, concise history of possession and exorcism, see Kelly, *The Devil, Demonology and Witchcraft,* 67–95.

39 For Asmodeus's place in the angelic orders, see Robert West, *Milton and the Angels,* 156–7; and see Kramer and Sprenger, *The Malleus Malificarum,* pt. 2, quest. 2, chap. 2, 168; and chap. 5, 178.

40 See Steadman, 'Eve's Dream and the Conventions of Witchcraft,' 573. He was preceded by Hunter, 'Eve's Demonic Dream' (1946), in *The Descent of Urania,* 46–55.

41 James Sharpe, *Instruments of Darkness,* 190–210, finds that witchcraft cases increasingly allege demonic causation, rather than human intermediaries, and observes that possession cases involve 'very stereotyped patterns of behaviour' (195). For the comedic exploitation of possession, see the fifth acts of *The Comedy of Errors* (ca. 1592–4) and of *Volpone* (1606) and *The Devil is an Ass* (1616).

42 Hunter, *The Descent of Urania,* 48. On Satan's motives, see also Bowers, 'Adam, Eve, and the Fall in *Paradise Lost.*'

43 For the iconographic tradition, see Lehnhof, '"Impregn'd with Reason,"' 38–40 and figs. 1–6.

44 See Caciola, *Discerning Spirits,* 172, fig. 13.

45 See, e.g., Crouzet, 'A Woman and the Devil,' 196.

46 Ginzburg, *The Night Battles,* 9, 10.

47 On these, see, e.g., D.P. Walker, *Spiritual and Demonic Magic,* 80–1 (incantation); and Ginzburg, *The Night Battles,* 8 (trance).
48 For prophecy, see Caciola, *Discerning Spirits,* 76, 122–3. She notes 'a recurrent topos about possession through the consumption of food' (42).
49 On levitation I am indebted to a stimulating paper by Carlos M.N. Eire, 'Saint Teresa, Reluctant Levitator'; see his essay, 'The Good, the Bad, and the Airborne.' For Simon Magus, see *The Acts of Peter,* in *The Apocryphal New Testament,* 401–23; quotation, 423. In 1647 a famous physician wrote that there were only two signs of genuine demonic possession: speaking in unknown tongues on unknown subjects and levitation. See Trevor-Roper, *Europe's Physician,* 355.
50 Ferber, *Demonic Possession and Exorcism in Early Modern France,* 115. Sherry, 'Milton's Raphael,' 231, states boldly, 'Eve has just been possessed in her sleep by Satan because she has mistaken his voice for that of her true love.' Van den Berg, 'Eve, Sin and Witchcraft in *Paradise Lost,*' 353, considers but quickly dismisses the possibility of demonic possession; so too Benet, 'Milton's Toad or Satan's Dream?' 41. I agree with van den Berg that Milton uses this material as a 'discourse' through which to explore relevant themes.
51 Ferber, *Demonic Possession,* 118.
52 See Caciola, *Discerning Spirits,* 42–3.
53 Stuart Clark, *Thinking with Demons,* 84. He cites Léon d'Alexis (1599) and Thomas Ady (1676).
54 See Angus Fletcher, *Allegory,* 40–2.
55 See the interesting logical analysis by Jacobus, *Sudden Apprehension,* 143–8, and the discussion by Bennett, *Reviving Liberty,* 109–18.
56 Stanglin, *Arminius on the Assurance of Salvation,* 152. See further den Boer, *God's Twofold Love,* 172–7.
57 Stein, *Answerable Style,* 109.
58 Kerrigan and Braden, *The Idea of the Renaissance,* 194–218; also Scodel, *Excess and the Mean,* 263–8. Lehnhof, 'Impregn'd with Reason,' 57–62, extensively elaborates on the sexual implications of Eve's temptation; see further the studies cited in his notes.
59 On the ability of fallen angels to copulate with women, see Robert West, *Milton and the Angels,* 169–73; and Walter Stephens, *Demon Lovers.*
60 See Labriola, 'The Aesthetics of Self-diminution.'
61 Kerrigan and Braden, *The Idea of the Renaissance,* 206.
62 On this topos, see Curtius, *European Literature and the Latin Middle Ages,* 195–200.

63 See Jacobus's helpful analysis, *Sudden Apprehension*, 160–5; on Satan's verbal manipulations, see also Leonard, *Naming in Paradise*, 199–213; and Kahn, *Machiavellian Rhetoric*, 224–35.

64 Sherry, 'Speech in *Paradise Lost*,' writes insightfully: 'A sign of separation is the disintegration of their converse as duologue gives place to monologue, a characteristically fallen mode of utterance in *Paradise Lost*' (259). I would extend this to monologue in the presence of another character.

65 Sherry, 'Speech,' 255–6. The observation now has become such a critical commonplace that Martin Evans could state without elaboration: 'Eve begins to think and talk exactly like Satan' (*Milton's Imperial Epic*, 99). The nuances still reward exploration, however.

66 First quotation, Thomas, *Religion and the Decline of Magic*, 478; second, Ferber, *Demonic Possession*, 26. Walter Stephens, *Demon Lovers*, 328–9, traces the symptom of inappropriate knowledge to Aquinas. D.P. Walker, *Unclean Spirits*, 12, lists this as one of four 'main marks of possession.' As Benjamin J. Kaplan remarks, the first three – speaking in tongues, clairvoyance, extraordinary strength – 'amounted to the same thing . . . powers attributable only to a devil.' See 'Possessed by the Devil?' 739. The fourth, revulsion at the sight of holy objects (Catholic) or the Bible (Protestant), was anachronistic for Milton's narrative.

67 Briggs, *Witches and Neighbors*, 389. On the Catholic-Protestant differences, see also Stuart Clark, *Thinking with Demons*, 414–18, and Thomas, *Religion and the Decline of Magic*, 477–92. Andrew Cambers, 'Demonic Possession, Literacy and "Superstition,"' considers the role of the Bible in Protestant exorcism.

68 See Nischan, 'The Exorcism Controversy and Baptism in the Late Reformation.' In England the second Edwardian Prayer Book banished exorcism from the baptism rite.

69 For the seminal episode, see Crouzet, 'A Woman and the Devil'; and D.P. Walker, *Unclean Spirits*, 4–5, 19–28; the larger phenomenon is discussed by Pearl, *The Crime of Crimes*.

70 Trans. Pearl, *The Crime of Crimes*, 53, from Bodin's *Démonomanie* (1580), bk. 3, chap. 6.

71 The rule specifies: 'Now the signs of a possessing demon are: the speaking of many words or the understanding of a speaker in an unknown tongue; the revealing of distant and occult things; the manifestation of powers beyond the nature of one's age or condition; and other things of this sort, which when several occur together are all the more decisive indications.' Trans. Kelly, *The Devil, Demonology and Witchcraft*, 64.

72 Kierkegaard, *Problema III*, 104.
73 See Stuart Clark, *Thinking with Demons*, 417, 421.
74 See D.P. Walker, *Unclean Spirits*, 80. Kallendorf, 'The Diabolical Adventures of Don Quixote, or Self-Exorcism and the Rise of the Novel,' 215–19, discusses a 1676 exorcism manual with a section of instructions for lay persons to perform self-exorcisms by prayers to Jesus Christ, a striking instance of the church's movement nearer to the Protestant position.
75 Quoted from Stuart Clark, *Thinking with Demons*, 401.
76 Bennett, *Reviving Liberty*, 86.
77 Summers, *The Muse's Method*, 177–8.
78 Wittreich, *Feminist Milton*, 99. See also Collier, *Milton's 'Paradise Lost'*, xi, for whom Eve is the 'true hero' of the story (cited by Wittreich, *Feminist Milton*, 100).
79 Sims, *The Bible in Milton's Epics*, 213.
80 John 11: 2, to the contrary, identifies the woman who 'wiped [Jesus's] feet with her hair' as Mary, sister of Martha and of Lazarus.
81 Maggi, *Satan's Rhetoric*, 116.
82 It may be pertinent that reminding demons of the Last Judgment (of which the first was a type), and thus their limited time and ultimate fate, was an approved tactic of exorcism.
83 In *Doctrine and Discipline of Divorce* the word 'solace' (from *solacium:* comfort) is used recurrently to define the purpose of marriage – for instance, in the argument to bk. 1, chap. 11: '*mariage the intended solace of life*' (*CPW* 2: 273).
84 As Kerrigan and Braden argue, *Idea of the Renaissance*, 216–18.
85 Latin letter (28 September 1654) to his friend Leonard Philaras, trans. *The Works*, 12: 71. I agree with Wollaeger, 'Apocryphal Narration,' that Milton 'had a host of personal reasons to feel a deep empathy with Tobit' (152), but not his speculation that the poet hoped for a restoration of his sight. Milton was too much of a rationalist for that. On the other hand, Wollaeger's suggestion that '*Michael* from *Adam's* eyes the Film remov'd' (11: 412) echoes Tobit's cure is convincing; father Adam sees his children with far less pleasure than does Tobit.
86 In the painting by Jan Massys or Massijs (Antwerp, 1564) the figure restoring Tobit's sight, I would argue, is not Tobias but the older, larger (wingless) angel. If so, the artist makes direct the intervention of providence, the medicine of God.
87 Milton is eloquent on just what constitutes heresy and heretics: 'He then who to his best apprehension follows the scripture, though against any

point of doctrine by the whole church receivd, is not the heretic; but he who follows the church against his conscience and perswasion grounded on the scripture' (*CPW* 7: 248). Mueller, 'Milton on Heresy,' usefully tracks occurrences of the term, possibly 'problematizing' them more than necessary.

6. Murder One: Blood, Soul, and Mortalism

1 Browne, *Pseudodoxia Epidemica*, bk. 5, chap. 4, p. 276.

2 Winstanley, *An Humble Request to the Ministers of Both Universities* (1650), in *The Works of Gerrard Winstanley*, 425.

3 Roland Frye, *Milton's Imagery*, 304.

4 Most helpful on the tradition are Henderson, 'Cain's Jaw-Bone,' and Barb, 'Cain's Murder-Weapon and Samson's Jawbone of an Ass.' Two later studies focus on Cain's punishment. See Mellinkoff, *The Mark of Cain*, and Quinones, *The Changes of Cain*.

5 Werman, *Milton and Midrash*, 227. This Midrash was translated into Latin by Willem Vorstius as *Capitula R. Elieser* (Leiden, 1644). See Werman, 44–5. The similarity was noticed first by Don Cameron Allen, 'Milton and Rabbi Eliezer.' Louis Ginzberg paraphrases another Midrash: 'Not knowing what injury was fatal, Cain pelted all parts of his body with stones, until one struck him on the neck and inflicted death.' *The Legends of the Jews*, 1: 109.

6 Cowley, *Poems*, 8 and 29, n. to stanza 16. The *Davideis* analogue is mentioned by Shumaker, *Unpremeditated Verse*, 204–5; and by Roland Frye, *Milton's Imagery*, 302. Cowley's note is quoted by Don Cameron Allen, *The Legend of Noah*, 178. Like Cowley, the most recent illustrator settles on a stone to the head. See Crumb, *The Book of Genesis Illustrated*.

7 Quoted Harvey, *The Anatomical Lectures of William Harvey*, 243.

8 See Crooke's [*Microcosmographia*]: *A Description of the Body of Man* (1615), bk. 2, v, 'Of the midriffe called Diaphragma,' 354; also, Primaudaye, *The French Academie* (1618), bk. 2, xxxvii, 449; and Vicary, *The English-Mans Treasure* (1633), 40.

9 Woodall, *The Surgions Mate* (1617), 'Of Wounds,' 125, 134 [126]. On Woodall, see Debus, 'John Woodall, Paracelsian Surgeon.'

10 See Hume, *Annotations on Milton's Paradise Lost*, 300–1. Hume's phrasing ('great Stone') may echo Cowley's note to *Davideis*.

11 See MacCallum, 'Milton and Figurative Interpretation of the Bible,' and Mulder, 'Typology,' in *A Milton Encyclopedia*. See further chap. 7 following.

12 Gilbert Cope, *Symbolism in the Bible and the Church,* 199; see also Roland Frye, *Milton's Imagery,* 300.

13 Browne, *Pseudodoxia Epidemica,* bk. 6, chap. 6, p. 345.

14 Winstanley, *A Letter to the Lord Fairfax* (1649), in *The Works,* 290.

15 Coppe, *A Fiery Flying Roll* (1650), pt. 1, chap. 1, in *Selected Writings,* 24.

16 See Christopher Hill, *The English Bible,* 205–15, 239–40, 242–6, 387–9; also *The World Turned Upside Down,* 117–19. See further King, *Milton and Religious Controversy,* 173–9; and Blythe, 'Cain and Abel in *Paradise Regained,*' who follows King in tracing the use of the siblings in contemporary polemics, religious and political.

17 The Muggletonian Thomas Tomkinson, quoted from Hill, *The English Bible,* 240. See also Seaver, *Wallington's World,* 51. Much earlier Gregory the Great had made the same association; see Emmerson, *Antichrist in the Middle Ages,* 20.

18 See, for example, Réau, *Iconographie de l'art chrètien,* 2, pt. 1, 961: 'Dans les Bibles moralisées, Cain est assimilé à Judas qui "bailla" son maitre Jesus aux Juifs pour le Crucifier.'

19 See Tuve, *Allegorical Imagery,* 95, fig. 18; and Braude, '"Cokkel in oure Clene Corn,"' 581 and fig. 11.

20 *Bible Moralisée: Codex Vindobonensis 2554* (London, 1995), 56. See the facsimile, 2vC, and Guest's comment on the typology, 31. The imputation of the Judas kiss to the Genesis narrative occurs more than once. The most notable precursor to the typological schemes of the *biblia pauperum* may be the altarpiece, attributed to Nicolas of Verdun, for the monastery of Klosterneuburg. One group in blue enamel and black niello against gold, dating from 1330, presents two types: above (*ante legem*), Cain strikes Abel with a hoe; below (*sub lege*), Joab slays Abner. Between them, the antitype shows Judas betraying Christ with a kiss. See Avril Henry, *Biblia Pauperum,* 10–12, and fig. 7B.

21 See Roland Frye, *Milton's Imagery,* 301–2.

22 For biblical and classical antecedents to the reaper or mower metaphor, see Don Cameron Allen, *Image and Meaning,* 130–1. As Erwin Panofsky noted, Death 'was represented with a scythe or sickle from very early times.' See *Studies in Iconology,* 77. The Codex 2554 illuminator figures Cain as Death by changing the colour of his costume from ochre (when he kisses Abel) to blue-black (as he strikes him with the hoe). Although the *OED* does not record the epithet 'Grim Reaper' before the nineteenth century, the pre-modern sense of *grim* as 'Fiercely angry' (*OED,* s.v. A.1.b) is suggestively like Milton's 'inly rag[ing]' reaper.

23 For these, see Arnold Williams, *The Common Expositor,* 142.

24 Crucial here is Hebrews 12: 24, 'and to Jesus the mediator of the new covenant, and to the blood of sprinkling, that speaketh better things than *that of* Abel.' For a summary of commentators on this comparison, see Lapide, *Commentarii in Scripturam Sacram*, 9: 1007; and, for Abel and Cain as types, see 1: 97, 100. Among Milton's contemporaries, John Bunyan uses Heb. 12: 24 to explain, 'as by the rule of contraries,' the progression from Law to Grace, the blood of Abel to the blood of Christ. See *An Exposition of the First Ten Chapters of Genesis*, in *Complete Works*, 3: 399.

25 See Susan Snyder, 'The Left Hand of God,' 53, 55–6. For the visual conventions of representing the suicide, see Cassell, 'Pier della Vigna's Metamorphosis.'

26 I am grateful to Michael Walton for pointing out the relevance of this text. On the different versions, see Kirsopp Lake, 'The Death of Judas.'

27 See, e.g., Ambrose, *De Cain et Abel*, bk. 2, chap. 8, in *The Fathers of the Church*, 42: 426–7.

28 Meccaby, *Judas Iscariot and the Myth of Jewish Evil*, 59. *The Book of Jubilees*, drawing on the legend of Cain as first city builder, has him die by the same weapon with which he committed his crime: 'His house fell on him, and he died inside it and was killed by the stones of it; for with a stone he had killed Abel, and by a just retribution he was killed by a stone himself.' See *The Apocryphal Old Testament*, 24.

29 Newton's note on the vision pauses over the conjunction of the blow to the diaphragm and the massive haemorrhage, citing Cowley for the one and Virgil for the other: 'Undantique animam diffundit in arma cruore' (*Aeneid 10:* 908). See *Paradise Lost*, ed. Newton, 2: 352–3. The circumstances in both of Newton's suggestions differ from Milton: Cowley's Cain hurls the stone at Abel's head and Aeneas slashes Mezentius's throat with a sword. Nonetheless, Newton's bracketing may have established the correct range. Virgil's phrase *animam diffundit* echoes Lucretius (3: 437), on which see *Aeneid 10*, 285, n. to l: 908. Bk. 3 of *De rerum natura* expounds on the mortality of the soul, a subject discussed later in this chapter.

30 Sermon No. 11, 'Preached at St. Pauls, upon Christmas day. 1622.' *The Sermons of John Donne*, 4: 293, 294.

31 See Park, 'The Organic Soul,' in *The Cambridge History of Renaissance Philosophy*, 64–8. See also Eckhard Kessler, 'The Intellective Soul,' idem, 485–534, for debate on the question of its immortality.

32 'Ipse vero est corpus tenuissimum, quasi non corpus et quasi iam anima, item quasi non anima et quasi iam corpus.' Quoted from Ficino, *Three Books on Life*, bk. 3, iii, 256–7. See also bk. 1, ii, 111. On *spiritus*, see 42–4;

Park, 'Organic Soul,' 469; D.P. Walker, *Spiritual and Demonic Magic;* Klein, 'Spirito Peregrino,' in his *Form and Meaning*, 62–85.

33 Quoted from *The Complete English Poems of John Donne*, ed. Patrides.

34 For this philosophic commonplace, see Waddington, '"All in All."'

35 Overton, *Man's Mortalitie*, 72. Overton provides the marginal note, 'Absurd.'

36 See Park, 'Organic Soul,' 476–84; quotation, 483. See also Temkin, *Galenism*, 143–9, on Telesius and Campanella.

37 Stephen Fallon, *Milton among the Philosophers*, 98–107, discusses the corporeality of the soul in Raphael's Book 5 speeches, arguing that, in effect, for Milton the rational displaces the immortal soul.

38 See Waddington, '"All in All,"' 56–7. *DDC* uses the topos directly to support traducianism: 'anima est tota in toto, et tota in qualibet parte' (*CPW* 6: 321–2 and n. 70).

39 See Hobbes, *Leviathan*, chap. 44, p. 425. For the contemporary reception of the work, see Mintz, *The Hunting of Leviathan*.

40 John Henry, 'Medicine and Pneumatology.' 23. See further D.P. Walker, 'Medical Spirits in Philosophy and Theology from Ficino to Newton.'

41 The three essays are from *P&P:* Hill, 'William Harvey and the Idea of Monarchy,' no. 27 (April 1964); Whitteridge, 'William Harvey: A Royalist and No Parliamentarian,' no. 30 (April 1965); and Hill, 'William Harvey (No Parliamentarian, No Heretic) and the Idea of Monarchy,' no. 31 (July 1965). They have been reprinted in Webster, *The Intellectual Revolution of the Seventeenth Century*, 182–96. Webster mediates the dispute in judging that, while Harvey's ideas did not change over time, 'critics are obliged to accept Hill's basic point that there are distinct differences of emphasis between *De motu cordis* and *De generatione*' (14). Hill's attention to the political uses of the circulation metaphor has been extended by Rogers, *The Matter of Revolution*, 16–38.

42 Hill, in *The Intellectual Revolution*, 161, 162. But see Whitteridge, *William Harvey and the Circulation of the Blood*, 215–21, in which she traces Harvey's thought on the primacy of heart or blood; and 191–2, 223–7, in which she revisits the spirit-in-blood issue.

43 French, *William Harvey's Natural Philosophy*, 130. For the reception of Harvey's ideas in England, see his chap. 6; and, on the Continent, chap. 9.

44 Fludd, *Doctor Fludds Answer unto M. Foster. Or, the Squeesing of Parson Fosters Sponge* (1631), 68–70; quotation, 70.

45 Helmont, *Oriatrike or, Physick Refined*, 793. See also 954 on the soul in the blood. Michael T. Walton discusses both Fludd and van Helmont as

chemists who read Genesis through the perspective of the Cabala. See 'Genesis and Chemistry in the Sixteenth Century,' 8–12.

46 The psalm was understood as an epitome of providence; for example, Robert Bellarmine explained, 'Davide praevidente Christi,' quoted from Lapide, *Commentarii in Scripturam Sacram*, 7: appendix, p. 57.

47 Debus, 'Harvey and Fludd: The Irrational Factor in the Rational Science of the Seventeenth Century,' 90. See further Debus, 'Robert Fludd and the Circulation of the Blood,' and 'The Sun in the Universe of Robert Fludd,' and French, *William Harvey's Natural Philosophy*, 123–32.

48 See Niebyl, 'Galen, Van Helmont, and Blood Letting.'

49 See French, *William Harvey's Natural Philosophy*, 2.

50 See John Henry, 'A Cambridge Platonist's Materialism,' and 'The Matter of Souls.'

51 More, *The Easie, True, and Genuine Notion and Consistent Explication of the Nature of a Spirit*, 90. See 112–22, 144, 152–62 for More's extended exposition and confutation of Holenmerianism. This is Glanvill's translation of chapters 27–8 from More's *Enchiridion metaphysicum* (1671). Presumably, the increased association with mortalism caused More to recant his earlier acceptance of the *tota in toto* concept in *Psychathanasia*, bk. 2, cant. 2, st. 32 and 37.

52 See More, *The Philosophical Poems of Henry More*, 169–72, for the Latin text. In 'Henry More's "Circulatio Sanguinis,"' Shugg concludes that it was written between 1651 and 1653.

53 See Shugg, 186–7, on these analogies.

54 Collop, *The Poems of John Collop*, ed. Hilberry, introduction, 6 (edition quoted hereafter).

55 Harvey, *Anatomical Exercitations* (1653), chap. 51, 280; also cited by Hilberry, ed., 203, n. to l. 12. The modern translation by Whitteridge, *Disputations Touching the Generation of Animals*, 245, eliminates the Latin tag, thereby obscuring the reference. Earlier in chap. 51 Harvey cites the Bible for the assertion that life and soul exist in the blood (Whitteridge trans., 243).

56 Marvell dallies coyly with these ideas in 'To His Coy Mistress': 'And while thy willing soul transpires / At every pore with instant fires' (35–6); 'though we cannot make our Sun / Stand still, yet we will make him run' (45–6). Smith annotates l. 46 with Psalm 19: 6.

57 Harvey, *Anatomical Exercitations*, chap. 52, 283 (see Hilberry's note on 'Of the Blood,' l. 34, 'Placing in him this tutelar Deity'). Whitteridge's translation again blunts the point: 'and that there the tutelary deities and the soul itself have set up their abode, no man can doubt' (243).

58 D.P. Walker, 'The Astral Body in Renaissance Medicine,' 131.

59 *The Apocryphal Old Testament,* par. 22, ll. 4–5, p. 152.

60 For James Harrington, 'the parliament is the heart which . . . sucketh in and gusheth forth the life blood of Oceana by a perpetual circulation.' *The Political Works of James Harrington,* 287. See further I. Bernard Cohen, 'Harrington and Harvey.'

61 Corns, *Regaining* Paradise Lost, 88.

62 Burns, *Christian Mortalism.* On the congruence of mortalism with traducianism (discussed in chap. 5 above), see Burns, 172–4. See also William B. Hunter, Jr, 'Mortalism' in *A Milton Encyclopaedia.*

63 See Christopher Hill, *Milton,* 317–23, particularly 321.

64 Christopher Hill, *Milton,* 333. For an assessment of the thesis, see Waddington, 'Milton Turned Upside Down.'

65 Burns, *Christian Mortalism,* 168.

66 For the presence of Lucretius in the poem, see Leonard, 'Milton, Lucretius, and "the void profound of unessential Night,"' and Quint, 'Fear of Falling,' 47–81; on mortalism see 871.

67 See Coldiron, 'Milton *in parvo,*' and Burbery, 'From Orthodoxy to Heresy.'

68 See Kerrigan, 'The Heretical Milton,' 145. He notes, 145–6, that both Overton and Hobbes use Enoch and Elijah as proofs of mortalism.

69 Christopher Hill, *Milton,* 317. Sugimura, '*Matter of Glorious Trial,*' 141–9, 153–7, argues – unconvincingly – that Milton's 'inherently metaphorical' language subverts his intended mortalism in both *PL* and *DDC.*

70 Burns, *Christian Mortalism,* 172–4, discussing Richard Overton and Milton; and see chap. 6 above. Luther was both mortalist (Burns, 27–32) and traducian (George HuntstonWilliams, *The Radical Reformation,* 788–98).

71 Burns, *Christian Mortalism,* 178. The extent to which mortalism and bodily resurrection were intertwined can be seen from the citations in *DDC* I, chapters 13 and 33 (*CPW* 6: 400–14, 619–21). In both, I Cor. 15 is the key text, frequently the same verses.

72 Quoted by Bynum, *The Resurrection of the Body in Western Christianity,* 21 and 42–3. On these treatises see Quasten, *Patrology,* 2: 282–4.

73 Bynum, *Resurrection,* 26; also Vidal, 'Brains, Bodies, Selves, and Science,' 942–3.

74 *Works* 16: 353, 352. I here prefer the Sumner translation to *CPW* 6: 620–1, where 'same identity' loses the specificity of *idem numero* (precisely or indistinguishably identical). The phrase 'numerically identical' was a staple of resurrection discourse. See Vidal, 'Brains, Bodies, Selves, and Science,' 940 and n. 48, 943, 946–7; also *CPW* 6: 621, n. 12. *DDC* uses the phrase *unum numero* to convey that Christ was a single person with two natures

(*CPW* 6: 423, 424), not only a man of flesh, but resurrected in the same flesh. Milton's contemporaries John Locke and Robert Boyle, however, dispensed with numerical identity (Vidal, 950–6).

75 Tertullian believed that the whole person, body and soul, commits the sin. See Bynum, *Resurrection*, 35–6.

76 Bynum, *Resurrection*, describes it as 'the oldest Christian metaphor' for bodily resurrection; see 3–6, 79–80, 176–8, 184–6, and passim. Vidal, 'Brains, Bodies, Selves, and Science,' 941–2, calls it 'the crucial metaphor.' For emblems of resurrection imaging the seed sown, see e.g. Wither, *A Collection of Emblemes* (1635), bk. 1, no. 21 (engraving from Gabriel Rollenhagen, *Nucleus emblematum selectissimorum*, Utrecht, 1613); and Joachim Camerarius, *Symbolorum et emblematum*, 'Spes Altera Vitae,' fig. 12 in Colie, *The Resources of Kind*.

77 Mellinkoff, *The Mark of Cain*, 17.

78 See Arnold Williams, *The Common Expositor*, 143–4; and Mellinkoff, *The Mark of Cain*, 60–72.

79 On Milton's concept of the covenant, see Duncan, *Milton's Earthly Paradise*, 139–47; and Shawcross, *John Milton*, 128–38, 154–8. He rejects a covenant of works; in *PL* there is only the covenant of grace.

80 *DDC*, bk. 1, chap. 26 (CPW 6: 515; see also 416).

81 Patrides, *Premises and Motifs*, 96–102, reviews the seed imagery in *PL* and cites contemporary examples.

82 See Susan Snyder, 'The Left Hand of God,' 32; and Mellinkoff, *The Mark of Cain*, 8.

83 See Mellinkoff, *The Mark of Cain*, 92–4; Susan Snyder, 'The Left Hand of God,' 32–3.

84 See *The Life of Adam and Eve*, pars. 25–43, in *The Apocryphal Old Testament*, 153–9. There is brief discussion of the *Vita* in Evans, Paradise Lost *and the Genesis Tradition*, 55–8.

7. Providential Design: The Death and Conversion of Adam

1 Cromwell in Commons debate, 26 December 1648; quoted by Robertson, *The Tyrannicide Brief*, 135.

2 Sterry, *A Discourse of the Freedom of the Will* (1675), 166.

3 Addison, *Spectator*, no. 369, quoted from Shawcross, *Milton: The Critical Heritage*, 216–17.

4 *CPW* 6: 353; Steadman, 'The Tree of Life As Messianic Symbol,' in *Milton's Epic Characters*, 82–4; and Arnold Williams, *The Common Expositor*, 102–4.

5 Quoted from Shawcross, *Milton 1732–1801,* 50; and for one discussion, see Edward W. Tayler, *Milton's Poetry,* 90–6.
6 Rogers, *The Matter of Revolution,* 176. For an account of the two expulsion rationales different from mine, see 147–53.
7 Rogers, *The Matter of Revolution,* 155. Cf. his paragraph on Arminius (159) with the section 'Arminius and Milton on Providence' in chap. 1 above. By 'self-limitation' I mean God's deferring his potential power to the requirements of justice, on which see den Boer, *God's Twofold Love,* 102–5.
8 On the simile, see Rogers, *The Matter of Revolution,* 172–4; quotation, 173; following quotations, 176.
9 Quotations, ibid., 174, 161. I pose both questions because Rogers sometimes writes of 'Milton's' conscious efforts, but more often the activity of the poem itself.
10 Since Rogers's concern is with mundane nature, I exclude two references to guiding stars. The first (5: 706) plays on 'influence' to explain Satan's ability to attract followers; the second (12: 362), whether special or extraordinary providence, is the *nova* guiding the Magi.
11 See Walton, *Genesis and the Chemical Philosophy.*
12 Quoted in Shawcross, *Milton: The Critical Heritage,* 217. Underlying Addison's terms 'color' and 'design' is his awareness of the great sixteenth-century artistic quarrel, Florentine *disegno* versus Venetian *colorito.*
13 Patrides, *The Grand Design of God,* 7.
14 Emmerson, *Antichrist in the Middle Ages,* 50, 14.
15 Edward Tayler, *Milton's Poetry,* 13, 14. Loewenstein, *Milton and the Drama of History,* 120–5, agrees that both linear and cyclical patterns are present, but argues they are in unresolved conflict, rather than the counterpoint that Tayler and I find. Rogers, *The Matter of Revolution,* 175, asserts, 'Milton attempts to impose a linear, temporal resolution onto the immanent contradictions in organizational philosophy that fracture the political theology of the entire poem.'
16 Yates, *Giordano Bruno and the Hermetic Tradition,* 1.
17 See Tayler, *Milton's Poetry,* 34–40; quotation, 40; see further the admirable study by Chambers, 'Christmas,' who comments, 'forward movement is retrogressive in effect, is a "looking back" or progressive means of returning to the New Song of Creation' (147). For linear and cyclical time in *PR,* see also Chambers, 'The Double Time Scheme in *Paradise Regained.*'
18 For a fuller diagram of the narrative structure, see Shawcross, *With Mortal Voice,* 145.
19 See Nicolson, 'Milton and the Telescope' (1935), reprinted in her *Science and Imagination;* for Ramism, Jackson Cope, *The Metaphoric Structure of* Paradise Lost, 26–35, and Martin, *The Ruins of Allegory,* 76–7, 121–7.

20 For chronology in the Garden, as well as the more vexed question of the complete chronology, see Zivley, 'The Thirty-Three Days of *Paradise Lost,*' and Welch, 'Reconsidering Chronology in *Paradise Lost.*' For temporal symbolism see Cirillo, 'Noon-Midnight and the Temporal Structure of *Paradise Lost,*' and on Plato, Edward Tayler, *Milton's Poetry,* 9, 12, 15–16.

21 Edward Lord Herbert's 'To his Watch, When He Could Not Sleep,' quoted from Howarth, *Minor Poets of the Seventeenth Century.*

22 See C.S. Lewis, *A Preface to 'Paradise Lost,'* 129.

23 The other issue, of course, is poetic quality. Louis Martz, for example, concedes the design, but believes there is a 'falling-off in Milton's poetic powers,' speculates that they have been 'exhausted,' and specifies various points at which 'deterioration in the quality of the writing is painful.' See *The Paradise Within,* quotations 142, 159. In one defence, Fish, *Surprised by Sin,* 300–7, relates the 'bareness' and 'controlled anonymity' to the 'expository rhetoric of God's speeches.' This is right in pointing to rhetoric, but does not do justice to the sophistication of God's rhetoric (both Father and Son), for which see Pallister, *Between Worlds,* 122–36; on the neglected subject of Michael's rhetoric, 138–47.

24 For these see, in order, Lewalski, 'Structure and the Symbolism of Vision in Michael's Prophecy, *Paradise Lost,* Books XI–XII,' Northrop Frye, *Five Essays on Milton's Epics,* 19–20, 55; Whiting, *Milton and This Pendant World,* 172–91; and MacCallum, 'Milton and Sacred History.' Some 'much revised' passages of the last appear in *Milton and the Sons of God,* chap. 5.

25 Book 3 reduplicates the pattern with divine sanction (see chap. 4 above); from vision to voice consistently is the progression.

26 See Summers, *The Muse's Method,* 206–8; Lewalski, 'Structure and the Symbolism of Vision'; and Sasek, 'The Drama of *Paradise Lost,* Books XI and XII.'

27 Rajan, *The Lofty Rhyme,* 82; see also Lewalski, 'Structure and the Symbolism of Vision,' 28–9.

28 Auerbach, *Mimesis,* 64.

29 Bryan, 'Adam's Tragic Vision in *Paradise Lost,*' discusses the catalogue in light of the *translatio imperii* tradition. On the 'progress' of history, see also Schultz, *Milton and Forbidden Knowledge,* 89–91.

30 On the 'second Adam' concept, see Pecheux, 'The Second Adam and the Church in *Paradise Lost.*' Also relevant is her companion piece, 'The Concept of the Second Eve in *Paradise Lost.*'

31 See Summers, *Muse's Method,* 198; MacCallum, 'Milton and Sacred History,' 158; and Lewalski, 'Structure and the Symbolism of Vision,' 29. I cannot follow Lewalski's extension of the Hebrews relationship through bk. 12, which seems more tenuous than the ages-of-history pattern.

32 See Jackson Cope, *The Metaphoric Structure* of Paradise Lost, 142–5.
33 See Emmerson, *Antichrist in the Middle Ages,* 20, 30.
34 On Nimrod as a figure for all tyrants, see Christopher Hill, *The English Bible,* 217–22; and 206–9 for Cain as a symbol of all persecution and exploitation. See also Arnold Williams, *The Common Expositor,* 160–3, on Nimrod. For Cain as city builder, see further Ginzberg, *The Legends of the Jews,* 1: 115; and Mellinkoff, *The Mark of Cain,* 47. In *The Readie & Easie Way* (*CPW* 7: 357) Milton uses the tower of Babel to comment on the failure of the Commonwealth.
35 For law and its relationship to liberty, see Northrop Frye, *Five Essays,* 88–93; and Barker, 'Structural and Doctrinal Pattern in Milton's Later Poems,' esp. 183–94.
36 On Adam's (and Eve's) idolatry, see Northrop Frye, *Five Essays,* 67–9, 79–80; also Steadman, *Milton and the Renaissance Hero,* 113–22, 127–31.
37 MacCallum, 'Milton and Sacred History,' 155–6. Northrop Frye, *Five Essays,* 129, remarks, 'Milton's view of baptism is an exception to his generally anti-sacramental attitude to biblical symbolism.' For a full account of Flood typology, see Daniélou, *The Bible and the Liturgy,* 70–85. See also *DDC* on baptism (*CPW* 6: 544–52).
38 See Pecheux, 'Abraham, Adam, and the Theme of Exile in *Paradise Lost.*' Shawcross, *With Mortal Voice,* rightly maintains that Exodus is a 'myth of linear time' (138), yet its recurrence in the Bible and the poem again complicates the linearity.
39 For the traditional implications of the setting, see George Huntston Williams, *Wilderness and Paradise in Christian Thought*; Christopher Hill, *The Experience of Defeat,* 301–3, traces the wilderness trope in seventeenth-century religious discourse. Milton initiates a chain of correspondences with the comparison of Adam and Eve to Deucalion and Pyrrha (11: 9–14): Adam is to Noah as Noah is to Christ. On the identification of Deucalion's flood with Noah's, see Arnold Williams, *The Common Expositor,* 213–14; and Don Cameron Allen, *The Legend of Noah,* 83, 176, 188.
40 Fish, *Surprised by Sin,* 280–2.
41 See Pecheux, 'The Second Adam,' 174–6.
42 See, e.g., MacCallum, 'Milton and Sacred History,' 156; and MacCaffrey, *Paradise Lost as 'Myth,'* 176. For a visual arts analogue that highlights the similarity of Creation and Flood imagery, see Gombrich, 'Bosch's Garden of Earthly Delights: A Progress Report,' in his *The Heritage of Apelles,* 83–90. He reinterprets the closed wings of the triptych as representing not the Creation but the recession of the Flood.

43 Daniélou, *The Bible and the Liturgy,* 72–5; quotation, 72; for baptism as a 'sacramental anticipation' of the Last Judgment, see 79.

44 Carruthers, *The Craft of Thought,* 197; on *pictura,* see 196–220.

45 Carruthers, *The Craft of Thought,* 217.

46 See Ettlinger, *The Sistine Chapel Before Michelangelo.*

47 See, e.g., MacCallum, 'Milton and Sacred History,' 165–6; Sasek, 'The Drama of *Paradise Lost,*' 352; and Lewalski, 'Structure and the Symbolism of Vision,' 27–8.

48 Lewalski, 'Structure,' 31; and Williamson, 'The Education of Adam,' 107.

49 See 10: 615–40; and cf. Herbert, 'The Church-floore,' 16–18: 'Sometimes Death, puffing at the doore, / Blowes all the dust about the floore: / But while he thinks to spoil the room, he sweeps.'

50 Under the aegis of general providence, *DDC* affirms that God set a 'definite limit to human life, beyond which no one can go' (*CPW* 6: 339).

51 See pars. 30–48, in *The Apocryphal Old Testament,* pp. 155–60; interestingly in view of the judgment, Eve's death comes without mention of pain (pars. 49–50, pp. 160–1). On the many Adam books, see Sparks's introduction, 141–7.

52 See Hendy, *Piero della Francesca and the Early Renaissance,* 79–82, and plates XV–XVIII, also fig. 28; for a perceptive analysis, see Beck, 'Piero della Francesca at San Francisco in Arezzo,' who argues that the young couple on the left are Adam and Eve in Paradise (at 54, 61–3).

53 Baldwin, 'Some Extra-Biblical Semitic Influences upon Milton's Story of the Fall of Man,' 382. For the thousand-year day, see also 2 Peter 3: 8. On the general problem of patriarchal chronology, see Arnold Williams, *The Common Expositor,* 139–41; and Egerton III, 'The Longevity of the Patriarchs.' *See DDC* bk. 1, chaps 12–13, for distinctions between physical and spiritual death; it comments that the word 'day' is commonly used to denote any given period of time (*CPW* 6: 623).

54 For the first two theories, see Baldwin, 'Some Extra-Biblical Semitic Influences,' 382–3. Browne, *Pseudodoxia Epidemica,* bk. 6, chap. 6, p. 347, remarks on 'that conceit of some, that Adam was the oldest man, in as much as he is conceived to be created in the maturity of mankind, that is, at 60 (for in that age it is set down they begat children) so that adding this number unto his 930, he was 21 years older than any of his prosterity [*sic*].'

55 Irenaeus, *Against Heresies,* bk. 4, chap. 23, quoted from *The Ante-Nicene Fathers,* 1: 551.

56 The commentators were encouraged in such directions by the biblical chroniclers' own tendencies toward symmetrical patterning, as for

instance in the ten generations that preceded the Flood and the ten from Noah to Abraham. On this, see *The New Catholic Encyclopedia* (New York, 1967), 10: 1097.

57 Browne, *Pseudodoxia Epidemica*, 346.

58 Ainsworth, *Annotations upon the First Book of Moses*, F1v.

59 See Arnold Williams, *The Common Expositor*, 144, on Lamech. Noah lived over a third of his life, 350 of his 950 years, after the Flood (Gen. 9: 28–9.). For his Latin epitaph by Jacobus Salianus (1620), see Don Cameron Allen, *The Legend of Noah*, 81.

60 Whiting, *Milton and This Pendant World*, 183. On Milton's modification of the Augustinian model, see Edward Tayler, *Milton's Poetry*, 71–2; and Loewenstein, *Milton and the Drama of History*, 178, n. 13.

61 Northrop Frye, *Five Essays*, 46–7, briefly remarks on this point.

62 Daniélou, *The Bible and the Liturgy*, 43, 42.

63 See Wunderli and Broce, 'The Final Moment before Death in Early Modern England.'

64 Daniélou, *The Bible and the Liturgy*, 77.

65 See Jackson Cope, *Metaphoric Structure*, 142–8; also MacCallum, 'Milton and Sacred History,' 154.

66 For this tradition, see Parish, 'Pre-Miltonic Representations of Adam as a Christian,' Steadman, '"Taught by His Example": Adam and the Prophesied Redeemer,' in *Milton's Epic Characters*, 72–81; and Patrides, '"*The first promise made to man*": The Edenic Origins of Protestantism,' in *Premises and Motifs*, 90–104.

67 *The Life of Adam and Eve* is suggestive concerning Michael's role here. The angel appears to Eve and Seth and announces, 'I am appointed by God to look after men's bodies.' See *The Apocryphal Old Testament*, par. 41, 2–3, p. 158.

68 See G.C. Taylor, *Milton's Use of DuBartas*, 88–90, 112–21; also Grant McColley, 'The Book of Enoch and Paradise Lost,' 28.

69 Bartas, *The Divine Weeks and Works of Guillaume de Saluste Sieur du Bartas*, 1: 401–2, ll. 767–74.

70 MacCallum, 'Milton and Sacred History,' 167–8. The proportions also reflect the disparity in duration between the first age and the much shorter postdiluvian ages.

71 Barker, 'Structural and Doctrinal Pattern,' 183.

72 In a book intended as a guide for teachers of undergraduates, Thickstun, *Milton's* Paradise Lost, 159, states an obvious truth: 'It is essential to the success of Milton's poem that Adam's story conclude with his salvation . . . the essential part of his story.'

73 Wall, 'Considerations Upon the Point of the Conversion of the Jews,' in Menasseh ben Israel, *The Hope of Israel* (corrected 2nd ed. 1652), 58; quoted by Katz, *Philo-Semitism and the Readmission of the Jews to England,* 188. Despite the subtitle, *The English Translation by Moses Wall, 1652,* the Méchoulan and Nahon edition presents a modernized text and omits Wall's 'Considerations,' as well as his 'Answer' to Sir Edward Spencer's *Briefe Epistle* (1650).
74 On these models see Cummings, *The Literary Culture of the Reformation,* 52–3, 60–4, 365–72. Charles Cohen, 'Two Biblical Models of Conversion,' noted less familiar types (Lydia in Acts 16: 14–15, and David in Ps. 51). McGee, *The Godly Man,* 55–64, 231, 250–1, usefully differentiates English attitudes toward conversion: 'Puritans made it sound hard and Anglicans made it sound easy' (59).
75 On the Tainos, see Ricardo E. Alegría, in *The Christopher Columbus Encyclopedia,* 1: 345–9. The feather skirts also were characteristic of the Tupinambé of Brazil and frequently illustrated (see pp. 338–9). For the many possible sources of the fig tree passage, see Svendsen, *Milton and Science,* 30–2; Edwards, *Milton and the Natural World,* 149–51, focuses more sharply on Ralegh's *Historie.*
76 See Evans, *Milton's Imperial Epic,* 94–103, esp. 95. On las Casas, see Benjamin Keen in *The Christopher Columbus Encyclopedia,* 2: 408–12.
77 Quoted from las Casas, *An Account, Much Abbreviated, of the Destruction of the Indies,* xxi. For the 'natural slaves' concept, notorious from las Casas's dispute with Juan Ginés de Sepulveda, see Hanke, *Aristotle and the American Indians.*
78 Quoted from Evans, *Milton's Imperial Epic,* 24.
79 See John F. Schwaller, 'Missionary Movement,' in *The Christopher Columbus Encyclopedia,* 2: 471–4; and Phelan, *The Millennial Kingdom of the Franciscans in the New World.*
80 See Axtell, 'Were Indian Conversions *Bona Fide?*' in his *After Columbus,* 100–21; quotations, 114, 114–15. Milton alludes to the Jesuit conversions (*CPW* 1: 966). For the insistence on civilizing Indians, see Axtell, *The Invasion Within,* 131–78. See also Charles Cohen, 'Conversion among the Puritans and Amerindians.' Cohen attributes the limited success of New England missionaries to the Indians' difficulty in accepting the transition from a god angry at man's sinfulness to a god of love, a problem shared by some readers of *PL* 12.
81 Axtell, *The Invasion Within,* 241.
82 See Axtell, *The Invasion Within,* 222–5, on John Eliot's procedure. Evans, *Milton's Imperial Epic,* 76, 98, sees the Raphael dialogues as 'replicating'

Eliot's 'evangelical technique.' Surprisingly, he does not extend the argument to bks 11–12.

83 *The covenant betweene God and Man* (1616), 60. Quoted by Fish, *The Living Temple*, 95. Despite the concluding palinode, this is a valuable study.

84 Evans, *Milton's Imperial Epic*, 97, cites Eve's gardening tools (9: 391) as proof that 'technological development' in Eden parallels that of the Amerindians. Their joint skill at sewing (9: 1112) might also be adduced. Evans's argument becomes tendentious in forced analogies to the guardian angels as colonists and Adam and Eve as exploited natives.

85 The allusion is discussed by Hamlin, *Psalm Culture and Early Modern English Literature*, 213–15, who notes that Psalm 51, 'the preeminent psalm of repentance' (173), is an Ash Wednesday text in *The Book of Common Prayer*. For its authority as a conversion narrative, see Charles Cohen, 'Two Biblical Models of Conversion.'

86 See the thorough study by Myers, 'Prevenient Grace and Conversion in *Paradise Lost*.'

87 See Axtell, *The Invasion Within*, 114–16; quotation, 116. On the difference between Catholic and Protestant attitudes to visual aids in religious instruction, see Green, *The Christian's ABC*, 15–16; for 'The Reformation of the Eyes' broadly considered, see Stuart Clark, *Vanities of the Eye*, chap. 5.

88 See particularly Green's substantial study, chap. 1, 'What is Catechizing?' in *The Christian's ABC*.

89 *The Works of George Herbert*, 256. On the facility of Indian converts in framing penetrating questions about Christianity, see Axtell, *The Invasion Within*, 232–4.

90 Herbert, *Works*, 258. For the extended debate on just how baptism is a preparatory stage, see Pettit, *The Heart Prepared*, and Green, *The Christian's ABC*, 519–39.

91 Herbert, *Works*, 257. Lares, *Milton and the Preaching Arts*, 158–68, maintains that Michael should be understood as a preacher who draws on two kinds of sermons, corrective in bk. 11 and consolatory in bk. 12. The argument is more persuasive for 12 than for 11 (and the visions are not 'iconic'). The distinction between pedagogical and homiletic, moreover, is exaggerated. Catechizing (unmentioned) is instruction.

92 Adam's faltering progress has attracted critical attention. Haskin, *Milton's Burden of Interpretation*, 232–6, presents him as learning to 'read' by coming to understand the difficulty of interpreting biblical 'places.' Martin, *The Ruins of Allegory*, describes Adam's 'journey' from a 'fallen mode of orality' emphasized by his 'constant liability to childish interpretive

errors' in bk. 11 to 'more thoughtful, readerly responses' required by the 'the complexly modulated lecture of book 12' (293, 292).

93 Quoted from Shawcross, *Milton: The Critical Heritage*, 217.

94 As Patrides has remarked, *Premises and Motifs*, 103. For baptism as a covenant, see Green, *The Christian's ABC*, 525–7, 538–9.

95 Rosenblatt, *Torah and Law in* Paradise Lost, 227, curiously contends, 'Somewhere between lines 564 and 565, Adam disappears as subject, relinquishing agency and identity, dying in Christ.' This is untenable for two reasons. First, it collapses temporal sequence. Adam makes an act of faith in response to prophecy ('to walk / As in his presence'); Christ will not exist for (by common compute) four millennia. Second, although many Protestants did regard baptism and entering the church as becoming 'incorporated' or 'engrafted' into the body of Christ, Rosenblatt ignores the Arminian and Miltonic commitment to resistible grace. Adam and Eve face nine centuries of trials; perseverance is everything.

96 Armitage, 'The Cromwellian Protectorate and the Languages of Empire,' 538; on the Western Design, see 536–46; and Robert Fallon, 'Cromwell, Milton, and the Western Design.'

97 For the textual history, see Shawcross, appendix, in *Achievements of the Left Hand*, 361–3. Robert Fallon, *Milton in Government*, 88–100, traces state correspondence regarding Spain, but finds no evidence for Milton's involvement with the *Declaration* (see 99–100).

98 See Shawcross, *The Arms of the Family*, 73–133; quotation, 123. He accepts Milton's authorship of the Latin translation. Paul Stevens, 'Milton's "Renunciation" of Cromwell,' 373–82, plausibly argues that Milton strongly supported the Spanish War 'as a defensive war driven by the threat of Catholic aggression in general and Spanish power in particular' (387); he also links Milton with Ralegh in a tradition of anti-Spanish providentialism. Although Stevens does not mention Phillips here, an earlier article, '*Paradise Lost* and the Colonial Imperative,' 9–10, uses the las Casas translation to frame the point that Sin and Death represent a critique of colonial abuse. Armitage, 'The Cromwellian Protectorate,' sees an indignant allusion to the failure of the Western Design in *The Readie & Easie Way* (*CPW* 7: 357).

99 Quoted from the British Library copy (George Thomason's), available as an on-line resource.

100 Quotations from *The Works*, 13: 515, 517, 561, 563.

101 Quotation from Robert Fallon, *Milton in Government*, 129. On this venture, see Capp, *Cromwell's Navy*, 87–91.

102 See Robert Fallon, *Milton in Government*, 139–51, and for a list of the state papers, 263. For the affinities of the Waldensians with radical protestants, see George Huntston Williams, *The Radical Reformation*, index; see further Audisio, *The Waldensian Dissent*, 198–207. Honigmann, editor of *Milton's Sonnets*, 162–6, thoroughly places Sonnet 18 in contemporary public discourse. Excommunicated in 1215, the Waldensians retorted they were persecuted because the papacy was in league with Antichrist. See Whitford, 'The Papal Antichrist,' 33.

103 I disagree with Robert Fallon, *Milton in Government*, who concludes that the subject of the Indian genocide 'had no apparent impact upon his imagination' (99). Achinstein, 'Imperial Dialectic,' 70–1, follows Fallon by contrasting Phillips's 'highly sympathetic' attitude toward Amerindian suffering to its 'absence' on Milton's part. But Adam's response to vision 4 speaks to all massacres; moreover, the Book 9 Indian analogy works both ways: what follows implies a method of conversion appropriate to the condition of the Amerindians. In the *Second Defense* Milton's apparent dismissal of 'Indians' as having degenerated into the dullest of humans (*Works* 8: 6, 'quae stolidissimos mortalium infamat Indos, degeneraverat') might be questioned. Whereas Helen North translates 'Indos' thus (*CPW* 4, pt. 1: 551), Robert Fellowes (Bohn Library ed.) renders it 'natives of Hindostan.' Similarly, 'Indian *Catharist*' (*CPW* 2: 590) probably means East Indian.

104 On Wall, see Popkin's note in *The Hope of Israel*, 165–70. Livewell Chapman, the bookseller responsible for the second edition of *The Hope* also sold Milton's *Hirelings* (1659) and *The Readie & Easie Way* (1660). Wall's extant letter to Milton (26 May 1659) expresses gratitude 'that you are pleased to honor me, with your letters' and discusses 'yor last Book,' presumably the *Treatise of Civil Power* (*CPW* 7: 510–13); also in Masson's *Life* (5: 601–3). The letter is discussed by Nicholas von Maltzahn, 'Making Use of the Jews,' 64–7.

105 *The Hope of Israel*, 101, 111.

106 *The Diary of Ralph Josselin*, 266 (20 December 1651). Quoted by Katz, *Philo-Semitism*, 145. This paragraph is directly indebted to his fine study.

107 Whereas 'To his Coy Mistress' ostensibly grants the lady ages to decide, the allusion means 'hurry up before it's too late.'

108 Quoted by Katz, *Philo-Semitism*, 151–2. Still another aspect of the conversion mania is suggested by such sensational titles as Thomas Warmstry's *The Baptized Turk* (1658).

109 On the identification of ten lost tribes with Amerindians, see Katz, *Philo-Semitism*, 127–57; for the motive of converting the Jews, 89–126, 167, 213–15; and, particularly for the Whitehall Conference, see Katz, *The Jews in the History of England*, 126–8. A half-century ago, Wolfe, 'The Limits of Miltonic Toleration,' considered Milton's failure to speak out on readmission, concluding sadly that, as with his adamant opposition to popery, this was beyond Milton's range of religious toleration. Arguably, admitting Jews in order to convert them might be seen as less, not more, tolerant. As von Maltzahn observes, the motives of those urging readmission never 'extended to a liberal or humanitarian regard for toleration and Jewish faith and culture' ('Making Use of the Jews,' 67). Milton's silence also might evidence his growing disbelief in an imminent millennium; Shawcross, 'Confusion: The Apocalypse, the Millennium,' sets the terminus at 1657. Von Maltzahn, 65, sees in Wall's letter an implicit reproach to Milton on this score. Guibbory, 'England, Israel, and the Jews in Milton's Prose, 1649–1660,' 34, concludes: 'It is hard to imagine that Milton viewed the possibility of Jewish readmission to England very sympathetically.' Yet, if Milton were simply opposed to readmission, it is hard to imagine that, despite his official role, he would not have contrived to say so.

110 Donnelly, *Milton's Scriptural Reasoning*, 187, worries that readers, mistaking 'the equipoise of epic closure,' will 'appeal to "Providence," the good end of the story, in order to fortify their own sloth, cowardice, license, or infidelity.' He and I understand Milton's Arminian providence differently.

111 Richard Bernard, *The Faithfull Shepheard* (1607), 69, 70; available as an electronic resource; enlarged editions in 1609 and 1621. Cited by Lares, *Milton and the Preaching Arts*, 166, n. 75.

112 'No persvasions can prevaile to turne them backe from God whome he hath chosen to be his' (Geneva gloss to Ruth 1: 16). The Argument to the book comments: 'Herein also is described howe Iesus Christ . . . proceded of Ruth.' Flannagan, *The Riverside Milton*, notes that 'for wither thou goest, I will go' had become proverbial for marriage.

113 Stuart Clark, *Vanities of the Eye*, 304, summarizes Christian attitudes toward dreams. Whereas 'false dreams were evil ones sent by the devil to tempt and corrupt,' 'True dreams were good dreams that came from God (or angels) and were spiritually improving, even revelatory, and might lead to conversion.'

114 *DDC*, bk. 1, chap. 26, states: 'The COVENANT of GRACE itself is first made public from God's point of view, Gen. iii.15' (*CPW* 6: 515).

Afterword

1 Cummings, *The Literary Culture of the Reformation*, quotations, 6, 5. Voicing a related complaint, Lares, *Milton and the Preaching Arts*, 159, observes, 'In our secular age, we might question whether the mere hearing of a sermon could be a valid religious experience.'
2 See Charles Taylor, *A Secular Age*. Rather than Taylor's own lengthy exposition of 'the buffered self,' I quote the succinct summary by Lloyd, *Providence Lost*, 6.
3 Charles Taylor, *A Secular Age*, 223–4.
4 See Martin, *Milton among the Puritans*, 311–16.
5 The providential guidance of insects was a familiar trope in writings, pro and con. M.P. Fontana composed a hexameter poem, *Formica sive de Divina Providentia* (1594); a decade earlier Giordano Bruno's *Lo spaccio de la bestia triofante* (1584) used dung beetles and bed bugs to parody 'a very orthodox method of expounding the activities of special Providence.' See Don Cameron Allen, *Doubt's Boundless Sea*, 144. Rochester's 'A Satyr against Mankind' is quoted on 201.
6 See Kubrin, 'Newton and the Cyclical Cosmos,' 327.
7 Lloyd, *Providence Lost*, 305.

Bibliography

Achinstein, Sharon. 'Imperial Dialectic: Milton and Conquered Peoples.' In *Milton and the Imperial Vision,* ed. Rajan and Sauer, 67–89. Pittsburgh, 1999.

Achinstein, Sharon, and Elizabeth Sauer, eds. *Milton and Toleration.* Oxford, 2007.

Ainsworth, Henry. *Annotations upon the First Book of Moses, Called Genesis.* Amsterdam, 1616.

Alciati, Andrea. *Emblemata cvm commentarii* . . . Padua, 1621.

Allen, Don Cameron. *Doubt's Boundless Sea: Skepticism and Faith in the Renaissance.* Baltimore, 1964.

– *Image and Meaning: Metaphoric Traditions in Renaissance Poetry.* Baltimore, 1960.

– *The Legend of Noah: Renaissance Rationalism in Art, Science and Letters.* 1949. Urbana, IL. 1963.

– 'Milton and Rabbi Eliezer.' *Modern Language Notes* 63 (1948): 262–3.

Allen, Michael J.B. *Nuptial Arithmetic: Marsilio Ficino's Commentary on the Fatal Number in Book VIII of Plato's* Republic. Berkeley and Los Angeles, 1994.

Almond, Philip C. *Adam and Eve in Seventeenth-Century Thought.* Cambridge, 1999.

Ambrose, St. *Hexameron.* In *The Fathers of the Church,* vol. 42. Trans. John J. Savage. New York, 1961.

Anglo, Sydney. *Machiavelli – The First Century: Studies in Enthusiasm, Hostility, and Irrelevance.* Oxford, 2005.

The Apocryphal New Testament. Rev. and ed. J.K. Elliott. Oxford, 1993.

The Apocryphal Old Testament. Trans. C.H. Charles and ed. H.F.D. Sparks. Oxford, 1984.

Arminius, James [Jacob]. *The Writings of James Arminius.* 3 vols. Trans. James Nichols (1–2) and W.S. Bagnall (3). 1853. Grand Rapids, MI, 1956.

Armitage, David. 'The Cromwellian Protectorate and the Languages of Empire.' *Historical Journal* 35 (1992): 531–55.

– 'John Milton: Poet against Empire.' In *Milton and Republicanism,* ed. Armitage, Himy, and Skinner, 206–25. Cambridge, 1995.

Armitage, David, Armand Himy, and Quentin Skinner, eds. *Milton and Republicanism.* Cambridge, 1995.

Audisio, Gabriel. *The Waldensian Dissent: Persecution and Survival, c. 1177–1570.* Trans. Claire Davison. Cambridge, 1999.

Auerbach, Erich. *Mimesis: The Representation of Reality in Western Literature.* Trans. Willard Trask. 1953. Garden City, NY, 1957.

Augustine, St. *The Literal Meaning of Genesis.* In *Ancient Christian Writers,* ed. Johannes Quasten, Walter J. Burghardt, and Thomas Comerford Lawler, no. 42, vol. 2. Trans. John Hammond Taylor. New York, 1982.

Axtell, James. *After Columbus: Essays in the Ethnohistory of Colonial North America.* Oxford, 1988.

– *The Invasion Within: The Contest of Cultures in Colonial North America.* Oxford, 1985.

Babington, Gervase. *Certaine Plaine, briefe, and comfortable Notes, vpon euery Chapter of Genesis.* London, 1596.

Bacon, Francis. *The Wisedome of the Ancients.* Trans. Sir Arthur Gorges. London, 1669.

– *The Works of Francis Bacon.* Ed. J. Spedding, R.L. Ellis, and D.D. Heath. 14 vols. London, 1857–74.

Baldwin, E.C. 'Some Extra-Biblical Semitic Influences upon Milton's Story of the Fall of Man.' *Journal of English and Germanic Philology* 28 (1929): 366–401.

Bangs, Carl. *Arminius: A Study in the Dutch Reformation.* Nashville, TN, 1971.

– 'Arminius and the Reformation.' *Church History* 30 (1961): 155–70.

Barb, A.A. 'Cain's Murder-Weapon and Samson's Jawbone of an Ass.' *Journal of the Warburg and Courtauld Institutes* 35 (1972): 386–9.

Barker, Arthur E. 'Structural and Doctrinal Pattern in Milton's Later Poems.' In *Essays in English Literature,* ed. Millar MacLure and F.W. Watt, 169–94. Toronto, 1964.

Barret, Robert. *The Theorike and Practike of Moderne Warres.* London, 1598.

Bartas, Guillaume de Saluste Sieur du. *The Divine Weeks and Works of Guillaume de Saluste Sieur du Bartas.* 2 vols. Trans. Joshua Sylvester. Ed. Susan Snyder. Oxford, 1979.

Beck, James. 'Piero della Francesca at San Francisco in Arezzo: An Art-Historical Peregrination.' *artibus et historiae* 47 (2003): 51–80.

Benet, Diana Traviño. 'Milton's Toad or Satan's Dream?' *Milton Studies* 45 (2006): 38–52.

Bennett, Joan S. 'Asserting Eternal Providence: John Milton through the Window of Liberation Theology.' In *Milton and Heresy*, ed. Dobranski and Rumrich, 217–43. Cambridge, 1998.

– *Reviving Liberty: Radical Christian Humanism in Milton's Great Poems.* Cambridge, MA, 1989.

Bernard, John. *Why Machiavelli Matters: A Guide to Citizenship in a Democracy.* Westport, CT, 2009.

Bernard, Richard. *The Faithfull Shepheard, or the Sheapheards Faithfulnesse.* London, 1607.

Berry, Boyd M. *Process of Speech: Puritan Religious Writing and* Paradise Lost. Baltimore, 1976.

Besly, Edward. '"To Reward Their Deservings": The Badge for the Forlorn Hope.' *The Medal*, no. 19 (autumn 1991): 20–7.

Betteridge, Maurice S. 'The Bitter Notes: The Geneva Bible and Its Annotations.' *Sixteenth Century Journal* 14 (1983): 41–62.

Bible Moralisée: Codex Vindobonensis 2554, Vienna, Österreichische Nationalbibliothek. Trans, Gerald B. Guest. London, 1995.

Bietti, Monica. In *da Pontormo & per Pontormo: Novità alla Certosa*, exhibition catalogue, 87–93. Florence, 1996.

Blythe, Joan. 'Cain and Abel in *Paradise Regained:* Fratricide, Regicide, and Cultural Equality.' In *Milton's Legacy*, ed. Kristin A. Pruitt and Charles W. Durham, 70–82. Selinsgrove, PA., 2005.

Boer, William Arie den. *God's Twofold Love: The Theology of Jacob Arminius (1559–1609).* Reformed Historical Theology 14. Göttengin, 2010. Trans. of *Duplex Amor Dei: Contextuele karakteristick van de theologie van Jacobus Arminius (1559–1609).* Apeldoorn, 2008.

– 'Jacobus Arminius: Theologian of God's Twofold Love.' In *Arminius, Arminianism and Europe*, ed. T.M. van Leevwen, K.D. Stanglin, and M. Tolsma, 25–50. Brill Series in Church History. Leiden, 2009.

Boethius. *The Consolation of Philosophy.* In *Boethius*, trans. H.F. Stewart, E.K. Rand, and S.J. Tester. Loeb Classical Library. Cambridge, MA, 1973.

Boll, Valérie. *Autour du couple ambigu crapard-grenouille: recherches ethnozoologriques.* Paris, 2000.

Bolzoni, Lina. *The Gallery of Memory: Literary and Iconographic Models in the Age of Printing.* Trans. Jeremy Parzen. Toronto, 2001.

Boswell, Jackson Campbell. *A Catalogue of the Remains of John Milton's Library and an Annotated Reconstruction of Milton's Library and Ancillary Readings.* New York, 1975.

Bouwsma, William. *John Calvin: A Sixteenth-Century Portrait.* New York, 1988.

Bowers, Fredson. 'Adam, Eve, and the Fall in *Paradise Lost.*' *PMLA* 84 (1969): 264–73.

Braude, Pearl F. '"Cokkel in oure Clene Corn": Some Implications of Cain's Sacrifice.' *Gesta* 7 (1968): 15–28.

Briggs, Robin. *Witches and Neighbors: The Social and Cultural Context of European Witchcraft.* New York, 1996.

Broadbent, J.B. *Some Graver Subject: An Essay on* Paradise Lost. New York, 1960.

Brooks, Douglas A., ed. *Milton and the Jews.* Cambridge, 2008.

Brown, Keith M. 'The Vanishing Empire: British Kingship and Its Decline, 1603–1707.' In *Scots and Britons: Scottish Political Thought and the Union of 1603,* ed. Roger A. Mason, 58–87. Cambridge, 1994.

Browne, Sir Thomas. *Pseudodoxia Epidemica.* 6th ed. London, 1672. Bound with *Religio Medici.* 7th ed. London, 1672.

Bryan, Robert A. 'Adam's Tragic Vision in *Paradise Lost.*' *Studies in Philology* 62 (1965): 197–214.

Bryson, Michael, 'The Mysterious Darkness of Unknowing: *Paradise Lost* and the God Beyond Name.' In '*Paradise Lost: A Poem Written in Ten Books'; Essays on the 1667 First Edition,* ed. Michael Lieb and John T. Shawcross, 188–212. Pittsburgh, 2007.

– *The Tyranny of Heaven: Milton's Rejection of God as King.* Newark, DE, 2004.

Buck, Lawrence T. '*Anatomia Antichristi:* Form and Content of the Papal Antichrist.' *Sixteenth Century Journal* 42 (2011): 349–68.

Bulstrode, Richard. *Memoirs and Reflections upon the Reign and Government of King Charles the Ist and Charles the IId.* London, 1721.

Bunyan, John. *The Complete Works of John Bunyan.* Ed. Henry Stebbing. 1859. 4 vols in 3. Marshallton, DE, 1968.

Burbery, Timothy. 'From Orthodoxy to Heresy: A Theological Reading of *Sonnets XIV and XVIII.*' *Milton Studies* 45 (2006): 1–20.

Burden, Dennis H. *The Logical Epic: A Study of the Argument of* Paradise Lost. London, 1967.

Burns, Norman T. *Christian Mortalism from Tyndale to Milton.* Cambridge, MA, 1972.

Burton, Henry. *The Seven Vials, or A briefe and plaine exposition vpon the 15 and 16 chapters of the Revelation.* London, 1628.

Bynum, Caroline Walker. *The Resurrection of the Body in Western Christianity, 200–1336.* New York, 1995.

Caciola, Nancy. *Discerning Spirits: Divine and Demonic Possession in the Middle Ages.* Ithaca, NY, 2003.

Calamy, Edmund, ed. *Cromwell's Soldier's Bible: being a Reprint, in Facsimile, of 'The Souldier's Pocket Bible,' compiled by Edmund Calamy.* London, 1895.

Calvin, John. *Calvin: Institutes of the Christian Religion.* Ed. John T. McNeill and trans. Ford Lewis Battles. 2 vols. Library of Christian Classics 20–1. Philadelphia, 1960.

Cambers, Andrew. 'Demonic Possession, Literacy and "Superstition."' *Past and Present* 202 (2009): 3–35.

Campbell, Gordon, and Thomas N. Corns. *John Milton: Life, Work, and Thought.* Oxford, 2008.

Campbell, Gordon, Thomas N. Corns, John K. Hale, and Fiona J. Tweedie. *Milton and the Manuscript of* De Doctrina Christiana. Oxford, 2007.

– (also David L. Holmes). 'The Provenance of *De Doctrina Christiana.*' *Milton Quarterly* 31 (1997): 67–117.

Caplan, Harry. 'Memoria: Treasure-House of Eloquence.' In his *Of Eloquence: Studies of Ancient and Modern Rhetoric,* 196–246. Ithaca, NY, 1970.

Capp, Bernard. *Cromwell's Navy: The Fleet and the English Revolution, 1648–1660.* Oxford, 1989.

Carruthers, Mary. *The Book of Memory: A Study of Memory in Medieval Culture.* Cambridge, 1990.

– *The Craft of Thought: Meditation, Rhetoric and the Making of Images, 400–1200.* Cambridge, 1998.

Carruthers, Mary, and Jan M. Ziolkowski, eds. *The Medieval Craft of Memory: An Anthology of Texts and Pictures.* Philadelphia, 2002.

Cartari, Vicenzo. *Imagine delli Dei de gli antichi* (facsimile of the Venice 1647 ed.). Intro. Walter Koschatzky. Graz, Austria, 1963.

Caryl, Joseph. *The Saints Thankfull Acclamation at Christs resumption of His great Power.* London, 1644.

Cassell, Anthony K. 'Pier della Vigna's Metamorphosis: Iconography and History.' In *Dante, Petrarch, Boccaccio: Studies in the Italian Trecento in Honor of Charles S. Singleton,* ed. Aldo S. Bernardo and Anthony I. Pellegrini, 50–60. Binghampton, NY, 1983.

Chambers, A.B. 'Christmas: The Liturgy of the Church and English Verse of the Renaissance.' *Literary Monographs* 6 (1975): 109–53.

– 'The Double Time Scheme in *Paradise Regained.*' *Milton Studies* 7 (1975): 189–205.

– 'Milton's Proteus and Satan's Visit to the Sun.' *Journal of English and Germanic Philology* 62 (1963): 280–7.

– 'Wisdom at One Entrance Quite Shut Out: *Paradise Lost,* III, 1–55.' *Philological Quarterly* 42 (1963): 114–19.

Chandos, John, ed. *In God's Name: Examples of Preaching in England, 1534–1662.* Indianapolis and New York, 1971.

Chernaik, Warren. *The Poet's Time: Politics and Religion in the Work of Andrew Marvell.* Cambridge, 1983.

– 'Victory's Crest: Milton, the English Nation, and Cromwell.' In *Early Modern Nationalism,* ed. Loewenstein and Stevens, 73–111. Toronto, 2008.

The Christopher Columbus Encyclopedia. 2 vols. Ed. Silvio A. Bedini. New York, 1992.

Cicero, Marcus Tullius. *Cicero III: De oratore.* Trans. E.W. Sutton and H. Rackham. Loeb Classical Library. 1942. London. 1967.

Cirillo, Albert R. ' "Hail Holy Light" and Divine Time in *Paradise Lost.' Journal of English and Germanic Philology* 68 (1969): 45–56.

– 'Noon-Midnight and the Temporal Structure of Paradise Lost.' *ELH* 29 (1962): 372–95.

– 'Tasso's *Il mondo creato:* Providence and the Created Universe.' *Milton Studies* 3 (1971): 83–102.

Clark, Donald Lemen. *John Milton at St. Paul's School: A Study of Ancient Rhetoric in English Renaissance Education.* New York, 1948.

Clark, Stuart. *Thinking with Demons: The Idea of Witchcraft in Early Modern Europe.* Oxford, 1997.

– *Vanities of the Eye: Vision in Early Modern European Culture.* Oxford, 2007.

Cockle, Maurice J.D. *A Bibliography of Military Books up to 1642.* 1900. London, 1957.

Coffey, John. *John Goodwin and the Puritan Revolution.* Woodbridge, 2006.

Cohen, Charles L. 'Conversion among the Puritans and Amerindians: A Theological and Cultural Perspective.' In *Puritanism: Transatlantic Perspectives on a Seventeenth-Century Anglo-American Faith,* ed. Francis J. Bremer, 233–56. Boston, 1993.

– 'Two Biblical Models of Conversion: An Example of Puritan Hermeneutics.' *Church History* 58 (1989): 182–96.

Cohen, I. Bernard. 'Harrington and Harvey: A Theory of the State Based on the New Physiology.' *Journal of the History of Ideas* 55 (1994): 187–210.

Cohen, Jeremy. *'Be Fertile and Increase, Fill the Earth and Master It.' The Ancient and Medieval Career of a Biblical Text.* Ithaca, NY, 1992.

Coldiron, A.E.B. 'Milton *in parvo:* Mortalism and Genre Transformation in Sonnet 14.' *Milton Quarterly* 28 (1994): 1–10.

Colie, Rosalie L. *The Resources of Kind: Genre-Theory in the Renaissance.* Berkeley and Los Angeles, 1973.

Collier, John. *Milton's 'Paradise Lost': Screenplay for Cinema of the Mind.* New York, 1973.

Collinson, Patrick. 'Biblical Rhetoric: The English Nation and National Sentiment in the Prophetic Mode.' In *Religion and Culture in Renaissance England,* ed. Claire McEachern and Debora Shuger, 15–45. Cambridge, 1997.

Collop, John. *The Poems of John Collop.* Ed. Conrad Hilberry. Madison, WI, 1962.

Condren, Conal, and A.D. Cousins, eds. *The Political Identity of Andrew Marvell.* Aldershot, 1990.

Cope, Gilbert. *Symbolism in the Bible and the Church.* London, 1959.

Cope, Jackson I. *The Metaphoric Structure of* Paradise Lost. Baltimore, 1962.

– 'Satan's Disguises: *Paradise Lost* and *Paradise Regained.*' *Modern Language Notes* 73 (1958): 9–11.

Coppe, Abiezer. *Selected Writings.* Ed. and intro. Andrew Hopton. London, 1987.

Corbett, Margery, and R.W. Lightbown. *The Comely Frontispiece: The Emblematic Title-page in England, 1550–1660.* London, 1979.

Corbett, Margery, and Michael Norton. *Engraving in England in the Sixteenth and Seventeenth Centuries. Part III: The Reign of Charles I.* Cambridge, 1964.

Corns, Thomas N. 'Milton's Antiprelatical Tracts and the Marginality of Doctrine.' In *Milton and Heresy,* ed. Dobranski and Rumrich, 39–48. Cambridge, 1998.

– *Regaining* Paradise Lost. London, 1994.

Cotgrave, Randle. *A Dictionarie of the French and English Tongues.* London, 1611.

Cowley, Abraham. *The Civil War.* Ed. Allan Pritchard. Toronto, 1973.

– *Poems (1656).* Scolar Press Facsimile. Menston, 1971.

Cox, Virginia. *The Renaissance Dialogue: Literary Dialogue in Its Social and Political Contexts, Castiglione to Galileo.* Cambridge, 1992.

Cressy, David. *Bonfires and Bells: National Memory and the Protestant Calendar in Elizabethan and Stuart England.* Berkeley and Los Angeles, 1989.

Crooke, Helkiah. *[Microcosmographia]: A Description of the Body of Man.* London, 1615.

Crouzet, Denis. 'A Woman and the Devil: Possession in Sixteenth-Century France.' In *Changing Identities in Early Modern France,* ed. Michael Wolfe, 191–215. Durham, NC, 1997.

Crumb, R. *The Book of Genesis Illustrated.* New York, 2009.

Crump, Galbraith Miller. *The Mystical Design of* Paradise Lost. Lewisburg, PA, 1975.

Cummings, Brian. *The Literary Culture of the Reformation: Grammar and Grace.* Oxford, 2002.

Cummins, Juliet, ed. *Milton and the Ends of Time.* Cambridge, 2003.

Curtius, Ernst Robert. *European Literature and the Latin Middle Ages.* Trans. Willard R. Trask. Bollingen Series 36. New York, 1953.

Cust, Richard. 'Charles I and Providence.' In *Religious Politics in Post-Reformation England,* ed. Fincham and Lake, 193–208. Woodbridge, 2006.

Daniélou, Jean. *The Bible and the Liturgy*. Notre Dame, IN, 1956.

Danielson, Dennis. *Milton's Good God: A Study in Literary Theodicy*. Cambridge, 1982.

Davis, J.C. 'Cromwell's Religion.' In *Oliver Cromwell and the English Revolution*, ed. Morrill, 181–208. London, 1990.

[Dawbeny, Henry] H.D. *Historie & Policie Re-viewed, in the Heroick Transactions of his Most Serene Highnesse, Oliver, Late Lord Protector, from his cradle to his tomb*. London, 1659.

Debus, Allen G. 'Harvey and Fludd: The Irrational Factor in the Rational Science of the Seventeenth Century.' *Journal of the History of Biology* 3 (1970): 81–105.

– 'John Woodall, Paracelsian Surgeon.' *Ambix* 10 (1962): 108–18.

– 'Robert Fludd and the Circulation of the Blood.' *Journal of the History of Medicine* 16 (1961): 374–93.

– 'The Sun in the Universe of Robert Fludd.' In *Le Soleil à la Renaissance: Sciences et Mythes*, 259–77. Travaux de l'Institut pour l' Étude de la Renaissance et de l'Humanisme 2. Brussels and Paris, 1965.

Dekker, Eef. 'Was Arminius a Molinist?' *Sixteenth Century Journal* 27 (1996): 337–52.

Demetz, Peter. 'The Elm and the Vine: Notes toward the History of a Marriage Topos.' *PMLA* 73 (1958): 521–32.

Dent, Arthur. *The Ruine of Rome, or, An Exposition vpon the whole Revelation*. 7th ed. London, 1633.

Diodati, John. *Pious and Learned Annotations upon the Holy Bible*. 4th ed. London, 1664.

Dobranski, Stephen B., and John P. Rumrich, eds. *Milton and Heresy*. Cambridge, 1998.

Donne, John. *The Complete English Poems of John Donne*. Ed. C.A. Patrides. Everyman's Library. London, 1985.

– *Devotions upon Emergent Occasions*. Ann Arbor, MI, 1959.

– *The Sermons of John Donne*. 10 vols. Ed. George R. Potter and Evelyn M. Simpson. Berkeley and Los Angeles, 1953–62.

Donnelly, Phillip J. *Milton's Scriptural Reasoning: Narrative and Protestant Toleration*. Cambridge, 2009.

Duncan, Joseph E. *Milton's Earthly Paradise: A Historical Study of Eden*. Minneapolis, 1972.

Dzelzainis, Martin. 'Milton and the Protectorate in 1658.' In *Milton and Republicanism*, ed. Armitage, Himy, and Skinner, 181–205. Cambridge, 1995.

– '"Undoubted Realities": Clarendon and Sacrilege.' *Historical Journal* 33 (1990): 515–40.

Edwards, Karen L. *Milton and the Natural World: Science and Poetry in* Paradise Lost. Cambridge, 1999.

Egerton, F.N. III. 'The Longevity of the Patriarchs: A Topic in the History of Demography.' *Journal of the History of Ideas* 27 (1966): 575–84.

Eire, Carlos M.N. 'The Good, the Bad, and the Airborne: Levitation and the History of the Impossible in Early Modern Europe.' In *Ideas and Cultural Margins in Early Modern Europe: Essays in Honor of H.C. Erik Middlefort*, ed. Marjorie Elizabeth Plummer and Robin B. Barnes, 307–23. Farnham, Surrey, 2009.

Elliott, Dyan. *Spiritual Marriage: Sexual Abstinence in Medieval Wedlock.* Princeton, 1993.

Ellis, Henry, ed. *Original Letters, Illustrative of English History.* Series 1, vol. 3. London, 1824.

Ellmann, Richard. *James Joyce.* 1959. New York, 1982.

Emmerson, Richard Kenneth. *Antichrist in the Middle Ages: A Study of Medieval Apocalypticism, Art, and Literature.* Seattle, WA, 1981.

Erasmus, Desiderius. *The Collected Works of Erasmus.* Vol. 76, *Controversies.* Ed. Charles Trinkaus and trans. Peter Macardle. Toronto, 1999.

Ettlinger, L.D. *The Sistine Chapel before Michelangelo: Religious Imagery and Papal Primacy.* Oxford, 1965.

Evans, J. Martin. *Milton's Imperial Epic:* Paradise Lost *and the Discourse of Colonialism.* Ithaca, NY, 1996.

– Paradise Lost *and the Genesis Tradition.* Oxford, 1968.

Fallon, Robert T. *Captain or Colonel: The Soldier in Milton's Life and Art.* Columbia, MO, 1984.

– 'Cromwell, Milton, and the Western Design.' In *Milton and the Imperial Vision*, ed. Rajan and Sauer, 133–54. Pittsburgh, 1999.

– *Milton in Government.* University Park, PA, 1993.

– 'A *Second Defence:* Milton's Critique of Cromwell?' *Milton Studies* 39 (2000): 167–83.

Fallon, Stephen M. '"Elect above the Rest": Theology as Self-Representation in Milton.' In *Milton and Heresy*, ed. Dobranski and Rumrich, 93–116. Cambridge, 1998.

– *Milton among the Philosophers: Poetry and Materialism in Seventeenth-Century England.* Ithaca, NY, 1991.

– 'Milton's Arminianism and the Authorship of *De doctrina Christiana.' Texas Studies in Literature and Language* 41 (1999): 103–27.

– *Milton's Peculiar Grace: Self-Representation and Authority.* Ithaca, NY, 2007.

Farris, Janna Thacher. 'Angelic Visitations: Raphael's Roles in the Book of Tobit and *Paradise Lost.*' In *Arenas of Conflict: Milton and the Unfettered Mind*, ed. Kristin Pruitt McColgan and Charles W. Durham, 183–92. Selinsgrove, PA, 1997.

Ferguson, George. *Signs and Symbols in Christian Art*. New York, 1954.

Fenton, Mary C. 'Hope, Land Ownership, and Milton's "Paradise Within."' *Studies in English Literature* 43 (2003): 151–80.

– *Milton's Places of Hope: Spiritual and Political Connections of Hope with Land*. Burlington, VT, 2006.

Ferber, Sarah. *Demonic Possession and Exorcism in Early Modern France*. London, 2004.

Ferry, Anne Davidson. *Milton's Epic Voice: The Narrator in 'Paradise Lost.'* Cambridge, MA, 1963.

Ficino, Marsilio. *De sole*. In *Renaissance Philosophy*, vol. 1, *The Italian Philosophers*, ed. and trans. A.B. Fallico and Herman Shapiro, 118–41. New York, 1967.

– *Three Books on Life*. Ed. and trans. Carol V. Kaske and John R. Clark. Binghampton, NY, 1989.

Filarete [Antonio Averlino]. *Filarete's Treatise on Architecture, Being the Treatise by Antonio di Piero Averlino, Known as Filarete*. Trans. John R. Spencer. 2 vols. New Haven, 1965.

Fincham, Kenneth, and Peter Lake, eds. *Religious Politics in Post-Reformation England: Essays in Honour of Nicholas Tyacke*. Woodbridge, 2006.

Finlayson, Michael. 'Clarendon, Providence, and the Historical Revolution.' *Albion* 22 (1990): 607–32.

The First Prayer Book of King Edward VI. Ed. Vernon Staley. The Library of Liturgiology and Ecclesiology for English Readers, vol. 2. London, 1903.

Fish, Stanley. *The Living Temple: George Herbert and Catechizing*. Berkeley and Los Angeles, 1978.

– *Surprised by Sin: The Reader in* Paradise Lost. New York, 1967.

Fixler, Michael. 'The Apocalypse within Paradise Lost.' In *New Essays on* Paradise Lost, ed. Kranidas, 131–78. Berkeley and Los Angeles, 1969.

– *Milton and the Kingdoms of God*. London, 1964.

Fleming, James Dougal. *Milton's Secrecy and Philosophical Hermeneutics*. Aldershot, 2008.

Fletcher, Angus. *Allegory: The Theory of a Symbolic Mode*. Ithaca, NY, 1964.

Fletcher, Harris. *Milton's Rabbinical Readings*. Urbana, IL, 1930.

Fludd, Robert. *Doctor Fludds Answer unto M. Foster. Or, the Squeesing of Parson Fosters Sponge, ordained by him for the wiping away of the Weapon-Salve*. London, 1631.

Foer, Joshua. *Moonwalking with Einstein: The Art and Science of Remembering Everything*. New York, 2011.

Forsyth, Neil. *The Satanic Epic*. Princeton, 2003.

F[otherby], J. *The covenant betweene God and Man. Playnely declared, in laying open the cheifest points of Christian Religion*. London, 1616.

Freeman, James A. *Milton and the Martial Muse:* Paradise Lost *and European Traditions of War*. Princeton, 1980.

French, Roger. *William Harvey's Natural Philosophy*. Cambridge, 1994.

Friedman, Donald M. 'Memory and the Art of Salvation in Donne's Good Friday Poem.' *English Literary Renaissance* 3 (1973): 418–42.

Friedman, John B. 'The Architect's Compass in Creation Miniatures of the Later Middle Ages.' *Traditio* 30 (1974): 419–29.

Frye, Northrop. *Five Essays on Milton's Epics*. London, 1966.

Frye, Roland M. *Milton's Imagery and the Visual Arts*. Princeton, 1978.

Fuller, Thomas. *The Holy State*. 3rd ed. London, 1652.

Gallagher, Philip J. *Milton, the Bible, and Misogyny*. Ed. Eugene R. Cunnar and Gail E. Mortimer. Columbia, MO, 1990.

– '"Real or Allegoric": The Ontology of Sin and Death in *Paradise Lost*.' *English Literary Renaissance* 6 (1976): 317–35.

The Geneva Bible: A Facsimile of the 1560 Edition. Intro. Lloyd E. Berry. Madison, WI, 1969.

Gentles, Ian, John Morrill, and Blair Worden, eds. *Soldiers, Writers and Statesmen of the English Revolution*. Cambridge, 1998.

Gilbert, Allan H. *On the Composition of* Paradise Lost*: A Study of the Ordering and Insertion of Material*. Chapel Hill, NC, 1947.

Ginzberg, Louis. *The Legends of the Jews*. 7 vols. Trans. Henrietta Szold. Philadelphia, 1909–38.

Ginzburg, Carlo. *The Night Battles: Witchcraft and Agrarian Cults in the Sixteenth and Seventeenth Centuries*. Trans. John and Anne Tedeschi. Baltimore, 1983.

Glanvill, Joseph. *Saducismus Triumphatus: Or Full and Plain Evidence Concerning Witches and Apparitions*. 2nd ed. London, 1682.

Godfrey, W. Robert. 'John Hales' Good Night to John Calvin.' In *Protestant Scholasticism: Essays in Reassessment*, ed. Carl R. Trueman and R. Scott Clark, 165–80. Carlisle, Cumbria, 1999.

The Golden Legend or Lives of the Saints as Englished by William Caxton. Ed. F.S. Ellis. Temple Classics. London, 1900.

Gombrich, E.H. *The Heritage of Apelles: Studies in the Art of the Renaissance*. Oxford, 1976.

– *Symbolic Images: Studies in the Art of the Renaissance*. London, 1972.

Goodwin, John. [*Apolytrosis Apolytroseos*] *Redemption Redeemed. Wherein the most glorious work of the redemption of the world by Jesus Christ, is . . . vindicated and asserted* . . . London, 1651.

Greaves, Richard L. 'Traditionalism and the Seeds of Revolution in the Social Principles of the Geneva Bible.' *Sixteenth Century Journal* 7 (1976): 94–109.

Green, Ian. *The Christian's ABC: Catechisms and Catechizing in England c. 1530–1740.* Oxford, 1996.

Guibbory, Achsah. 'England, Israel, and the Jews in Milton's Prose, 1649–1660.' In *Milton and the Jews*, ed. Brooks, 13–34. Cambridge, 2008.

– 'John Donne and Memory as the Art of Salvation.' *Huntington Library Quarterly* 43 (1980): 261–74.

Hakewell, George. *An Apologie of the Power and Providence of God in the Government of the World.* London, 1627.

Hale, John K. 'The Significance of the Early Translations of *Paradise Lost.*' *Philological Quarterly* 63 (1984): 31–53.

Hales, John. *Golden Remains, of the ever Memorable Mr. John Hales of Eton College.* London, 1673.

Hamilton, Gary D. 'Milton's Defensive God: A Reappraisal.' *Studies in Philology* 69 (1972): 87–100.

Hamlin, Hannibal. *Psalm Culture and Early Modern English Literature.* Cambridge, 2004.

Hammond, Gerald. *Fleeting Things: English Poets and Poems, 1616–1660.* Cambridge, MA, 1990.

Hanford, James Holly. *John Milton, Poet and Humanist.* Cleveland, OH, 1966.

Hanke, Lewis. *Aristotle and the American Indians: A Study in Race Prejudice in the Modern World.* London, 1959.

Harley, David. 'Spiritual Physic, Providence and English Medicine.' In *Medicine and the Reformation*, ed. Ole Peter Grell and Andrew Cunningham, 101–17. London, 1993.

Harrington, James. *The Political Works of James Harrington.* Ed. J.G.A. Pocock. Cambridge, 1977.

Harrison, Peter. *The Fall of Man and the Foundations of Science.* Cambridge, 2007.

Harvey, William. *Anatomical Exercitations, Concerning the Generation of living animals.* London, 1653.

– *The Anatomical Lectures of William Harvey.* Ed. and trans. Gweneth Whitteridge. Edinburg, 1964.

– *Disputations Touching the Generation of Animals.* Trans. Gweneth Whitteridge. Oxford, 1981.

Haskin, Dayton. *Milton's Burden of Interpretation.* Philadelphia, 1994.

Hawkins, Edward. *Medallic Illustrations of the History of Great Britain and Ireland.* Ed. A.W. Franks and H.A. Grueber. 2 vols. 1885. London, 1978.

Heitsch, Dorothea, and Jean-François Vallee, eds. *Printed Voices: The Renaissance Culture of Dialogue.* Toronto, 2004.

Held, Julius S. 'Rembrandt and the Book of Tobit.' In Held, *Rembrandt Studies*, 118–43. Princeton, 1991.

Helm, Paul. 'Calvin (and Zwingli) on Divine Providence.' *Calvin Theological Journal* 29 (1994): 388–405.

– *John Calvin's Ideas*. Oxford, 2004.

Helmont, Jean Baptiste van. *Oriatrike or, Physick Refined*. Trans. J.C. London, 1662.

Henderson, George. 'Cain's Jaw-Bone.' *Journal of the Warburg and Courtauld Institutes* 24 (1961): 108–14.

Hendrickson, Robert. *The Facts on File Encyclopedia of Word and Phrase Origin*. Rev. ed. New York, 1997.

Hendy, Philip. *Piero della Francesca and the Early Renaissance*. London, 1968.

Heninger, Jr, S.K. *Touches of Sweet Harmony: Pythagorean Cosmology and Renaissance Poetics*. San Marino, CA, 1974.

Henry, Avril. *Biblia Pauperum: A Facsimile and Edition*. Aldershot, 1987.

Henry, John. 'A Cambridge Platonist's Materialism: Henry More and the Concept of Soul.' *Journal of the Warburg and Courtauld Institutes* 49 (1986): 172–95.

– 'Henry More versus Robert Boyle: The Spirit of Nature and the Nature of Providence.' In *Henry More (1614–1687): Tercentenary Studies*, ed. Sarah Hutton, 55–76. Dordrecht, 1990.

– 'The Matter of Souls: Medical Theory and Theology in Seventeenth-Century England.' In *Medicine, Religion and Natural Philosophy in the Seventeenth Century*, ed. Roger French and Andrew Wear, 87–113. Cambridge, 1989.

– 'Medicine and Pneumatology: Henry More, Richard Baxter, and Francis Glisson's Treatise on the Energetic Nature of Substance.' *Medical History* 31 (1987): 15–40.

Herbert, George. *The Works of George Herbert*. Ed. F.E. Hutchinson. 1941. Oxford, 1959.

Hill, Christopher. *Antichrist in Seventeenth-Century England*. London, 1971.

– *The English Bible and the Seventeenth-Century Revolution*. London, 1993.

– *The Experience of Defeat: Milton and Some Contemporaries*. New York, 1984.

– *God's Englishman: Oliver Cromwell and the English Revolution*. 1970. New York, 1972.

– *Milton and the English Revolution*. New York, 1978.

– *The World Turned Upside Down: Radical Ideas during the English Revolution*. New York, 1972.

Hill, John Spencer. *John Milton, Poet, Priest and Prophet: A Study of Divine Vocation in Milton's Poetry and Prose*. Totowa, NJ, 1979.

Hind, Arthur M. *Engraving in England in the Sixteenth and Seventeenth Centuries II: James I*. Cambridge, 1955.

Hirst, Derek. '"That Sober Liberty": Marvell's Cromwell in 1654.' In *The Golden and the Brazen World: Papers in Literature and History, 1650–1800*, ed. John M. Wallace, 17–53. Berkeley and Los Angeles, 1985.

Hobbes, Thomas. *Leviathan*. Ed. Richard Tuck. Cambridge, 1996.

Holberton, Edward. *Poetry and the Cromwellian Protectorate: Culture, Politics, and Institutions*. Oxford, 2008.

Hoopes, Robert. *Right Reason in the Renaissance*. Cambridge, MA, 1962.

Horapollo. *Hieroglyphica*. Paris, 1551.

Howarth, R.G., ed. *Minor Poets of the Seventeenth Century*. Everyman's Library. London, 1963.

Howison, Patricia M. 'Memory and Will: Selective Amnesia in *Paradise Lost*.' *University of Toronto Quarterly* 56 (1987): 523–39.

Hughes, Kevin L. *Constructing Antichrist: Paul, Biblical Commentary, and the Development of Doctrine in the Early Middle Ages*. Washington, DC, 2005.

Hughes, Merritt Y. 'The Filiations of Milton's Celestial Dialogue.' In his *Ten Perspectives on Milton*, 104–35. New Haven, 1965.

Hume, Patrick. *Annotations on Milton's Paradise Lost*. In *The Poetical Works of Mr. John Milton*. London, 1695.

Hunt, John Dixon. *Andrew Marvell: His Life and Writings*. London, 1978.

Hunter, William B. *The Descent of Urania*. Lewisburg, PA, 1988.

– 'Holy Light in *Paradise Lost*.' *Rice Institute Pamphlets* 45 (1960): 1–14.

– gen. ed. *A Milton Encyclopedia*. 9 vols. Lewisburg, PA, 1978–83.

– 'The War in Heaven: The Exaltation of the Son.' In *Bright Essence*, ed. Hunter, Patrides, and Adamson, 114–30. Salt Lake City, 1973.

Hunter, William B., C.A. Patrides, and J.H. Adamson. *Bright Essence: Studies in Milton's Theology*. Salt Lake City, UT, 1971.

Hutchinson, Lucy. *Memoirs of the Life of Colonel Hutchinson*. In *Politics, Religion and Literature in the Seventeenth Century*, ed. William Lamont and Sybil Oldfield, 183–5. London, 1975.

Hyamson, Albert M. *A Dictionary of English Phrases*. London, 1922.

Ide, Richard S. *Possessed with Greatness: The Heroic Tragedies of Shakespeare and Chapman*. Chapel Hill, NC, 1980.

Irenaeus of Lyons. *Against Heresies* (*Adversus Haereses*). In *The Ante-Nicene Fathers*. Vol. 1. Ed. Alexander Roberts and James Donaldson. Rev. ed. Grand Rapids, MI, 1957.

Jacobus, Lee A. *Sudden Apprehension: Aspects of Knowledge in* Paradise Lost. Studies in English Literature 94. The Hague, 1976.

Jones, Mark. *A Catalogue of the French Medals in the British Museum*. Volume 2, *1600–1672*. London, 1988.

Jones, Rufus M. 'Peculiar People.' In *Encyclopedia of Religion and Ethics*, ed. James Hastings, vol. 9, 701–3. New York, n.d.

Josselin, Ralph. *The Diary of Ralph Josselin.* Ed. Alan Macfarlane. London, 1976.

Judt, Tony. *The Memory Chalet.* New York, 2011.

Kahn, Victoria. *Machiavellian Rhetoric from the Counter-Reformation to Milton.* Princeton, 1994.

Kallendorf, Hilaire. 'The Diabolical Adventures of Don Quixote, or Self-Exorcism and the Rise of the Novel.' *Renaissance Quarterly* 45 (2002): 192–223.

Kaplan, Benjamin J. 'Possessed by the Devil? A Very Public Dispute in Utrecht.' *Renaissance Quarterly* 49 (1996): 738–59.

Katz, David S. *The Jews in the History of England, 1485–1850.* Oxford, 1994.

– *Philo-Semitism and the Readmission of the Jews to England, 1603–1655.* Oxford, 1982.

Kelley, Maurice. Introduction. *Complete Prose Works,* vol. 6, 3–99. New Haven, 1973.

– 'Letter to the Editor.' *Times Literary Supplement,* 5 September 1975, p. 997.

– 'The Theological Dogma of *Paradise Lost* III, 173–202.' *PMLA* 52 (1937): 75–9.

– *This Great Argument: A Study of Milton's 'De Doctrina Christiana' as a Gloss upon 'Paradise Lost.'* Princeton, 1941.

Kelly, Henry Ansgar. *The Devil, Demonology and Witchcraft: The Development of Christian Beliefs in Evil Spirits.* Garden City, NY, 1968.

Kendall, R.T. *Calvin and English Calvinism to 1649.* Oxford, 1979.

Kerrigan, William. 'The Heretical Milton: From Assumption to Mortalism.' *English Literary Renaissance* 5 (1975): 125–66.

– *The Prophetic Milton.* Charlottesville, VA, 1974.

Kerrigan, William, and Gordon Braden. *The Idea of the Renaissance.* Baltimore, 1989.

Kierkegaard, Søren. *Fear and Trembling, Repetition.* Ed. and trans. Howard V. Hong and Edna H. Hong. Princeton, 1983.

King, John N. *Milton and Religious Controversy: Satire and Polemic in* Paradise Lost. Cambridge, 2000.

Kirkconnell, Watson. *The Celestial Cycle: The Theme of 'Paradise Lost' in World Literature with Translations of Major Analogues.* Toronto, 1952.

Klein, Robert. *Form and Meaning: Writings on the Renaissance and Modern Art.* Trans. Madeline Jay and Leon Wieseltier. Princeton, 1981.

Knapp, Henry M. 'John Owen's Interpretation of Hebrews 6: 4–6: Eternal Perseverance of the Saints in Puritan Exegesis.' *Sixteenth Century Journal* 34 (2003): 29–52.

Knoppers, Laura Lunger. *Constructing Cromwell: Ceremony, Portrait, and Prose, 1645–1661.* Cambridge, 2000.

Kramer, Heinrich, and James [Jakob] Sprenger. *The Malleus Malificarum.* Trans. Montague Summers. 1928. New York, 1971.

Kranidas, Thomas, ed. *New Essays on Paradise Lost*. Berkeley and Los Angeles, 1969.

Kubrin, David. 'Newton and the Cyclical Cosmos: Providence and the Mechanical Philosophy.' *Journal of the History of Ideas* 28 (1967): 325–46.

Labriola, Albert C. 'The Aesthetics of Self-diminution: Christian Iconography and *Paradise Lost*.' *Milton Studies* 7 (1975): 292–7.

– 'Christus Patiens: The Virtue Patience and *Paradise Lost*, I–II.' In *The Triumph of Patience: Medieval and Renaissance Studies*, ed. Gerald J. Schiffhorst, 138–46. Orlando, FL, 1978.

– '"Thy Humiliation Shall Exalt": The Christology of *Paradise Lost*.' *Milton Studies* 15 (1981): 29–42.

– 'The Medieval View of Christian History in *Paradise Lost*.' In *Milton and the Middle Ages*, ed. John Mulryan, 115–32. Lewisburg, PA, 1982.

Lake, Kirsopp. 'The Death of Judas.' In *The Beginnings of Christianity. Part I: The Acts of the Apostles*, ed. F.J. Foakes Jackson and Lake, 5: 22–30. London, 1933.

Lake, Peter. 'Anti-popery: The Structure of a Prejudice.' In *Conflict in Early Stuart England: Studies in Religion and Politics 1603–1642*, ed. Richard Cust and Ann Hughes, 72–106. London, 1989.

– 'Introduction: Puritanism, Arminianism and Nicholas Tyacke.' In *Religious Politics in Post-Reformation England*, ed. Fincham and Lake, 1–15. Woodbridge, 2006.

– 'The Significance of the Elizabethan Identification of the Pope as Antichrist.' *Journal of Ecclesiastical History* 31 (1980): 161–78.

Lamont, William. 'Arminianism: The Controversy That Never Was.' In *Political Discourse in Early Modern Britain*, ed. Nicholas Phillipson and Quentin Skinner, 45–66. Cambridge, 1993.

– 'Comment: The Rise of Arminianism Reconsidered.' *Past and Present* 107 (1985): 227–31.

– *Puritanism and Historical Controversy*. London, 1996.

– 'The Religion of Andrew Marvell: Locating the "Bloody Horse."' In *The Political Identity of Andrew Marvell*, ed. Condren and Cousins, 135–56. Aldershot, 1990.

Lapide, Cornelius a [Cornelissen van den Steen]. *Commentarii in Scrituram Sacram*. 10 vols. 1618–29. Lyon and Paris, 1858–60.

Lares, Jameela. *Milton and the Preaching Arts*. Pittsburgh, 2001.

Las Casas, Bartolomé de. *An Account, Much Abbreviated, of the Destruction of the Indies*. Trans. Andrew Hurley. Ed. and intro. Franklin W. Knight. Indianapolis, IN, 2003.

– *The Tears of the Indians being An Historical and True Account Of the Cruel Massacres and Slaughters of above Twenty Millions of innocent people; Committed by the Spaniards.* [*Brevíssima relación de la destruición de las Indias*] Trans. John Phillips. London, 1656.

Lehnhof, Kent R. '"Impregn'd with Reason": Eve's Aural Conception in *Paradise Lost.*' *Milton Studies* 41 (2002): 38–75.

Lemmi, Charles W. *The Classical Deities in Bacon: A Study in Mythological Symbolism.* 1933. New York, 1971.

Leonard, John. 'Milton, Lucretius, and "the void profound of unessential Night."' In *Living Texts: Interpreting Milton,* ed. Kristin A. Pruitt and Charles W. Durham, 198–217. Selinsgrove, PA, 2000.

– *Naming in Paradise: Milton and the Language of Adam and Eve.* Oxford, 1990.

Lewalski, Barbara K. 'Innocence and Experience in Milton's Eden.' In *New Essays on* Paradise Lost, ed. Thomas Kranidas, 86–117. Berkeley and Los Angeles, 1969.

– *Protestant Poetics and the Seventeenth-Century Religious Lyric.* Princeton, 1979.

– 'Structure and the Symbolism of Vision in Michael's Prophecy, *Paradise Lost,* Books XI–XII.' *Philological Quarterly* 42 (1963): 25–35.

Lewis, C.S. *A Preface to 'Paradise Lost.'* 1942. New York, 1969.

Lewis, Rhodri. 'Of "Originian Platonisme": Joseph Glanvill on the Pre-existence of Souls.' *Huntington Library Quarterly* 69 (2006): 267–300.

Lieb, Michael. 'Paradise Lost, Book III: The Dialogue in Heaven Reconsidered.' In *Renaissance Papers 1974,* ed. Dennis G. Donovan and A. Leigh DeNeef (1975): 39–50.

– *Poetics of the Holy: A Reading of* Paradise Lost. Chapel Hill, NC, 1981.

– *Theological Milton: Deity, Discourse and Heresy in the Miltonic Canon.* Pittsburgh, 2006.

Lieb, Michael, and John T. Shawcross, eds. *Achievements of the Left Hand: Essays on the Prose of John Milton.* Amherst, MA, 1974.

Lithgow, William. *A Most Delectable and Trve Discovrse of an Admired and Painfull Pergrination from Scotland, To the Most Famous Kingdomes in Evrope, Asia and Affricke.* London, 1616.

Lloyd, Genevieve. *Providence Lost.* Cambridge, MA, 2008.

Loewenstein, David. *Milton and the Drama of History: Historical Vision, Iconoclasm, and the Literary Imagination.* Cambridge, 1990.

Loewenstein, David, and Paul Stevens, eds. *Early Modern Nationalism and Milton's England.* Toronto, 2008.

Low, Anthony. *Love's Architecture: Devotional Modes in Seventeenth-Century English Poetry.* New York, 1978.

Lugt, Frits. 'Man and Angel, II.' *Gazette des Beaux-Arts,* ser. 6, vol. 25 (1944): 321–46.

McAdoo, H.R. *The Spirit of Anglicanism: A Survey of Anglican Theological Method in the Seventeenth Century.* London, 1965.

Macaulay, Thomas Babington. *Literary Essays Contributed to the Edinburgh Review.* 1913. London, 1932.

MacCaffrey, Isabel Gamble. Paradise Lost *as 'Myth.'* Cambridge, MA, 1959.

– 'The Theme of *Paradise Lost,* Book III.' In *New Essays on Paradise Lost,* ed. Kranidas, 58–85. Berkeley and Los Angeles, 1969.

MacCallum, Hugh R. 'Milton and Figurative Interpretation of the Bible.' *University of Toronto Quarterly* 31 (1962): 397–415.

– 'Milton and Sacred History: Books XI and XII of *Paradise Lost.*' In *Essays in English Literature,* ed. Millar MacLure and F.W. Watt, 149–68. Toronto, 1964.

– *Milton and the Sons of God: The Divine Image in Milton's Epic Poetry.* Toronto, 1986.

Maclure, Millar, and F.W. Watt, eds. *Essays in English Literature from the Renaissance to the Victorian Age Presented to A.S.P. Woodhouse.* Toronto, 1964.

McColley, Diane Kelsey. *Milton's Eve.* Urbana, IL, 1983.

McColley, Grant. 'The Book of Enoch and *Paradise Lost.*' *Harvard Theological Review* 31 (1938): 21–39.

McDannell, Colleen, and Bernhard Lang. *Heaven: A History.* 1988. 2nd ed. New Haven, 2001.

McGee, J. Sears. *The Godly Man in Stuart England: Anglicans, Puritans, and the Two Tables, 1620–1670.* New Haven, 1976.

McGinn, Bernard. *Antichrist: Two Thousand Years of the Human Fascination with Evil.* New York, 1994.

McGrath, Alister E. *Iustitia Dei: A History of the Christian Doctrine of Justification.* 2 vols. Cambridge, 1986.

MacLean, Gerald. 'Milton, Islam and the Ottomans.' In *Milton and Toleration,* ed. Achinstein and Sauer, 293–304. Oxford, 2007.

Machiavelli, Niccolò. *Nicholas Machiavel's Prince.* Trans. E[dward] D[acres]. London, 1640. Scolar Press Facsimile. Menston, 1969.

McLeod, Bruce. 'The "Lordly eye": Milton and the Strategic Geography of Empire.' In *Milton and the Imperial Vision,* ed. Rajan and Sauer, 48–66. Pittsburgh, 1999.

McWilliams, John. 'Marvell and Milton's Literary Friendship Reconsidered.' *Studies in English Literature* 46 (2006): 155–77.

Maggi, Armando. *Satan's Rhetoric: A Study of Renaissance Demonology.* Chicago, 2001.

Maltzahn, Nicholas von. 'Making Use of the Jews: Milton and Philo-Semitism.' In *Milton and the Jews,* ed. Brooks, 57–82. Cambridge, 2008.

– 'Milton, Marvell and Toleration.' In *Milton and Toleration,* ed. Achinstein and Sauer, 86–104. Oxford, 2007.

Marshall, Peter. *Beliefs and the Dead in Reformation England.* Oxford, 2002.

– '"The Map of God's Word": Geographies of the Afterlife in Tudor and Early Stuart England.' In *The Place of the Dead: Death and Remembrance in Late Medieval and Early Modern Europe,* ed. Gordon and Marshall, 110–30. Cambridge, 2000.

Martin, Catherine Gimelli. 'Eliding Absence and Regaining Presence: The Materialist Allegory of Good and Evil in Bacon's Fables and Milton's Epics.' In *Thinking Allegory Otherwise,* ed. Brenda Machosky, 208–34. Stanford, CA, 2009.

– 'The Enclosed Garden and the Apocalyptic Moment versus Transcendent Time in Milton and Marvell.' In *Milton and the Ends of Time,* ed. Cummins, 144–68. Cambridge, 2003.

– *Milton among the Puritans: The Case for Historical Revisionism.* Burlington, VT, 2010.

– 'Rewriting Cromwell: Milton, Marvell, and Negative Liberty in the English Revolution.' *Clio* 36 (2007): 307–32.

– *The Ruins of Allegory: 'Paradise Lost' and the Metamorphosis of Epic Convention.* Durham, NC, 1998.

Martz, Louis L. 'Meditation as Poetic Strategy.' *Modern Philology* 80 (1982): 168–74.

– *The Paradise Within: Studies in Vaughan, Traherne, and Milton.* New Haven, 1964.

– *The Poetry of Meditation.* 1954. Rev. ed. New Haven, 1962.

Marvell, Andrew. *The Poems and Letters of Andrew Marvell.* Ed. H.M. Margoliouth. 2 vols. 2nd ed. Oxford, 1963.

– *The Poems of Andrew Marvell.* Ed. Nigel Smith. Rev. ed. Harlow, 2007.

– *The Prose Works of Andrew Marvell.* Ed. Martin Dzelzainis and Annabel Patterson. 2 vols. New Haven, 2003.

Masson, David. *The Life of John Milton: Narrated in Connexion with the Political, Ecclesiastical, and Literary History of his Time.* 6 vols. 1877. Gloucester, MA, 1965.

Mazzeo, Joseph A. *Medieval Cultural Tradition in Dante.* Ithaca, NY, 1960.

– *Structure and Thought in the 'Paradiso.'* Ithaca, NY, 1958.

Meccaby, Hyam. *Judas Iscariot and the Myth of Jewish Evil.* London, 1992.

Mellinkoff, Ruth. *The Mark of Cain.* Berkeley and Los Angeles, 1981.

Menasseh ben Israel. *The Hope of Israel: The English Translation by Moses Wall, 1652.* Ed. Henry Méchoulan and Gérard Nahon. Oxford, 1987.

Mendelson, Michael. '"The Business of those Absent": The Origin of the Soul in Augustine's *De Genesi Ad Litteram* 10.6–26.' *Augustinian Studies* 29 (1998): 25–81.

Milton, Anthony, ed. *The British Delegation and the Synod of Dort (1618–1619).* Church of England Record Society 13. Woodbridge, 2005.

– *Catholic and Reformed: The Roman and Protestant Churches in English Protestant Thought, 1600–1640.* Cambridge, 1995.

Milton, John. *Complete Prose Works of John Milton.* Gen. ed. Don M. Wolfe. 8 vols in 10. New Haven, 1953–82.

– *Joannis Miltonis Angli De Doctrina Christiana Libri Duo Posthumi.* Ed. Charles Richard Sumner. Brunswick, 1827.

– *John Milton: Complete Poems and Major Prose.* Ed. Merritt Y. Hughes. New York, 1957.

– *Milton's Sonnets.* Ed. E.A.J. Honigmann. New York, 1966.

– *Paradise Lost.* Ed. Thomas Newton. 2 vols. 1749. 4th ed. London, 1757.

– *Paradise Lost.* Ed. Alastair Fowler. 2nd ed. Harlow, 2007.

– *The Riverside Milton.* Ed. Roy Flannagan. Boston, 1998.

– *The Second Defence of the People of England.* Trans. Robert Fellowes. In *The Prose Works of John Milton.* Ed. J.A. St. John. Bohn Standard Library. 5 vols. 2: 214–300. London, 1853.

– *The Works of John Milton.* Gen. ed. Frank Allen Patterson. 18 vols in 21. New York, 1931–8.

Mintz, Samuel I. *The Hunting of Leviathan: Seventeenth-Century Reactions to the Materialism and Moral Philosophy of Thomas Hobbes.* Cambridge, 1962.

Molina, Luis de. *On Divine Foreknowledge (Part IV of the* Concordia*).* Trans. Alfred J. Freddoso. Ithaca, NY, 1988.

Mollenkott, Virginia R. 'The Pervasive Influence of the Apocrypha in Milton's Thought and Art.' In *Milton and the Art of Sacred Song,* ed. J. Max Patrick and Roger H. Sundell, 23–43. Madison, WI, 1979.

More, Ellen. 'John Goodwin and the Origins of the New Arminianism.' *Journal of British Studies* 22 (1982): 50–70.

More, Henry. *The Easie, True, and Genuine Notion and Consistent Explication of the Nature of a Spirit.* In Joseph Glanvill, *Saducismus Triumphatus,* 89–162. Trans. Glanvill. London, 1682.

– 'Henry More's 'Circulatio Sanguinis': An Unexamined Poem in Praise of Harvey.' Comment. Wallace Shugg. Trans. Walter Sherwin and Jay Freyman. *Bulletin of the History of Medicine* 46 (1972): 180–9.

– *The Philosophical Poems of Henry More.* Ed. Geoffrey Bullough. Manchester, 1931.

Morrill, John. 'The Making of Oliver Cromwell.' In *Oliver Cromwell and the English Revolution,* ed. Morrill, 19–48. London, 1990.

– ed. *Oliver Cromwell and the English Revolution.* London, 1990.

Moyles, R.G. *The Text of* Paradise Lost: *A Study in Editorial Procedure.* Toronto, 1985.

Mueller, Janel. 'Milton on Heresy.' In *Milton and Heresy*, ed. Dobranski and Rumrich, 21–38. Cambridge, 1998.

Muller, Richard A. *God, Creation, and Providence in the Thought of Jacob Arminius.* Grand Rapids, MI, 1991.

Murrin, Michael. *The Allegorical Epic: Essays in Its Rise and Decline.* Chicago, 1980.

Myers, Benjamin. 'Prevenient Grace and Conversion in *Paradise Lost.' Milton Quarterly* 40 (2006): 20–36.

Nicolson, Marjorie Hope. *Science and Imagination.* Ithaca, NY, 1965.

Niebyl, Peter H. 'Galen, Van Helmont, and Blood-Letting.' In *Science, Medicine and Society in the Renaissance: Essays to Honor Walter Pagel*, ed. Allen G. Debus, 2: 13–23. New York, 1972.

Nischan, Bodo. 'The Exorcism Controversy and Baptism in the Late Reformation.' *Sixteenth Century Journal* 18 (1987): 31–51.

Norbrook, David. *Writing the English Republic: Poetry, Rhetoric and Politics, 1627–1660.* Cambridge, 1999.

Norford, Don P. 'The Sacred Head: Milton's Solar Mysticism.' *Milton Studies* 9 (1976): 37–75.

O'Connell, Robert J. *The Origin of the Soul in St. Augustine's Later Works.* New York, 1987.

Ogden, H,V.S. 'The Crisis of *Paradise Lost.' Philological Quarterly* 36 (1957): 1–19.

Ong, Walter J., SJ. 'Logic and the Epic Muse: Reflections on Noetic Structures in Milton's Milieu.' In *Achievements of the Left Hand*, ed. Lieb and Shawcross, 239–68. Amherst, MA, 1974.

– *Ramus, Method and the Decay of Dialogue.* Cambridge, MA, 1958.

Orpheus. *The Hymns of Orpheus.* Trans. *Thomas Taylor, the Platonist: Selected Writings*, ed. Kathleen Raine and G.M. Harper, 209–93. Princeton, 1969.

Overton, Richard. *Man's Mortalitie.* Ed. Harold Fisch. Liverpool, 1968.

Pagels, Elaine. *Adam, Eve, and the Serpent.* New York, 1988.

Pallister, William. *Between Worlds: The Rhetorical Universe of* Paradise Lost. Toronto, 2008.

Panofsky, Erwin. *Meaning in the Visual Arts.* Garden City, NY, 1955.

– *Studies in Iconology: Humanistic Themes in the Art of the Renaissance.* 1939. New York, 1962.

Parish, John E. 'Milton and an Anthropomorphic God.' *Studies in Philology* 56 (1959): 619–25.

– 'Milton and the Well-Fed Angel.' *English Miscellany* 18 (1967): 87–109.

– 'Pre-Miltonic Representations of Adam as a Christian.' *Rice Institute Pamphlet* 40 (1953): 1–24.

Park, Katherine. 'The Organic Soul.' In *The Cambridge History of Renaissance Philosophy*, ed. Charles B. Schmitt and Quentin Skinner, 164–84. Cambridge, 1988.

Parker, William Riley. *Milton: A Biography*. 2 vols. Oxford, 1968.

Parnham, David. *Sir Henry Vane, Theologian: A Study in Seventeenth-Century Religious and Political Discourse*. Madison, NJ, 1997.

Partee, Charles B. 'Calvin on Universal and Particular Providence.' In *Readings in Calvin's Theology*, ed. Donald K. McKim, 69–88. Grand Rapids, MI, 1984.

Patrides, C.A. *The Grand Design of God: The Literary Form of the Christian View of History*. London, 1972.

– *Milton and Christian Tradition*. 1966. Hamden, CT, 1979.

– *Premises and Motifs in Renaissance Thought and Literature*. Princeton, 1982.

– 'Renaissance and Modern Views on Hell.' *Harvard Theological Review* 57 (1964): 217–36.

Patterson, Annabel. *Marvell and the Civic Crown*. Princeton, 1978.

Paul, Robert S. *The Lord Protector: Religion and Politics in the Life of Oliver Cromwell*. London, 1955.

Pearl, Jonathan L. *The Crime of Crimes: Demonology and Politics in France, 1560–1620*. Waterloo, ON, 1999.

Pecheux, Mary Christopher. 'Abraham, Adam, and the Theme of Exile in *Paradise Lost*.' *PMLA* 80 (1965): 365–71.

– 'The Concept of the Second Eve in *Paradise Lost*.' *PMLA* 75 (1960): 359–66.

– 'The Image of the Sun in Milton's Nativity Ode.' *Huntington Library Quarterly* 38 (1975): 315–33.

– 'The Second Adam and the Church in *Paradise Lost*.' *ELH* 34 (1967): 173–87.

Pettit, Norman. *The Heart Prepared: Grace and Conversion in Puritan Spiritual Life*. New Haven, 1966.

Phelan, John Leddy. *The Millennial Kingdom of the Franciscans in the New World*. Rev. ed. Berkeley and Los Angeles, 1970.

Pico della Mirandola, Giovanni. *On the Dignity of Man, On Being and the One, Heptaplus*. Trans. Charles Glenn Wallis, Paul J.W. Miller, and Douglas Carmichael. Library of Liberal Arts. Indianapolis, IN, 1965.

Pitkin, Hanna F. *Fortune Is a Woman: Gender and Politics in the Thought of Niccolò Machiavelli*. Berkeley and Los Angeles, 1984.

Plett, Heinrich F. 'Topik und Memoria.' In *Topik: Beiträge zur interdisziplinären Diskussion*, ed. Dieter Breuet and Helmut Schanze, 307–33. Munich, 1981.

Poole, William. *Milton and the Idea of the Fall*. Cambridge, 2005.

Pope, Elizabeth Marie. *'Paradise Regained': The Tradition and the Poem*. Baltimore, 1947.

Popkin, Richard H. 'A Note on Moses Wall.' In Menasseh ben Israel, *The Hope of Israel*, ed. Méchoulan and Nahon, 165–70. Oxford, 1987.

Primaudaye, Pierre de la. *The French Academie*. Trans. T.B. London, 1618.

Quasten, Johannes. *Patrology*, vol. 2, *The Ante-Nicene Literature after Irenaeus*. Utrecht-Antwerp-Westminster, MD, 1962.

Quinones, Ricardo J. *The Changes of Cain*. Princeton, 1991.

Quint, David. 'Fear of Falling: Icarus, Phaethon, and Lucretius in *Paradise Lost*.' *Renaissance Quarterly* 57 (2004): 847–81.

Raab, Felix. *The English Face of Machiavelli: A Changing Interpretation, 1500–1700*. London, 1964.

The Racovian Catechism, with Notes and Illustrations. Trans. Thomas Rees. 1818. Lexington, KY, 1962.

Radzinowicz, Mary Ann. *Milton's Epics and the Book of Psalms*. Princeton, 1989.

Rahe, Paul A. *Against Throne and Altar: Machiavelli and Political Theory under the English Republic*. Cambridge, 2008.

Rahner, Hugo. *Greek Myths and Christian Mysteries*. Trans. Brian Battershaw. London, 1963.

Rajan, Balachandra. *The Lofty Rhyme: A Study of Milton's Major Poetry*. London, 1970.

– Paradise Lost *and the Seventeenth-Century Reader*. New York, 1948.

Rajan, Balachandra, and Elizabeth Sauer, eds. *Milton and the Imperial Vision*. Pittsburgh, 1999.

Ralegh, Sir Walter. *The History of the World*. London, 1614.

Randall, David. 'Providence, Fortune, and the Experience of Combat: English Battlefield Reports, circa 1570–1637.' *Sixteenth Century Journal* 35 (2004): 1053–77.

Raymond, Joad. 'Framing Liberty: Marvell's First Anniversary and the Instrument of Government.' *Huntington Library Quarterly* 62 (2001): 313–50.

Réau, Louis. *Iconographie de l'art chrètien*. 3 vols. Paris, 1956–9.

Resbury, Richard. *Some Stop to the Gangrene of Arminianism, Lately Promoted by Mr. John Goodwin in his Book entitled Redemption Redeemed*. London, 1651.

Revard, Stella P. 'The Dramatic Function of the Son in *Paradise Lost*: A Commentary of Milton's "Trinitarianism."' *Journal of English and Germanic Philology* 66 (1967): 45–68.

Riebling, Barbara. 'Milton on Machiavelli: Representations of the State in *Paradise Lost*.' *Renaissance Quarterly* 39 (1996): 573–97.

Robertson, Geoffrey. *The Tyrannicide Brief: The Story of the Man Who Sent Charles I to the Scaffold*. New York, 2005.

Rogers, John. *The Matter of Revolution: Science, Poetry, and Politics in the Age of Milton*. Ithaca, NY, 1996.

Roldan-Figueroa, Rady. '*Filius Perditionis:* The Propagandistic Use of a Biblical Motif in Sixteenth-Century Spanish Evangelical Bible Translations.' *Sixteenth Century Journal* 37 (2006): 1027–55.

Rosen, Jonathan. 'Return to Paradise.' *The New Yorker,* 2 June 2008, 72–6.

Rosenblatt, Jason. *Torah and Law in* Paradise Lost. Princeton, 1994.

Ross, Alexander. *Mystagogus poeticus.* 2nd ed. London, 1648.

Rossi, Massimiliano. 'Alessandro Vellutello e Giovanni Britto che "per sé fuoror." Sul corredo grafico della "Nove esposizione"' (1544). In *Un Giardino per le arti: 'Francesco Marcolino da Forlì,' la vita, l'opera, il catalogo,* ed. Paolo Procaccioli et al., 365–82. Bologna, 2009.

Rossi, Paolo. *Logic and the Art of Memory: The Quest for a Universal Language.* Trans. Stephen Clucas. Chicago, 2000.

Røstvig, Maren-Sofie. '*Ars Aeterna:* Renaissance Poetics and Theories of Divine Creation.' *Mosaic* 3 (1970): 40–61.

– 'Structure as Prophecy: The Influence of Biblical Exegesis upon Theories of Literary Structure.' In *Silent Poetry: Essays in Numerological Analysis,* ed. Alastair Fowler, 32–72. London, 1970.

Rowe, Violet A. *Sir Henry Vane the Younger: A Study in Political and Administrative History.* London, 1970.

Russell, William R. 'Martin Luther's Understanding of the Pope as the Antichrist.' *Archiv für Reformationsgeschichte* 85 (1994): 32–44.

[Rust, George]. *A Letter of Resolution Concerning Origen and the Chief of His Opinions.* Facsimile Text Society. New York, 1933.

Ryken, Leland. *The Apocalyptic Vision in 'Paradise Lost.'* Ithaca, NY, 1970.

Samuel, Irene. 'The Dialogue in Heaven: A Reconsideration of *Paradise Lost,* III, 1–417,' *PMLA* 72 (1957): 601–11.

The Sarum Missal, Edited from Three Early Manuscripts. Ed. J. Wickham Legg. 1916. Oxford, 1969.

Sasek, Lawrence A. 'The Drama of *Paradise Lost,* Books XI and XII.' In *Milton: Modern Essays in Criticism,* ed. Arthur E. Barker, 342–56. New York, 1965.

Sauer, Elizabeth M. 'Milton's Peculiar Nation.' In *Milton and the Jews,* ed. Brooks, 35–56. Cambridge, 2008.

Scafi, Alessandro. *Mapping Paradise: A History of Heaven on Earth.* Chicago, 2006.

Schultz, Howard. 'Christ and Antichrist in *Paradise Regained.' PMLA* 67 (1952): 790–808.

– *Milton and Forbidden Knowledge.* New York, 1955.

Schwartz, Regina M. *Remembering and Repeating: Biblical Creation in* Paradise Lost. Cambridge, 1988.

Scodel, Joshua. *Excess and the Mean in Early Modern English Literature.* Princeton, 2002.

Scudder, H.H. 'Satan's Artillery.' *Notes and Queries* 195 (1950): 334–47.

Seaver, Paul S. *Wallington's World: A Puritan Artisan in Seventeenth-Century London.* Stanford, CA, 1985.

Sellin, Paul R. 'John Milton's *Paradise Lost* and *De Doctrina Christiana* on Predestination.' *Milton Studies* 34 (1996): 45–60.

Setton, Kenneth M. *Europe and the Levant in the Middle Ages and the Renaissance.* London, 1974.

Sharpe, James. *Instruments of Darkness: Witchcraft in England 1550–1750.* London, 1996.

Sharpe, Kevin. *The Personal Rule of Charles I.* New Haven, 1992.

Shawcross, John T. *The Arms of the Family: The Significance of John Milton's Relatives and Associates.* Lexington, KY, 2004.

– 'The Balanced Structure of "Paradise Lost."' *Studies in Philology* 62 (1965): 695–718.

– 'Confusion: The Apocalypse, the Millennium.' In *Milton and the Ends of Time,* ed. Cummins, 106–19. Cambridge, 2003.

– *The Development of Milton's Thought: Law, Government, and Religion.* Pittsburgh, 2008.

– *John Milton: The Self and the World.* Lexington, KY, 1993.

– ed. *Milton: The Critical Heritage.* London, 1970.

– ed. *Milton 1732–1801: The Critical Heritage.* London, 1972.

– 'The Son in His Ascendance: A Reading of *Paradise Lost.*' *Modern Language Quarterly* 27 (1966): 388–401.

– *With Mortal Voice: The Creation of Paradise Lost.* Lexington, KY, 1982.

Sherry, Beverley, 'Milton's Raphael and the Legend of Tobias.' *Journal of English and Germanic Philology* 78 (1979): 227–41.

– 'Speech in *Paradise Lost.*' *Milton Studies* 8 (1975): 247–66.

Shumaker, Wayne. *Unpremeditated Verse: Feeling and Perception in 'Paradise Lost.'* Princeton, 1967.

Simpson, Ken. 'The Apocalypse in *Paradise Regained.*' In *Milton and the Ends of Time,* ed. Cummins, 203–23. Cambridge, 2003.

Sims, James H. *The Bible in Milton's Epics.* Gainesville, FL, 1962.

Sloane, Thomas O. 'Rhetoric, "Logic" and Poetry: The Formal Cause.' In *The Age of Milton: Backgrounds to Seventeenth-Century Literature,* ed. C.A. Patrides and R.B. Waddington, 307–37. Manchester, 1980.

Smarr, Janet Levarie. *Joining the Conversation: Dialogues by Renaissance Women.* Ann Arbor, MI, 2005.

Smith, Nigel. *Literature and Revolution in England, 1640–1660.* New Haven, 1994.

– *Perfection Proclaimed: Language and Literature in English Radical Religion, 1640–1660.* Oxford, 1989.

Smythe, John. *Certain Discourses Military.* Ed. J.R. Hale. Ithaca, NY, 1964.

Snyder, Jon R. *Writing the Scene of Speaking: Theories of Dialogue in the Late Italian Renaissance.* Stanford, CA, 1989.

Snyder, Susan. 'The Left Hand of God: Despair in Medieval and Renaissance Tradition.' *Studies in the Renaissance* 12 (1965): 18–59.

Sprigge, Joshua. *Anglia Rediviva: England's Recovery.* Intro. Harry T. Moore. Scholars' Facsimiles & Reprints. Gainesville, FL, 1960.

Stachniewski, John. *The Persecutory Imagination: English Protestantism and the Literature of Religious Despair.* Oxford, 1991.

Stallybrass, Peter, Roger Chartier, J. Franklin Mowery, and Heather Wolfe. 'Hamlet's Tables and the Technologies of Writing in Renaissance England.' *Shakespeare Quarterly* 55 (2004): 379–419.

Stanglin, Keith D. '"Arminius *avant la letter*": Peter Baro, Jacob Arminius, and the Bond of Predestinarian Polemic.' *Westminster Theological Journal* 67 (2005): 51–74.

– *Arminius on the Assurance of Salvation: The Context, Roots, and Shape of the Leiden Debate, 1603–1609.* Leiden, 2007.

Stavely, Keith W.F. 'Satan and Arminianism in *Paradise Lost.*' *Milton Studies* 25 (1989): 125–39.

Steadman, John M. 'Eve's Dream and the Conventions of Witchcraft.' *Journal of the History of Ideas* 26 (1965): 567–74.

– 'The God of *Paradise Lost* and the *Divina Commedia.*' *Archiv für das Studium der Neueren Sprachen* 195 (1959): 273–89.

– *Milton and the Renaissance Hero.* Oxford, 1967.

– *Milton's Epic Characters: Image and Idol.* Chapel Hill, NC, 1968.

Stein, Arnold. *Answerable Style: Essays on Paradise Lost.* Minneapolis, 1953.

– 'The Paradise Within and Without.' *Modern Language Quarterly* 26 (1965): 586–600.

Sterry, Peter. *A Discourse of the Freedom of the Will.* London, 1675.

Stevens, Paul. 'How Milton's Nationalism Works: Globalization and the Possibilities of Positive Nationalism.' In *Early Modern Nationalism,* ed. Loewenstein and Stevens, 273–301. Toronto, 2008.

– 'Milton and the New World: Custom, Relativism, and the Discipline of Shame.' In *Milton and the Imperial Vision,* ed. Rajan and Sauer, 90–111. Pittsburgh, 1999.

– 'Milton's "Renunciation" of Cromwell: The Problem of Ralegh's Cabinet Council.' *Modern Philology* 98 (2001): 363–92.

– *'Paradise Lost* and the Colonial Imperative.' *Milton Studies* 34 (1996): 3–21.

– Review of S. Fallon, *Milton's Peculiar Grace. Modern Philology* 108 (2011): 177–82.

Stevens, Walter. *Demon Lovers: Witchcraft, Sex, and the Crisis of Belief.* Chicago, 2002.

Stewart, Stanley N. *The Enclosed Garden: The Tradition and the Image in Seventeenth-Century Poetry.* Madison, WI, 1966.

– *George Herbert.* Twayne's English Authors Series 428. Boston, 1986.

Strong, Roy. *Henry, Prince of Wales and England's Lost Renaissance.* London, 1986.

Stuart Tracts, 1603–1693. Intro. C.H. Firth. New York, 1964.

Stuckenbruck, Loren T. 'The "Fagius" Hebrew Version of Tobit: An English Translation Based on the Constantinople Text of 1519.' In *The Book of Tobit: Text, Tradition, Theology,* ed. Géza G. Xeravits and Jozsef Zsengellér, 189–219. *Supplements* to *The Journal for the Study of Judaism* 98. Leiden, 2005.

Sugimura, N.K. *'Matter of Glorious Triall': Spiritual and Material Substance in* Paradise Lost. New Haven, 2009.

Summers, Joseph H. *The Muse's Method: An Introduction to* Paradise Lost. Cambridge, MA, 1962.

Sutcliffe, Matthew. *The Practice, Proceedings, and Lawes of Armes.* London, 1593.

Svendsen, Kester. *Milton and Science.* Cambridge, MA, 1956.

Tachau, Katherine H. 'God's Compass and *Vana Curiositas:* Scientific Study in the Old French *Bible Moralisée.' Art Bulletin* 80 (1998): 7–33.

Taft, Barbara. '"They that pursew perfaction on earth . . . ": The Political Progress of Robert Overton.' In *Soldiers, Writers and Statesmen,* ed. Gentles, Morrill, and Worden, 286–303. Cambridge, 1998.

Tanner, John. *Anxiety in Eden: A Kierkegaardian Reading of* Paradise Lost. Oxford, 1992.

Tasso, Torquato. *Gerusalemme liberata.* Ed. Lanfranco Caretti. Bari, 1961.

– *Jerusalem Delivered.* Trans. Edward Fairfax. Ed. Henry Morley. Carisbrooke Library. London 1890.

Tayler, Edward W. *Milton's Poetry: Its Development in Time.* Pittsburgh, PA, 1979.

Taylor, Charles. *A Secular Age.* Cambridge, MA, 2007.

Taylor, G.C. *Milton's Use of DuBartas.* Cambridge, MA, 1934.

Temkin, Owsei. *Galenism: The Rise and Decline of a Medical Philosophy.* Ithaca, NY, 1973.

Tertullian. 'A Treatise on the Soul' (*De anima*). In *The Ante-Nicene Fathers,* ed. Alexander Roberts and James Donaldson, vol. 3. Trans. Peter Holmes. Rev. ed., Grand Rapids, MI, 1957.

Thickstun, Margaret Olafson. *Milton's* Paradise Lost: *Moral Education*. New York, 2007.

Thomas, Keith. *Religion and the Decline of Magic*. New York, 1971.

Topsell, Edward. *The Historie of Foure-Footed Beastes*. London, 1607.

– *The Historie of Serpents. Or, The Seconde Booke of Living Creatures*. London, 1608.

Trapp, Joseph. *Thoughts Upon the Four Last Things: Death; Judgement; Heaven; Hell. A Poem in Four Parts*. London, 1734–5.

Trevor-Roper, Hugh. *Europe's Physician: The Various Lives of Sir Theodore de Mayerne*. New Haven, 2006.

Tuve, Rosemond. *Allegorical Imagery: Some Medieval Books and Their Posterity*. Princeton, 1966.

Tyacke, Nicholas. *Aspects of English Protestantism, c. 1530–1700*. Manchester, 2001.

– *Anti-Calvinists: The Rise of English Arminianism c. 1590–1640*. Oxford, 1987.

Ussher, James. *A Body of Divinitie, or The Summe and Substance of Christian Religion*. London, 1645.

van den Berg, Sara. 'Eve, Sin and Witchcraft in *Paradise Lost*.' *Modern Language Quarterly* 47 (1986): 347–65.

Valeriano, Piero. *Hieroglyphica*. Basel, 1575.

Vander Molen, Ronald J. 'Providence as Mystery, Providence as Revelation: Puritan and Anglican Modifications of John Calvin's Doctrine of Providence.' *Church History* 47 (1978): 39–47.

Vergil, Polydore. *An Abridgement of the Works of the most Learned Polidore Virgil. Being An History of the Inventors*. Ed. T[homas] Langley. London, 1659.

Vicary, Thomas. *The English-Mans Treasure: With the true Anatomie of Mans Body*. 8th ed. London, 1633.

Vidal, Fernando. 'Brains, Bodies, Selves, and Science: Anthropologies of Identity and the Resurrection of the Body.' *Critical Inquiry* 26 (2002): 930–74.

Virgil. *The Aeneid 10*. Trans. and comment. S.J. Harrison. Oxford, 1991.

Waddington, Raymond B. '"All in All": Shakespeare, Milton, Donne and the Soul-in-Body Topos.' *English Literary Renaissance* 20 (1990): 40–68.

– 'Lutheran Hamlet.' *English Language Notes* 27 (1989): 27–42.

– 'Melancholy against Melancholy: *Samson Agonistes* as Renaissance Tragedy.' In *Calm of Mind: Tercentenary Essays on 'Paradise Regained' and 'Samson Agonistes*,' ed. Joseph A. Wittreich, Jr, 259–87. Cleveland, OH, 1971.

– 'Milton Turned Upside Down.' *Journal of Modern History* 51 (1979): 108–12.

– Review of N.K. Sugimura. *Milton Quarterly* 45 (2011): 3–6.

– 'The Sun at the Center: Structure as Meaning in Pico della Mirandola's *Heptaplus*.' *Journal of Medieval and Renaissance Studies* 3 (1973): 69–86.

Walker, D.P. 'The Astral Body in Renaissance Medicine.' *Journal of the Warburg and Courtauld Institutes* 21 (1958): 119–37.

– *The Decline of Hell: Seventeenth-Century Discussions of Eternal Torment*. Chicago, 1964.

– 'Medical Spirits in Philosophy and Theology from Ficino to Newton.' In *Arts du spectacle et histoire des idées: Recueil offert en homage à Jean Jacquot*, 287–300. Tours, 1984.

– *Spiritual and Demonic Magic from Ficino to Campanella*. London, 1958.

– *Unclean Spirits: Possession and Exorcism in France and England in the Late Sixteenth and Early Seventeenth Centuries*. Philadelphia, 1981.

Walker, William. Paradise Lost *and Republican Tradition from Aristotle to Machiavelli*. Turnhout, Belgium, 2009.

Wallace, Jr, Dewey D. 'Puritan and Anglican: The Interpretation of Christ's Descent into Hell in Elizabethan Theology.' *Archiv für Reformationsgeschichte* 69 (1978): 248–87.

– *Puritans and Predestination: Grace in English Protestant Theology, 1525–1695*. Chapel Hill, NC, 1982.

Wallace, John M. *Destiny His Choice: The Loyalism of Andrew Marvell*. Cambridge, 1968.

Walsham, Alexandra. *Providence in Early Modern England*. Oxford, 1999.

Walton, Michael T. *Genesis and the Chemical Philosophy: True Christian Science in the Sixteenth and Seventeenth Centuries*. Brooklyn, NY, 2012.

– 'Genesis and Chemistry in the Sixteenth Century.' In *Reading the Book of Nature: The Other Side of the Scientific Revolution*, ed. Allen G. Debus and Walton, 1–14. Sixteenth Century Essays and Studies 41. Kirksville, MO, 1998.

Watson, J.R. 'Divine Providence and the Structure of *Paradise Lost*.' *Essays in Criticism* 14 (1964): 148–55.

Watt, Tessa. *Cheap Print and Popular Piety, 1560–1640*. Cambridge, 1991.

Webb. Henry J. *Elizabethan Military Science: The Books and the Practice*. Madison, WI, 1965.

Webster, Charles, ed. *The Intellectual Revolution of the Seventeenth Century*. London, 1974.

Welch, Anthony. 'Reconsidering Chronology in *Paradise Lost*.' *Milton Studies* 41 (2002): 1–17.

Werman, Golda. *Milton and Midrash*. Washington, DC, 1995.

West, Robert H. *Milton and the Angels*. Athens, GA, 1955.

West, William N. 'Memory.' In *The Encyclopedia of Rhetoric*, ed. Thomas O. Sloane, 482–93. Oxford, 2001.

Whitford, David M. 'The Papal Antichrist: Martin Luther and the Underappreciated Influence of Lorenzo Valla.' *Renaissance Quarterly* 61 (2008): 26–52.

Whiting, George W. *Milton and This Pendant World.* Austin, TX, 1958.

Whitteridge, Gweneth. *William Harvey and the Circulation of the Blood.* London, 1971.

Wigler, Stephen. 'The Poet and Satan before the Light.' *Milton Quarterly* 12 (1978): 59–64.

Willet, Andrew. *Sacrorum Emblematum Centuria Una (1592?).* Intro. Bettie Anne Doebler. Scholars' Facsimiles & Reprints. Delmar, NY, 1984.

Williams, Arnold. *The Common Expositor: An Account of the Commentaries on Genesis, 1527–1633.* Chapel Hill, NC, 1948.

Williams, George Huntston. *The Radical Reformation.* 3rd ed. Sixteenth Century Essays and Studies 13. Kirksville, MO, 1992.

– *Wilderness and Paradise in Christian Thought.* New York, 1962.

Williams, Grant, and Christopher Ivic, eds. *Forgetting in Early Modern English Literature: Lethe's Legacies.* London, 2004.

Williamson, George. 'The Education of Adam.' *Modern Philology* 61 (1963): 96–109.

Wind, Edgar. *Pagan Mysteries in the Renaissance.* 1958. Rev. ed. New York, 1968.

Winstanley, Gerrard. *The Works of Gerrard Winstanley.* Ed. George H. Sabine. 1941. New York, 1965.

Wither, George. *A Collection of Emblemes, Ancient and Modern.* London, 1635.

Witt, Ronald G. 'Boncompagno and the Defense of Rhetoric.' *Journal of Medieval and Renaissance Studies* 16 (1986): 1–31.

Wittreich, Joseph. *Feminist Milton.* Ithaca, NY, 1987.

Wolfe, Don M. 'The Limits of Miltonic Toleration.' *Journal of English and Germanic Philology* 60 (1961): 834–46.

Wollaeger, Mark A. 'Apocryphal Narration: Milton, Raphael, and the Book of Tobit.' *Milton Studies* 21 (1985): 137–56.

Woodall, John. *The Surgions Mate (1617).* Intro. John Kirkup. Bath, 1978.

Woodhouse, A.S.P., ed. *Puritanism and Liberty: Being the Army Debates (1647–9) from the Clarke Manuscripts.* 1951. Chicago. 1965.

Woolrych, Austin. 'Cromwell as a Soldier.' In *Oliver Cromwell and the English Revolution,* ed. Morrill, 93–118. London, 1990.

– 'Milton and Cromwell: "A short but Scandalous Night of Interruption"?' In *Achievements of the Left Hand,* ed. Lieb and Shawcross, 185–218. Amherst, MA, 1974.

Worden, Blair. 'Andrew Marvell, Oliver Cromwell, and the Horatian Ode.' In *Politics of Discourse: The Literature of History in Seventeenth-Century England,* ed. Kevin Sharpe and Steven N. Zwicker, 147–80. Berkeley and Los Angeles, 1987.

– 'John Milton and Oliver Cromwell.' In *Soldiers, Writers and Statesmen*, ed. Gentles, Morrill, and Worden, 243–64. Cambridge, 1998.

– *Literature and Politics in Cromwellian England: John Milton, Andrew Marvell, Marchamont Nedham*. Oxford, 2007.

– 'Oliver Cromwell and the Sin of Achan.' In *History, Society and the Churches: Essays in Honour of Owen Chadwick*, ed. Derek Beales and Geoffrey Best, 125–45. Cambridge, 1985.

– 'Providence and Politics in Cromwellian England.' *Past and Present* 109 (1985): 55–99.

Wortham, Christopher. 'Marvell's Cromwell Poems: An Accidental Triptych.' In *The Political Identity of Andrew Marvell*, ed. Condren and Cousins, 16–52. Aldershot, 1990.

Wunderli, Richard, and Gerald Broce. 'The Final Moment before Death in Early Modern England.' *Sixteenth Century Journal* 20 (1989): 259–75.

Yates, Frances A. *The Art of Memory*. London, 1966.

– *Giordano Bruno and the Hermetic Tradition*. Chicago, 1964.

Young, R.V. *Doctrine and Devotion in Seventeenth-Century Poetry: Studies in Donne, Herbert, Crashaw, and Vaughan*. Studies in Renaissance Literature 2. Cambridge, 2000.

Yu, Anthony C. 'Life in the Garden: Freedom and the Image of God in *Paradise Lost*.' *Journal of Religion* 60 (1980): 247–71.

Zivley, Sherry Lutz. 'The Thirty-Three Days of *Paradise Lost*.' *Milton Quarterly* 34 (2000): 117–27.

Index

www.ingramcontent.com/pod-product-compliance
Lightning Source LLC
LaVergne TN
LVHW090151080826
844660LV00013B/758/J
9781442643420